I Wanna Wrock!

I Wanna Wrock!

The World of Harry Potter–Inspired "Wizard Rock" and Its Fandom

PAUL A. THOMAS

McFarland & Company, Inc., Publishers
Jefferson, North Carolina

All song lyrics herein were reprinted with the permission of the original artists.

This book has undergone peer review

LIBRARY OF CONGRESS CATALOGUING-IN-PUBLICATION DATA

Names: Thomas, Paul A., 1992– author.
Title: I wanna wrock! : the world of Harry Potter-inspired "wizard rock" and its fandom / Paul A. Thomas.
Description: Jefferson, North Carolina : McFarland & Company, 2019 | Includes bibliographical references and index.
Identifiers: LCCN 2018046322 | ISBN 9781476673035 (softcover : acid free paper) ∞
Subjects: LCSH: Wizard rock—History and criticism.
Classification: LCC ML3534 .T538 2019 | DDC 781.66—dc23
LC record available at https://lccn.loc.gov/2018046322

BRITISH LIBRARY CATALOGUING DATA ARE AVAILABLE

ISBN (print) 978-1-4766-7303-5
ISBN (ebook) 978-1-4766-3464-7

© 2018 Paul A. Thomas. All rights reserved

No part of this book may be reproduced or transmitted in any form or by any means, electronic or mechanical, including photocopying or recording, or by any information storage and retrieval system, without permission in writing from the publisher.

Front cover image based on an image © 2019 Craig Swart/iStock

Printed in the United States of America

McFarland & Company, Inc., Publishers
 Box 611, Jefferson, North Carolina 28640
 www.mcfarlandpub.com

Trina, Thanks for agreeing to write
wizard rock with me those many years ago.
It's been a magical ride.

Table of Contents

Acknowledgments — viii
Notes on Terminology — x
Preface — 1
Introduction — 7

1. Wizard Rock: A History — 19
2. DIY Wrock; or, How to Make Your Own Band — 47
3. Wrocking the Library: Live Wizard Rock — 72
4. "I *Am* Harry Potter": A Closer Look at Role-Play — 96
5. The Structure and Demographics of the Community — 112
6. Wizard Rock and the "Muggle World" — 131
7. The Wider World of Wizard Rock — 150
8. Why Do They Wrock So Hard? — 172

Conclusion — 183
Chapter Notes — 185
Appendix A: List of Major Wrock Bands — 205
Appendix B: Wizard Rock EP of the Month Club Releases — 220
Bibliography — 223
Index — 241

Acknowledgments

Given that a book—much like a wizard rock album—is rarely the work of a single person working in total isolation from the outside world, I would like to use this space to thank all those whose contributions and assistance made this project possible:

First, I would like to thank J.K. Rowling (for writing the *Harry Potter* books) and Paul and Joe DeGeorge (for creating what we now know as "wizard rock"). Without these individuals, the peculiar style of music that is the subject of his book would have never been born.

Second, I would like to thank my immediate family, and especially my mother and father, Julia and Mark. They not only put up with my musical *Harry Potter* obsession, but also encouraged it by buying me my first guitar as well as my first professional microphone.

Third, I would like to extend a special thanks to all those who answered my questions, provided me with photographs, or allowed me to use their lyrics: Cherra Acosta, Ashley Aisyah, Steph Anderson, Christopher Bee, Russ Benoit, Mary Bertke, Ariel Factor Birdof, Paige Breisacher, Phillip Carter, Holly Casio, Jessica Cicale-Mahon, Rachael Clawson, Mary Clow, Lauren Cook, Grace Dow, Drama, Adam Dubberly, Sam Durcharme, Nikki Ebright, Lauren Fairweather, Amanda Finlaw, Yaritza Gonzalez, Georgia Greenberg, Lara Griffith, Aya Esther Hayashi, James Hinsey, Sarah Frances Holder, Kristina Horner, Theodore Hwa, Will Jackson, Freya Jansen, Myles Kane, Grace Kendall, TK Lawrence, Sarah Leal, Anu Lingappa, Margaret Lingas, Matt Maggiacomo, Bradley Mehlenbacher, Claudia Morales, Christie Dawn Mowery, Wilbur Nether, the Niffler, Heather Nolis, Mehera Nori, Stacy Pisani, Erin Pyne, Sara Rasmussen, Jonathon Rosenthal, Brian Ross, Lauren Amanda Smith, Amy Snow, Denni Towle, Scott Vaughan, Andrew W. Wright, Spirit-Rose Waite, Karin Westman, Wrock Snob, Julia Weinstein, Amelie WT, and Susannah (of *Your Wizard Rock Resource*).

Fourth, I would like to thank those wizard rock scholars who came before me and helped make this work a reality: Melissa Anelli, Aya Esther

Hayashi, Sarah Frances Holder, Kelli Rohlman, Suzanne Scott, Anne C. Smith, Lauren Amanda Smith, and Jennifer Terrell—to name just a few. Hayashi in particular deserves extra kudos, as she shared her finalized dissertation with me via email, read over and commented upon a draft of this book, and discussed some key ideas with me. Her help has truly been invaluable. Special thanks also goes to Grace Kendall, whose extensive (and impressive!) "Museum of Wizard Rock" exhibit made researching the history of wizard rock much easier.

Fifth, I would like to thank all those who read my drafts and offered constructive criticism: Bess Carnan, Paul DeGeorge, Yaritza Gonzalez, and Aya Esther Hayashi, several anonymous peer reviewers, and the talented editors at McFarland. Your feedback has made this book much stronger. (Paul deserves additional thanks for also answering an avalanche of questions I had about his band, their recordings, and their creative process.)

And finally, special thanks goes to Trina Thomas, my musical partner and my loving wife, without whom I may have never gotten interested in wizard rock in the first place:

Thank you for reading drafts of this book and discussing ideas with me…

Thank you for listening as I blathered on for hours about the minutia of wizard rock…

But perhaps most importantly, thank you for all the magical, musical memories.

Notes on Terminology

"Wizard rock," when it is used as a noun phrase in this book, appears in full. However, when the term is invoked as an adjectival phrase (e.g., "wizard rock band"), it is rendered simply as "wrock." Relatedly, people who play in wizard rock bands are referred to as "wrockers." This was done not only to cut down on unwieldy modifiers, but also to reflect actual fandom usage. This practice is confined to the author's text; quotes and text snippets excised from other works retain their original spellings.

All unique nouns or terms that were created or reinterpreted by Rowling (e.g., "Muggle," "Patronus") are capitalized, whereas terms created or used by fans and fandom scholars (e.g., "fanon," "fan fiction") are in lowercase. This follows the style established by Lisa Brenner in her 2016 book *Playing Harry Potter*. While this book assumes that the reader has a basic understanding of the *Harry Potter* novels and films, unique terms coined by Rowling are briefly defined in the endnotes of the chapter in which they first appear.

Finally, the endnotes of this book use the following abbreviations for the *Harry Potter* novels:

SS—*Harry Potter and the Sorcerer's Stone*
CS—*Harry Potter and the Chamber of Secrets*
PA—*Harry Potter and the Prisoner of Azkaban*
GF—*Harry Potter and the Goblet of Fire*
OP—*Harry Potter and the Order of the Phoenix*
HBP—*Harry Potter and the Half-Blood Prince*
DH—*Harry Potter and the Deathly Hallows*
CC—*Harry Potter and the Cursed Child*
FB—*Fantastic Beasts and Where to Find Them*

Preface

This book is a holistic, detailed, and historio-ethnographic study of the phenomenon known as "wizard rock" (or "wrock")—i.e., the genre of music about the *Harry Potter* book series by British author J.K. Rowling, and the fannish community of musicians who write, record, and perform this type of music. While this eccentric genre—having been formally founded by the band "Harry and the Potters" in 2002—has been around for over 16 years, only a handful of academic journal articles, book chapters, and Ph.D. dissertations have been devoted to exploring this unique musical subculture. In fact, this is the first published book to focus solely on wizard rock.

The chapters within this book explore a wide variety of topics, and because each is self-contained, they can be viewed by the reader as their own individual works of analysis. However, I believe they are best viewed as comprising a single, comprehensive look at the entirety of the wizard rock community. The outline of the book is as follows:

Chapter 1 provides a detailed history of wizard rock. In this section of the book, I first survey the antecedents (viz. punk rock, filk music, and fan fiction) that preceded and, in many ways, came to influence wizard rock. I then delineate the evolution of wizard rock itself, starting with what is considered the first wrock song by the band Switchblade Kittens before ending with a survey of the existing state of the scene. While much of this chapter focuses on the role that the band Harry and the Potters had in developing wizard rock, I also take into account the many other musical groups who have influenced the community, such as The Parselmouths, Draco and the Malfoys, The Whomping Willows, The Remus Lupins, and The Moaning Myrtles.

Chapter 2 is concerned with the ways in which musicians form bands, record songs, and distribute music. I open this section by stressing the importance of a band's name, which I argue often functions as a critical indexical that lets potential listeners know what *kind* of wizard rock they will be listening to. I then proceed to discuss wizard rock's musical diversity, as well as the "lyrical sub-genres" that musicians commonly employ when writing songs. Following this, I discuss how bands approach the recording process. I then look at the methods bands make use of to distribute their music to others. After considering how social media sites like MySpace, Facebook, and Twitter have propagated wizard rock in the online sphere, I close the chapter with a brief discussion of wrock merchandise.

Chapter 3 provides an ethnographic examination of live wizard rock shows. First, I define and explore "wizard rock space" by surveying the various venues at which musicians perform; during this portion of the chapter, I place particular emphasis on libraries, arguing that these places are favored by wrockers because they are conducive to "rituals of rebellion." I also discuss the importance of house shows and explore the logistics of touring. After outlining the history of a number of wrock events (such as The Yule Ball, Wrockstock, the Hallows and Horcruxes Ball, Wrock Chicago, Wrock the Boat, and LeakyCon), my focus pivots slightly, and I discuss the sense of community and solidarity felt during live shows in regard to theories developed by the sociologist Émile Durkheim.

Chapter 4 focuses on wizard rock role-play, its importance, and its prevalence at live shows. First, I discuss the nature of this behavior by comparing and contrasting it to what one might call "traditional" role-play, as well as to the fannish practice of cosplay. To further elucidate wizard wrock role-play, I then analyze this most curious phenomenon in regard to Judith Butler's seminal re-interpretation of performativity. I conclude that role-play is a performative exercise that allows wizard rock musicians to shape their own identity by citing character elements with which they themselves want to be associated in what one might call the "real world."

Chapter 5 revolves around the results of a survey that I administered in 2017, which documented the demographic makeup of the wrock community in regard to nationality, gender, sexual orientation, and race. Large portions of this chapter explore one of wizard rock's greatest paradoxes: while many within the community stress the importance of diversity and the dangers inherent in passively accepting hegemonic structures, the community is often defined by those very things against which it strives to fight. (For instance, while most wizard rock musicians and fans are female, the most popular groups are male-fronted. Furthermore, people of color make up a disproportionately smaller percentage of the movement when compared to white individuals.) In this section of the book, I explore these contradictions and seek to answer the questions they raise by contrasting community demography with rhetoric, and critically analyzing the results.

Chapter 6 considers the many ways in which the world of wizard rock has affected the "real world." I first explore wizard rock's connection to activism, noting that ever since its beginning, the wizard rock community has heartily embraced political and social engagement, championed pro-literacy causes, fought for gender equality, and opposed authoritarianism. In this chapter, I also look at the "dark side" of wizard rock by exploring the sexual and emotional abuse scandals that very nearly destroyed the community in 2014; I argue that these scandals prove that even in a community like wizard rock—which self-conceives of itself as a movement of the good fighting the evil—there are still those who abuse their power and privilege, hurting others in the process.

The penultimate chapter of the book considers the elements of wizard rock that exist on the periphery of the community but are still of utmost importance, namely: radio stations, online music encyclopedias, documentaries, fandom musical critics, and award shows. The topics discussed in this chapter heavily suggest that wizard rock, in addition to being a distinct type of music, is also an interconnected and varied community of individuals, all of whom contribute to the wider world of wizard rock through various modes of fandom engagement.

The book's final chapter considers a number of hypotheses as to why many are encouraged in the first place to write songs about the *Harry Potter* book series. In this portion of the book, I explore whether wrockers are motivated by the promise of financial gain, the potential to feel empowered, the desire to escape social alienation and belong in a group, or the appeal of a community that embraces and actively encourages "unlimited enthusiasm."

This book also includes two appendices. The first alphabetically catalogues the more popular wrock bands in the community, providing brief description of the groups, as well as listing the names of their members and their studio releases. The second appendix lists the 37 Wizard Rock EP of the Month Club releases, organized by month and year.

Much of this book takes on the form of an ethnography, attempting to explain the behavior endemic in the wrock community. Since 2009, I have been an active member of this community, attending numerous concerts and performing in my own band, The 8th Horcrux. This is important to note, given that ethnographic research is generally carried out by an unaffiliated "outsider" studying a culture of which they are not considered a part. This means that by documenting my own subcultural niche, I am filling both the role of the scholarly researcher as well as the "native" whose culture is being described. To account for this seeming contradiction, I have made use of a methodological approach known as "autoethnography"—a variant of standard ethnography in which the researcher "retrospectively and selectively write[s] about epiphanies that stem from, or are made possible by, being part of a culture and/or by possessing a particular cultural identity [and then] analyze[s] these experiences" to come to some understanding about a larger culture.[1] This approach is perhaps most evident in how I frame many of the chapters with short vignettes that illustrate certain aspects of the scene from my own subjective perspective before moving on to a deeper consideration from a different, more impartial (and perhaps less solipsistic) angle.

But while I explicitly identify myself as being an active member of the wrock community, in this work I still often employ the customary divide between ethnographic researcher and cultural informant; after all, much of the information found in this book was garnered not from my own personal experiences but rather from interviews with wrock fans and musicians, many of whom were involved in the creation of the genre. This was done to strike a methodological middle ground between the radically subjective style of autoethnography that focuses on the self at the expense of the object, and what one might call the "traditional" style of ethnography that focuses on the object and downplays the importance of the researcher. In this way, I am able to highlight my own subjective experiences within the scene, while at the same time recognizing that my personal experiences are not—and should not be—the *only* experiences worth describing.

Ultimately, with this work, it has been my goal to do three main things: First, I have attempted to provide an extensive and accurate history of the wrock movement, starting from the beginning and continuing up to the present. While there exist a handful of sources that have attempted something similar, most either treat the history of wizard rock in a cursory manner or are simply outdated. And in terms of historical approach, this book is unique because it explores the development and impact of those things which other reference works tend to overlook (e.g., fansites, radio programs, documentaries, music critics). By also focusing on these sorts of activities, I have attempted to document a more complete and inclusive history of wizard rock—and not just a history of the most popular bands.

Second, I have tried to approach and analyze the wrock movement through a critical lens. I embraced this attitude largely after corresponding with the musicologist Aya Esther Hayashi, who pointed out that most existing treatments of wizard rock have a tendency to heap lavish praise upon the scene, presenting it as some kind of perfect subculture devoid of problems that plague similar groups. While admittedly I think highly of the wrock scene (what with my being an active member and all), I also recognize that admiring the good of the community while ignoring the bad is not only imperceptive, it is also poor scholarship. Thus, this work lays bare both the positive and the negative aspects of wizard rock to better illustrate how complicated and nuanced the wrock community—like all human communities—actually is.

Third and finally, I have not been content to simply describe the wrock community and its members—rather, I have tried my hardest to explain *why* wrockers and fans do the things that they do in the first place. It is perhaps this question of "why?" that is often so difficult for an ethnographer to answer, simply because human behavior is so incredibly diverse and almost always resists easy classification and categorization. But if the researcher ignores the integral question of "why," they can only come to a surface-level understanding of any given behavior or activity. In the context of this project, that would mean failing to more thoroughly understand a phenomenon as complex, varied, and fascinating as wizard rock.

Before we move onto my findings, I would like to note that this book, as with most scholarly works, was written while standing on the shoulders of giants, and I feel that it is my duty to discuss those scholars whose research I found myself consulting time and time again. First and foremost, I must emphasize the influence of scholar and "aca-fan" Henry Jenkins on the entirety of this work. While Jenkins has never written about wizard rock in as extensive and narrowly focused a way as this book, his ideas—especially those that he first laid out in his works *Textual Poachers* (1992), *Fans, Bloggers, and Gamers* (2006), and *Spreadable Media* (2013)—heavily influenced the way I approached and interpreted my subject matter.

I have also made extensive use of Melissa Anelli's 2008 book *Harry, a History*, specifically its sixth chapter, "Rocking at Hogwarts." In addition to her role as the webmaster of the popular *Harry Potter* fansite The Leaky Cauldron, Anelli is notable in the wrock community for being the first to publish a comprehensive history of the genre, and while today her book is a bit dated (having been published over a decade ago), it is nonetheless a wonderful resource that any scholar of wizard rock should have in their collection. Without Anelli's book, it would have been extremely difficult to write this work's first chapter on the history of wizard rock.

Finally, I have also consulted a number of Ph.D. dissertations and master's theses, including: Kelli Rohlman's thesis "Identity, Rhetoric and Behavior: The Contradictory Communities of Wizard Rock" (Texas Tech, 2010), Suzanne Scott's dissertation "Revenge of the Fanboy: Convergence Culture and the Politics of Incorporation" (USC, 2011), Jennifer Terrell's dissertation "Constructing Rooms of Requirement: The Ethnographic Study of Digitally Transmediated Sociality" (Indiana University, 2015), Sarah Frances Holder's thesis "'Get Your Geek On': Online and Offline Representations of Audiotopia Within the GeekyCon Community" (University of Tennessee, Knoxville, 2017), and Aya Esther Hayashi's dissertation "Musicking, Discourse, and Identity in Participatory Media Fandom" (CUNY, 2018). These works have proven to be goldmines of information, and without many of their ingenious ideas off of which to springboard, I would have likely been unable to get as far on this work as I did.

Per the above, I would like to stress that while this book might be the first to treat wizard rock in a comprehensive fashion, I make no claim that all the ideas and hypotheses discussed and promoted in this book are mine and mine alone. In fact, many of the concepts I consider were first developed to discuss various aspects of fandom or *Harry Potter* fan culture at large. With that said, I have made use of these ideas in appropriate and sometimes novel ways, either by affirming/denying their continued relevance, building off them to reach a new point, or—perhaps most commonly—explicitly reframing them to exclusively consider the nature of wizard rock, rather than fandom or *Harry Potter* fan culture in general.

Introduction

I first learned about the curious musical movement known as "wizard rock" when I was 16.

It was mid-2008. I was wandering the streets of my adopted hometown, Lawrence, Kansas, when I noticed a somewhat tattered poster hanging below the marquee of a downtown event space. Emblazoned upon it, in large, stylized letters, were the words:

HARRY and THE POTTERS, LIVE!

Underneath this bold declaration was a minimalistic but memorable depiction of a guitar being struck by a bright-white bolt of lightning.

It was readily apparent from both their poster as well as their name that this group was devoted to playing songs about the *Harry Potter* book series. I was no stranger to the idea of writing songs about beloved works of pop culture (I am, after all, a fan of "Weird Al" Yankovic and his parodic odes to fictional franchises like "Yoda" or "Jurassic Park"). However, I had never heard of any band that dedicated its entire catalogue to one—and only one—book series. *They must be really enthusiastic about Harry Potter*, I thought to myself.

And really nerdy.

Fast-forward a year later, to the summer of 2009. There was a girl named Trina with whom I was smitten. For a few weeks, we had been involved in one of those awkward teenage courting rituals (you know the type—where one individual tries to let the other know that they like them without explicitly saying as much). In a rare moment of courage and frankness, I asked her if she would like to go to the movies and see the newest *Harry Potter* film: *The Half-Blood Prince*. At the time, I did not know if she enjoyed *Harry Potter*—I just assumed that it would be a nice way to spend time with her. Much to my excitement, she agreed.

After the show, as we walked out of the dark theater into the summer heat, we took to discussing aspects of the Potter fandom. From this conversation, I learned that Trina was quite the Potter fan. Hoping to impress her,

I blurted out, "Did you know that there is a band called 'Harry and the Potters' that sings songs about *Harry Potter*?" Trina informed me that she had in fact heard of them before, but that she had never taken the time to listen to their music.

At the first available opportunity, we scoured the Internet for a track or two, and what we discovered in the process we could hardly believe: there was not just one band that wrote songs about *Harry Potter*, but a whole community of them, ranging from punk bands to techno-groups. These musicians called what they did "wizard rock." We were so intrigued we spent the rest of the night talking about this most unusual type of music.

But over the next few weeks, our opinion about wizard rock changed: we began to view it less as a morbid curiosity and more as a genuine fascination. Whenever we would meet, the conversation would inevitably return to wizard rock. Trina would inform me of new bands she had discovered, and I would tell Trina about Harry and the Potters' latest updates.

Eventually, we developed song ideas of our own. Being musicians, we decided it would be fun to record these tunes for our own personal enjoyment. On July 31 (Harry Potter's birthday of all days!), we jammed in my basement, and within a few hours, we had started to work out our first song. By the time the weather had cooled and autumn had arrived, we were a bona fide wrock band working on our first album. Nine years later, The 8th Horcrux, as we decided to call ourselves, is still going strong.

I feel as if I should also mention that Trina and I were married in October 2017.

Given the above, it is no understatement to say that wizard rock has been a major part of my life. But the magnitude of this reality only dawned upon me around the summer of 2016. In June of that year, I graduated from the University of Chicago with a master's degree in social science. During the preceding dozen or so months, I had been critically examining everything from North American horse cultures to contemporary video games through the lenses of media theory and anthropology, and when I left the academy and no longer had any graduate papers to write, I turned this critical examination inward, looking at those things in my own life that had so far escaped scrutiny. It was during this period of self-contemplation that I truly realized the role wizard rock had played in shaping who I was as a person. This in turn led to my asking questions I had never really considered before. What exactly *is* wizard rock? What makes it different from other genres of music or fan productions? How has it affected other people's lives? And perhaps most importantly, *why* do fans feel the need to make this sort of music? This book is my attempt to answer (or, at the very least, explore) these questions.

* * *

Introduction 9

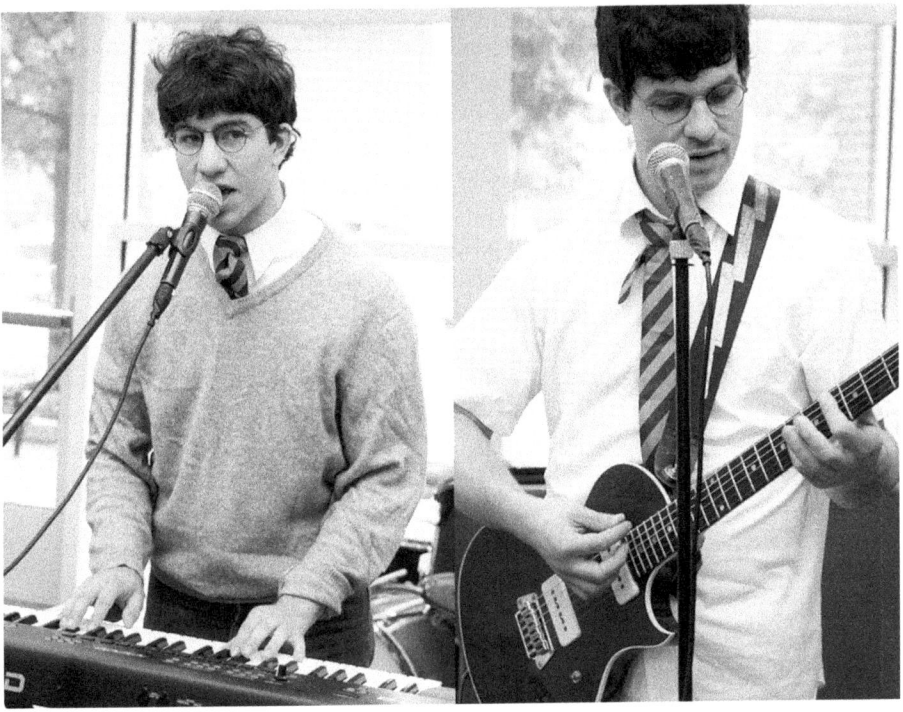

Harry and the Potters play at a library in 2009. The group, which comprises the brothers Joe (left) and Paul DeGeorge, is today credited with creating and popularizing the genre of Wizard Rock (courtesy Grace Kendall).

Wizard rock (often just called "wrock," /raːk/) is the name given to a unique type of music focused solely on the *Harry Potter* book series by British author J.K. Rowling. While the roots of this movement stretch to the turn of the millennium, most date the beginning of wizard rock–proper to the summer of 2002, when the brothers Paul and Joe DeGeorge of Norwood, Massachusetts, started the band Harry and the Potters. In the years that followed, hundreds of similar bands have formed and thousands of songs have been written, all dedicated to a fictional boy wizard and the magical world in which he lives. Unfortunately, while wizard rock has occasionally caught the attention of sites like MTV and NPR over the years, and a handful of academics have found the movement worthy of scholarly attention, the genre remains firmly an underground and under-studied phenomenon. *I Wanna Wrock* is an attempt to rectify this issue.

But before I dive into the fascinating world of wizard rock, perhaps I should briefly look at that which spawned wizard rock in the first place: the *Harry Potter* series. For the uninitiated, the books follow the adventures of the eponymous young boy wizard, Harry Potter, whose parents were murdered by the evil Lord Voldemort when he was only a year old. Harry was also targeted by this dark wizard, but somehow survived the attack. What is more, in the fray, Voldemort himself was vanquished, seemingly by Harry, who, it must be stressed, was only a baby. After the death of his parents, Harry is sent to live with his Muggle[1] relatives, the Dursleys, and upon his eleventh birthday, he is whisked away to Hogwarts School of Witchcraft and Wizardry. At this magical boarding school, he begins to train and hone his abilities; along the way, he befriends Ron Weasley (a loyal and somewhat lackadaisical wizard) and Hermione Granger (an often pedantic but all the same brilliant witch). He also comes under the protection of Albus Dumbledore, the benevolent, quasi–Machiavellian headmaster of the school, and arguably the most powerful wizard of his time. Harry eventually learns that Voldemort desires to become immortal, and that he had targeted a young Harry because of a prophecy, which predicted that Harry would be the one to vanquish him.

The first book in the series, *Harry Potter and the Sorcerer's Stone*, is frequently described as playfully lighthearted. However, as Harry (and, often the reader) grows and matures, the tone of the books changes and becomes much more somber. In the fourth book, *The Goblet of Fire*, Voldemort is reborn and once again goes about waging a highly destructive war against those who oppose him. After Dumbledore is murdered in the climax of the series' sixth book, *The Half-Blood Prince*, all seems lost, but in the final book, *The Deathly Hallows*, Harry and his friends are able to muster enough courage and determination to defeat Voldemort once and for all.

While the *Harry Potter* series is sometimes written off as "just another children's book," many of the book's central topics are surprisingly complex and rather dark. Epitomic of this is the series' central interest in the nature of death and the process of becoming its "Master." For different characters, this title holds different meanings. Voldemort so fears death that he seeks immortality by any means necessary, but, ironically, his obsessive desire to avoid his own demise ends up being his downfall. Harry and Dumbledore, on the other hand, seek not to conquer death, but rather to come to terms with it. Their realization that death is natural and unavoidable provides them with the strength to die for others, while at the same time becoming almost Messianic characters, who return from the grave (in various ways) and triumph over Voldemort and his minions.

The series' other central topic concerns love and how it, above all else, will inevitably allow victory over the legions of the wicked. While on the surface, "love conquers all" may seem trite and saccharine, Rowling does an excellent job of writing her characters so that they—while motivated by this most positive emotion—are nuanced, complicated, and often problematic.

Introduction

Perhaps the best example is Severus Snape, a rather cantankerous and cold professor of potions. Snape, throughout the series, is motivated to protect Harry by a deep and unending love for Harry's now-deceased mother, Lily—a love the readers only learn about in the final book. But while Snape is eventually revealed to be a "good guy," he constantly treats Harry cruelly because the boy reminds him of Lily's husband, James, who bullied Snape as a child. As such, Snape is regarded by many as one of the series' most complex and interesting characters, because, while his actions are ultimately motivated by goodness, his general behavior is usually reprehensible.

Over the years, many have been drawn to the *Harry Potter* series, and during the late 1990s and early 2000s, millions were swept up in what the critics called "Pottermania": the books began flying off the shelves of stores, library patrons struggled to get a hold of copies, and whenever a new novel was announced, fans would rush to nearby stores and camp out until the book's midnight release. Each successive novel drew in more fans than the last, leading the series to continuously set, break, and re-set records for the most copies sold upon release. The popularity of the series was also bolstered by highly successful cinematic interpretations of the books starring actors Daniel Radcliffe, Emma Watson, and Rupert Grint as Harry, Hermione, and Ron, respectively. The franchise has even spawned a massive and lucrative theme park chain called the Wizarding World of Harry Potter that attracts thousands of visitors (and dollars) every day.

Despite the first *Harry Potter* book being over 20 years old, the series has continued to remain very popular with readers, young and old alike. People enjoy the books for a variety of reasons, although most fans will claim that they fell in love with the series because of the colorful characters, the expansive world, the emotionally compelling themes, the allure of magic, or possibly Rowling's accessible writing style. And for many fans, this love has served as a creative catalyst, motivating them to produce their own paratexts, such as pieces of fan art or works of fan fiction that are directly inspired by the book series. A subset of these fans has translated their love for the series into original musical compositions. They are called wizard rockers (from here on out referred to as "wrockers," /ˈrɑː.kɚs/) and they are the subject of this present book.

But why focus on wizard rock of all things? Is it not just another instance of fans being weird? (During the course of writing this book, I was asked this more than I care to admit.) While such questions are understandable—after all, for many people in- and outside the *Harry Potter* fandom, wizard rock is seen as a fringe activity at most—they are ultimately shortsighted. The study of fan groups like the wrock community is important because these groups, whether consciously or not, are often reacting to or embracing the power structures, sociocultural constructs, belief systems, hegemonic norms, or hierarchies in a given society. Thus, by studying the world of wizard rock, we will not only learn a great deal about the people directly involved in penning songs, but also about the social, political, and economic contexts in which the movement emerged and continues to operate. For another thing, groups like the wrock community often function as microcosm of the larger world. So, for instance, by studying how fans interact at wrock shows or share songs via social media platforms, we can come to better understand the ways people communicate with one another, create identity, or generate distinct communities in general. In other words, the study of fan communities like wizard rock is important because in the end we will learn more about those very processes that help shape human culture at large.

What Is "Wizard Rock"? Defining the Magic

> We're rocking at Hogwarts
> Rocking the Room of Requirement
> We're rocking at Hogwarts
> And there's no one that can stop the wizard rock
>
> —Harry and the Potters, "Rocking at Hogwarts" (Featuring the first recorded instance of the term "wizard rock")[2]

When I inform people that I play in a wrock band, they often ask me incredulously, "What does that even *mean*?" I then tell them that I perform "*Harry Potter* songs," which generally sates their curiosity. But when you look at it, such an explanation is extremely broad, and encompasses material generally not considered part of the "official" wrock canon. For instance, are works by John Williams (i.e., the composer of several of the *Harry Potter* movies) like "Hedwig's Theme" or "Christmas at Hogwarts" wizard rock? Despite being not only inspired by the *Harry Potter* universe but also featured in the movies themselves, almost all wrock fans would agree that these should be seen as film scores, *not* wrock tracks. What about songs that briefly reference or allude to the *Harry Potter* universe, but are otherwise unrelated to the series (e.g., the song "Voldemort" by the pop punk band With Confidence)? Are they to be viewed as a part of wizard rock, too?

One of the key difficulties for someone wishing to write about a given topic is first defining the very thing about which they hope to write: after all, definitions are rarely objective, constraints are almost always artificial, and there is usually some outlier that resists being put into a neat little box. But because a working definition of wizard rock is essential to this project, I propose that wizard rock should be seen as a musical style and subculture that (a) focuses on *Harry Potter*; (b) emphasizes performance and performativity;

and (c) is united by a sense of community. By embracing this tripartite definition, I am able to entextualize wizard rock, separate it from related but distinct musical traditions,[3] and explore it in greater detail.

Wizard Rock Focuses on Harry Potter

Perhaps the most obvious and uncontroversial element of wizard rock is its focus on the *Harry Potter* book series. In particular, wrockers hold the series' "canon" (a term repurposed from theological discourse that denotes what is considered "real" or "true" within a fictional universe), as defined by the author J.K. Rowling, to be of paramount importance; the writer Rob Yoho, for instance, argues that for wrockers, "the *Harry Potter* books establish the basis for the master narrative while all other *Potter* iterations [e.g., the movies] must be qualified as offshoots from the original."[4] Wrockers embrace Rowling's view of the world, first because she is recognized by the fandom as its creator and thus its sole arbiter (Paul DeGeorge of Harry and the Potters, for instance, once described her as "our creator in a sense [and] kind of like … God"[5]), and second, because it allows wrockers to start from the same place, enabling common understanding.

There are, however, those bands that *do* deviate from Rowling's understanding of the canon. Given the nature of the movement itself, this is to be expected—by the act of creating their own independent works, wrock bands are expanding upon, reinterpreting, and purposely differing from the source material to suit their own ends.[6] Sometimes this deviation is done in the style of what one might call "traditional" fan fiction (a type of amateur fan literature that is discussed further in Chapter 1). For instance, a wrocker might select a character about which not much is known and then write an entire song about that character, effectively "making it all up" as they go. There are many wrock songs that fall into this category. However, with many of these creative works, wrockers still respect or acknowledge what Rowling has or has not confirmed; according to the classicist and wrock scholar Anne C. Smith, these individuals take "on an authorial role to generate new characters and events in the *Harry Potter* universe" [but] "also restrict their own authorial and participatory power."[7] Smith argues that this is because these fans, while creating their own original paratexts, often hold to an understanding that, in the end, Rowling is the One True Author, and that they are ultimately just readers without the power to change "real" canon.[8]

At other times, wizard rock breaks wildly from Rowling's canon. Often, this deviation is done to make some sort of (generally humorous) point. A classic example is the song "Brotherly Love" by Gred and Forge, which details a lewd, incestuous and decidedly non-canon relationship between the brothers Fred and George Weasley. The humor of this song, aside from the obvious shock value, is derived from the lyrics' self-aware break from the series' official canon. Another example in this vein is the entirety of Tianna Mignogna's 2012 EP entitled *Fangz 2 Raven*, focusing exclusively on the infamous *Harry Potter* fan fiction *My Immortal*.⁹ The EP's songs humorously present *My Immortal* as if it were canonical. By doing this, Mignogna is not suggesting that she actually believes *My Immortal* to be Rowling-level canon; rather Mignogna is pretending to privilege the work as canon to highlight its absurdity.¹⁰ But while songs like "Brotherly Love" or records like *Fangz 2 Raven* might break from Rowling's understanding of canon, it is important to emphasize that they still exist in relation to and directly play off that canon, thereby highlighting its utmost importance (as contradictory as that might seem).

Of course, after one accepts the perhaps straightforward point that wizard rock is about *Harry Potter*, the question soon arises: What makes the *Harry Potter* book series so special that there exists a large group of fans dedicated to writing songs about it and it alone? Perhaps it is because the *Harry Potter* universe is simply so sprawling. These sorts of big fictional universes are ripe for the creation of fan-made paratexts (such as songs), as they more easily allow individuals to hone in on undeveloped portions of the world (like minor characters, briefly mentioned locations, or alluded-to stories) and expand them to their heart's content. But there are a number of large fictional universes out there, and hardly any of them have inspired the same sort of musical interest as the world of *Harry Potter* has—for example, why has *Star Wars* or *Lord of the Rings* not inspired large-scale musical movements akin to wizard rock?¹¹

For one thing, wizard rock emerged during a very specific historical and technological context. In 2002, Pottermania was part of the zeitgeist, with the books having ensnared an entire generation of children, as well as countless teenagers and adults. At the same time, technological breakthroughs had decreased the price of recording equipment, and more and more people were connecting online thanks to newfound high-speed Internet access. While fans had been composing songs for years about their favorite media franchises, these recent advances meant that fans could not only write their own songs but also easily record and distribute them to others via the Internet. To (ab)use an idiom, wizard rock simply started in the right place at the right time.

In addition to material conditions, I believe it best to also consider how the very spirit of the *Harry Potter* series led to the emergence of wizard rock. While *Harry Potter* is no doubt cut from the same monomythic cloth as other great works like *Star Wars* or *Lord of the Rings*, there is something particularly youthful—and dare I say it, angsty—about the adventures of the Boy Who Lived. Harry and his friends are first and foremost teenagers, and although our heroes deal with all sorts of supernatural threats, it is the real, youthful struggle of surviving adolescence and rebelling against older, corrupt generations that is most often foregrounded in the series. There is something about this narrative focus that recalls the ethos of rock—a music genre that often expresses the frustrations of youth and chastises the failings of previous generations. In fact, there is so much overlap between the spirit of both the books and rock music that Paul DeGeorge once even wrote in his diary, "If you want real rock, you have to go to Hogwarts."[12]

Wizard Rock Emphasizes Performance and Performativity

The second feature of wizard rock that needs to be considered is its emphasis both on performance and performativity. The word "performance" has many definitions, but here I use it to mean a "tangible, bounded event that involves the presentation of rehearsed artistic actions [by] a performer (someone doing something) [to] a spectator (someone observing something)".[13] Provided with this definition, categorizing wizard rock as a type of performance seems uncontroversial. For one thing, wizard rock is clearly bounded and temporal; at wrock concerts, the performances are delineated by things such as venue space and costuming, all of which clearly demarcate where and when shows begin and end. For another, wizard rock is highly self-aware, with both audience members and bands being "in on" the routine.

One could argue that these elements of performance are not unique to wizard rock and are instead endemic to almost every genre and style of music out there. While this is true, it is important to note the ways in which the performance elements of wizard rock differ when compared to other musical traditions or genres. For one thing, wrockers often eschew convention and perform in places that do not normally host concerts, like libraries. And, so often do bands play in these sorts of locations that the concept of "playing a show in the library" has become a trope that is not laughed about but rather one that is actively embraced within the wrock community. By explicitly situating their performances within environments that they otherwise "do not belong," these musicians are thus highlighting the central role that performance plays in wizard rock.

But, perhaps more importantly, wrock performances often make heavy use of role-play (i.e., the mimetic act in which an individual temporarily assumes the role of a specific character). This feature of wizard rock is perhaps best exemplified by Harry and the Potters, comprising brothers Paul and Joe DeGeorge, both of whom contend that they each *are* Harry Potter when putting on a show. Consider the unique way in which they often begin their concerts:

PAUL DEGEORGE: "I'm Harry Potter!"
JOE DEGEORGE: "And *I'm* Harry Potter!"
PAUL AND JOE: "And *we're* Harry and the Potters!"[14]

Arguably, it is this sort of character inhabitation that is most often associated with wrockers in the popular consciousness, and most write-ups about the scene generally include some sort of reference to role-playing within at least the first few paragraphs. Often, this behavior is considered in relation to other fannish activities, such as cosplay.

A discussion of wizard rock's penchant for role-play necessarily leads into a discussion of the movement's performative nature. "Performativity" is a social scientific term introduced by the linguist J.L. Austin that originally described speech acts that, once they are uttered by an individual, actually create certain aspects of sociocultural reality.[15] The gender theorist Judith Butler borrowed and modified the term to refer to actions that, when enacted, change or even create aspects of an individual's identity.[16] Despite the narrowness of Butler's initial use of the term—she originally invoked this retooled definition of performativity to consider how the citation of gendered actions gives rise to *gender* identity—"performativity" has become a major concept in a number of academic disciplines and is often invoked in discussions about any activity that changes reality through enactment.[17]

Arguably, wizard rock is one such activity. How so? As we have discussed above, wrockers often don the role of certain characters and then perform as those characters during shows. By jumping into the role of a specific character, a wrocker is not only bringing them to life, but they are also establishing an "intimate connection" between that character and themselves. This "intimate connection" inevitably transfers onto the wrocker those traits associated with that character, and this transfer in turn influences how others perceive that wrocker in real life.[18] In other words, wrock role-play is a form of self-expression, and by connecting themselves to specific characters in some way, wrockers can shape their own identities.

What all of this means is that in order to fully understand wizard rock itself, it is important to understand the role that both "performance" and "performativity" play in the movement. Taken together, these two elements demonstrate that wizard rock is not simply "songs about *Harry Potter*," but rather an elaborate and extended routine, in which musicians inhabit specific roles, in specific places, and in specific ways to achieve specific ends.

Wizard Rock Is a Community

The third—and, arguably, most important—feature of wizard rock is its communal aspect. When discussing wizard rock, many refer to it simply as a genre, akin to "alternative rock" or "hip-hop." While this term is technically correct (wizard rock, after all, is a distinct style of music, set apart from other styles by its shared lyrical content), there is something lacking about the way it is often used. Perhaps this is because the term "genre" does not even come close to describing the sense of "togetherness" felt by many wrock bands and fans. Given the deficiency of the term "genre" then, perhaps it is best to describe wizard rock as a community. According to the sociologist Elizabeth D. Hutchison, "Attempts to reach agreement on the definition of community have centered on the report that [most definitions] in the sociological literature included the same three elements: [shared] geographic area, social interaction, and common ties."[19] With these three features in mind, Hutchison thus defines community as "people who are bound either by geography or by webs of communication, sharing common ties, and interacting with one another."[20] Wizard rock, as we shall soon see, satisfies all of the criteria in Hutchison's definition.

While it is a fact that wrock bands are to be found disproportionately in the United States, wizard rock is not by definition restricted to any specific region or area[21]; indeed, there are wrock bands the world over, from Australia to Russia. But while there is no single geographic area in the "real world"[22] that wrock bands share in common, there does exist a sort of "virtual geography" that almost all wrock bands share: closely bound social media circles. The importance of social media in regard to wizard rock cannot be understated. When their movement was just beginning, wrockers made heavy use of sites like MySpace to discuss and propagate wizard rock. These sites allowed like-minded individuals to congregate closely in one simulated "place," obviating the limits of real-world geography. Even today, those within the wrock scene still rely on sites like Twitter and Facebook to stay connected. Ultimately, it is these social media sites—these virtual "areas" of interaction— that allow many of wizard rock's tight-knit relationships to form and flourish.[23]

This online sense of "space" inevitably leads to the emergence of what Hutchinson would call "webs of communication."[24] These virtual avenues facilitate interaction between people who might never otherwise meet (e.g., bands who have never performed live shows, or fans who are isolated from one another in the real world by thousands of miles). As the previous paragraph established, these online hubs of interaction ultimately allow wizard rock to flourish. Now, it must be noted that interaction between wrockers is by no means confined entirely to the digital world. Indeed, during live shows, both bands and fans alike step away from the comfortable glow of their computers and engage with one another in spatio-temporal "real life." With that said, it does seem that the webs of communication which emerge in "real life" are often engendered by their online counterparts (e.g., fans meet and come to know each other online before actually meeting in real life at a wrock concert).

And as to whether wrockers share common ties with one another or not, this seems demonstrably to be true. For one thing, the members of this movement are unified by their enjoyment of a shared set of texts: the *Harry Potter* series. But perhaps more significantly, wrockers are united by their level of *enthusiasm* for these texts—after all, there are many fans of *Harry Potter* out in the world, but only a small number are devoted enough to write songs about the series. This love of and enthusiasm for the books has led to many wrockers embracing their own shared "fannish cosmology" (if you will), based on *Harry Potter*: those who enjoy or produce wizard rock are seen as good wizards fighting against the evil Dark Arts, "Voldemort" is used as a metaphor for any source of evil or malady in the world, music is viewed as an extremely powerful form of magic, and books are a particularly effective weapon against the forces of darkness. These ideas are frequently heard during wrock shows and are often touched upon in songs themselves. Of course, wrockers understand that this "cosmology" is a fiction (for instance, you would be hard-pressed to find wrockers who truly believe that Harry Potter is an actual person),[25] but they embrace it all the same because it provides them with a mutual grounding—a collective "understanding of the world" that creatively enables individuals to recognize the ties that unite them as one community.

Finally, it should be noted that many within the wrock scene are open about the sense of alienation they felt before they discovered the wide world of wizard rock; these same individuals are also open about the extreme happiness they felt once they became "part of" the scene. This oft-described movement from isolation to acceptance by a larger group suggests that, indeed, there is some*thing* into which would-be wrockers can join. It is this "thing" that I consider to be the wrock community.

1

Wizard Rock: A History

At 2017's MISTI-Con, attendees were greeted by a surprise: a veritable wrock museum, documenting the scene from its inception to the present day. Spread out across the tops of a number of strategically placed tables and pasted onto walls, the exhibit unfolded chronologically, exploring the story of wizard rock through textual snippets, hundreds of photographs, and various pieces of physical evidence, like ticket stubs, t-shirts, lyric sheets, CDs, setlists and a plethora of assorted merchandise.

Grace Kendall, the display's curator and a wrocker who records music under the name "Snidget," spent a month researching the history of the movement, collecting items, designing the exhibition, and whittling a photography collection composed of 12,000 unique photos down to just 300. In an interview, Kendall told me:

> My friend Jenn Levine and I have talked for years about doing a wizard rock museum, but when I decided to go to MISTI-Con and saw the theme was "Coming Home" I just felt like this was the right time to do it.... I accepted almost every item that was loaned to me—the people I reached out to had great taste and were selective about what posters, setlists, and notebooks they offered. I used to heavily photograph the scene so I knew I wanted a lot of photos, and I tried to choose images that represented the community and highlighted some of the bigger events that took place.... [The whole exhibit] was less learning new things and more being reminded of old things I'd forgotten.[1]

While the primary purpose of this exhibit was to nostalgically remind people of days gone by, it also reinforced the fact that quite a bit has happened in wizard rock's relatively short life.

Wizard rock is just under two decades old, but in this brief stretch of time, the community has experienced just as many developments as other older and more established musical genres: twists and turns, fortuitous accidents, brief feuds, and the possible threat of irrelevance. But wizard rock— to the surprise of many—has surmounted most obstacles, and while still being very much an underground phenomenon continues to thrive. In this chapter, I explicate the colorful history of wizard rock, starting with three key traditions (viz. punk rock, filk music, and fan fiction) that preceded and arguably influenced the movement. I then explore wizard rock's origins, expound how it evolved, and end with a survey of the current state of the scene.

Antecedents

New ideas rarely, if ever, arise from a total vacuum, as there is almost always some precursor that engenders their emergence. While to many, wizard rock is a truly unique movement and thus an exception to the rule, it too is not exempt from this reality. Unfortunately, because it is often considered to be one of kind and unprecedented, many who discuss the history of wizard rock either briefly touch upon or entirely gloss over that which came before it, instead choosing to begin by immediately considering the movement's oft-recounted "origin story." I would like to rectify this issue by first considering three key traditions that, in their own ways, preceded and ultimately came to influence wizard rock: punk rock, filk music, and fan fiction.

The first of these, punk rock, is the one that is most often discussed by music critic, but this connection is rarely explored beyond a paragraph or two at the most.[2] This is unfortunate, given that these two musical traditions share much in common, with perhaps the biggest similarity being that both are defined by a raw and unpolished sound, as well as a do-it-yourself (DIY) work ethic. Most scholars trace the origins of the punk rock tradition to the homegrown "garage rock" scene of the mid–20th century.[3] Members of these bands were often restless youths, craving "to escape ... suburbia,"[4] and their music was generally simple, raw, and sometimes sloppy (musically speaking), reflecting their relative inexperience as musicians.[5] This did not matter to them, as writer Ryan Cooper argues that these groups were interested in "break[ing] the rules ... of music" more so than conforming to a standard that society arbitrarily considered correct.[6] By 1971, music critic Dave Marsh had developed the term "punk rock" to better describe a number of these youthful groups,[7] many of whom began to espouse rebellious philosophies in their lyrics.

The beginning of the 1970s saw the formation of a number of bands who would go on to be influential within the eventual punk movement, like MC5, The New York Dolls, Television, The Fugs, The Stooges, and The Velvet Underground.[8] Then, in 1973–75, a major economic recession affected parts of the industrial world, leading to torpid economic growth, monetary inflation, and high unemployment. Without a livelihood to look forward to, many young individuals living in effected nations became despondent and picked up instruments to vent their frustrations through fast, raw, and aggressive music.[9] By the middle of the decade, bands like The Ramones and The Sex Pistols had signed to major labels and were releasing albums, charting singles, and causing controversy with their "stick-it-to-the-Man" antics.[10] During this time, punk was mostly confined to the U.S. and the UK, but during the close of the 1970s, the genre became world (in)famous. By the Reagan-Thatcher era, punk had further distilled itself into a variety of styles,[11] and by the mid–1990s, a more radio-friendly variant now commonly referred to as "pop punk" became popular thanks to California-based bands like Bad Religion, Green Day, NOFX, The Offspring, and Rancid.[12]

Quite a few early punk rockers saw then-popular music as "fake" and far too pretentious, and so they distanced themselves from the mainstream music industry by emphasizing a stripped-down, raw sound.[13] Within this community, there emerged a widespread understanding that punk music did not have to necessarily be "good," but it *did* have to be authentic. Michael Stewart Foley in a monograph centered on the Dead Kennedys' 1978 debut album *Fresh Fruit for Rotting Vegetables*, succinctly explained this philosophy by saying, "What mattered [to punk rockers] was truth—being true to onself, to one's community and to anyone else who would listen.... Status derived from wealth or some other mainstream calculus of success simply did not matter to them."[14] Adherents of this philosophy hold that the worst crime a wannabe punk rocker could commit was trying to join the scene or pen a tune without understanding what the movement "meant."

As discussed earlier, when the punk movement emerged in full-force, the world was in a state of economic turmoil. This context led to many of the biggest punk bands espousing inflammatory political opinions that derided the current state of the world, with quite a few punkers specifically choosing to compare contemporary political figureheads to the leaders of dictatorial regimes like Nazi Germany: The Sex Pistols, for instance, blasted the Queen of England for being a fascist monstrosity in their song "God Save the Queen," and the Dead Kennedys heavily implied that California Governor Jerry Brown was cut from the same cloth as Adolf Hitler in their debut single "California Über Alles."[15] This overt and abrasive rejection of the ruling status quo has led to punk rock being intimately associated with progressive, leftist, and revolutionary politics (although it should be noted that rightwing punk bands do indeed exist).

Given the above, it can perhaps be seen why punk and wizard rock are often compared. For one thing, many wrock bands embrace a stripped-down, raw style that recalls the 1970s punk sound; Yaritza Gonzalez (an administrator of the popular Facebook group "Wizard Rock Revival"), for instance, argued that Harry and the Potters' "first album is in a lot of ways reminiscent of The Ramones."[16] Wizard rock also mirrors punk's attitude about authenticity and talent, in that the community is fairly forgiving of poor musicianship as long as the musicians in question are motivated by a sense of enthusiasm and love for the *Harry Potter* series, and not by the desire to gain fame or fortune.[17] Moreover, like their punk comrades, wrock bands often concern themselves with (generally leftist) politics or issues of social justice, with many wrockers choosing to compare certain contemporary political leaders not to Nazis, but rather to Voldemort, his henchmen, or the complicit Ministry of Magic. Finally—and perhaps most importantly—punk and wizard rock are united in their embracing of a DIY philosophy, or an ethical system generally associated with anti-consumerism and a desire to become independent of the whims of materialistic, capitalist culture. This ethos is often driving, inspiring these bands to book their own shows, record their own songs, and burn or press up their own albums.

These overlapping characteristics have led many within the wrock scene to readily adopt the punk label in tandem with that of wizard rock. Steph Anderson of Tonks and the Aurors,[18] for instance, argued on a Facebook post that her band is based around and inspired by the ethos of the punk subgenre "riot grrrl."[19] On the same post, Amanda Leigh Lepelstat of The Restricted Section wrote something similar, stressing that her band "is *specifically* punk."[20] In a personal interview, Holly Casio of the Shrieking Shack Disco Gang[21] echoed the previous comments by arguing that her band's music is situated within "the wider context of concept punk."[22] Finally, Paul and Joe DeGeorge of Harry and the Potters—arguably the founders of wizard rock—are upfront about the influence that punk rock played in the formation of their group, describing their music as "if Harry Potter quit the Quidditch[23] team and started a punk rock band."[24] In an interview with Fuse, Paul further said:

> [Our band] kind of came out of the books. Harry ... has got this mistrust of authority. He's not afraid to speak his mind. I sort of saw a lot of that in my punk rock heroes. So I thought, "Wouldn't it be cool if Harry Potter started his own punk rock band?"[25]

However, a major problem of ideology soon emerges. Punk, as I noted earlier, is often associated with an anti-consumerist line of thought due to its embrace of DIY ethics.[26] If this is the case, it seems that there is a very real contradiction at the heart of wizard rock: On one hand, the movement claims to be punk, eschewing corporatization and commercialization. On the other, the movement is not only intimately connected to but ultimately dependent on consumer culture, given that it is built upon the decidedly commercial works of J.K. Rowling and Warner Brothers. How can wizard rock claim to be "punk" when it so keenly embraces rampant consumerism?

But perhaps this is a false dilemma. After all, taking an existing commercial property and reinterpreting it does not inherently make one a corporate shill or a peon to the whims of stockholders. On the contrary, it may actually make one a true rebel.

One of the first media theorists to argue something like this was Henry Jenkins, who introduced the concept of "textual poaching" in his essay "*Star Trek* Rerun, Reread, Rewritten" (1988) and then expanded upon it in his book *Textual Poachers* (1992). Citing the ideas of the social theorist Michel de Certeau, Jenkins proposed that fans who take existing media and repurpose them to serve their own interests should be seen as "textual poachers," who:

> reclaim works that others regard as "worthless" trash, finding them a source of popular capital. Like rebellious children, fans refuse to read by the rules imposed upon them by the schoolmasters. For the fan, reading becomes a kind of play, responsive only to its own loosely structured rules and generating its own kinds of pleasures.[27]

Jenkins argues that the concept of textual poaching functions as "a powerful counterimage to prevailing stereotypes of fans as passive consumers and cultural dupes."[28] By applying Jenkins's hypothesis to wrockers, one could argue that they are really rogue content creations, who—far from (literally) buying into "The Man" by celebrating the Boy Who Lived—choose instead to "reject the rules that have forcibly been foisted upon them."[29]

While a number of scholars have sought to move fan studies away from Jenkins' formulation of "textual poaching" (this idea was, after all, developed almost thirty years ago when fan studies was in its relative infancy), I think that that the idea applies nicely when considering the intersection of punk and wizard rock, especially when one takes into account the perspectives of the wrockers themselves, many of whom believe they are bucking authority and reclaiming *Harry Potter* when they pen wrock tunes. Paul DeGeorge, for instance, once contended in an interview that his band actively promotes "the *anti*-corporatization of Harry Potter"[30] [emphasis added]—and if that is not in the spirit of punk rock, then I do not know what is.

For many, Jenkins's idea of "textual poachers" may recall a different type of musical movement—one that is intimately associated with fans taking pre-existing texts and reinterpreting them to serve some new musical purpose: filk. This idiosyncratic term[31] refers to a genre of music, loosely defined as being made up of songs inspired by sci-fi or fantasy franchises; Jenkins, through the act of quoting the pseudonymous filker "Sourdough Johnson," more colloquially defines filk music as "the folk songs of fandom."[32]

The origins of filk are hazy, but most agree that the tradition emerged in the context of 20th century sci-fi and fantasy conventions ("cons"). At these events, some musically-inclined fans would meet up in in open spaces conducive to jamming (which came to be called "filk rooms"). They would then arrange themselves in a circle and take turns performing and discussing songs that they had written (this sort of get-together is called a "filksing" or a "filk circle").[33] When it was in its infancy, filking was decidedly ad hoc, as there were not many established "rules" governing the scene. Over time, however, filking "etiquette" began to develop, and nowadays filking is a sophisticated practice that is integral to what one might call "con culture."[34] And while modern cons might feature things like elaborate "filk concerts," it is still very common to see people performing in filk rooms (just like the filkers of yesteryear).[35]

According to Melissa Tatum, detailing the (sub)cultural milieu from which filk emerged is not a problem for the ethnomusicologists, but the same cannot be said about delineating the quiddity of the genre. Part of this is because filk encompsses a broad range of topics and musical styles. Tatum writes:

> Some [filk songs] use original lyrics; some use lyrics based on characters and universes created by other people; and some set poems or other written words to music. The lyrics can be poignant, witty, even ribald; they can celebrate an event, critique a work, provide social commentary, poke fun, or tell an original story.... The tunes for filk songs come from a variety of places. When many people think of filk, their first thought is of parody—someone taking a well-known tune that is subject to copyright, stripping the lyrics, and writing new ones, a sort of ["Weird Al"] Yankovic for the science fiction set. And although that is certainly common, it is far from the only form of filk. The melodies for filk songs can also be drawn from the public domain, and many filk songs are set to original compositions.[36]

But despite the rather nebulous nature of the movement, a filker named Gary McGath, via an online manifesto cited by Tatum, attempted to provide a thorough, accurate, and succinct definition of the genre by describing it as "a musical movement among fans of science fiction and fantasy fandom and closely related activities, emphasizing content which is related to the genre or its fans, and promoting broad participation. Filkers are people who participate in this movement."[37] Given its simplistic yet thorough nature, McGath's definition has gained popularity in the filk and fandom studies scene, and it is this definition that I use in this book.

Since filk includes, among other things, music based on fantastical media, parallels can be drawn between it and wizard rock. For one thing, both traditions are composed largely of amateur musicians who sing about fictional universes. For another, both filkers and wrockers are sometimes known to take popular hits and rewrite their lyrics to be about a different, fannish subject (i.e., "parody songs," often informally—and, in some cases, confusingly—called "filks"). What is more, both wizard rock and filk have also remained fairly underground movements, popular only with a select group of fandom-minded people. Finally, filk and wizard rock have both found homes at fan conventions.

Given the above similarities and the fact that filk emerged as its own

The Blibbering Humdingers preform at Camelot Treasures in Cary, North Carolina, in 2009. The band, made up of Kirsten and Scott Vaughan, has one foot in both the filk and wizard rock genres (courtesy Selena N.B.H)

movement decades before the rise of wizard rock, it seems almost undeniable that filk either helped set the stage for wizard rock or influenced how the movement evolved in some regard. But some people, including a number of academics[38] have taken this comparison a step further, arguing that wizard rock should really only be considered a niche sub-division of the filk community. While the theorist of fan cultures Suzanne Scott notes that it *is* "tempting to view wrock simply as evolved filk for the MySpace age," she cautions that "a number of factors trouble such a reading."[39]

For one thing, she notes that wrockers embrace a "performer/audience ... binary" that favors bands actively playing music to passive audiences, whereas filkers embrace a non-binary, "democratic, [and] spontaneous creative enterprise" (e.g., the filksing) in which all those involved are also actively participating.[40] In an interview, Scott Vaughan of the filk/wrock band The Blibbering Humdingers, told me something similar when said that wrock musicians are "more focused on 'being a band' ... and playing concerts" to fans, whereas in the filk community, "most of the performing happens in casual circles" amongst a small group of "musicians hav[ing] a good time."[41] This filk/wrock performance distinction is perhaps made most cogently by Tatum, who writes that "wizard rock ... promotes performance to a particular crowd [whereas filk focuses on] building a community of performers who perform for each other."[42]

This divide in performance styles is indicative of a deeper divide in identity. According to Tatum, filkers as a whole have a specific understanding of what it *means* to filk. Wrockers on the other hand, have a specific understanding of what it *means* to wrock out. These two understandings give rise to different behaviors, presumptions, and—ultimately—identities that shape how members of filk or wizard rock think about their respective subcultures.[43] For instance, some wrockers to whom I talked rejected the "filk" descriptor simply because they believed that it was not an appropriate label fot their shtick. Still other wrockers—including several of those who founded the movement—told me that they had never even heard of filk when they started their bands. Perhaps best exemplifying this sort of unfamiliarity was Paul DeGeorge, who said: "I didn't know anything about filk when Joe and I started [Harry and the Potters]. It makes sense to me that filk exists but that is certainly not where we came from."[44]

Still other wrockers do not take on the filk label because they simply have not found acceptance in wider filk circles. Steph Anderson, for instance, commented the following on a Facebook post discussing the relationship between wizard rock and filk:

> While I think some [wizard rock] musicians cross over to filk, I don't think most of us would consider [ourselves] a part of [that scene]. I think wizard rock would exist if filk hadn't arrived. *I would also expect to have been accepted more by filk at large if we were considered filk, which I can personally say has not been the case in my 10 years of participation in wizard rock* [emphasis added].[45]

I agree with Anderson, as my band, The 8th Horcrux, exclusively performs fannish parody songs (a type of music, as mentioned earlier in this section, that is stereotypically associated with filkers), yet we have been unable to break into the wider filk community.

What this means is that referring to wizard rock as only "a filk subculture" is problematic because such an assertion ignores the importance of self-identity.[46] Of course, this is not to say that filk did not influence the way wizard rock evolved over time; this seems patently untrue, given that a few wrock groups are upfront about their movement from the world of filk into the world of wizard rock. Nor does this suggest that there is not *any* overlap between the two traditions whatsoever; this too is false, as many performers, such as the aforementioned Blibbering Humdingers or Alex Boyd, take part in both the filk and wrock scenes and have identities associated with both. Rather, it simply means that filk and wizard rock are two separate albeit related traditions with distinct conceptions of what their respective movements "mean." Similarities between the two should be noted but lumping them into one blanket category is at best simplistic and at worst just plain wrong.

The final antecedent to be considered is not a music tradition, but rather a form of amateur literature: fan fiction. According to Patrik Wikstrom and Christina Olin-Scheller, the term "fan fiction" refers to stories "based on well-established characters and structures, but written by the fans of these well-established characters rather than by the original author."[47] Sometimes, fan fiction (often just called "fanfic") focuses on a media franchise's more popular characters; conversely, other works focus on "minor characters" (i.e., characters who appear "in the background" or who otherwise remain undeveloped within a given text), or new characters that the fan fiction writers have themselves created ("original characters," often abbreviated online as "OCs"). From a technical standpoint, works of fan fiction are what one might call "unauthorized," given that they are fan-created paratexts and not the "official" creations of a media franchise's original author(s). Consequently, most fanfics are viewed by readers as being separate from a franchise's main "canon."[48]

Many of the behaviors endemic to fan fiction circles have crossed over into the realm of wizard rock. For instance, fan fiction helped popularize the aforementioned appropriating of established characters and reinterpreting them in new contexts—something that wizard rock does, only in a musical setting. Fan fiction also assisted in the popularization of "shipping" (a term, pared down from "relationshipping," referring to "the act of supporting or wishing for a particular romantic relationship ... by discussing it, writing ... about it, or creating other types of fanworks exploring it"[49])—a concept with which wrockers have also taken and run.

Furthermore, because both wrock songs and works of fan fiction are unofficial and unapproved paratexts, their authors have greater freedom to put forth different interpretations of the source material. This leads to some wrockers and fan fiction writers alike breaking from established canon if they fear that the author (be it J.K. Rowling or possibly Warner Brothers) is not treating the original series in a way that they believe is appropriate. These fans purposely "undo" or go against that which they dislike to keep their interpretation of *Harry Potter* intact. Henry Jenkins, in his essay "*Star Trek* Rerun, Reread, Rewritten," refers to this as a fannish form of the "moral economy," in which groups of people justify their actions by appealing to fairness, and ideals such as "the wider consensus of the community."[50] While the concept of a moral economy was developed to explain peasant revolts, Jenkins repurposes the term and situates it firmly within fan studies, writing: "Fans respect the original texts yet fear that their conceptions of the characters and concepts may be jeopardized by those who wish to exploit them."[51] Jenkins's original use of the term was in regard to the *Star Trek* fandom, but his points can still be applied to the world of wizard rock, as some wrockers may deviate wildly from what is official canon to preserve that which they feel is special about the series in the first place.

Given the amount of overlap between the two fan traditions, calling wizard rock a type of "musical fan fiction" may in fact be appropriate—although, as we shall explore throughout this book, wizard rock is much more nuanced than what any single, snappy phrase can get across.

The First "Wrock" Songs (2000–02)

Many, both in and outside the community, argue that wizard rock as a genre owes its existence to the song "Ode to Harry," released at the tail end of 2000 by the Southern California–based pop punk band Switchblade Kittens.[52] This song was the brainchild of the group's frontwoman, Drama, who had developed the idea after reading the *Chamber of Secrets*. While Drama thoroughly enjoyed the book, she was somewhat off-put by the main characters' treatment of Ginny Weasley; she explained, "Ginny ... was not getting a fair shake in the book. Ginny is always around.... Hermione, Ron, and Harry [but they] did not include her."[53] This was a disappointment for Drama because she believed Ginny to be one of the series' more promising characters, who had "the possibility of ... stand[ing] up for herself in a major heroic way [and] becoming a true riot grrrl."[54]

To sublimate these concerns, Drama decided to write a Switchblade Kittens single, sung from the point of view of a young Ginny, which expresses the character's irritation at always being left out of Harry's adventures. The first stanza goes as follows:

> I can't help but blush when you're near me
> But you just exclude me from your circle of three
> I'm right in front of you, but you don't see
> You treat me like I'm a Colin Creevey

While the lyrics are similar to those of many pop songs that discuss the pain of exclusion and unrequited love, they are set apart by their copious *Harry Potter* references. The band dubbed the final track "Ode to Harry"—and just like that, the first wrock song was arguably born.[55]

Unfortunately, because Switchblade Kittens was signed to a record label, Drama and her bandmates were unable to release songs for sale without approval from label executives. Given the mountain of legal paperwork that such a release would inevitably entail, the label passed on the idea of sanctioning the song as an official single. But because Switchblade Kittens so wished to unleash their creation into the world, they released "Ode to Harry" as free digital download during December 2000.[56] The group also let *Harry Potter* fan sites host the digital track if they were so inclined. Much to the surprise of Drama and her bandmates, the song exploded in popularity, and within a few short months of release had been downloaded a staggering three million times.[57]

While playing various stops on the Vans Warped Tour, the members of Switchblade Kittens also started to see many *Harry Potter* fans attend their sets, and in several instances, fans even leaped onto the stage to sing "Ode to Harry" with Drama.[58] Drama was initially astounded—and, to be honest, a bit perplexed—that the song had resonated with so many people, considering that it had not been officially released by a label. Nevertheless, she was pleased with how the song was received and soon came to the realization that "Potterheads are everywhere."[59]

"Ode to Harry" would not be the only time Switchblade Kittens would dabble in wizard rock. In 2006, they returned to the *Harry Potter* universe with their album *The Weird Sisters*, comprising 13 *Harry Potter*-inspired songs. On the band's website, Drama wrote:

> [After the release of "Ode to Harry"] I literally received thousands of e-mails begging me to write an entire CD about *Harry Potter*.... After [a] record deal fell through I experienced the toughest time in my entire life.... I made it through by reading about Harry and his trials; I can honestly say that *Harry Potter* may have saved my sanity.... I returned the [favor] to Harry by writing this 13 song CD called *The Weird Sisters*. It is not a collection of songs about plot summaries but a reaction to the emotion and strengths that are encountered in the books and in a magical life.[60]

Given their contributions, Switchblade Kittens—and Drama in particular—are seen by many as the progenitors of what we now know as wizard rock (although Drama prefers the more eclectic and humorous title "cool aunt of wizard rock").[61]

For many years, it was supposed that no other wrock songs were recorded between the release of "Ode to Harry" and the rise of Harry and the Potters. But a revelation in October 2016 challenged this long-held belief. Near the end of the month, during an interview with BBC Radio 2, Bruce Springsteen let slip that prior to the 2001 release of the *Harry Potter and the Sorcerer's Stone* film, he had recorded a song entitled "I'll Stand by You Always" that he had hoped would be used in the movie. Springsteen described the song, which he had written for his son, as "very uncharacteristic of something [he]'d sing [himself and] something that [he] thought would have fit lovely" somewhere in the film.[62] Alas, the producers turned him down, and the song went into Springsteen's vault, where it languished for almost fifteen years until it leaked online in February 2017. Given that the song was inspired by the *Harry Potter* series, many like to argue that "I'll Stand by You Always" is the second wrock song to have ever been written.[63]

It should be noted that the identification of "Ode to Harry" and "I'll Stand by You Always" as the first wrock songs was *post facto*; Bruce Springsteen, for instance, never embraced the label "wizard rock,"[64] and Switchblade Kittens only adopted it after the movement took off. This is not an indictment of either group, or an attempt to argue that "Ode to Harry" and "I'll Stand by You Always" are not *real* wrock songs. Rather, it is to elucidate the wrock scene's canonical "meta-narrative" on how their movement began. Once Harry and the Potters had firmly established themselves as the popularizers of the movement, there was a desire to look back and find the scene's roots. It was at this point that "Ode to Harry" (and later "I'll Stand by You Always," once its existence became known) was retroactively added to the wrock canon.

The Rise of Harry and the Potters (2002–04)

While at the turn of the millennium, underground groups like Switchblade Kittens and established musicians like Bruce Springsteen were toying around with songs inspired by *Harry Potter*, it was not until 2002 that what most currently recognize as "wizard rock" emerged in full force. It was in this year that Harry and the Potters, comprising brothers Paul and Joe DeGeorge, burst onto the scene and paved the way for other like-minded *Harry Potter* enthusiasts.

The DeGeorges grew up in the quiet Massachusetts city of Norwood, not far from the heart of Boston.[65] While both Paul (born 1979) and Joe (born 1987) were fascinated with science and mathematics, the two were also creative souls, who shared a deep love for the preforming arts: Paul played guitar in a wistful synth-pop band called The Secrets, ardently curated Christmas and indie music, and even ran a small record label named Eskimo Laboratories out of his parents' house.[66] Likewise, Joe acted in high school plays and performed in the eccentric rock band Ed in the Refridgerators [*sic*], whose quirky songs included "Windows 95 Ding," "Mary had a Little Lamb in C Minor (with Spaghettios)," and "The Pope Song."[67]

On June 22, 2002, Joe had organized a concert and barbeque jamboree in his parents' backyard shed, at which Ed in the Refridgerators was slated to perform alongside Paul's band The Secrets and the lo-fi one-man-band Soltero.[68] Unfortunately, due to extenuating circumstances, the latter two bands canceled at the last minute, and when the hour of the concert finally arrived, only about a half-dozen of Ed in the Refridgerators' loyal fans even bothered to attend. But even a few people is still an (albeit diminutive) audience, and Paul did not want to disappoint them by calling off the show, so he suggested to Joe that they perform as "Harry and the Potters."[69]

This idea, which Paul had been thinking about for some time, can trace its genesis back to 2001. That year, Paul had finally read all the then-released *Harry Potter* books. Having always been drawn to punk rock, he was immediately impressed by the "punk" ethos of Harry and his friends.[70] This revelation, along with his love for oddball bands like The Zambonis (a group from Bridgeport, Connecticut, that writes songs about hockey) and BlöödHag (a "biographical grindcore" band from Seattle, Washington, that wrote songs about sci-fi and fantasy authors), inspired him to draft up a concept band in

Paul DeGeorge (pictured) developed the idea for what would become Harry and the Potters the summer of 2001, after reading all the then-released Harry Potter books (courtesy Andrew Warren).

which the musicians would also role-play as distinct characters from the *Harry Potter* novels.[71] He even came up with the perfect "silly name" for the project: Harry and the Potters.[72] But despite this burst of enthusiasm, the idea stalled, and there is a strong chance that "Harry and the Potters" would have eventually lost Paul's interest and faded from his memory had it not been for that fateful concert in 2002.[73]

With his original show in jeopardy of collapsing, Joe agreed to Paul's request. Lacking additional members, the two immediately tweaked Paul's initial concept and decided that Harry and the Potters would be a musical duo in which both brothers role-played as Harry. To justify this idiosyncratic choice, they came up with an equally idiosyncratic explanation: Joe, they claimed, was Harry in his fourth year at Hogwarts, whereas Paul was Harry in his seventh.[74] (And how did two versions of Harry from different time periods form a band with themselves? In an interview with *Paste* magazine, Paul mused, "It's a magical world, so it's not going too much further to suppose that Harry could swipe a Time-Turner[75] and then start a band with himself.")[76] Down to the wire, Paul and Joe grabbed a keyboard and a guitar and quickly wrote several short, punky songs—including such ditties as "I Am a Wizard," "Wizard Chess," "Platform 9 and ¾," "Diagon Alley," and "Problem Solving Skillz"[77]—and just like that, Harry and the Potters was born.

While Joe tinkered with a few of these songs later that summer, by the end of 2002, Harry and the Potters slipped largely from the brothers' minds. Flash-forward to early 2003. The world was abuzz with chatter about the impending release of the long-awaited fifth Harry Potter book, *The Order of the Phoenix*. All this *Harry Potter* talk jogged Paul and Joe's memory. Given that mania for the series was at a record high, the brothers correctly reasoned that the timing was perfect for a *Harry Potter* concept band, and so they hatched a plan: They would record a rough demo tape of some of their songs and use it to book a show or two. And where would a band that sings about a book series perform? Why, naturally, a bookstore! Consequently, they dropped their demo off at a local Borders chain with a polite note asking if they could play in-store on or around June 21 (the date of the book's release). The request was passed around from one contact to another before it eventually wound up in the hands of an amiable events coordinator for the company. Upon listening to their tape, she enjoyed the concept and scheduled them to play at not just one but five Borders locations in the Greater Boston area.[78]

When the DeGeorges got the news that their shows had been approved, they were elated, but immediately realized that they almost had more shows booked than they had songs written. To remedy this situation, the brothers hurriedly began writing and recording what would become their debut album in April 2003.[79] According to Paul, the entire process mostly took place in his parents' living room over the course of a few weekends and was rather haphazard, as the idea to record their tracks came only at the last minute:

> As we were writing these songs ... we decided we should just record them and treat the book release as an album release. So we were working on a pretty tight deadline.... Most of the songs were recorded [with a Korg Digital 12 track audio recorder] in just a couple takes, often immediately after the song had been written. We were moving so quickly that Joe and I recorded much of the album and then decided we should add some drums. We had our friend Ernie [Kim] come over on a weekend and set up his drums ... and overdub the drums onto our tracks—it's just crazy [work] to overdub drums, but that's what we did. I think "These Days Are Dark" is one of the only songs where the drums and instruments were recorded together live. We double-tracked a lot of the vocals to make it sound like we could sing better. It fooled no one.[80]

After recording wrapped up in early May, the band cut the tracklist down to 18 songs, and Paul ordered 1,000 professionally pressed CDs from Bellwether Manufacturing.[81] Around this time, the brothers also started to think about their stage presence; to make their performances really pop, they decided to buy grey sweaters and Gryffindor ties so that they could not only role-play as Harry on stage, but dress like him, too.[82]

Just before their Borders gigs, the band also agreed to play at an acquaintance's graduation party. This show—the group's first official concert since 2002—was, according to Paul, really just "a warm-up gig for our true public debut: the [*Order of the Phoenix*] release."[83] The days leading up to and following this event were a whirlwind of activity, as Paul explained:

> When [*Order of the Phoenix*] came out, we played two gigs on June 20 (leading up to midnight) and three gigs on June 21 (official release day)—all at Borders bookstores. After those went over well, we booked a handful of gigs later in the summer mostly at branches of the Boston Public Library. Those library gigs did seem to generate a bit of buzz and by the end of summer, we had a pack of 10 year-olds singing along to the songs.[84]

But despite this small cult following of *Potter*-obsessed children, the band was virtually unknown outside their Eastern Massachusetts stomping grounds. Late 2003 saw this change when *Harry Potter* fan sites started posting about the group. (Most of these sites, in turn, had discovered Harry and the Potters thanks to positive comments made in September on LiveJournal by then-fan fiction celebrity and future author of *The Mortal Instruments* series Cassie Claire.)[85] Then, in the spring of 2004, the student paper of Barnard College, the *Barnard Bulletin*, published a rather critical review of the band, in which tastemaker critic Jessica Plummer wrote:

> Potterites, you're in luck because I'm bringing you news of the craziest Potter shenanigans since the books first appeared—a rock band.... The best thing about Harry and the Potters is not how silly the whole concept is or the faithfully accurate retelling of the books but how very bad the band is. Neither brother has a strong voice, and they're not particularly fine musicians. Furthermore, the songwriting is uninspired and the lyrics are vapid.... So why should you listen to Harry and the Potters? Actually, their very badness makes them a must-listen. It's a sort of "hurts so good" approach to music that's endearing while providing hours of amusement trying to imitate the singer's drone on "The Yule Ball" just right.[86]

Whether Plummer meant for the review to be taken literally or ironically did not matter, as it only increased the band's visibility, which in turn earned them a larger audience.

By May 2004, Harry and the Potters' diminutive but growing fanbase was yearning for new music, and so Paul and Joe retreated to their parents' house and began writing and recording a sophomore album. This record, based on the stories and themes of *The Order of the Phoenix*, would eventually be released under the catchy title *Voldemort Can't Stop the Rock!* Paul explained that when it came time to work on this album: "We were a bit better prepared and gave ourselves a bit more time to record ... but it was a pretty similar experience to the first album, [being] home-recorded on the [Korg]

D12, mostly in our parent's living room and the shed behind the house."⁸⁷ Sonically, *Voldemort Can't Stop the Rock!* is reminiscent of the band's debut album (albeit a bit more polished), but as many have noted, its lyrics are darker and more political at times.⁸⁸ Nevertheless, the record (released on June 29, 2004) did not lose the sense of fun and enthusiasm that defined the band's first album. In fact, *Voldemort Can't Stop the Rock!* would go on to be very popular, as it included a number of songs that have since become fan-favorites, such as "The Human Hosepipe"⁸⁹ and "The Weapon"—the latter of which is arguably the band's signature song

Up until early 2004, the band had never performed shows outside the Greater Boston area. In April 2004, this changed when the band played shows at Vassar College in Poughkeepsie, NY and a middle school in Doylsetown, PA in a single weekend. Soon thereafter, the band decided to embark on a massive tour of the United States to better promote *Voldemort Can't Stop the Rock!*⁹⁰ As to why the band decided to finally start touring, Joe DeGeorge told me:

> Reading the ... tour diaries [of the punk band] Atom and his Package made us realize how it was possible to tour on your own.... So when people started emailing us asking us when we would start touring or playing in their towns, it [soon] seemed entirely possible to us. [In 2004] we put an announcement on our website and asked for help. [We] booked a national tour [by] working with enthusiastic Harry Potter fans and cold calling libraries across the country.⁹¹

The resultant circuit kicked off June 30, 2004, at the Boston Public Library, and for several months thereafter, the brothers travelled across the country in a car that they lovingly called the "Potter Mobile,"⁹² playing "libraries, bookstores, backyards, basements, pool parties, a bike shop, a doughnut shop, and even a pirate supply store."⁹³ In 2005, the band expanded the scope of their tour by playing a few shows in Canada, and by year's end, the DeGeorges had even managed to hop across the pond and perform in the United Kingdom and the Netherlands.⁹⁴ This tour had a major impact on the future of wizard rock, as it broadcast the antics of Harry and the Potters to a huge number of people across the United States—many of whom would eventually decide to follow in the band's footsteps a few years later.⁹⁵

It was around this time that something truly remarkable happened. The infamously persnickety music site *Pitchfork* (a pacesetter for hipsters and bohemians that was notorious for occasionally awarding albums that they disliked a 0.0 out of 10 score) applauded the band's live shows, writing: "Unless you frequent MuggleNet.com, you probably aren't aware that the greatest rock and roll tour of the year took place this past summer in public libraries across America." The site emphatically ended their review by declaring, "The Decemberists *wish* they could lit-rock like" Harry and the Potters.⁹⁶ This newfound attention was, simply put, incredible. The band's previous audiences had been made up mostly of librarians and kids. Now professional, established music critics were taking notice and positively comparing them to The Decemberists of all bands!

Unfortunately, copyright holders were taking notice, too, and in early 2005, the band was served a much-dreaded—but long-anticipated—legal notice from Warner Brothers. Thankfully, what could have become a massive brouhaha was soon defused by Marc Brandon, a member of Warner Brothers' Worldwide Anti-Piracy Operations group. Brandon contacted the DeGeorges and told them that Warner Brothers did not want to sue them—in fact, he implied that his company did not have issues with the band's music at all. The company did, however, have a problem with their merchandise (e.g., t-shirts), much of which heavily borrowed the aesthetic design of "real" WB products. While Brandon was firm in his resolve to protect his company's copyrights, he was also willing to cut the goofy tribute band a deal: if they stopped selling merch online (excepting their CDs), Warner Brothers would ignore their activities as well as any merch sold at live shows. If they failed to comply, there would be legal consequences. The brothers accepted the arrangement and never heard from Brandon or his company again.[97]

With Warner Brothers satisfied, the stage was set for wizard rock's spread.

Wizard Rock in Bloom (2004–05)

As news of Harry and the Potters spread, the first "wave" of wrock groups began to form. The earliest of these bands was The Parselmouths, made up of Kristina Horner and Elle Viane Sonnet[98] from Renton, Washington. The high school-aged duo was inspired to dabble in wizard rock after attending a Harry and the Potters concert in the summer of 2004 at a branch of Seattle's famed University Bookstore.[99] For the two self-described *Harry Potter* fanatics, that initial performance resonated deeply—Horner later told *Salon* in 2007, "I just [knew] sometime after first seeing Harry and the Potters, we wanted to sing about *Harry Potter*, too."[100]

When they started writing music, Horner and Sonnet initially desired to become the "female Harry and the Potters" by basing their group around one canonical character (their website, for instance, notes that they briefly considered both "The Moaning Myrtles" and "The Pansy Parkinsons" as band names).[101] But upon further consideration, they decided to eschew this style in favor of performing as their own character creations. This choice was made for several reasons, with perhaps the most important one being that it did not require them to meticulously conform to *Harry Potter*'s rigid system of canon; by crafting their own in-universe identities, Horner and Sonnet could, as their band's website notes, "write about virtually anything they wanted" with complete, authorial control.¹⁰² But who exactly would these characters be? After realizing that "there's a boy band about a Gryffindor [but no] girl band about Slytherins," the two decided to role-play as "normal girls" belonging to the latter house.¹⁰³ According to their website:

> The premise of [The Parselmouths] was to create and portray very real Slytherin girls because to them, Pansy Parkinson and Millicent Bullstrode are very two dimensional, and Kristina and [Elle] wanted to try to give depth to a house that is usually slammed for just being a bunch of spoiled rich kids. They have put themselves into the *Harry Potter* world as silly, boycrazy, mean Slytherin girls, but the Parselmouths hope that you'll see the deeper message in a lot of their songs. Just as Draco showed his weakness in *Harry Potter and the Half Blood Prince*, Kristina and [Elle] of the Parselmouths try to show that Slytherins aren't all just evil.¹⁰⁴

In late July 2004, The Parselmouths created a LiveJournal account and began promoting their Slytherin-centric music online, often in rather creative

The Parselmouths preform at the 2007 Hallows and Horcruxes Ball. The band was formed in 2004 by Kristina Horner (left) and Elle Viane Sonnet, and is considered the second wrock band to have been founded (courtesy Julia Weinstein).

ways. One particularly ingenious method—necessitated at first by Horner and Sonnett's lack of professional recording equipment—involved recording song demos on their cellphones and then setting these recordings as their default voicemail greetings. This way, when people called them, they could hear some of the band's tunes.[105] To promote this veritable "dial-a-song,"[106] Horner and Sonnet posted their phone numbers online with the message, "Look forward to hearing more songs on our voicemail!"[107] (Incidentally, when Paul and Joe DeGeorge learned of Horner and Sonnett's unique tactic, they though it was "awesome," as it reminded them of a similar tactic pioneered by the alternative rock band They Might Be Giants in the 1980s.)[108]

By late 2004, news of The Parselmouths and their variant of wizard rock began to circulate around Seattle, earning them both library gigs and mentions from local news outlets.[109] Around this time, Harry and the Potters accidentally began to convert others on the East Coast to the wrock cause when they performed at a house party in 2004 thrown by a Woonsocket, Rhode Island, musician named Matt Maggiacomo. According to Maggiacomo's website, he routinely hosted these sorts of parties so that musicians—including himself and his friends, half-brothers Brian Ross and Bradley Mehlenbacher—could perform in front of a sympathetic and supportive audience. Maggiacomo had first come to hear of the DeGeorges when at a previous show, Tim Howard of the band Soltero (the same band, in fact, that had canceled on the DeGeorges in the summer of 2002, leading to the creation of wizard rock as we now know it) mentioned a fun novelty act called "Harry and the Potters" that played shows in the New England area. Understandably, Maggiacomo was intrigued by the concept of a *Harry Potter* tribute band, and so he reached out to the DeGeorges, asking them if they were interested in performing at one of his future get-togethers. Always game to play in whatever venue might have them, Harry and the Potters replied in the affirmative, and in November 2004, they dutifully showed up on Maggiacomo's doorstep, ready to spread the gospel of wizard rock.[110]

The house show was a smash hit. Maggiacomo, Mehlenbacher, and Ross were thoroughly amused by the band's antics and greatly appreciated the mixture of fannish love and unlimited enthusiasm that powered Paul and Joe's performance. (Mehlenbacher, for instance, told me in an interview, "I loved the songs and concept. The whole thing was super fun and completely lived up to my expectations. [I] definitely had the feeling that you get when you meet someone and know you will be friends for a very long time.")[111] Maggiacomo hoped to follow up that initial show with another sometime in the winter of 2005, and while tentative plans were made, Harry and the Potters were forced to postpone at the last minute. In the interim, Ross joked to Mehlenbacher that they should write their own songs about Harry Potter and play in the band's stead. Mehlenbacher was intrigued by the suggestion, and he countered with the idea that they write songs not about the Boy Who Lived but rather the Slytherin thug, Draco Malfoy; in an interview, he explained: "We're both big wrestling fans, and our favorites were always the bad guys, so it was easy to write like we [as Draco] were Roddy Piper and [the DeGeorges as Harry Potter were] Hulk Hogan."[112] Ross thought this idea was a good one, and soon thereafter, he and Mehlenbacher began developing lyric ideas, writing riffs, and composing vocal melodies. Soon, they had songs of their own.[113]

The two decided to keep their project a secret until April 2005. It was in this month that Maggiacomo scheduled another house show at which Harry and the Potters were once again asked to play. When they received this invitation, the DeGeorge brothers had reasonably assumed that they would be the only wrock band performing. One can thus imagine their surprise when the night of the show arrived and Mehlenbacher and Ross opened the house show by performing as the "evil wizard rock" band "Draco and the Malfoys." During their hilarious and subversive set, Mehlenbacher and Ross parodied (albeit gently) the DeGeorges' antics by donning Slytherin-green ties and playing a handful of songs with titles like "My Dad Is Rich," "99 Death Eaters," and "Potions Yesterday."[114] Maggiacomo—who had been one of the few in on Mehlenbacher and Ross's secret—decided to take part in this friendly ribbing, too. However, his performance was decidedly more avant-garde. Positioning himself in the middle of the room sans guitar or other musical instrument, he introduced himself as "The Whomping Willow[115]: professional critic and interpretive dancer." Maggiacomo first delivered a hyperbolic roast of Harry and the Potters (whom he disparaged for the silliest of defects), before arguing that

The Whomping Willows perform at Wrockstock III in 2009. The band, which is the solo project of Matt Maggiacomo (pictured), was formed to playfully poke fun at the antics of the DeGeorge brothers (courtesy Grace Kendall).

the rock band Kansas's hit song "Carry on Wayward Son" represented "the pinnacle of rock music's potential."¹¹⁶ As the comedic *pièce de résistance*, he played the song on a stereo to his bewildered audience while he "danced" to the beat. According to Maggiacomo's website, "This performance was initially met with scattered laughter, followed by five or six minutes of uncomfortable silence."¹¹⁷

Regardless, the overall show was fun for everyone involved, and afterwards, Maggiacomo, Mehlenbacher, and Ross started to develop additional wrock song ideas that they hoped to perform at future house shows with the DeGeorges. Paul and Joe, who were more than willing to share the stage, welcomed their new friends with open arms; they even asked the novice wrockers to perform with them at select shows in 2005, including the inaugural Yule Ball.¹¹⁸ But once these musicians were made aware of the delicate agreement that the DeGeorges had made with Warner Brothers, they all agreed to "stay below the radar as best [they] could"¹¹⁹ by not promoting their acts without Harry and the Potters' consent. While restrictive, deferring to the DeGeorges was viewed by all as the safest possible move—after all, no one wanted to be sued and have their livelihoods ruined because of a goofy *Harry Potter* tribute band.¹²⁰

The year 2005 would prove to be a turning point for the wrock movement. It was during this year that another wrock band burst onto the scene—and nearly caused a crisis.

This new group was The Remus Lupins,¹²¹ based out of Beverly Hills and fronted by Alex Carpenter. The band began (as it seems most wrock bands do) by accident, when Carpenter posted a short, *Harry Potter*-inspired song on MySpace during the summer of 2005. The song had been written in jest and recorded just for fun, but it nonetheless garnered the attention of hundreds of *Harry Potter* fans, many of whom demanded that Carpenter write more. Carpenter quickly grasped the potential of what he had accidentally stumbled upon, and he amassed quite the fan following in Los Angeles County after churning out several more songs under the moniker "The Remus Lupins."¹²² Part of Carpenter's success was due to his willingness to communicate with his fans¹²³ and swiftly respond to their demands; in an interview with the *Etownian*, he noted: "I just did things as people asked me to. 'We want more songs,' so I wrote them. 'We want an EP,' so I made one. Then, 'We want shows,' so I played them."¹²⁴ But another perhaps more important aspect of Carpenter's success was due to his masterful use of MySpace—a platform through which he assiduously advertised and self-promoted.¹²⁵

Separated by over 2,000 miles, Carpenter and the East Coast wrockers operated in ignorance of one another for a time, but soon news of Carpenter reached New England. When this happened, the East Coast wrockers began to worry.¹²⁶ As Mehlenbacher explained to me, "We were already kind of protective [of wizard rock] and … there was definitely a worry that someone might ruin it by not being careful.… Alex raised [our] eyebrows by being pretty aggressive social media wise."[127] The problem that the East Coast wrockers had with Carpenter was twofold: First, it appeared that Carpenter was commodifying *Harry Potter* not necessarily out of a love for the books,[128] but rather to further his own ends (e.g., earn money, attract women,[129] and get signed to a record label).[130] This approach to wizard rock was different—almost antithetical—to that taken by the East Coast wrockers, and it was certainly harder to defend to copyright holders.[131] Second, Carpenter—who knew not of the deal that the DeGeorges had struck with Marc Brandon—was active in the heart of Warner Brothers' sprawling media empire.[132] (As Melissa Anelli rhetorically writes in her book *Harry, a History*, "What if a Warner Brothers person just showed up [at one of Carpenter's shows] and saw Potter themed merchandise on sale?")[133] Given that they had been so meticulous as to not "poke the bear," the East Coast wrockers rightly worried that Carpenter's antics could result in copyright holders rescinding their agreement to let the wrock scene be, thereby causing the whole thing to go up in flames.[134]

After privately fretting for some time, the East Coast wrockers eventually reached out to Carpenter via email. They tried to be transparent and helpful by laying out the legal precariousness of the nascent wrock movement, but they were also frank, telling Carpenter, in essence, to knock it off. This initial message became the opening salvo in a brief East vs. West Coast wrock "feud." Carpenter, who was caught off guard by the email, was unhappy with the demands. Stubbornly refusing to yield, he argued that he had just as much right to form a *Harry Potter* concept band as anyone else.[135] For a time, the East and West Coast bands sparred online before the former recognized the inevitability of bands like The Remus Lupins forming. And so the East Coast wrockers made peace with Carpenter and obviated the requirement that all bands defer decisions to the DeGeorges.[136] With caution thrown to the wind, the East Coast wrockers fully embraced their acts,[137] and by 2006, both Draco and the Malfoys, and The Whomping Willows had released their debut albums and were soon booking solo shows.[138] It was then, to quote Bradley Mehlenbacher "that it was really off to the races"[139]: By the end of 2005, only about five or six bands were active, but by the next year, 40 bands were performing wizard rock.[140]

The "Golden Age" (2006-10)

In many ways, 2006 could be considered the start of wizard rock's "golden age," as this year saw dozens of soon-to-be influential bands form and begin recording music, including: Gred and Forge, Justin Finch-Fletchley and the Sugar Quills, and The Mudbloods. Even "mainstream" musicians began joining in on the fun: for instance, Mark Jennings, Jason Munday, and Aaron Nordyke of the major label Christian rap-rock group 38th Parallel teamed up with Luke Conard, Jeremy Jennings, and Ryan Seiler to create the synth-pop boy band Ministry of Magic,[141] which would go on to be one of the more popular groups in the community during the late oughts and early 2010s. Wizard rock's sudden growth even caught the attention of MTV, who published an article entitled *"Harry Potter* Fandom Reaches Magical New Level Thanks to Wizard-Rock Bands."[142] This inevitably brought more exposure to the movement and in turn inspired even more bands to form.

This year also saw the creation of another important wrock band: The Moaning Myrtles, comprising Lauren Fairweather and Nina Jankowicz. While they officially formed in 2006 in Hillsborough, New Jersey, this group can trace its origins back to 2004, when a high school-aged Fairweather attended a Harry and the Potters concert. Prior to the show, Fairweather had peripherally been aware of wizard rock's existence.[143] However, in an interview, she told me that it was not until she actually attended that concert in 2004 that she "fell in love with the [wrock] community and the idea of writing songs about [her] favorite books."[144] Much like others before her, it seems that seeing Harry and the Potters earnestly perform song after song kindled within Fairweather a desire to write music about a beloved book series. Soon thereafter, she started dreaming up song concepts, but for whatever reason, these ideas never quite coalesced into anything concrete.[145]

This would change in November 2005, when Fairweather attended another Harry and the Potters concert, this time with her best friend Nina Jankowicz. It seems that Jankowicz was just as affected by live wizard rock as Fairweather, because after the show, Jankowicz suggested to her friend that they create their own band[146]; Jankowicz, in fact, was the one who proposed that they role-play as Moaning Myrtle.[147] Regardless of whether Jankowicz was joking when she first mentioned the idea to Fairweather (as some sources claim),[148] this jocular facade quickly melted away and the two began to explore the idea in earnest on November 27 of that year. According to Fairweather: "We recorded a [demo of 'And Then I Died' in 2006] and uploaded [it] on social media where people could find [it]. We were blown away by the response and the rest is history."[149] At the time, The Moaning Myrtles were quite unique, because they broke from the standard style of wizard rock by heavily emphasizing the piano in most of their songs.

As their name suggests, the band chose to write songs from the perspective of Moaning Myrtle, a weepy ghost who haunts an oft-deserted girls bathroom at Hogwarts. According to Fairweather, "We thought she'd be the most fun to play around with because, while she's usually pretty emo, she's unintentionally hilarious … which, of course, provides lots of room for us to joke around in the lyrics."[150] Fairweather and Jankowicz were also drawn to Myrtle because she is an ancillary character who does not appear that often in the *Harry Potter* books, meaning that they had a certain flexibility in regard to how they could portray her.[151]

Today, The Moaning Myrtles are lauded not only for their music, but also for their role in ensuring the movement's continued success in the mid- to late 2000s.

Wizard rock's "Golden Age" was also a time of increased musical and creative growth: bands were honing their skills, performances were getting more fine-tuned, and songs were becoming increasingly complex. This sort of growth is perhaps best epitomized by Harry and the Potter's third album, *Harry and the Potters and the Power of Love*, based on *The Half-Blood Prince*. Paul DeGeorge explained:

> [*The Power of Love*] is where we really "leveled-up" both our song-writing and recording process. In the year and a half since we'd released *Voldemort Can't Stop the Rock*, we'd done a lot of touring and gotten pretty good at performing. We still couldn't sing, but we felt we were a pretty good live band, and our albums didn't really represent that at all. So we wanted to make an album that better represented what we do.... Before recording, we probably spent about 3–6 months writing, demo-ing, and editing. Before going into the studio, we created a mixtape that was full of a whole bunch of different songs that pointed to the sort of sounds and mood we were looking for in creating a new full length. There was a lot of Bruce Springsteen, but also a bunch of stuff that was further afield like Blood Brothers and Les Savy Fav.
>
> [In early 2006] we started working on *Power of Love* ... at a house in Cambridge, MA outside of Harvard Square. My friend Farhad [Ebrahimi] owned this huge house and a bunch of people from my favorite Boston bands were living there at the time. My friend Kevin Micka had set up a recording studio in two of the rooms on the ground floor. So recording in a home felt pretty familiar, but Kevin had a lot better equipment and was far more qualified behind the mixing board.... We had practiced most of the songs a few times with Ernie, so we put down the basic tracks without too much problem. Then it was on to the overdubs where we put in a lot of time. We tried really hard to add some new instrumentation to the lineup.... We brought in some strings and a melodica. There was a bunch more saxophone. We had our pal Brian [Church] play bass on a few songs. We ported some rough mixes to our D12 and then recorded timpani drums and tubular bells in the basement of our old high school. We were trying to make something epic that could stand alongside the *Harry Potter* stories, where the stakes were getting increasingly high.... [*The Power of Love*] was the first album we were really happy with the recording. I still find it mostly lis-tenable and only wish we had cut a couple songs from the tracklist.[152]

Harry and the Potters and the Power of Love was released on July 4, 2006, and almost instantly became a classic, bolstered by such tracks as the Twisted Sis-ter–soundalike "New Wizard Anthem," the 30-second earworm "This Book Is So Awesome," the sprightly "Save Ginny Weasley from Dean Thomas," and the sad-but-uplifting "Dumbledore." Given the quality of the record's tracks, it is not hyperbolic to suggest that the record may be one of the best wrock albums ever recorded.

Around this time, Paul DeGeorge was shocked at just how big wizard rock had gotten, and he began dreaming up ways to better showcase the rapidly expanding scene. These ideas developed into the "Wizard Rock EP of the Month Club," which would offer subscribers one EP a month[153] from a different wrock group. In an interview, Paul told me:

> I was always enamored with these exclusive record clubs—like Sub Pop Singles Club, stuff like that—so that was certainly my primary source of inspiration. You're signing up on faith because you trust whoever is making the judgement as to what to put on the disc. I thought, "This could be fun." It could be a really great way to expose some emerging wizard rock bands to a wider audience. We could use our reputations—and some of the bigger bands at the time—to allow other, younger, less experienced bands to "ride our coattails" and get their music out to just as many people.[154]

In mid-2006, DeGeorge began to coordinate with interested musicians and groups, and eventually, after months of preparation, the Wizard Rock EP of the Month Club launched in January 2007. For every monthly release, around one thousand CDs were pressed up. Eight hundred copies of each release were shipped to those who signed up for the club, while the remaining 200 were given to the band-of-the-month free of charge, which they could then sell at their leisure. All the club's proceeds were donated to a variety of charities, such as First Book and the Harry Potter Alliance.[155]

The first year of the club featured several of the biggest names in wizard rock at the time, such as Harry and the Potters, Draco and the Malfoys, The Parselmouths, and The Remus Lupins. But in addition to well-known wrock groups, the EP of the Month Club also released records by more obscure groups, such as The Hungarian Horntails (a "hardcore dragon rock" band fronted by then-8 year old Darius Wilkins, who sang songs from the perspective of the eponymous species of dragon),[156] The Fleur Delacours (a group that Paul lovingly described to me as "Riot grrrl wrock"),[157] and Dumbledore (a "wizard rap" side-project of the DeGeorges that featured a number of guest vocalists, like Bradley Mehlenbacher of Draco and the Malfoys, and Neil Cicierega of *Potter Puppet Pals* fame).[158] Other groups released by the EP of the Month Club would eventually go on to be among the more popular bands in the community, such as Tonks and the Aurors. The Wizard Rock EP of the Month Club would ultimately come to distribute almost forty EPs, and in December 2009, the club shipped perhaps its most ambitious release, the CD/DVD combo *Live at the Yule Ball* by Harry and the Potters.[159]

Sadly, 2009 would be the last year that the Wizard Rock EP of the Month Club operated. In mid-2010, Paul DeGeorge wrote on the club's official website:

There's no 2010 edition of the EP club. It was a ton of work, so I just needed to take a step back and put my efforts into other projects. Putting out 12 discs a year and all the corresponding mailings is more than most small record labels would attempt, so I'm pretty proud of the 3-year streak we had. I'm even more proud of the quality of music that we released. Thirty [seven] CDs ... and a DVD, each one of them really unique and special. From 2007 through 2009 we did our best to document some of our favorite bands in wizard rock. Some of these bands probably would have never made a record, so it feels good to have helped usher something like that into existence.[160]

Impressively, the Wizard Rock EP of the Month Club helped raise over $50,000 for charity during its three-year run.[161]

For many, the logical culmination of Pottermania was the release of the final *Harry Potter* book *The Deathly Hallows* on July 21, 2007. The night before this event, fans—young and old alike—waited in lines at bookstores, hoping to get their hands on the novel and read it before all their friends. Naturally, wrock bands were swept up in this excitement, with many playing shows at libraries and area bookstores to crowds of hundreds if not thousands of people: That night, for instance, Harry and the Potters and Draco and the Malfoys played a show at Harvard Square to an audience of approximately 16,000—which *Washington Post* journalists Joshua Zumbrun and Sonya Geis noted is "an enormous audience for this type of niche band."[162]

Because *The Deathly Hallows* would be the final installment in the *Harry Potter* saga, many in the media predicted that the wrock movement would collapse within a few short months of the book's release. As it turns out, these doomsday fortune-tellers were quite immature in their prophecies: immediately following *The Deathly Hallows*, wizard rock was still alive and well. In fact, 2008 saw a number of ambitious wrock conventions being hosted, as well as the release of two documentaries (Josh Koury's *We Are Wizards* and Mallory and Megan Schuyler's *The Wizard Rockumentary*) and a book (Melissa Anelli's *Harry, a History*) that further explored the inner machinations of the scene. During the end of this year, "wizard rock" even became an official Library of Congress Subject Heading, thanks to the efforts of California State University Fullerton (CSUF) librarians Joy Lambert and Annette Anderson-Ma (the former of whom has humorously taken to titling herself as a "wizard rock librarian").[163] By the close of 2009, bands were still putting out elaborate records,[164] and the scene had grown to a staggering 800 bands worldwide.[165] Part of the reason for the movement's continued growth was because the *Deathly Hallows* novel provided bands with plenty of material to work with, and the final few *Harry Potter* films were still playing in theatres, wooing fans with their dazzling visuals.

The Post-Potter Nadir and the "Second Wave" (2011–present)

An intense interest in wizard rock could not be maintained forever, and following the release of the final *Deathly Hallows* film in the summer of 2011, the genre ceased to be in vogue. Before long, fans grew bored and began wandering from the community. With each passing year, the exodus grew more and more severe, and soon wizard rock was imploding:

This collapse was arguably presaged in mid-2010, when the popular web-based wrock encyclopedia Wizrocklopedia began to experience technical issues, flickering on- and offline a number of times before finally ceasing to update for years.[166]

Then, in October 2011, "Wrockstock" (an annual all-wizard rock music festival started in 2007) was held for the last consecutive time.[167]

Two months later, Draco and the Malfoys shocked the community by breaking up.[168] Around this time, several other "big name" bands began laying down their wands and guitars and walking away, too.[169]

In 2013, MySpace—which up until then had been a major bastion for the wizard rock movement—was "updated" to the point of being almost unrecognizable. This massive change led to an untold number of bands abandoning the site, leaving it little more than a desolate, digital wasteland.[170] The downfall of MySpace compounded the disastrous loss of the Wizrocklopedia a few years earlier, and given that these two sites were for many the heart and soul of wizard rock, the online community quickly became "decentralized" (to quote musicologist Aya Esther Hayashi), collapsing into a state of total disarray.[171]

But perhaps most traumatically, in 2014, a horrendous sexual abuse scandal involving members of The Remus Lupins and Ministry of Magic devastated the remaining wrock scene, making many fans reconsider where they devoted their time and energy.[172]

By 2015, the community was a feeble shadow of its former self. Had death finally come for wizard rock, as those pessimists had predicted several years earlier? Not quite. As Stacy Pisani of the group Swish and Flick told *Broadly*:

> Even after the last movie came out (years after the [last] book) ... there were still active wizard rock bands (and new ones forming all the time), active online communities, active meet-up groups, podcasts, several conventions being held every year. The fandom never died after the books were completed. It had just lost the attention of popular media for a few years when there had been no tie-ins, like books and movies. [But] there are seven books with endless ideas to draw from.... New songs don't need to be about new content; they can be about content that J.K. Rowling wrote 19 years ago.[173]

Indeed, while this period was marked by the dissolution of several of the bigger wrock groups, there were other bands who never showed any sign of slowing down. Harry and the Potters, for instance, kept touring (and even managed to release an extravagant live album on vinyl). Other bands like Seen and Unforeseen, Tonks and the Aurors, The 8th Horcrux, and Tianna and the Cliffhangers continued to write songs and put out full-length records.

But while a number of bands remained active, it is likely that wizard rock would have faded away into the annals of pop culture history had it not been for one thing: new media releases. First, in September 2013, Warner Brothers announced that they would be producing five films based on the 2001 charity book *Fantastic Beasts and Where to Find Them*. Then, three months later, it was revealed that J.K. Rowling herself was developing a stage play that would serve as a sequel to the *Harry Potter* series. On July 30, 2016, the aforementioned play, entitled *Harry Potter and the Cursed Child*, officially debuted at Palace Theatre in London. This release gave *Harry Potter* fans plenty of material to talk (or complain) about. Then, in November 2016, the initial *Fantastic Beasts* movie was screened to audiences worldwide. The first cinematic journey back into Rowling's magical world, this movie quenched the thirst that many fans had had for anything Potter-related. Fans once again came together to witness the adventures of characters new and old like Newt Scamander, Tina Goldstein, and Albus Dumbledore on the silver screen.

These new media releases piqued the interest of many a former wrocker, and some (including, most notably, Mehlenbacher and Ross) began to recall the glory days of wizard rock. Many subsequently returned to the scene, turning their attention once more to their hibernating wrock projects. In fact, so fruitful was the end of 2016 and the beginning of 2017 that this period could in many ways be considered the start of wizard rock's "second wave."[174] Since this time, new bands have formed (e.g., The Lovegoods, Flitwick and the Charmers, Ludo Bagman and the Trash), old bands have reunited (e.g., The Mudbloods), and new material is once again being released at a fairly consistent and steady rate (Harry and the Potters, for instance, debuted parts of their long-awaited *Deathly Hallows*-centered studio album at a live show on March 30, 2018, and later teased that it would feature, among others, the vocal talents of anti-folk star Kimya Dawson; likewise in October 2018, Lauren Fairweather released her first wrock album in years, titled *With You Whatever Happens*).[175] And with more *Fantastic Beasts* films, fan conventions, and wrock house shows on the horizon, the community will likely continue to experience a sense of renewal. While no one can say for sure what the future holds for wizard rock, its prospects nonetheless look bright.

2

DIY Wrock; or, How to Make Your Own Band

When Trina and I officially decided to start a wrock band, the first thing we did was choose a name. After briefly considering "Potterwatch" and "Accio Awesome"[1] (both of which we later used as album titles), we settled upon "The 8th Horcrux."[2] Trina came up with the phrase, and we immediately liked it for several reasons: It was original. It was a bit nonsensical. But perhaps most importantly, it was humorously self-deprecating—it insinuated that our music needed to be destroyed so that Voldemort might be conquered. I would like to think that our name lets potential listeners know that we above all else strive to make people laugh.

From the get-go, Trina and I agreed that we would only write parodies. I had always been a big fan of the American comedy musician "Weird Al" Yankovic and needless to say found writing parodies to be quite amusing. Trina enjoyed writing them as well, but her delight seemed to stem more from successfully matching the original song's musical style and lyrical meter.

We also decided that, unlike bands such as Harry and the Potters or Draco and the Malfoys, we would sing from the viewpoint of many characters. It was our belief that doing so would provide us with greater flexibility and creative freedom, as we would not be bound to only one perspective.

In late July and early August 2009, The 8th Horcrux began work on our first spoof,[3] which was a sendup of The Who's 1969 single "Pinball Wizard" (after all, with a name like that, the song was just begging to be re-written about *Harry Potter*). Following a few days of brainstorming parody ideas, we eventually came up with lyrics that concerned Harry's unearned success in potions class thanks to the mysterious Half-Blood Prince, as described in the sixth *Harry Potter* novel. The first verse goes as follows:

> Ever since I was at Hogwarts
> I've sucked at potions class
> But under Slughorn's guidance

> I thought that I might pass
> But then one day while browsing
> Through a book of potion spells
> I met this Half-Blood Prince bloke
> And he knows his potions spells!

What did we name our creation? Why, "Potions Wizard" of course!

At this point, we found ourselves at a crossroads: we could either spend time and money recording our song, or we could just keep this parody to ourselves and perform it at live shows. Hoping to bestow our labor of love upon the world, we opted for the former. But then another problem arose: there were not any affordable recording studios in the area, and we did not have any professional recording equipment at our disposal.

Perhaps because we had come so far, we were determined to see our efforts through, and over the course of a few weeks, Trina and I created a makeshift studio in my basement, which was the only space big enough to hold all our amps and musical miscellanea. To create a "sound booth," I borrowed a $20 Logitech microphone from a friend and haphazardly taped it to a wobbly music stand. To curtail any rogue "s" and "p" sounds during recording, we made a windscreen out of a bent hanger and an old article of clothing. I ran the microphone's line-out cable into an ancient computer, which at the time was running an operating system about ten years out of date. All our tracks were recorded and mixed using the free sound editor Audacity. Our musical equipment was limited mostly to what we owned at the time of recording (namely, a bright-pink Squire Stratocaster guitar loaned to us by another friend, a low-power Fender amp, and Trina's 50-year old classical guitar), but we also pooled our money and purchased a few new instruments like a jaw-harp, and a tambourine. (We also borrowed a vibraslap from our high school bandroom!) This setup was decidedly ad hoc, but it served its purpose.

Trina and I recorded the album on the weekends, often on Sundays, working late into the night. During some of these sessions, we would focus on writing and recording new songs. During others, we tried to mix and master what we had managed to record.

We had originally planned on recording maybe three or four songs and then releasing a limited-edition, hand-made EP, but by October 2009, we had written and recorded an entire album's worth of parodies, which we decided to call *Potterwatch!* After sharing our creations with friends and family, we were encouraged by the positive response, and so Trina and I ordered 100 professionally made copies of our album from DiscMakers, which we sold out of our lockers at school to our classmates. We also set up Facebook, Tumblr, and MySpace accounts and began emailing wrockers that we admired, begging them to take a listen to our tunes. During The 8th Horcrux's first year in existence, we did not play a single live show, but by the dawning of the band's second year together, we had a respectable following—both in person and online—all thanks to word-of-mouth and the power of social media.

* * *

The vignette that begins this chapter is intended to illustrate one thing: when Trina and I started tinkering with wizard rock, we quickly realized that there was no official "rule book" that told us how to start a band, record songs, or release records. Rather, we were effectively making it up as we went. We later found out that for a wrock group this is generally par for the course. Indeed, as a movement, wizard rock is infused with a DIY spirit, and bands both new and old are encouraged to write their own songs, record their own material, and then self-release their own records. This self-reliant philosophy has become so widespread that it is often seen as a defining feature of what might be called the "wrock aesthetic." But while the prospect of doing everything yourself can seem liberating, it can also be a daunting task, especially for someone new to the community. Where exactly should a novice wrocker start?

The purpose of this chapter is therefore twofold. First, it seeks to document the most common ways that wrock bands form, choose names, write and record music, and then circulate that music. Second, this chapter functions as a "how to" guide, providing helpful information for the would-be wrocker. It must be stressed that what follows is not an official guide on how to start a wrock band, nor does it detail the *only* ways in which a person can start such a band. Rather, it is a general outline of the steps that are most often followed by new wrock groups. These steps are not set in stone, and can indeed be reordered, modified, or even skipped. Wizard rock, after all, is highly malleable.

What's in a Name?

Generally, the first task for all new wrock bands is to choose a name. It could be argued that this is, of course, the first step for all new bands, regardless of whether they are penning songs about the Boy Who Lived. However, when it comes to wizard rock, a band's name is one of its most important attributes, as it does not just identity the group, but often broadcasts to listeners what *type* of wrock band this group is going to be. In other words, the name can function as a critical indexical, letting a potential audience know if the band is going to, for instance, extol the virtues of the books' heroes or laud the actions of the series' main villains. According to Sam Ducharme of Flitwick and the Charmers:

> [Names] can act as something of a *signal flare* to fans of the wrock scene…. Let's say I'm a casual wizard rock enthusiast. I know about [Harry and the Potters, and Draco and the Malfoys] and some of the other better-knowns. If I see a band name pop up that's something like "Dudley and the Dursleys" (Oooh, that's a good one!) or "Dobby and the Free Elves," *there's a pretty good chance I know what they're all about, or at least I can make a good inference* [emphasis added].[4]

Likewise, Will Jackson, who performs "wizard rap" under the name MC Gryf, notes:

> My artist name is MC Gryf. It took me awhile to kind of perfect what I wanted because I was interested in creating rap music from the perspective of my house [i.e., Gryffindor], but the imagery was difficult to nail down. Most of the imagery we associate with hip-hop music is somewhere between self-indulgence and great ambition for popularity and monetary success, which are generally way more Slytherin concepts, and while my genre wouldn't feel right without that stuff I had a hard time fitting rap into the frame of being a Gryffindor. But *I wanted my name to say "rapper" and "Gryffindor" so that there would be no mistake whatsoever about exactly what you were getting into when you turn it on* [emphasis added].[5]

As both of these quotes illustrate, a name can quickly and efficiently indicate to a potential listener what sort of music they are about to hear.

However, this trend is not a rigid and unbreakable rule. As Steph Anderson of Tonks and the Aurors puts it, "Musical name versus content is a totally personal thing."[6] Ducharme agrees, noting that while there often exists a connection between group name and lyrical content, "correlation isn't a guarantee."[7] In fact, some groups strategically choose names that broadly allude to the *Harry Potter* universe, without being too restrictive (e.g., Let's Lumos!, The 8th Horcrux, Swish and Flick, The Butterbeer Experience); this allows these groups to sing about whatever topics interest them.

When wizard rock was in its relative infancy, bands often made use of a standard naming formula, which goes as follows: [First name of *Harry Potter* character] and the [Pluralized last name of the aforementioned character]. Examples of this type of construction abound, with perhaps the preeminent examples being Harry and the Potters, and Draco and the Malfoys. It seems almost certain that this peculiarly ubiquitous naming formula was due to the massive influence of the aforementioned bands. Grace Kendall of Snidget notes:

> [The standard] naming convention absolutely came from the fact that all of the bands were modeling after each other. Harry and the Potters started the scene, and their friends formed Draco and the Malfoys in direct response to that, so when other bands started out, they were modeling that [style]. The Whomping Willows and The Remus Lupins were other early members of the scene that people were emulating, so a whole community of names started there. I think a lot of that had to do with people following their established pattern of representing a specific character.[8]

As Kendall touches on near the end of their statement, this type of naming structure often prompts band members to take on the persona of the character(s) referenced in their band's name. For instance, Harry and the Potters perform *as* Harry Potter, and Draco and the Malfoys perform *as* Draco Malfoy. The connection between name and the character personas that they often give rise to thus reveals the importance of role-play in wizard rock (which will be discussed in Chapter 4).

Musical Possibilities

Wizard rock is often referred to as a "genre," but unlike other genres (into which bands are categorized based on a shared style of music), wizard rock is defined more by a shared *lyrical* theme.[9] This means that the term "wizard rock" itself is actually a bit of a misnomer, as there is no canonical musical style to which *all* wrock songs conform. This flexibility is important because, as the classicist and wrock scholar Anne C. Smith argues, the musical style or "setting" employed by a wrock band often "underscores the lyrical message" of their songs.[10] Bands are therefore known to jump from style to style, employing the motifs, tropes, trends, and traditions associated with those styles to make certain points.[11] (For instance, according to Smith, The Parselmouths' song "My Obsession" employs an "eerie 'Phantom of the Opera' flavor" so as to better accent and emphasize "the song's dark parallels between lust and hatred.")[12] Ultimately, the ability for wrockers to choose one or more styles of music is "an additional channel for negotiating meaning."[13]

This musical variety also makes wizard rock more enjoyable and accessible to a wider range of people. Indeed, it seem as if there is a style of wizard rock for any musical predilection: One can start with the acoustic stylings of KwikSpell, proceed to Flitwick and the Charmers' jaunty third-wave ska, and finish by blasting the heavy metal band Voldemort—all while staying firmly immersed in the *Harry Potter* universe. How many established genres of music allow for that sort of versatility? With that said, it is no secret that the vast majority of wrock bands gravitate toward the styles of indie, alternative, or punk rock. A contributing factor to this is likely because the first few wrock bands (namely Harry and the Potters, and Draco and the Malfoys) embraced a raw, rock-oriented sound. This eventually gave rise within the movement to an understanding of what "conventional" wizard rock sounds like, in turn leading to new bands emulating this sound. It has also been argued that because the wrock community is disproportionately white (see Chapter 5 for more on this topic), it came to unconsciously embrace music styles that are often associated with whiteness,[14] such as indie or punk rock.[15]

Brian Ross (of Draco and the Malfoys, left) helps Stacy and John Pisani (background) of Swish & Flick perform their track "My Dad Is Rich (On a Boat)" in 2009. The Pisanis' group is one of the most popular "wizard rap" acts in the wrock community (courtesy Grace Kendall).

But as I have established, other styles of wizard rock do indeed exist. Arguably, the most popular non-rock variant is known as "wizard rap" (sometimes called "wiz-hop" or "wrap"). Notable bands in this sub-category include MC Kreacher, Swish and Flick, Danny Dementor, Big Whompy, LiL iFFy, and Dumbledore. However, while rap groups such as these are to be found in the wrock community, they are substantially less-represented than their rock comrades. When asked about the limited number of wizard rap acts, Will Jackson, told me:

> We call ourselves "wizard rappers" ... but we're all usually perfectly happy being included in the group with wizrock, and when you look at any major collection of wizard rock tracks, there's usually a couple stray wizrap artists in there, be it Undesirable No. 1, Swish and Flick, yours truly MC Gryf, or one of the many others.
> One of the things about rap is that it often doesn't seem hugely organic—despite some obvious exceptions, with famous rappers like Nelly or Eminem often having original guitar and drum tracks for some of their biggest hits ... rap is often composed of an electronic backbeat and a vocalist, and to a lot of people it probably seems a bit overproduced versus the perception of indie rockers kinda grabbing an acoustic [guitar] and just singing from the heart in their basement, which definitely [harkens back] to the time and place where wizrock started. So, there's quite a ten-

dency when you've got a genre based on very feelzy books to make the music seem more like a soulful, indie-hippie, coffee shop kind of experience, or a super politicized dive bar punk show. So naturally most people who want to make or listen to wrock kinda jump to those genres. Rap then seems a little out of the way to them. But we're here.[16]

While "wrappers" might be under-represented in the broader wrock community, they are by no means intentionally ignored, disparaged, or side-lined—quite the opposite! In fact, many of my informants were quick to point out that some of their favorite wrock bands are those which could be categorized as "wrappers," such as the extremely beloved group Swish and Flick, composed of Stacy and John Pisani, whose humorous rap tracks include "Cho Chang (Shake Your Thang)" and "My Dad Is Rich (On a Boat)."[17] Given the relative popularity of this band and others like them, perhaps it is only a matter of time before wizard rap groups make up a proportionate size of the community.

Some wrock bands eschew writing their own music and instead pen parody songs,[18] which pair *Harry Potter*-inspired lyrics with a pre-existing song's musical track.[19] Numerous examples abound, such as The Parselmouths' "Heartbreaker" (which combines the musical structure of Pat Benatar's 1979 song of the same name with lyrics about love in the wizarding world). Whether or not a band writes parodies depends on their sensibilities: some bands never write parodies, others occasionally dabble in parodies, and still other groups make parodies the heart of their shtick.

People seem to take pleasure in parody songs, but why might this be? Mary Ann Rishel argues that it is due to "our delight in imitation, an intellectual pride in knowing an original source so well that we can brilliantly reimagine it in new ways that mirror the original."[20] Differing slightly from this assertion, I contend that people enjoy parodies, not merely because the songs imitate some source, but because these spoofs are inherently incongruous (i.e., they distort reality). Philosophers like Søren Kierkegaard and Arthur Schopenhauer have all argued that incongruity is at the root of humor itself, with Kierkegaard in particular proposing that something is funny when an outcome contradicts expectations; in other words, humor is due to the "disparity between what is expected and what is experienced."[21]

This seems to be case with wrock parody songs. Often, when an individual hears such a spoof for the first time, they erroneously assume that they are listening to the original. But once they hear the new *Harry Potter*–centered lyrics, their expectations are violated and they are thrown for a loop. For an example, consider this write-up from the *University Daily Kansan*, which describes my band, The 8th Horcrux, performing a parody song called "Witch" (a send-up of Meredith Brooks's '90s hit "Bitch") in a library:

> Surrounded by books, youthful grins and skeptical glances, the duo that is The 8th Horcrux prepares to dive into the beginning chords of "Bitch" by Meredith Brooks. Trina [Thomas], singer and guitarist, introduces the song: "This song is about Hermione Granger and how she liked Ronald Weasley." ... [Trina] said [that] when they start to play this song she can see parents' worried expressions fill the ... library.... "The parents, *they're nervous about it at first*, but then when I start singing the chorus and it's just about witches, *they start laughing with relief*" [emphasis added].[22]

At the concert in question, many of those who were familiar with the original song were nervously anticipating Trina to begin swearing in the library. But once the chorus hit and Trina simply began singing, "I'm a witch/Born from Muggles/I think elves/Just want cuddles," they were caught off guard. This incongruity—between what they expected and what they actually heard—caused them to laugh.

There is also the bonus that a wrock parody song might allow a person to indulge in several of their interests all at once. Consider, for example, my band's song, "Voldemort Is Going Down," which is a parody of the American pop punk band Green Day's 1995 single "When I Come Around" rewritten to detail Harry, Ron, and Hermione's hunt for horcruxes in *The Deathly Hallows*. For someone who is both a fan of Green Day and *Harry Potter*, this song might appeal to two different sensibilities because this parody combines two things that they enjoy. And the exact opposite can be true: a band that despises Green Day may enjoy the spoof because it not only skewers a group they hate but also "sanitizes" one of their tunes by making it about *Harry Potter*.[23]

Lyrics and "Lyrical Sub-Genres"

When a band settles upon a genre (or genres), they often begin to mull over lyrical possibilities.

In 2010, Lauren Amanda Smith published a scholarly blog post in which she argued, among other things, that there are six main "lyrical sub-genres" of which wrockers commonly make use.[24] The following list is based heavily on her delineation, although it has also been supplemented and synthesized with ideas put forth by other fan scholars (namely Henry Jenkins) regarding the different ways that fan creators "rewrite" media objects.[25]

Sub-genre #1: Songs sung from the perspective of a canonical character: A vast majority of wrock songs are sung from the perspective of a specific, canonical character. "Ode to Harry" by Switchblade Kittens is the premiere example of this lyrical sub-genre,[26] as it is presented from the viewpoint of Ginny Weasley, with lyrics like:

2. DIY Wrock

> Do you know you're the one I adore?
> Next year at Hogwarts you'll see I've transformed
> I will hold my head up high, I'm a Gryffindor
> And you won't need to save me anymore

Smith argues that this type of song is so popular because many of the first wrock bands (such as Harry and the Potters, or Draco and the Malfoys) embraced this lyrical style. Since subsequent bands often took to emulating early wrock bands, these new recruits also adopted the unique way in which the first bands wrote their lyrics.[27]

While most songs in this lyrical sub-genre are sung from the perspective of *main* characters, this is by no means a requirement[28]; the Giant Squidstravaganza, for example, sings songs from the viewpoint of the giant squid that lives in the lake near Hogwarts—a minor character to say the least. Jenkins refers to this focus on "secondary or tertiary characters" as "refocalization." This practice allows fans to "reclaim" minor characters who only exist on the peripheries of the series, or whom fans believe have been unfairly overlooked or sidelined in some way.[29] The resultant wrock songs therefore allow otherwise marginalized characters to "achieve their full potential."[30]

One rather freeing aspect of this lyrical sub-genre is that it enables musicians to sing behind character constructs, allowing them to more easily express emotions that they might normally have trouble conveying through "Muggle music." In the documentary film *We Are Wizards*, Bradley Mehlenbacher of Draco and the Malfoys noted:

> I've tried to write songs ever since I've been able to play guitar, but I could never do it. I think it was because I could never be confident enough that I had something to say about the world that people would care about. When I started writing songs from a fictional character's perspective, it just shattered that [insecurity]. It just came flooding out. I think that freed a lot of [other] people ... too.[31]

Myles Kane (who performs "wizard rap" under the moniker MC Kreacher) touched on this same idea in an interview when he told me:

> Intimacy and vulnerability [can] stifle creativity. Like trying to sing about love or something. You just feel [like], "I can't sing about this. I can't get away with singing about love." But the second you put on this mask of another character and channel his thoughts and feelings, sing about his heartache, you could write anything you want. It's still the real you, but you have [the] protection of this mask.[32]

Sub-genre #2: Songs detailing events that explicitly occurred in the *Harry Potter* books: Closely related to the first lyrical sub-genre but distinct in its own right is that group of songs detailing events that explicitly occurred in the *Harry Potter* books. Consider "Ginny, Are You OK?" by The 8th Horcrux, which details the plot to *The Chamber of Secrets*. The first verse goes as follows:

> In Diagon Alley,[33] we saw Malfoy with his daddy
> He gave you a journal; [it] was a Horcrux and infernal
> You took it without question; you were put under possession
> So you threw it in the bathroom, where I found it—it was our doom

Songs such as this are popular for a number of reasons. For one thing, they allow fans to closely and creatively re-examine a scene that they might consider compelling, emotional, funny, or otherwise memorable.[34] But perhaps more importantly, these types of songs allow wrockers to temporarily become *the* storyteller of a pre-existing text,[35] and thereby, in the words of Joelle Paré, "produce a new text from an original text."[36] For many, there is a certain allure in this opportunity.

Sub-genre #3: Songs building upon story elements only hinted at in the books: Some songs focus on story elements that are only alluded to, hinted at, or which "Rowling's narratives [otherwise] elide over."[37] For instance, "Bacon" by Harry and the Potters hypothesizes that Harry's favorite food is, as the title suggests, bacon: a conclusion that is not explicitly stated in the books, but that Paul and Joe DeGeorge nevertheless came to after realizing how often Harry ate bacon throughout the series.[38] The song begins with the following introduction:

> PAUL DEGEORGE: Hey, Harry?
> JOE DEGEORGE: Yes, Harry?
> PAUL: What's your favorite food?
> JOE: Oh, you know my favorite food is bacon

This lyrical sub-genre is often embraced by those who write about romantic pairings about which there is limited but existent textual support,[39] such as Draco Malfoy and Pansy Parkinson[40]—a pairing which, for instance, is referenced in songs like "Pansy (You Are the Girl of My Dreams)" by Draco and the Malfoys, and "Pansy" by The 8th Horcrux.

In his consideration of how fans can rewrite an established media universe, Jenkins differentiates between "recontextualization" (in which writers "fill in the gaps[41] in … the material and provide additional explanations for the character's conduct"),[42] and "expanding the series timeline" (in which fan writers latch onto "hints or suggestions" sprinkled throughout the series and use these as "openings for their own stories").[43] This differentiation is subtle, with the former focusing on characters, and the latter focusing on events. But regardless of their differences, both allow for fans to take elements which have not been explicitly canonized, and creatively explore them in greater detail.

Sub-genre #4: Songs that consciously deviate from Rowling's understanding of canon: There are also a number of songs that deviate from the official "canon" of the series.

2. DIY Wrock 57

As was discussed in the Introduction, this deviation comes largely in two "flavors," the first of which includes wrock songs that feature new characters or story elements but that still respect Rowling's canon to some degree. Consider for example the song "Imperius Regrets" by The Mudbloods. The song details the somber story of a wizard who was put under the Imperius[44] curse and committed extreme acts of evil:

> I don't remember these things I did.
> Just what I read in the papers,
> And what they said.
> I swear I didn't do it,
> Yeah you know it was not me,
> Who Crucio-ed[45] my daughter,
> And then murdered both my sons,
> And my poor old husband never even saw the wand.
> But you know he made me do it,
> Yeah you know it was not me.

While the character in the song—a "good herbologist"[46] who served as "a gardener in [a] sleepy little town"—is a non-canon creation of Adam Dubberly (the frontman of The Mudbloods), the song strives to keep the character and her motives/behaviors consistent with the parameters of the world that Rowling has created.

Unfortunately, this sort of "personalization" (as Jenkins refers to it) can lead to the accusation that bands are creating "Mary Sue" characters (i.e., poorly written characters that are brilliant and attractive, with no discernable character foibles).[47] The term "Mary Sue" generally carries with it an implicit gendered critique and is sometimes leveled by (generally male) "consumers" against *any* original female characters, whether or not the original creator deserves it.[48] The Parselmouths were occasionally the victims of this sort of accusation early in their career, as they note on their website: "At times they have been accused of writing themselves into the *Harry Potter* world ... as 'Mary Sues' ... but they would like to stomp this rumor out. They admit their grades are lousy, that Harry Potter doesn't pay any attention to them, and that they're not really hardcore Deatheaters [*sic*] or You-Know-Who's right hand women."[49]

The second flavor of deviation includes songs that completely abandon (or sometimes actively rebut) the canon of the series. This flavor itself has many sub-categories, but perhaps the most popular is fanon "eroticization," in which wrockers turn the *Harry Potter* universe into what Jenkins would call "an erogenous zone of sexual experimentation" by taking characters who otherwise show no attraction toward one another in the canonical text and re-writing their characterization so that they do indeed feel some sort of attraction.[50] For instance, "In Which Draco and Harry Secretly Want to Make

Out" by The Whomping Willows discusses Harry and Draco's romantic feelings for one another—something that is never expressed or even hinted at in the main canon:

> Draco and Harry sitting in a tree
> S-N-O-G-G-I-N-G
> It's Draco and Harry sitting in a tree
> F-A-L-L-I-N-G in love

Other popular sub-categories of "canon abandonment" include wrock tunes that realign, invert, or otherwise adjust the morals of characters; songs that place *Harry Potter* characters in unfamiliar settings or in some new plot; and songs in which characters crossover into other (usually fictional) universes.[51] Tianna Mignogna's EP *Fangz 2 Raven* (2012) is perhaps the premiere example of these exercises in "canon abandonment," as it focuses on the infamous *Harry Potter* fan fiction *My Immortal*, which is notorious in the fandom for its single-minded fixation on gothic culture and its apparent ignorance of the established canon of the books. Mignogna's record, however, is set apart from others in that it is self-consciously embracing the tropes of "canon abandonment" for the sake of humor.

Smith argues that songs abandoning the canon of *Harry Potter* "reflect the general tendency within wrock to do something simply because it is fun and not take oneself too seriously."[52] At the same time, there are songs that break from the series' canon not to make people laugh but rather to preserve the original work from any possible damage caused by supposed meddling (e.g., the release of a shoddy tie-in). Consider, for instance, the number of wrock songs that disparage the stage play *The Cursed Child* for its egregious plotholes, characterization inconsistencies, and shoddy writing. And because a number of wrockers consider this work to not only be subpar, but also to counter or retcon important aspects of the *Harry Potter* novels, many have explicitly rejected the play's canonicity in their lyrics. Epitomic of this is the aptly titled "*Cursed Child* Isn't Canon" by Losing Lara, the chorus of which goes:

> *Cursed Child* isn't canon
> It's bad fan fiction
> Your story really sucks
> Didn't give any fucks
> Not worth a second read
> Not a thing I need
> The only thing that's right
> Is Hermione isn't white

Henry Jenkins writes that some fans who buck canon "perceive themselves as rescuing the [original text] from its producers, who have manhandled its characters and then allowed it to die."[53] This is clearly the case with songs like "*Cursed Child* Isn't Canon," which reject the canonicity of *The Cursed*

Child so as to prevent the "true spirit" of the *Harry Potter* series from being perverted or otherwise tarnished in some way by a bad sequel.

Sub-genre #5: Songs about wizard rock or the *Harry Potter* fandom itself: Wizard rock is also dotted with songs that self-reflexively comment upon the movement or the *Harry Potter* fandom itself. These are referred to in the fandom as "metawrock" songs.[54]

"Post Potter Depression" by Lauren Fairweather, a song in which the singer autobiographically recalls her life as a wrocker, is an excellent example. As illustrated below, the lyrics are rife with in-jokes that reference both the wizard rock and the *Harry Potter* fandoms:

> And I wanna grow up to be Melissa Anelli[55]
> Kristina Parselmouth[56] is pretty and I'm jealous
> Matt Maggiacomo[57] is my Patronus
> Yeah, Matt Maggiacomo is my Patronus

Another example is the rather tongue-in-cheek "Wizard Rock Heart Throb" by The Whomping Willows, in which Matt Maggiacomo both discusses the wrock scene, and humorously compares his relative attractiveness to that of other "wrock stars":

> He's not as cute as Joe and he's not as cute as Paul[58]
> He's not as cute as Brian or Bradley at all[59]
> He's not as cute as Alex Carpenter—but then again who is?
> He's not as cute as Patrick from the Hinky Punks[60]
> 'Cuz he's packing way too much junk in the trunk
> He might be a bit cuter than that guy from Hollow Godric[61]
> But that's not saying much, no, that's not saying much

While metawrock tunes often contribute to the overall sense of community in the wrock scene, they can also be among the genre's most esoteric, for if one is not familiar with the goings-on of the *Harry Potter* fandom or the wrock community, these tracks make little to no sense.

Sub-genre #6: "Tribute songs," dedicated to fictional characters or actual people: Finally, there exist a number of "tribute songs," which are dedicated to both fictional characters as well as actual people. As Smith points out, many of these are dedicated to J.K. Rowling,[62] such as "For Jo" by Riddle™:

> So, Ms. Rowling, here is a song I wrote for you
> 'Cuz I'm grateful for all that you've taught me and inspired me to do
> You showed me good triumphs over evil
> And you taught the whole world how to read
> So thank you, Ms. J.K. Rowling
> Thank you so much for Harry

Riddle™ comprising the sisters Georgia (left) and Victoria Minnear, performing at Wrockstock III in 2009. The band's musical ode to J.K. Rowling, "For Jo," is an example of a wrock "tribute" song (courtesy Grace Kendall)

Songs such as this allow fans to express gratitude by praising either characters they adore, or individuals whom they admire in real life.

It should be stressed that these six categories are not the *only* lyrical sub-genres out there, nor is it true that songs can only be sorted into *one* of these categories. Rather, they are useful but artificial constructs that can be used to more productively explore how wrockers write their lyrics.

Recording Wrock

Most wrockers tend to embrace a certain DIY approach to music production, recording their tracks in what might be considered "non-studio" environments, like living rooms, basements, garages, or bedrooms. At the start of the movement, this was largely done for pragmatic reasons: wrock bands were simply having fun and thus could not justify spending huge sums of money to have their silly tunes professionally recorded, as Will Jackson notes:

> The concept of "record in the basement" is [a] reality.... I could rent studio space and professional help to run a power mixing board and record in a sound-specific environment, but I'm not Lil Wayne and I didn't just drop a few gold records and so it's hard to justify even the most successful wizard rock artists spending that type of money so that they can rap about Nargles[63] when the resources are right in front of us.[64]

However, as wizard rock grew in popularity, the concept of "recording in the basement" became a defining element of the scene, as it helped further shift attention away from showmanship toward what many wrockers believe really matters—pure enthusiasm.

This general eschewing of professional recording more often than not results in a distinctly lo-fi sound quality. But surprisingly, this sometimes-questionable quality of wizard rock is rarely seen in a bad light within the community itself; in fact, it is often implicitly encouraged, as one of the central ethos of wizard rock is that *anyone*, regardless of age or even talent, can pen songs about *Harry Potter*, record them, and then share them with other fans. This attitude was espoused by Paul DeGeorge in *The Wizard Rockumentary* when he exclaimed: "It doesn't matter if you have ever played an instrument before, that stuff is so irrelevant to the fact that you *can* make music."65 Matt Maggiacomo of The Whomping Willows championed a similar attitude when he wrote online:

> There are no bad wizard rock bands. Half of these bands are just kids fucking around with GarageBand or whatever free program they can get their hands on.... We, as the elder statespeople of wizard rock, should not be encouraging young people to worry about categorization and public image. We should be encouraging them to have fun.66

Maggiacomo further argues that because many within the scene "are just learning to play an instrument and record music," wizard rock serves as a "learning experience."67 Sam Ducharme concurs, noting, "I definitely [embrace] the rough-around-the-edges-style of wrock, if for no other reason than I've been teaching myself about recording/mixing audio as I go."68

With this said, some bands do strive for a "polished" sound, with perhaps the epitome being Ministry of Magic, a synth-pop band whose music is notable for being highly produced.69 Other groups even opt for professional studios, such as Harry and the Potters, who recorded their extended play *Scarred for Life* (2006) and the untitled split EP with the Zambonis (2006) at Soundtrack Boston.70 Paul DeGeorge told me:

> In January 2006, we did a session at Soundtrack Boston with Dan Brennan, our friend from the band Uncle Monsterface. Soundtrack Boston is a super fancy professional studio, mostly used for a lot of post-production work for TV and film. Dan got us in to there to record for free on the weekends and we recorded 5 songs: the 3 tracks on the *Scarred for Life* 7" and the two tracks for the split 7" with the Zambonis. These are two pretty high-concept [EPs]71 and we just loved executing them as individual stand-alone [releases] rather than connecting the songs back to our next full length. We spent the majority of the time at Soundtrack working on the *Scarred for Life* songs and laid down a lot of overdubs (lots of guitars, gang vocals, even several piano tracks) to create a pretty massive soundscape. We were liberated from our [Korg D12 Digital 12 track machine] and went pretty wild.72

Working in a studio resulted in a group of songs that have an exceptional sonic quality to them. Unfortunately, many amateur musicians are not lucky enough to have recording studio connections, and—given that the expense of laying down just one song at a "real studio" can usually cost a band at the very least $300—most wrock groups are perfectly content with haphazardly setting up microphones and amps in their basements, garages, or living rooms, and capturing everything onto a personal computer.

Bands who record their own music employ a variety of digital audio workstations (DAWs), with perhaps the most rudimentary but accessible being Audacity.[73] A free, open source program that runs on most major operating systems, Audacity is easily downloaded, fairly straightforward to operate, and relatively flexible in terms of use. It also comes with a number of useful tools, like the ability to remove background static from tracks, the option to change pitch and tempo, and the capability to add multiple tracks to one project. Yet Audacity does have its limitations: its plugins are useful but not particularly powerful, and its rudimentary controls are not the best at mixing or mastering tracks. Nevertheless, a number of albums were recorded using Audacity, including Romilda Vane and the Chocolate Cauldrons' first record *Hogwarts, a Mystery* (2007), The 8th Horcrux's debut and sophomore albums *Potterwatch!* (2009) and *Accio Awesome* (2010), and Madam Pince and the Librarians' sole release *Stacked!* (2010).[74]

Quite a few wrockers use Macintosh computers, and as a result, have selected GarageBand as their DAW of choice. This program, which comes pre-loaded as part of the Macintosh operating system, is fairly sophisticated and substantially more complicated than Audacity or other free audio editors. One of GarageBand's biggest assets is that it features a "tracks area," or a space in which you can record instruments or add loops and samples. The benefit of GarageBand's tracks area is that it is directly connected to the program's tempo setting, meaning that pre-recorded drum tracks or other loops will automatically respond to changes in the master tempo. This makes it much easier to craft songs that have stable beats per minute. GarageBand also includes a number of software instruments, which allow wrockers to add unique sounds (ranging from string bass to 80s synthesizers) to their tracks, even if they do not have access to these instrument in real life. GarageBand also has rather sophisticated sound controls, meaning that mixing and mastering can be done much more easily than on a free audio editor. Notable wrock albums that were recorded using GarageBand include Draco and the Malfoys' eponymous debut (2006), The Whomping Willows' album *Welcome to the House of Awesome* (2007), and Tonks and the Aurors' first two releases, *The Pink Album* (2007) and *The Hogsmeade Diaries* (2008).[75]

Finally, some bands purchase professional DAW software. Among the more popular, commercially available DAWs are Ableton Live, Audition, FL Studio, Logic, PreSonus, and Pro Tools. These programs are professional-grade, meaning that users can easily create high-fidelity, radio-quality songs, provided one has the right equipment and sufficient training. However, the downsides to these programs are perhaps fairly obvious: professional DAWs are quite expensive and they can also be rather difficult to use if one does not have the necessary experience. Nevertheless, the potential that professional DAWs offer is quite alluring.

Getting Music "Out There"

Creating *Harry Potter*-inspired music for its own sake can be a lot of fun, but more often than not, wrockers—like fan fictions writers, with whom they share much in common—are eager to see their songs and albums consumed by other *Harry Potter* fans.

Interestingly, wrock bands have resisted what many consider the most effective way of having their music distributed to a wider audience—signing with labels.[76] When I asked my informants as to why wrockers eschewed labels, several expressed the same fear: that label executives might interfere in their creative process. Nevertheless, a handful of what could rightly be considered "wrock record labels" have come into existence over the years,[77] with the most influential arguably being Cheap Rent, helmed by Matt Maggiacomo (of The Whomping Willows) and Kate Aubin. However, for the two, Cheap Rent was not so much a label in the traditional sense as it was a unique way to simply help wrockers release their music to a wider audience.[78] In an interview with the *Detroit Metro Times*, Maggiacomo explained his motivations:

> I've always been concerned that a corporate record label might try to step in and take advantage of Wizard Rock bands who haven't learned from experience how corporate labels can screw people. So Cheap Rent works to provide advice to bands for free, helping them to become self-sufficient so they won't feel like they need assistance from any corporate entity.[79]

Groups that eventually released albums with the help of Cheap Rent included The Parselmouths, Gred and Forge, The Butterbeer Experience, The Mudbloods, and The Moaning Myrtles.[80]

With or without the help of labels, most wrock bands get their music "out there" by producing and distributing CDs. Bands for the most part have two options: they can hand-make CDs, or they can have discs replicated/duplicated through sites like DiscMakers or Kunaki.[81] While the latter method is perhaps more commonly used (especially by established bands), wrock fans—given their appreciation for the DIY aesthetic—are unlikely to turn their nose up at a band just because they release their tunes on burnt CD-Rs. In fact, many bands start out by burning their own discs and only switch to professional disc-making sites out of convenience. According to Lauren Fairweather of The Moaning Myrtles:

> We started out burning CDs ourselves to raise money [but then we realized] it actually ends up being much more expensive when you consider how long it takes to individually make every CD yourself.... [We] moved to Kunaki once we realized that was an option for us.... Though, Kunaki isn't the most professional of the CD-making services I've used, they don't have a minimum [order], so anyone who wanted to could literally make one CD using [the service].[82]

If a band chooses to use an online CD replication/duplication service, this will generally entail the need for liner notes, album art, and a disc design. Most online services provide free editors that their patrons can use to create quick and easy graphics; this is especially useful for groups that are newly formed and have not released albums before. Other more seasoned bands eschew these editors and instead hire experienced graphic designers to create the necessary artwork.

In regard to financing physical media, many wrock bands take to crowd-sourcing sites like Kickstarter and Indiegogo, asking fans for money in exchange for future rewards (e.g., CDs, t-shirts, posters). Often, these fundraising campaigns function as veritable pre-orders, with several added bonuses. For one thing, they let bands know just how many people want their music, allowing them to estimate how many albums they ought to press up. For another thing, they enable bands to receive money *before* they replicate/duplicate a batch of CDs, thereby taking the stressful risk of an up-front investment away from the musicians themselves. Notable albums that were funded via crowdsourcing include The Whomping Willows' *1975*,[83] and The Mudbloods vinyl re-issue of their 2007 EP, *The Animals That Have Left Me*.[84]

But despite the number of bands that sell physical media, arguably the more popular as well as convenient way of distributing wizard rock is by uploading tracks onto the Internet, either for free download or for purchase. There are myriad sites that allow for users to upload tracks that can freely be listened to and downloaded. During wizard rock's heyday, one of the most-often used sites was Last.fm, which enabled bands to create accounts and upload a few tracks that their fans could then download at their leisure. Given that the site facilitated the listening and dissemination of wizard rock, it came to be a major avenue through which individuals discovered new bands. Trina, for instance, told me:

> Through the site, I learned the names of bands.... I was able to listen to different genres within this one genre.... We had a page, and I put our stuff up on there. I thought, "Oh hey, it's another way to get people to listen to our music!" It was before Bandcamp was a thing.[85]

Unfortunately, within the last few years, Last.fm redesigned its interface and expunged older files, meaning that many of the wrock songs that had been hosted on the site are now lost.

Another commonly used but fortunately extant platform for online distribution is YouTube, a video-streaming site onto which wrockers and fans alike have uploaded wrock videos. Most of the times, these uploads are little more than "lyric videos"—slideshows that display a track's lyrics while the song itself plays in the background. Though simple, these videos are popular because they allow fans to not only hear a song, but also learn the lyrics. Other wrock videos on YouTube are more creative (for instance, some pair wrock tracks with spliced footage from the *Harry Potter* films), and some bands even shoot extravagant music videos.

While YouTube videos can be monetized, most are uploaded for free. This means that bands who are interested in earning money through digital distribution should consider other options, such as iTunes, the almost ubiquitous online music marketplace. When iTunes was in its relative infancy, independent musicians had to negotiate with Apple directly to get their music into the store. Given that Apple had very stringent requirements for who they accepted,[86] bands who did manage to have their music hosted via iTunes were often seen by those in the wrock community as having "made it." Thankfully, over the years, services like CD Baby, TuneCore, and DistroKid have enabled independent bands to more easily get their music onto the service (as well as other platforms, like Spotify).

An alternative to iTunes—and perhaps a more appropriate platform for the novice wrocker—is Bandcamp. This site functions much like iTunes, allowing bands to upload their songs and then sell them to their fans directly. However, unlike with iTunes, purchasers who use Bandcamp are able to listen to whole songs regardless of whether they purchase the music, as well as share links to songs/albums on other social media sites. For musicians, signing up for Bandcamp does not cost anything, and the company only keeps a small cut of the profits—if and when they are made. Bandcamp therefore functions in many ways like a useful cross between iTunes and a platform like YouTube, in that it allows bands to make money, but it also provides a medium through which fans can freely listen to, share, and—if they want—download their favorite tracks.

Between the fall of MySpace (discussed in the next section) and the release of the first *Fantastic Beasts* film, wizard rock arguably reached its nadir; a lack of new books or movies meant that while the *Harry Potter* fandom did not disappear, it certainly ebbed until only a core group was left. The continued use of Bandcamp, therefore, was a factor that kept the movement afloat, as it provided a place where wrockers could freely upload their music and their fans could easily find it. In fact, it was Bandcamp that hosted the 2016, 2017, and 2018 Wizard Rock Samplers (free, digital albums curated by Grace Kendall to "remind people that wizard rock is alive and well"),[87] and it was Bandcamp that the Wizrocklopedia chose to house their MySpace wrock archive.

Because wizard rock is an underground phenomenon, potential audiences are limited, and bands are unlikely to become rich by selling their albums. Nevertheless, a few lucky wrock bands have managed to shift a substantial number of units: Harry and the Potters, for instance, revealed in 2009 that they had sold a combined 10,000 copies of their first three studio albums.[88] Around that time, it was also reported that Harry and the Potters had sold a staggering 1.3 million copies of their track "Save Ginny Weasley," and that Draco and the Malfoys had sold 289,000 copies of their song "My Dad is Rich."[89] Considering that both Harry and the Potters and Draco and Malfoys are independent "novelty" bands, these numbers are quite astounding.

The Importance of Social Media Platforms

In their influential book, *Spreadable Media* (2013), media scholars Henry Jenkins, Joshua Green, and Sam Ford introduced the somewhat idiosyncratic term "spreadability." An alternative to the impersonal concepts of "virality" and "memetics,"[90] spreadability refers to the "increasingly pervasive forms of media circulation [as well as] the potential—both technical and cultural—for audiences to share content for their own purposes."[91] Jenkins et al. contended that successful instances of spreadable media make use of technology to facilitate the process of sharing; in particular, the authors stress, "Spreadability recognizes the importance of the social connections among individuals, connections increasingly made visible and amplified by social media platforms."[92] In other words, content creators who make use of social media often end up with highly spreadable—and thus by extension, highly successfully—content.

It is perhaps this element of the spreadability theory that best explains why wizard rock was so successful in the first place. At the onset of their musical movement, wrockers eagerly embraced the potential of the Internet by logging onto social media sites. Because these bands were one of the first groups of like-minded musicians to promote their music *en masse* by almost entirely and exclusively posting it onto key social media sites, social media became imbedded in the very foundation of the movement. And because social media not only stimulates spreadability but also was (and is) a major aspect of wizard rock, it seems likely that the social media aspect of wizard rock contributed to the movement becoming so eminently spreadable.

During wizard rock's heyday, the go-to social media platform was MySpace, and any serious consideration of wizard rock would not be complete without discussing it. Brought into this world in late 2003 by two perceptive entreupeneurs named Tom Anderson and Chris DeWolfe, MySpace enabled users to set up profiles and socialize with others in the online sphere. In its early years, MySpace was ground-breaking due to its highly customizable elements: a user could, for instance, tailor an account to their liking through the manipulation of HTML markup. This meant that user profiles, while all serving the same purpose, often looked radically different from one another. Whether it was due to the tantalizing promise of being able to modify their own account, or simply the appeal of something new, people (Millennials, in particular) began flocking to the site in droves. Within a few short years of its launch, MySpace had become a bona fide pop culture phenomenon, and by 2005 it had grown into the most-trafficked social networking site in the United States.[93]

In addition to the individual, the site also catered toward bands, enabling them to establish accounts of their own. These pages became major communication portals, through which musicians could directly "talk" to fans via private messages, public posts, and blogs. Bands could also post tour dates on their profile, upload pictures, and—perhaps most importantly—showcase some of their own tracks (some of which could even be downloaded for free). MySpace's innovations revolutionized the music industry and even led to bands like Artic Monkeys, Panic at the Disco, The Devil Wears Prada, Colbie Caillat, and Owl City landing record deals and breaking into the mainstream. Part of the reason for the site's success was because it was a win-win for both bands and their fans: Bands were able to upload tracks with ease and quickly gain an audience. Likewise, fans were able to freely listen to, download, and then share their favorite songs with their MySpace "friends"—who in turn might just become fans themselves. To quote Melissa Anelli, "MySpace made music easy to hear and easy to *spread*" [emphasis added].[94]

While a huge number of wrockers came to recognize the site's potential, the first group credited with whole-heartedly embracing MySpace was The Parselmouths; Kristina Horner and Elle Viane Sonnet realized in 2005 that the platform allowed fans who might otherwise be unable to come to one of their shows to still hear their music.[95] Alex Carpenter of The Remus Lupins was the next major wrocker who leveraged MySpace to his advantage. He did this by using his account to orchestrate elaborate online contests that drastically increased his number of digital "friends."[96] Harry and the Potters, too, soon joined the social media site, creating an account in late 2005, and within a year's time, they had an astounding 30,000 friends.[97] In time, more and more groups graviatated toward the site, leading to it becoming a veritable wrock stronghold.

MySpace was so important to the wrock community because it brought fans and bands together and facilitated immediate discussion in a way that no other platform had done before. According to Paul DeGeorge:

> MySpace created a mechanism for fans to directly give appreciative feedback to bands. You could post on their wall, "Cool song!" You could post it right there, and they'd see it, and they think, "I'll make another!" So it would create this sort of virtuous cycle where fans could give feedback to bands, which would inspire bands to create even more. This in turn would inspire other bands to think, "Whoa! If they can do this, I can do this!"[98]

Today, the period stretching from roughly 2006 to 2009 is considered by many to be the "golden age" of wizard rock, largely due to the ease with which wrock bands and fans alike were able to connect, discuss, and share music via MySpace.

Suffice it to say, MySpace was beloved by the wrock community. (Even today, I fondly recall when Trina and I set up The 8th Horcrux's account in mid-2009 and began reaching out to other wrock bands and fans, desperate to make as many "friends" as possible and spread our music along the way.) Unfortunately, the MySpace that many knew and loved came to a cataclysmic end in 2013. It was during this year that the site was overhauled and relaunched, and this major renovation unfortunately entailed the removal of key features like blogs, comment sections, private messages, and videos.[99] While band accounts and the songs that were uploaded to them were preserved, the download feature that had previously facilitated the spread and circulation of wrock tunes was removed, trapping an untold number of wrock songs unavailable elsewhere in a sort of digital limbo. To further complicate matters, many bands broke up and forgot their login credentials, meaning that some groups became nigh impossible to contact. In response to this disaster, the popular fan site Wizrocklopedia announced in December 2016 their "Music Archive." The purpose of this endeavor was to locate and collect hard-to-find songs and deposit them in one convenient, reliable, and easily shareable place. According to the website:

> With MySpace fading away, and [the] changes they made a few years back to wipe out a lot of features and available music, it's been tougher to (legally) find older music from bands that are no longer around.... After some discussions with [Wizrocklopedia] staff members, along with some current and former wizard rock bands, we decided to open up a new searchable wizard rock archive that features bands and music that have not been available online for some time.... If you're a wizard rock fan and there's some music you'd like to be able to download once again, let us know in the comments below! We'll do our best to contact the bands to see what we can do.[100]

The post quickly spread across other forms of social media, eliciting positive responses from those within the wrock community. As of June 2018, the archive, which is hosted on Bandcamp, has 23 complete albums available for sharing and download. While this is only a fraction of the tunes still in musical limbo, efforts to track down other rare songs and albums are ongoing.

The good news for the wrock scene is that as MySpace slipped into obscurity, content creators and fans began to migrate to other social media sites, such as Twitter and Facebook.[101] According to Jennifer Terrell:

> Because wizard rock is centered on the production of music and not directly tied to any platform, the medium through which people interact migrates as the community members migrate to new media. Eventually as people began to adopt Facebook and it became the dominant social medium of the time, wizard rockers also preferred Facebook to Myspace. Around the same time Twitter began to gain popularity, and many prominent members of wizard rock began to use that platform as well.[102]

Many in the wrock scene were eager to embrace Facebook and Twitter because these platforms more easily facilitated communication between bands and fans. These sites also increased spreadability of wizard rock-related content, as features like Twitter's retweet ability or Facebook's share button meant that new songs, bands, music videos, announcements, or other bits of information could be spread with just the swift click of a mouse.

And much like Bandcamp, continued social media use has also proven essential in preserving the momentum of the movement. When the community entered into a period of relative dormancy between the release of *Harry Potter and the Deathly Hallows, Pt. II* (2011) and *Fantastic Beasts and Where to Find Them* (2016), those who were still active within the wrock scene were able to come together and connect via sites like Twitter and Facebook. In fact, a group page made on the latter entitled "Wizard Rock Revival" has played a critical role in the recent revitalization of the scene by circulating wrock-related news.

Had the wrock community never embraced social media, it is likely that the movement would have quickly sputtered out. New bands might have formed and new songs might have been recorded, but without those online social media connections that quickly and easily link people the world over, hardly anyone might have known. In other words, the spreadability factor of the movement would have been near zero. One might contend that concerts provide an avenue through which content can spread, but the problem with this argument is that while live shows are an extremely important aspect of the community, a vast number of wrock bands never play a single concert.[103] Ultimately, wizard rock needs social media in order to survive and thrive.

Don't Forget the Merchandise!

Wrock bands, like almost all other musical groups, supplement their performance fees and their CD sales by selling other types of wrock-themed bobbles or wares. While T-shirts, posters, buttons, and stickers are perhaps the most common items for sale, some groups offer truly one-of-a-kind items to their fans: Draco and the Malfoys, for instance, once sold guitar-shaped USB drives that held their entire discography, and Harry and the Potters are famous within the community for selling "Golden Snitchwiches" (which are sandwiches filled with peanut butter and Golden Grahams cereal that must be caught in one's mouth—"just like Harry Potter did in his first Quidditch match").[104]

Much of the merchandise sold by wrock bands is professionally produced by established print-on-demand companies (e.g., t-shirts screen-printed by Red Bubble, posters and records reproduced by DiscMakers). Unfortunately, sinking money into the production of professionally produced merchandise can be a risky investment—especially for new bands who have limited or nonexistent funds. This has led some musicians to forgo the selling of merchandise altogether. Other groups, who are otherwise determined to produce more than just music, have chosen to save on production costs by

Wrock bands produce a wide variety of merchandise to supplement their performance earnings. Pictured here is merch table for The Whomping Willows, The Moaning Myrtles and Justin Finch-Fletchley and the Sugar Quills in 2009 (courtesy Oak Grove Library).

screenprinting their own t-shirts or silkscreening their own posters. Zines[105] are also popular (with perhaps the most striking—and idiosyncratic!—being Paul DeGeorge's 13-page work of "fan non-fiction" entitled *The Need to Regulate Cauldron Bottom Thickness*, which resembles a report of the same name referenced in *Harry Potter and the Goblet of Fire*). But even if a band chooses to eschew expense by hand-making their own products, it still must be remembered that doing so can be a major time commitment.

Wrock bands sell their physical records from a variety of places: while many groups have online stores from which a would-be fan can purchase albums, the vast majority of items are sold during live shows. The fandom and media scholar Suzanne Scott speculates that this is due to the early legal pressures that molded the way the scene developed.[106] As recounted in Chapter 1, Paul and Joe DeGeorge were contacted by Warner Brothers and told to refrain from selling their items in the digital sphere. They were, however, allowed to sell merchandise surreptitiously at their live shows. And because Harry and the Potters was the first wrock band, newer groups looked to the DeGeorge brothers and began to emulate their behavior—including how and where they sold their merchandise. In other words, what began as a legal restraint evolved into tradition that the community, for the most part, has been content to continue.

Music from the Cupboard Under the Stairs

Given the amount of freedom and independence allotted to each wrock band by the very nature of the movement, no two musical groups are likely to approach the writing, recording, and releasing of music the same way. Nevertheless, there are common steps—namely: deciding on a name, choosing a genre, considering lyrical possibilities, writing and recording tracks, distributing songs via CDs or the Internet, creating and using social media accounts, and purchasing or making merchandise—that most bands take when they are first starting out. In this chapter, I have attempted to explicate these phases and arrange them into a general, logical outline. I must stress that it is not my intention to catalogue these steps merely for academic purposes; I fully intend for this chapter to be consulted by novice wrockers, who might otherwise feel paralyzed by the daunting task of creating a band.

3

Wrocking the Library: Live Wizard Rock

The first wrock show that I attended was a Harry and the Potters concert in July 2010. The venue? The Lawrence, Kansas, Public Library.

I had learned about the show in January of that year after ordering the band's *Live at the Yule Ball* EP. Enclosed in my mailing envelope was a nifty little card, hand-written by Paul DeGeorge, announcing that Harry and the Potters would be performing in Lawrence on July 7. I informed Trina, and we excitedly made plans to attend.

In the days leading up to the concert, our anticipation began to build. But with this anticipation also came a feeling of nervousness. After all, we were both wrock neophytes at the time, and we had no idea what exactly to expect.

Eventually, the day of the show arrived. Neither Trina nor I had our licenses yet, but my mother was kind enough to drive us to the library. Unfortunately, she was not nearly as enthusiastic about the concert as we were (she thought wizard rock was a bit weird).

After we entered the building I approached a librarian sitting behind the circulation desk and asked, perhaps somewhat sheepishly, where the wrock show was. The librarian smiled and gestured to a closed door directly across from where I was standing. Lined up outside of the door were wrock fans—dozens of them—of all ages: children, middle-aged adults, and even older folk were all to be found in the crowd. Some of these people were even decked out in Hogwarts gear or waving handmade wands. Others were wearing worn and well-loved "Save Ginny!" shirts, which had been screen-printed way back in 2003 and sold by Harry and the Potters during their very first shows. Still other attendees were dressed more inconspicuously (wearing what insiders might call "Muggle clothes").

Eventually, the doors opened up and we shuffled into a large auditorium. Inside the room, amidst the crowd, Paul DeGeorge was walking around doing last-minute checks on the band's equipment. Trina and I were slightly starstruck, but we decided to muster up the courage to go and talk to him. After telling him how much of an inspiration his band had been, we presented him with a gift bag that included our embarrassingly amateur debut CD, *Potterwatch!* I'm not sure if he and Joe ever listened to it (and part of me hopes that they have not, given its quality!) but regardless, he was appreciative of the gift.

After talking to Paul, Trina and I then stood around in the crowd of people, and we waited for the show to begin. Finally, after what felt like an eternity, Paul and Joe DeGeorge came rushing into the crowd. The brothers were dressed identically, wearing jeans, white dress shirts, and iconic Gryffindor ties. Joe began doling out costumes to audience members so that we too could dress up; I selected an exact replica of Dumbledore's hat and Trina snagged some Quidditch goggles. After Paul grabbed his acoustic guitar, and Joe positioned himself behind both a keyboard and a glockenspiel, the concert began. The show was staged centrally, with the band surrounded on all sides by a sea of fans. While the brothers had placed a small microphone in the middle to strengthen their voices, the performance was, for the most part, sans amplification. To compensate, Paul and Joe took turns walking about the perimeter of the performance space, directing their voices to all those who were in attendance.

The concert was highly interactive: fans sang along with the band, the audience clapped enthusiastically to the beat, and everyone in the auditorium jeered and cheered when Voldemort and the Order of the Phoenix were mentioned, respectively. Joe served as the event's MC, and at times he would shout out to the audience, "Can I get a Magic Check?" to which we promptly waved our fingers and said "Ooooo!" As a follow-up, he would ask, "Can I get a fun check?" which resulted in the crowd screaming and yelling. Finally, he would ask—for reasons left hilariously unexplained—"Can I get a cat check?" Our response? We all meowed.

At one point, a string on Paul's guitar broke—which he attributed to one of Voldemort's nasty "string-breaking curses"—and he darted off to the corner of the room to hastily make a repair. To buy some time, Joe began telling extremely corny *Harry Potter* puns:

> Where do canines go to learn magic? *Dog*warts!
> Where do baby frogs go to learn magic? *Polly-wog*warts!
> Where do those cardboard milkcaps from the 90s learn magic? *Pog*warts!

The audience amiably laughed as he went through a litany of every-increasingly groan-worthy puns. Then, at the eleventh hour, just when Joe was nearly out of wizardly word-play, Paul came bounding back to center stage with his restrung guitar, and the show-as-scheduled resumed.

For over an hour the band played their hits—ranging from the self-explanatory "I Am a Wizard" to the 20-second ditty "Hagrid"—before closing the show with a crowd-assisted rendition of their song, "Save Ginny Weasley." When the band's set was completed, the DeGeorges were met with a prolonged ovation from dozens of wrock fans.

After the music had stopped and the crowd had started to drift apart, Trina and I approached the DeGeorge brothers and took a few group pictures. Paul was even generous enough to sign my copy of their album *Harry and the Potters and the Power of Love*, adding the tag "Let your heart explode with love!" right under his signature.

Trina and I bought some Harry and the Potters t-shirts, and soon thereafter, we left the Lawrence Public Library in a wrock-induced euphoria—the energy from the show still coursing through our veins. As we drove home, we played Harry and the Potters on the car stereo and reveled in the bliss of the moment.

Before that library concert, we considered ourselves wrock fans, but afterwards, we came to appreciate wizard rock on a completely new level.

(My mother, on the other hand, still thought we were weird.)[1]

* * *

According to Lauren Fairweather, "One really wonderful thing about wizard rock is that it exists primarily online. [But] while I found wizard rock online first, it wasn't until I attended a few concerts that I really became motivated to write my own music."[2] This sentiment was echoed by many of my informants, all of whom argued that while the Internet is often rightly considered the lifeblood of the movement, live shows still play an extremely significant role that should not be so readily forgotten.[3]

It seems that the importance placed on live shows has much to do with the limitations of the Internet itself. As discussed in this book's introduction, the Internet has been essential to the development of the wrock community, allowing otherwise isolated wrockers to "congregate" online in virtual rather than physical space, removing obstacles posed by geography. However, it cannot be denied that even when individuals are connecting online, they are still in many ways separated from one another. To better illustrate this point, imagine if you will that you are attending a concert in spatio-temporal reality. At this event, because you are physically present, you can interact with others via your five major senses: you can see fellow concert-goers gathered all around you, you can feel the deep thump of a bass or the hits of a snare drum in your chest, you can smell a litany of (both pleasant and unpleasant) scents that waft throughout the venue, you can brush up against people around you, etc. Now in contrast imagine that you are alone in your house talking to someone online (e.g., via Skype). This situation, sensorially speaking, is substantially different, as you are only able to speak, hear, and see others with the aid of additional—and often low quality—layers of mediation, like microphones, headphones, computer screens, etc. You will also find that the senses of smell, taste, and touch are—for better or worse—neglected or entirely ignored.

The two examples that I have just provided illustrate the point of this section: while online spaces can and do cause communities to form, it is those physical, "offline" gatherings that are often necessary for a community like wizard rock to *fully* develop, because it is only these sorts of gatherings that allow for full-sensory, spatio-temporal interaction. The social scientist Jeffrey S. Debies-Carl, in a consideration of punk rock space, argues something similar, noting that "the need to physically gather with like-minded people persists"[4] in the scene because there is a recognition that "the importance of face-to-face interaction ... cannot be replaced by virtual interaction over the internet."[5] He thus concludes that "in order for subcultures to flourish, [not only must] a certain density of people with shared interests [be] present in a given area [but there must also be] a *place* for such people to [actually] *congregate* and *participate* in a culturally meaningful activity" [emphasis added].[6] The fandom and filk scholar Sally Childs-Helton echoes Debies-Carl's argument, writing, "In-person, real-time, deeply immersive co-created experience reinforces a strong sense of community, making face-to-face interaction highly valued."[7] What all this means is that live shows are critical to scenes like wrock because the Internet is inherently limited in its interactional capabilities and cannot by itself a full community make.

At the same time, I must stress that I am neither arguing that the online part of wizard rock is inferior nor that the online aspect should be entirely disregarded. Instead, I am merely saying that both the on- and offline worlds are significant albeit different elements of the wrock community and that any study that focuses on only one is bound to be incomplete.

Given that in the previous chapter, I considered in part the important roles that the Internet and social media have played in the wrock movement, in this chapter, I explore the live wrock experience, placing particular emphasis on the role it plays in community formation. First, I focus on *venues*: places that allow wrockers and fans to meet each other, perform music for one another, and be surrounded by like-minded individuals in spatio-temporal reality. I then take a closer look at specific wrock events like conventions, as well as wrock tours. Following this, I pivot slightly, entering the world of social science wherein I consider the live wrock experience in light of theories proposed by the social scientist Émile Durkheim. With these theories in mind, I argue that the wrock community is held together by a "common consciousness"—which emphasizes a love of *Harry Potter* as well as wizard rock itself—that is fully realized during live shows. This shared system of belief pervades the scene, and when it is made manifest during concerts, it helps to create and maintain a tight-knit sense of community. I then assert that at these shows, participants experience unifying periods of collective effervescence.

Locating Wrock Space

Due to the fact that wizard rock is a rather strange type of music, it might not be surprising to learn that wrockers have shown a willingness to perform in rather strange places. This trend was started by Harry and the Potters, who since their founding have actively sought out spots to play that "normal" musicians would otherwise avoid, such as "art [galleries], bookstores, basements, backyards, and pizza places all over the world."[8]

Other bands have followed in Harry and the Potters' footsteps: On a Facebook post discussing the most idiosyncratic locations at which wrockers had performed, Bradley Mehlenbacher of Draco and the Malfoys discussed how he and Brian Ross once performed a show in an indoor soccer complex while a soccer game was going on, Tianna Mignogna commented that she once performed a show in a moving elevator, and Ariel Factor Birdoff described how she once livestreamed a set while a passenger in a car.[9] As long as a location is somewhat conducive to a concert, it seems that most wrockers are willing to embrace it as performance space.

But if you ask a large number of wrockers what their favorite is, many will almost certainly respond: "libraries!" For those outside of the community, this might seem like an odd choice. After all, in the public consciousness, libraries are seen as the home of controlling librarians, hell-bent on shushing all those who dare to raise their voices above a mere peep. Should not a boisterous musical performance in a library therefore be anathema? But the surprising reality is that for many in the wrock community, the library is not just a place to perform, but rather *the* place to perform. Why might this be the case? What exactly makes the library so special?

In seeking to understand the allure of the library as a performance space, I should first consider the rather prosaic possibility that libraries are simply favored because of their practicality. In an interview with *Mashable*, Brian Ross was quoted as saying:

> We're playing a lot of libraries. That's a very important aspect of [the] tour to touch on: libraries are a total win-win-win situation. We need a place to play, that can be an all-ages venue, parents will feel comfortable letting their kids go [there], the library wants people who are our fans' age, and these kids want to go to a wizard rock show. So everybody wins with a library show.[10]

The 8th Horcrux, made up of myself (left) and my wife Trina Thomas perform at the Cass County Public Library in Belton, MO (2012). Libraries are among the most popular places for wrock bands to play shows (courtesy Trina Thomas).

While one could cite this quote as evidence that wrockers embrace libraries simply due to their pragmatic utility, I would argue that this interpretation misconstrues what Ross is really getting at. For one thing, it assumes that libraries are the *only* places that, to quote Ross, are "a total win-win-win." In reality, they are not; many cities have youth clubs, community centers, or churches that fulfill Ross's requirements. For another thing, this understanding does not come close to explaining the sense of enthusiasm that motivates people either to set up shows in libraries, or to journey to their local library to see their favorite wrock bands play. In regard to this point, it must also be remembered that those who produce and enjoy wizard rock are often avid readers, and by extension, heavy library-users. For these people, there is surely something special about hearing music based on their favorite book series reverberating throughout the same place in which they might have first discovered the series. In other words, the allure of library shows has a strong emotional component that cannot so easily be ignored.

Additional postulations have also emerged which seek to explain why libraries have become popular wrock venues. Amanda Finlaw, the host of the

YouTube channel Amanda Aesthetic, argues that because libraries serve as the intersection of "our lives in physical spaces and our lives in fandom and stories,"[11] it logically follows that these spaces would be the ideal place for a liminal activity like wizard rock that otherwise blurs the line between the "real" (i.e., our "Muggle" identities) and the "fictional" (i.e., our "wizard" identities). Sara Rasmussen, one of the co-creators and former co-hosts of the popular wrock radio show *The Wizarding Hour*, contends that: "Libraries are really incredible spaces at the center of community, civic engagement, and literacy. I think those values really align with the underlying themes of *Harry Potter* and of this fan culture."[12] While their hypotheses differ in many ways, both Finlaw and Rasmussen are united in their belief that libraries are veritable intersections, connecting different aspects of the human experience.

But there is a final reason libraries are popular, and it has to do with wizard rock's streak of rebelliousness and its undeniable punk rock influence. As was mentioned at the start of this section, libraries are stereotypically thought of as somber "dens of silence."[13] This stereotype has given rise to the idea that making noise in a library is an unforgiveable taboo, meaning that there is something exhilarating and decidedly anti-authoritarian about playing music in a library—especially boisterous rock music. Such a sentiment was expressed by Melissa Anelli in her book *Harry, a History* when she wrote, "It was yet another slight dig at The Man to be turning up the volume intentionally in a place that wanted you to quiet your speech."[14]

With this quote, Anelli seems to suggest that libraries can be viewed as part of The System which is to be fought against, but there is something about this sentiment that does not seem quite right. For one thing, many librarians are self-described wrock fans (some, such as Ariel Factor Birdoff, are even wrockers themselves). For another thing, almost all wrock shows are library-sanctioned. How can wrock bands be sticking it to The Establishment if The Establishment is taking an active part in encouraging their rebellion? Given this paradox, perhaps it is best to view these shows as a type of *socially sanctioned* "dig at The Man." This is not as oxymoronic as it sounds; in fact, the anthropological record contains many examples of this behavior, which scholars call "rituals of rebellion." The first to explicitly formulate this idea was the anthropologist Max Gluckman in a book chapter concerning the Bantu peoples of South Africa. Gluckman observed that these peoples occasionally celebrated rites in which social norms were inverted, and open hostility was directed at the king or those in positions of power; however, when the rites ended, so too did this simulated "rebellion against authority."[15]

Gluckman thus argued that these behaviors were not random bursts of degenerate behavior, but rather actions that "proceed[ed] within an established and sacred traditional system, in which there [was] a dispute about particular distributions of power, and not about the structure of the system itself. This allow[ed] for instituted protest, which in complex ways renew[ed] the unity of the system."[16] In other words, these rituals are cathartic releases, which upend the power structures in the society, allowing the powerless to temporarily turn on the powerful and vent their frustrations in an institutionally approved way. And given that this outlet for emitting bottled-up frustrations is permitted by those in power, it inherently upholds and consequently strengthens the established social order even as it lays bare social tensions in a society.[17]

While modern American society might not feature many obvious "rituals of rebellion,"[18] I would argue that wrock library shows can be productively viewed in this light. For one thing, the act of playing loud rock music in a library is a clear example of usual power structures being inverted: the silenced become the boisterous, and the silencers temporarily lose their power to hush. What is more, many wrockers hold strong socio-political beliefs and use their music to critique the status quo. So not only are wrock shows in libraries disrupting the norm, but they are often doing so while laying bare social issues that wrockers would like to address. Finally—and perhaps, most importantly—a wrock show in a library manages to reaffirm the power and importance of the library itself, even as the musicians themselves temporarily reject the authority of the library to silence them. For a simple example, consider the lyrics to "The Library Song" by Tonks and the Aurors:

> Just ask Hermione Granger
> What she would do when faced with a problem
> Where can you find the answers to all of your questions?
> Inside of one room...
> Let's all go to the library!

These lyrics praise libraries as a space where problems—including, I would argue, social ills[19]—can be combatted. But in a somewhat contradictory manner, when Steph Anderson performs this song at a library, she is often singing into a microphone and loudly playing an electric guitar—behavior that would normally violate any library's rules!

Performances of tracks like Anderson's "The Library Song" consequently illustrate the seemingly contradictory nature of library shows: while wrockers temporarily reject the authority of the library to enforce silence, they are still affirming the importance and power of libraries. Thus, this incongruous behavior is in many ways analogous to the behaviors of the Bantu people, who protest the king's power during rituals of rebellion, but by doing so affirm that power.

Besides library gigs, house parties are for many the *de facto* type of wrock show. These are generally small, intimate gatherings in which a select group of musicians and fans come together in someone's house to perform songs for one another. Parties such as this function not only as social gatherings in which attendees can enjoy conversation and music, but also as "wrock workshops," in which bands can unveil new projects and receive constructive criticism from their peers. Brian Ross of Draco and the Malfoys, in particular, is known for his semi-annual house parties at his residence in Woonsocket, Rhode Island, which have been collectively dubbed the "House Show Series at Malfoy Manor." These gatherings showcase both up-and-coming wizard rock bands as well as perennial favorites like The Whomping Willows and Lauren Fairweather, thus letting the "old guard" of wizard rock perform with some of the scene's newest members.

This gathering of the "new and the old" (to quote Grace Kendall) in a small, intimate setting where everyone is assumed to be on equal footing facilitates the development of interpersonal relationships, which in turn engenders a tightknit sense of community. It was perhaps the fandom writer and activist Claudia Morales who best described this sentiment in the forward to her zine *Rocking the Room of Requirement, or Our House (In the Middle of Our Scene)*[20] when she wrote:

> [When] I walked into my first house show [at Malfoy Manor, I] immediately felt at home. I kept looking around at all my friends and all the familiar faces.... It was like the parties I thought I was missing out on in high school, populated with people I never thought I'd get to see in a place like this.... There's something so special about [Malfoy Manor]—a basement with lights woven through the rafters, our own little enchanted ceiling; a living room with couches and a fireplace and all the comfort and community of a common room; an entire great hall's worth of cupcakes. There's something so special about going down to the basement, packed full of people, and seeing bands that have been around since the very beginning playing alongside bands making their wizard rock debuts.[21]

In an interview, Sam Ducharme echoed her thoughts, humorously describing Ross's house shows as being "like a family reunion where I actually *like* everybody there."[22]

Additionally, Kendall has argued that Ross's house shows have helped re-anchor the wrock community after years of fragmentation and post–MySpace centerlessness:

> Small local communities have kept wizard rock powered for years, and at the heart of them have been reliable, safe-space venues—places like.... Brian's house in Rhode Island.... [His] basement gives people in wizard rock an unhesitating place to go.... By creating these regularly scheduled events, Brian and the others involved in organizing these shows are inviting a certain type of new life and expression with our community. These spaces take our community off of the internet—where it floats, with no real home since the days of MySpace and the Wizrocklopedia—and gives it a reliable gathering space in the physical world. Without a place to gather, we are scattered—but these reliable spaces allow us to concentrate our energies and to truly come together.[23]

(And I should add that it also seems fitting that this "re-anchoring" is occurring in New England—the very region where wizard rock was born.)

Wrock Concerts, Cons and Festivals

During the movement's early years, wrock concerts were generally small and intimate—rarely above a few dozen people. But as the movement grew in popularity, bands began to organize larger and larger shows to accommodate the increasing size of their audiences.

One of the earliest of these "large-scale" wrock concerts was "The Yule Ball," which Harry and the Potters describe as "a family friendly, all ages event … for wizards to get a little crazy and get dressed up all fancy."[24] The inaugural Yule Ball was organized in 2005 by the DeGeorge brothers and thrown at The Middle East Downstairs venue in Cambridge, Massachusetts. According to Paul, the inspiration for the event and the choice of venue has much to do with the antics of another Bostonian band:

> I'm a big fan of Christmas music and holiday traditions in general, but I think this event is most directly influenced by the Mighty Mighty Bosstones' Hometown Throwdown, where—even at the peak of [their] popularity—the band would do a weeklong holiday stand at the Middle East Downstairs. I loved that the Bosstones would always bring along so many great local and national acts for those shows, and the Throwdown really felt like an important and special local tradition. The only problem with the Bosstones's event was that only one of those shows would be all-ages and that was a tough ticket to get when I was in high school. Kudos to the Middle East for always letting our event be all ages and for being down to clown when I first brought them a list of wizard cocktails (and mocktails) 12 years ago. We couldn't ask for a better partner on this event.[25]

To this day, Harry and the Potters consider the Yule Ball their "biggest [and] most exciting annual show," and they often emphasize that "it's not just a fun concert. It's an event."[26]

At the December 21, 2008, Yule Ball, Paul and Joe had their performance professionally filmed and recorded, and the resulting product, a CD/DVD combo entitled *Harry and the Potters at the Yule Ball 2008*, was issued as the final release of the Wizard Rock EP of the month club in December 2009. Those curious as to what exactly the Yule Balls are like but who are otherwise unable able to attend are encouraged to consult this release, which the DeGeorge brothers described on their personal website as "a blistering 25+ song live document of all the wizardly holiday cheer that makes the Yule Ball one of our favorite shows of the year."[27]

Since its inception, the Yule Ball has hosted myriad wizard rock bands as well as other forms of wacky, Potter-centric entertainment (like Neil

Cicierega's popular puppet troupe *Potter Puppet Pals*), and because of this, it has remained one of the most beloved and well-attended wrock events.[28] In fact, the Yule Ball has become so popular within the wrock community that Harry and the Potters now regularly play several smaller Yule Balls, all of which lead up to the main event held at The Middle East Downstairs. Tickets for these shows generally cost around $20, of which a large percentage is donated to charities, such as the Harry Potter Alliance, which over the last decade has earned well over $40,000 exclusively from Yule Ball ticket sales.[29]

While the inaugural Yule Ball helped to somewhat satisfy the ballooning wrock scene's need for larger and more extravagant shows, wizard rock soon began to spill over into other domains, and by 2006–07, bands were performing at *Harry Potter* fan conventions and academic symposia (such as Lumos, held July 27–30, 2006; or Phoenix Rising, held May 17–21, 2007) to large groups of people who were not necessarily wrock fans. While initially taking a backseat to other aspects of fandom at these events, wizard rock soon began to "steal the show" (so to speak), steering some of the focus away from the books and toward fan-made music.[30]

It was at this point in time that people began to recognize the need for new wrock-only conventions. One of those who began to contemplate this idea was the dedicated wrock fan Abby Hupp, who told me: "I'd been to [wrock] library shows and seen the crowds that turned out at [the *Harry Potter* convention] Phoenix Rising in 2007 and figured wizard rock needed its own big event....

Paul DeGeorge performs at the 2016 Yule Ball. This event was first organized by Harry and the Potters in 2005. Since its inception, it has managed to raise over $35,000 for the Harry Potter Alliance (courtesy Grace Kendall).

Nobody had done a 100% wrock weekend event."[31] Hupp quickly got to work, and after months of planning, she announced to the community her project: the "Wrockstock Spooktacular," which she scheduled for late 2007.[32] This festival—which would eventually become an annual event known simply as "Wrockstock"—is considered by most within the wrock community to be the first largescale, all-wrock convention.[33]

Wrockstock's inaugural session was held from October 26–28, 2007, at the YMCA Trout Lodge in Potosi, Missouri. Being located in the middle of Southeast Missouri Ozarks, the event was secluded from the rest of the world, and, as author Erin Anne Pyne notes, "felt like summer camp with all your best friends. Cell phones did not work, Internet access was nonexistent. Shut off from the world, [attendees] truly felt like wizards in hiding from the Muggles."[34] Unlike other wrock shows that are generally free, tickets to Wrockstock cost around $100. However, almost all of the earnings were given to charity,[35] with Hupp informing me that much of the proceeds were donated to Andrew Slack, who used them to start up the Harry Potter Alliance.

During the first year, only a few hundred people trekked out to the wilds of the Missouri Ozarks for the event, but as wizard rock began to further explode in popularity, so too did Wrockstock's attendance. By 2009, over 500 people were taking part in the wizardly festivities (some of whom had journeyed from far-flung places like Northern Europe and Africa)[36] and within no time, organizing the festival become an enormous task, as Hupp told me:

> [It] was a full time [and] year-round job for me. I oversaw everything, plus [I] personally managed all the marketing, branding, band communications, and guest services. Then there were teams of dedicated volunteers who managed registration, and transport (we were two hours drive from the closest airport and ran our own shuttles). There was a stage management team [directed] magnificently ... by Steph from Tonks and the Aurors (before she even took the stage herself), there was a merch team (we had a full-blown merch room run by [Wrockstock] staffers), and there was also a crafts and activities team for daytime summer camp fun. [And] there was no budget—if we didn't sell enough tickets to pay the bills for using the property, I paid [for Wrockstock] out of my own pocket.[37]

During Wrockstock's zenith, generally between twelve to fifteen bands "headlined" the event, all of whom were among the most popular within the community, such as The Remus Lupins, Swish and Flick, The Parselmouths, Ministry of Magic, Draco and the Malfoys, The Whomping Willows, and The Moaning Myrtles. These groups performed in a large room at the Trout Lodge dubbed the "Room of Wrockquirement."[38] And just outside the lodge, in a large and spacious teepee, the Wrockstock staffers set up a space that was eventually nicknamed the "Wampum Willow," where newly formed, up-and-coming, or relatively unknown groups were able to play short sets.[39] A number of now-popular wrock bands got their start performing at the Wampum Willow, most notably Tonks and the Aurors.

Wrockstock was held from 2007 until 2011. Unfortunately, by 2011 the festival was unable to remain fiscally solvent, and in January 2012, the concert organizers took to their Facebook page, announcing that there would not be a 2012 Wrockstock. This statement was met with great sadness, and for a little over a year and a half, wrockers bemoaned the fact that they did not have a yearly Wrockstock to look forward to. This changed in early 2013, when it was announced that a final "Wrockstock Reunited" session would be held in St. Louis from July 26–28, 2013.[40] Unlike previous years, this session functioned less like a summer camp, and more like a joyous class reunion, providing musicians and fans with the opportunity to watch their favorite bands perform live while also reminiscing about the days of old.

After the success of Wrockstock's inaugural session in 2007, others began to plan large-scale shows of their own. One of the first of these, the Hallows and Horcruxes Ball, was organized in early 2008 by students and staff at Kansas State University (K-State) in Manhattan, Kansas.

The genesis of this event can be traced back to August 2007, when Dr. Karin Westman—the head of K-State's Department of English, as well as the faculty advisor for the campus group "Children's and Adolescent Literature Community"—took a trip to Prophecy, an academic *Harry Potter* conference. At this symposium, she witnessed several prominent wrock groups perform their music to a rapt crowd. Upon her return to Manhattan, she relayed her experience to her *Harry Potter*–loving students, and they began to toy with the idea of hosting their own wrock concert.[41] Their ideas eventually morphed into the inaugural "Hallows and Horcruxes Ball," which was held on March 8, 2008.[42] Over 200 people showed up to see some of the biggest bands in wizard rock perform.[43] Due to the success of the initial event, K-State decided to continue hosting the Hallows and Horcruxes Ball for seven consecutive years. During its long run, a number of prominent wrock bands performed at the event, including Draco and the Malfoys, The Moaning Myrtles, The Parselmouths, The Mudbloods, The Whomping Willows, Tonks and the Aurors, Gred and Forge, Justin Finch-Fletchley and the Sugar Quills, The Remus Lupins, and Ministry of Magic.[44]

Tickets for the Hallows and Horcruxes Ball cost $12, and almost all the proceeds were donated to the nonprofit First Book of Geary County—an organization that donates books to children in poverty.[45] According to the charity's co-chair, Sarah Jones, the Hallows and Horcruxes Ball had a major impact on their organization by providing it with much needed funding. Alisha Sommerville, a student at K-State in 2010, told *The Collegian*, "It's good to be a part of the donation process, especially when the donations are

Trina Thomas (left) and the author attend the 2011 Hallow & Horcruxes Ball, in Manhattan, KS (courtesy Trina Thomas)

going to such a good cause."[46] Westman expressed similar sentiments, telling the paper that she was proud that the concert stressed "the importance of helping others in your community."[47]

The last Hallows and Horcruxes Ball was organized on March 8, 2014. Although many at K-State were still enthusiastic about the event and wizard rock in general, the post–*Death Hallows* blues had taken its toll on the audience size, and it simply became too much work to host the massive concert every year. And while it has been several years since the last Hallows and Horcruxes Ball was held, many former attendees—both in and outside the Manhattan area—remember it fondly. In 2014, K-State alumna Anne Sisley told the school's student newspaper, *The Collegian*: "I grew up in Manhattan, so I've been to all six years [and] I've become friends with lots of the band members.... I'm sad this is the last year, but ... it's cool we're all still meeting and hanging out together."[48] Sisley's comments are sentimentally similar to those of Matt Maggiacomo, who told the paper two years earlier, "This event is special to me [because in 2010], my fiancée [i.e., Lauren Fairweather] and I got engaged here. It sets this event aside in a sense because of the emotional attachment we will forever have for it."[49]

As a Kansas resident and an attendee of the 2011 Hallows and Horcruxes Ball, I too am sad that the show has been defunct for years, as it was an eccentric tradition in the middle of an exceedingly conventional state. But at least we still have the memories.

A few months after the inaugural Hallows and Horcruxes Ball, the coordinators of Terminus (a five-day *Harry Potter* fan and academic conference) organized "Wrock Chicago" on August 8, 2008 at the Hilton Chicago Hotel. While the concert was technically a sub-event of the larger Terminus festivities, Wrock Chicago functioned in many ways as a stand-alone wrock convention. A grand total of 24 bands performed at the event, including Draco and the Malfoys, Harry and the Potters, Tonks and the Aurors, The Remus Lupins, The Whomping Willows, and Switchblade Kittens, making it the largest gathering of wrock bands that had, at that time, ever been held.[50]

In her dissertation "Revenge of the Fanboy: Convergence Culture and the Politics of Incorporation," Suzanne Scott provides a brief description of the convention, describing it almost like a scaled-down, indoor Lollapalooza or Warped Tour:

> The event was structured like a conventional music festival. Lesser known bands played one of two "stages" throughout the day, set up in hotel conference rooms, and the chosen "headliners" performed in the evening on the "main stage" [which was a hotel] ballroom, the only space that could accommodate all of Wrock Chicago's attendees, which numbered around 1,000.... During the day, a separate ballroom in the hotel was designated as a merchandise space, with many of the smaller bands opting to sell CDs and t-shirts. The evening "headliners" show featured an integrated retail space, with a wider array of products (e.g., multiple t-shirt designs, multiple albums on both CD and vinyl, etc.).[51]

This description suggests that while the wrock community was by no means jettisoning the "rocking in the library" mentality, by 2008 it was showing a willingness to emulate the feel and aesthetic of "traditional" large-scale concerts or music festivals.

While the Terminus events were unfolding, perhaps the most idiosyncratic wrock event of all time was being planned: the "Wrock the Boat" cruise, which as its name suggests was an almost week-long wrock concert and sea voyage all rolled into one. The event was orchestrated and directed by Pattie Beaven in an attempt to combat "the worst case of post–Potter depression [she] had ever experienced" after returning from the *Harry Potter* symposium Prophecy.[52] According to Beaven:

> Right after the [symposium], I was sitting out by a café, looking out at the Mississippi River. I watched as The Carnival [Cruise Lines ship] *Fantasy* sailed passed, with all her passengers on deck to bid a Bon Voyage. I sipped my smoothie and thought about some of the fantastic times I had on cruises in the past. [Then] I began to think not

just of my great vacations on cruises, but my exciting adventures with my friends in the *Harry Potter* Fandom.... My mind sorta worked like this: Cruises. *Harry Potter.* *Harry Potter.* Cruises. And now you could see the light bulb above my head and my eyes fill with hope and wonder! What in the world? A *Harry Potter* Cruise![53]

Soon thereafter, Beaven reached out to Carnival Cruise Line and began working on her distinctively off-beat idea.

After weeks of intense planning, scheduling, and negotiating, she secured the use of the very ship that had inspired the idea in the first place, the *Fantasy*, and with the assistance of Brian Ross of Draco and the Malfoys, she organized a floating wrock concert for Halloween 2008. When it was announced, the idea of a "wrock cruise" resonated with the community, and during the first two month of tickets being available, more than 200 were sold. The *Fantasy* set sail on October 27, 2008, from New Orleans. Over five days, the ship traversed the Gulf of Mexico and the Caribbean Sea. During this journey, passengers intermingled in the "Great Hall" (i.e., the ship's main atrium) and relaxed while listening to several wrock bands (including Draco and the Malfoys, Justin Finch-Fletchley and the Sugar Quills, Witherwings, Remus and the Lupins, and Catchlove) perform their greatest hits.[54]

Any section that discusses the concert and events of wizard rock would not be complete without discussing LeakyCon. Founded in 2009 and originally run by the Leaky Cauldron *Harry Potter* fansite (hence its name), the event was created to "celebrate" the *Harry Potter* fandom.[55] However, when Pottermania began to wane around 2011–14, the event programmers wisely decided to broaden LeakyCon's appeal by catering to other areas of pop culture like *Doctor Who* and *Game of Thrones*.[56] Today, LeakyCon is run by a group called Mischief Management, which offers a number of other fannish events—such as GeekyCon, BroadwayCon, and Con of Thrones—alongside the convention that started it all.[57]

It must be stressed that LeakyCon always accommodated a wide, diverse audience and was never a wrock-only convention like the Yule Balls or Wrock Chicago. Nevertheless, soon after its founding, wrock bands and fans alike quickly found a home at LeakyCon, and in time, large portions of the event were dedicated to wrock performances. And today—almost a decade after it was founded—there is still a fondness in the hearts of many wrockers for LeakyCon; according to Grace Kendall, this is at least in part due to it being:

> the only major con that kept going for so long—especially if you include their Geeky-Cons under that umbrella. While most other cons and festivals were one-off events, LeakyCon ... [was one of] the biggest and most frequently occurring events that kept a big focus on wizard rock. People could see what a great time their friends had and get caught up in the media outpouring that happens during and right after a con, and they could say: "That's it, I'm not missing this next year." When there are only one or

two events that happen [as] reliably [as] LeakyCon] ... it's easy for those to become big gathering spaces in the community. LeakyCon also had a tendency to book the same really popular acts from year to year, so people who really wanted to see Harry and the Potters or Draco and the Malfoys could buy tickets [knowing] that these big-name bands would most likely be there. And because it was a big event with huge crowd energy, those shows were some of the best performed by those bands: full band, full performance, [makes for] some of the best sets in the scene.[58]

It has been over a decade since the first Wrockstock took place, and in that span of time, a large number of wrock conventions and concerts have been hosted—so many, in fact, that an exhaustive list would take up far too much space. And while in the last few years, the frequency of these sorts of events has decreased (largely in proportion to the popularity of wizard rock as a whole), it is likely that these events will continue to be hosted the world over, wherever interest in wizard rock is high enough.

Hitting the Road

In an episode of the BBC's film news series *Talking Movies*, Josh Koury—the director of the documentary *We Are Wizards* (2007)—expressed the following sentiment while discussing the nature of wizard rock: "For me [the movement is] not an online community that stays shelled in a room; it's an online community that then expands onto the stage [and then] expands out on the road, and into the world."[59]

Regardless of whether Koury meant his final point in a metaphorical or literal way, the reality is that numerous wrock bands, provided they have sufficient resources and free time, organize large-scale wrock tours, generally of the United States. These often see bands piling into beat-up old vans, performing shows in any venue that will allow them entrance, and sleeping in the living rooms of kind-hearted hosts. These tours also have a tendency to be somewhat improvised and spontaneous, with bands scheduling shows as they go. Because of this, they often feel sincere and intimate, suggesting that the bands are not in it for the money or the fame, but rather for the *experience*: the chance to meet people, intermingle with fellow fans, and sing *Harry Potter*-inspired tunes in as many cities as possible.

This is not to say that wrock tours are always haphazardly thrown together. Indeed, quite the opposite: many of the "bigger" tours require some level of preparation, coordination, and planning, lest they fall apart entirely. Steph Anderson told me:

> For a summer tour in June or July, [for instance] I'll begin booking shows in November or December after I've found that most libraries book summer programs and finalize budgets by early January. So while it's hard to get moving that early, it

absolutely pays off in advance. You've got to plan a route, start a budget, and just start booking. The only way I've been successful long term is to start asking for money to cover travel expenses sooner rather than later![60]

Some bands are even able to meticulously organize and execute cross-continental tours; Harry and the Potters, for instance, have organized elaborate circuits in the United Kingdom (2005),[61] as well as several in Scandinavia (2010, 2015, and 2016).[62] However, these sorts of tours often necessitate that a band has both achieved a certain level of fame as well as secured contacts in the intended host countries.

For the average band—especially those just starting out—tours tend to be much smaller, and sometimes groups will perform at only a handful of places. For instance, in the summer of 2011, The 8th Horcrux embarked on what we called the *Mini-"Summer Tour Extravaganza,"* during which we played a string of shows at various eastern Kansas and western Missouri libraries, bookstores, and other assorted locations. By the end of the tour, we had performed around a dozen shows, all the while having never strayed more than 70 miles from the greater Kansas City area. In many ways, this "tour" gave us the best of both worlds: we were able to get a taste of the touring experience, but we were also able to do so in a way that did not require us to put our regular lives on hold (we both had summer jobs, after all). This last factor is important, given many wrock bands are made up of high school or college students, who might not be able to dedicate large swaths of time outside school vacations to touring in far-off locations.

And whether a wrock tour is going to be large or small, cost must be factored into the equation—after all, travelling is generally not cheap. According to Lauren Fairweather:

> Organizing tours can be tough depending on [if] venues ... have the funding to host shows.... I'd say the toughest thing is affording it; the cost of the vehicle, gas, hotels, merch, food, equipment, and everything else associated with touring made it tough for us to keep doing it. We tried to keep ticket prices free or as low as we could, so we relied on merchandise sales and show planners with the budgets to pay us when we were touring full-time.[63]

In addition to selling merchandise, wrock bands have also set up projects on crowdsourcing websites like Kickstarter or Indiegogo, promising perks (e.g., albums, t-shirts, stickers, posters) to donors in return for money. The benefits of using crowdsourcing platforms to raise money for a tour are similar to those discussed in the last chapter's section on CD replication/duplication. Namely, these platforms reduce upfront financial risk, and they allow a band to gauge potential interest; after all, if no one pledges money, it is likely that the tour is not going to be well-attended. Tours that have secured funding through crowdsourcing include: *Riddikulus!: A Rolling Wizard Rock*

Festival (a 2012 tour organized by The Whomping Willows, Lauren Fairweather, Justin Finch-Fletchley and the Sugar Quills, Tonks and the Aurors, Snidget, and I Speak Tree)[64]; *Go West, Young Wizards: A Wizard Rock Summer Tour* (a 2013 tour organized by Tonks and the Aurors, Justin Finch-Fletchley, and Kirstyn Hippe)[65]; and *Yes All Witches: Route 66 Edition* (a 2016 tour organized by Tonks and the Aurors).[66]

Solidarity, Collective Effervescence and Live Wizard Rock

In interviews with those active in the wrock community, time and time again I was told that the scene exudes a certain power that brings people closer together and allows them to connect on a different level. Importantly, almost all my informants emphasized that this sense of solidarity was the strongest and almost palpable during live shows. But while most of those whom I interviewed described this sense of intense unanimity (often with similar language), almost no one had a detailed explanation for its cause. Thus, the question becomes: what is the nature of the solidarity on display at wrock concerts, and where does it come from?

The answer to this question is complex, and it will require a brief foray into social scientific theory of the late 1800s. It was during this time that a French philosopher named Émile Durkheim, while studying at the Sorbonne, became fascinated with how individuals are connected to society, and how society itself is held together. He eventually focused much of his principal dissertation *The Division of Labour in Society* (1893) on trying to solve this problem. In this work, Durkheim postulated the existence of a "common consciousness,"[67] or "the totality of beliefs and sentiments common to the average members of a society [which] forms a determinate system with a life of its own."[68] In other words, the common consciousness is a system of shared beliefs that becomes imparted into a society, encouraging, as the social scientist Ken Morrison puts it, "social likeness and similarities among all members."[69] Durkheim also maintained that "it is independent of the particular conditions in which individuals find themselves," and that while "individuals pass on … it abides."[70] By this he did not mean that the common consciousness was an autonomous, supernatural "thing" floating "above" society, but rather that it has a community-level existence, thus explaining why humans obey social rules (or "facts") that they or people they know did not formulate.[71]

The composition and strength of this common consciousness, Durkheim argued, is intimately tied to what kind of "solidarity" unites a society, of which he proposed two different types: mechanical and organic.[72]

3. Wrocking the Library   91

Mechanical solidarity comes about when a group of people feel a connection thanks to shared moral/spiritual values, belief systems, or rituals. Because they collectively share in these ideals and practices, it could be said that these individuals are effectively "thinking the same thing." Thus, the common consciousness of the group is wide-spread[73] and intense, and consequently the "social links" uniting the society's members are robust. Additionally, in societies united by mechanical solidarity, the content of the common consciousness is often religious, extra mundane or mystical in nature, emphasizing the importance of community and supra-individual interests.[74]

Conversely, organic solidarity is based not around some perceived "sameness," but rather the division of labor in modern, capitalist societies, which leads to highly atomized individuals cooperating with one another to survive and prosper. In such a society, individuals have stronger attachments to one another more so than they do with society at large. This weakens the pervasiveness and intensity of the common consciousness, since the members of this society are no longer all necessarily "thinking the same thing." This of course is not to say that shared social beliefs or behaviors cease to exist, just that they are far more heterogeneous and less universal. And since the common consciousness still exists but is now uniting people who hold disparate and diverse beliefs, its content becomes "secular," focusing less on the numinous and more on the "here and now" of human affairs.[75]

The wrock community is not a full-blown "society" in the way that Durkheim used the term, meaning that any application of his sociological theories is bound to be somewhat simplistic. With that said, the wrock scene is a community, and one that is strongly unified by a commonality: a love of the *Harry Potter* universe. Trina articulated this view when she told me:

> Everyone has a different opinion about what the best book is or whether or not the movies are garbage, but at the end of the day, *we can all sing songs about Harry Potter*—it's accepted and it's safe.... [The 8th Horcrux] played a show awhile back, and we got to see a cross-section of wizard rock: acoustic filk, folk, wiz-hop, and parody. [The different groups] were all there. And *we all had the same purpose ... a common goal ... a common interest*: publicly expressing our love about this one book series.[76] [emphasis added]

Anu Lingappa, who ran the *Witching Hour* radio show for a time at Whitman College, expressed a similar sentiment when she argued, using very Durkheimian language, that "wizard rock [is] a statement of *solidarity between people who are all manners of obsessed* with *Harry Potter*" [emphasis added].[77]

Quotes like these support the idea that the wrock community is united primarily by this love of *Harry Potter* and, by extension, a general interest in wizard rock itself. These values thus come to comprise the "totality of beliefs and sentiments common to the average members of" the wrock community.

In other words, these values make up the contents of the community's very own common consciousness. And because these values are strongly held by almost everyone in the community, this common consciousness is pervasive and intense, engendering robust social links that bring members together. In this way, wizard rock comes to resemble a society held together more so by mechanical rather than organic solidarity. Thus, to return to the question posed at the start of this section, it is this mechanical solidarity that is so strongly felt during live shows, produced by the concertgoers' all-pervading, passionate, and shared love of *Harry Potter*. Arguably proving this is that behaviors which promote mechanical "oneness" are clearly on display at wrock concerts: bands and fans sing as one, audience members clap to the beat, performers emotionally stress the unity of those in attendance, and—perhaps most importantly—there is a pervading sense of "energy" flowing through and uniting the crowd.

It is this aforementioned sense of "energy" this is often brought up by wrockers when they discuss the power of live shows. For instance, Lauren Fairweather told me, "One of the most intriguing and inspiring things about wizard rock is getting to experience the energy of the concerts for the first time.… The energy at a wizard rock show is unlike anything I've ever experienced."[78] Scott Vaughan of the Blibbering Humdingers likewise told me, "The raw energy of a live show can be a natural high."[79] What exactly is this mysterious "energy" that Fairweather and Vaughan (and many others) speak of, and where does it come from? To answer this question, let me turn once again turn to the theories of Durkheim.

During his study of Australian aboriginal totemism, Durkheim argued that indigenous life seemed to be composed of two distinct "phases": the "profane" (in which individuals eschew gathering, keep to themselves, and focus mostly on "material life"), and the "sacred" (in which individuals communally celebrate religious rites or ceremonies).[80] Most of human existence takes place in the arguably boring world of the profane, with individuals focusing on as Alex Law puts it, their own "private egos and mundane interests."[81] However, when it is time to celebrate religious ceremonies, these individuals leave behind the world of the profane for the communal world of the sacred—a world in which individual concerns are subordinated to the concerns of society at large.[82] Because these people are now focusing on what unites them as one, sacred life becomes energized and affective, and soon those gathered are able to experience periods of what Durkheim calls "collective effervescence."[83] He writes:

> The very fact of the concentration acts as an exceptionally powerful stimulant. When [people united by a collective sentiment][84] come together … a sort of electricity is formed by their collecting which quickly transports them to an extra-ordinary degree

of exaltation. Every sentiment expressed finds a place without resistance in all the minds, which are very open to outside impressions; each re-echoes the others, and is re-echoed by the others. The initial impulse thus proceeds, growing as it goes, as an avalanche grows in its advance.... One can readily conceive how, when arrived at this state of exaltation, a man does not recognize himself any longer. Feeling himself dominated and carried away by some sort of an external power which makes him think and act differently than in normal times, he naturally has the impression of being himself no longer.... Everything is just as though he really were transported into a special world, entirely different from the one transported where he ordinarily lives, and into an environment filled with exceptionally intense forces that take hold of him and metamorphose him.[85]

It is important to note that, as the sociologist Karen Fields puts it, "[The] force experienced as external to each individual is the agent of that transformation, but the force itself is created by the fact of assembling and temporarily living a collective life that transports individuals beyond themselves."[86] In other words, it is a sort of chicken-egg situation: People believe that there are two worlds (the "routine everyday" and the "effervescent corroboree") which causes them to gather, but it is the act of gathering itself that results in people feeling as if they have been carried to some different realm of existence.[87]

Something similar occurs for those who attend wrock concerts. Prior to these events, individuals spend their time in what one could emically call the "Muggle world" (analogous to "the profane"). In this realm of existence, wrock musicians and fans alike are generally separated from one another as they focus on their "conventional" jobs and their "normal" relationships. And because of this, their obsession with *Harry Potter* and wizard rock is often of secondary importance. But during wrock concerts, the opposite is true: these same individuals assemble specifically to indulge in their fannish obsession. This interest quickly manifests during shows and, thanks to the number of like-minded fans present, is echoed and re-echoed until there is a collective "feeling" flowing through the crowd. This sense of "energy"—which, to paraphrase Fields, feels as if it is external to the individual, even though it was produced by the act of the wrockers and fans gathering together—is transformative, and soon the concert-goers find that they are no longer in the mundane Muggle world, but rather in what one might call the "world of wizards" (analogous to "the sacred"). This state of existence continues until the show ends, the bands put their instruments away, and the fans shuffle out the door. It is at this point that collective effervescence ceases, and everyone once again enters into the Muggle world.[88]

Since scholars have invoked collective effervescence to explain why people come together "as one" during sporting matches,[89] raves,[90] and mainstream music concerts,[91] it seems reasonable to extend Durkheim's line of thinking to explain wrock shows. At the same time, it must be stressed that Durkheim developed the concept of collective effervescence initially to explain *religious* life, and in this chapter I am concerned with fan activity. The two are *not* the same. In fact, many scholars (such as Henry Jenkins and Sean McCloud)[92] caution against casually comparing religion and fandom, arguing that such an association is at best simplistic and at worst entirely specious.

Luckily, Durkheim himself draws explicit parallels between religious ceremonies and "feasts" (i.e., large-scale celebrations that need not be religious), writing:

> Every feast, even when it has purely lay origins, has certain characteristics of the religious ceremony, for in every case its effect is to bring men together, to put the masses into movement and thus to excite a state of effervescence, and sometimes even of delirium, which is not without a certain kinship with the religious state. A man is carried outside himself and diverted from his ordinary occupation and preoccupations. Thus, the same manifestations are to be observed in each case: cries, songs, music, violent movements, dances, the search for [excitants], which raise the vital level, etc.[93]

It is thus best to view wrock concerts not as religious rituals but rather as "fandom feasts," which by their very nature share characteristics of those religious ceremonies that can induce collective effervescence. By approaching wrock concerts from this angle, I can side step the controversial issue of directly comparing fan activities to religious phenomena.[94]

An Energy Unlike Anything Else

In mid–August 2017, I reached out to a number of wrockers on Facebook and asked them what made the live aspect of wizard rock so important. Scott Vaughan of The Blibbering Humdingers told me: "There's just something about being in a room with two hundred people who all geek out over the same stuff—jumping up and down, banging their heads and shouting 'Dobby!' … there's just something surreal about the experience.… It really is magic."[95] The fan and scholar Lauren Cook seconded this opinion, arguing that "meeting other people who 'get it' is amazing.… The vibe is always so great and loving."[96] Finally, wrock fan James Hinsey poignantly explained, "At [many] shows, the performers and audience form a connection which is almost a one-on-one relationship.… A wrock show is the medium that intertwines us in that love for *Harry Potter*. [It] brings so much meaning into our lives and connects us all."[97]

These quotes serve to illustrate the overriding point of this chapter: wrock shows are integral to the formation of the community, as they bring disparate people together in spatio-temporal reality and allow them to "feel" as one. It is at these shows that wrock bands and their fans merge into one collective, entering into a world where the only cares are about the Boy Who Lived and the music that he inspires. And regardless of whether this is the result of collective effervescence or something else, one thing is for sure: it would be foolish to brush off what fans experience during live shows or chalk their experiences up to fans once again just "being weird." There is something about wrock shows that make them a unique form of fan expression, and it is this sort of expression that deserves study.

4

"I *Am* Harry Potter": A Closer Look at Role-Play

In December 2016, The 8th Horcrux was asked to perform at a large *Harry Potter* event in Kansas City—an event at which a number of the more popular wrock bands would be playing, including Tonks and the Aurors, Swish and Flick, and Draco and the Malfoys.

This invitation was a significant moment for us as a band, as up until that point, Trina and I had mostly been lone wolf wrockers. While it is true that we had performed shows with other musicians, these were few and very far in between. We were isolated in the middle of the country, after all, and did not have a reliable means (or opportunity) to tour extensively. Given our circumstances, we had long ago resigned ourselves to the fate of usually having to perform alone.

Needless to say, when the opportunity presented itself to play a massive gig with other wrockers—including not just one but three of the biggest names in wizard rock—Trina and I were thrilled and excitedly accepted the offer.

But perhaps we were too excited, because—due to an oversight on my part—we showed up at the venue about three hours earlier than we were expected. We managed to kill some time by meticulously setting up our instruments and double-checking all of our equipment, but soon we had little to do.

We were eventually saved from the tediousness of waiting when Steph Anderson of Tonks and the Aurors arrived at the venue. We greeted her in the event space's green room, and as she unpacked her equipment and tuned her guitar, we cordially chatted about music and books.

About an hour later, Stacy and John Pisani of the wizard rap group Swish and Flick arrived. While a bit more reticent than Anderson, the two genially introduced themselves to Trina and myself before devoting their attention to setting up myriad guitar pedals and to cueing up the right backing tracks for their performance.

4. "I Am Harry Potter" 97

Brian Ross (who was performing solo as Draco and the Malfoys that night) arrived about an hour before the event started. Given that Brian is one of the "founding fathers" of wizard rock, Trina and I were both star-struck to be in his presence. When we finally summoned the courage to chat with him before the show, we found him to be quite approachable. For several minutes, he happily entertained us with conversation, and when we told him we wrote parody songs, he expressed a genuine interest in our music, telling us how he too liked writing the occasional parody.

Trina and I were the second to play that night (following on the heels of the local filker, Alex Boyd), and after our performance, we set up camp near the merch table, eager to see our wizardly acquaintances wrock out on the big stage.

We have always been pretty good at gauging people's personalities after we get a chance to talk to them and, given that all the wrockers that we had met that night were sociable and fairly reserved, we were confident that we had a decent understanding of our fellow performers. But once their performances started, something extraordinary happened: These people—who we thought we had so correctly assessed—changed dramatically.

Brian was the first to step on stage, and his soft-spoken gregariousness melted away once he picked up his guitar and inhabited the role of Draco Malfoy; he opened his performance with a scathing diatribe against Harry Potter, referring to him as "this kid at Hogwarts who gets far too much attention for his own good." He then proceeded to sing a number of songs that praised the "virtues" of Voldemort and made fun of Harry Potter because his parents were dead. For anyone who has listened to Draco and the Malfoys, this sort of lyrical content might not be that surprising. But for someone like myself, who had never seen Brian perform live, his performance certainly caught me off guard, given that he was animated with such a gleefully snarky energy that contrasted with his "real life" composure.

Next, Steph took the stage and immediately captivated the audience with her performance as Nymphadora Tonks—a performance which can only be described as Bruce Springsteen-meets-riot grrrl. While Steph is by no means timid in what you might call "real life," when she was on stage and in-character, her aura was particularly powerful. At one point, during her song "Yes All Witches!" she began fist-pumping and shouting the eponymous phrase. With each punctuated gesticulation, the crowd grew more and more energized until almost everyone in the audience was singing along, and her message was reverberating throughout the venue.

The Pisanis closed out the concert. John stayed largely in the background, switching from vocoder to fuzz pedal with the greatest of ease, all the while playing a dizzying array of guitar riffs. Stacy, on the other hand, positioned herself front and center. Donning the role of Astoria Greengrass,[1] she began rapping over electronica-tinged beats about a diverse (and suggestive!) range of topics, including Cho Chang dancing rather provocatively, brawling with Hogwarts students, and engaging in light BDSM with none other than Draco Malfoy. The performance was scandalous, shocking... and highly entertaining.

But then, after Swish and Flick played their last tune, the concert ended and the lights came back on. All of a sudden, these musicians were back to their normal selves.

Trina and I were a bit taken aback; after all, we had just witnessed these individuals transform into *very* different people (Trina, in particular, was struck by the Pisanis' performance, given how easily the two had cast aside their introversion and playfully embraced the role of wrock provocateurs). Now of course, this was not a Jekyll and Hyde situation, and Trina and I were both fully conscious that everyone who stood on the stage that night was merely role-playing as characters within the *Harry Potter* universe. All the same, we were struck by the peculiar fact that these wrockers had role-played on stage for only a short period of time, but their performances had nonetheless left an imprint in our minds and informed how we now conceived of them as humans. On the drive home that night, Trina and I began further to ponder the nature of what we had just witnessed. Why do wrockers so eagerly embrace this sort of character role-play? From where does this behavior stem? And—perhaps most importantly—what impact does it have on a performer's personal identity?

* * *

At Harvard University's 2008 convocation, the school's guest speaker—J.K. Rowling herself—told a captivated audience, "Unlike any other creature on this planet, humans can think themselves into other people's minds, [and] imagine themselves into other people's places."[2] As the author Ethan Gilsdorf recounts in his book *Fantasy Freaks and Gaming Geeks* (2009), the members of both Harry and the Potters, and Draco and the Malfoys were in attendance, watching from afar. Was J.K. Rowling aware of this fact when she gave her speech? Almost certainly not, but it was nonetheless an interesting coincidence, given that those wrockers in the crowd regularly "think themselves into other people's minds, imagine themselves into other people's places," and then write songs from their perspectives. In other words, they role-play.

It is not an exaggeration to say that almost all wrock bands dabble in role-play at some time or another. However, this sort of behavior is not monolithic and comes in a variety of what you might call "styles." Some groups choose to role-play as only one character within the *Harry Potter* universe, such as Harry and the Potters. Other groups role-play not as one but rather

4. "I Am Harry Potter"

as many characters. For instance, my band The 8th Horcrux writes songs from the viewpoints of various individuals, and we choose which character(s) to inhabit based on the topics or themes about which we wish to sing. This means that our band's "viewpoint" is fluid and not fixed, in turn allowing us to engage in role-play without being restricted to the perspective of only one fictional individual. Lena Gabrielle of the Butterbeer Experience, who also embraces this style of role-play, agrees with the latter point, noting that she chose this style because she "had a lot of stuff [she] wanted to say [and she] really didn't want to be limited" to only one character.[3]

And there are also those bands that do not overtly role-play as *Harry Potter* characters and are instead content to merely sing about *Harry Potter* from an "out-of-universe" perspective. But while these performers do not necessarily insert themselves into the fictional world as readily as others, they almost always employ some elements of role-play (for instance, by pretending as if those who are listening to wizard rock are magic-users, by using in-universe terms or idioms earnestly and without explanation, or by wearing "wizard attire" during concerts). Because these groups do not explicitly intend to embrace role-play and yet to some extent still often do, they are perhaps the best examples of how this mimesis is embedded in the very heart of wizard rock.

In this chapter, I explore the complexities of wrock role-play. In the first portion, I define the activity, situating it in the wider tradition of role-play. I also delineate factors that make the behavior unique when compared to what one might call "traditional" role-play. Next, I compare and contrast wrock role-play with the related fannish behavior known as cosplay. In the chapter's final portion, I explore wrock role-play in regard to identify formation. In particular, I invoke Judith Butler's seminal reinterpretation of the concept of performativity to argue that wrock role-play is popular because it is an effective and unique method by which wrockers—through the process of citing character elements with which they themselves want to be associated in the real world—can shape their own personal identities.

What Is It?

To avoid any presumptuous conclusions, perhaps it is best to first consider whether wrock role-play actually *is* a type of role-play.

At the start of this book, I defined "role-play" rather simplistically as being the "mimetic act in which an individual temporarily assumes the role of a specific character." In the article "Social Reality in Roleplaying Games," the game scholar Markus Montola provides a more robust definition, arguing that role-play is ultimately a behavior in which people "manipulat[e]

Steph Anderson, performing as Tonks & the Aurors. Anderson sings songs from the perspective of the auror Nymphadora Tonks. When Tonks attended Hogwarts, she was a member of Hufflepuff House, hence Anderson's use of a yellow sweater (courtesy Steph Anderson).

an imaginary world together, following a power hierarchy, where at least some participants portray beings living in that world."[4] Inherent in this definition are three key aspects, which Montola refers to as the "three invisible rules" of role-play:

    1. "The World Rule": "Role-playing is an interactive process of defining and re-defining the state, properties, and contents of an imaginary game world";

    2. "The Power Rule": "The power to define the game world is allocated to participants of the game. The participants recognize the existence of this power hierarchy";

    3. "The Character Rule": "Player-participants define the game world through personified character constructs, conforming to the state, properties, and contents of the game world."[5]

In order to determine whether or not it is a form of role-play, it is necessary to consider the unique type of character inhabitation on display at wrock shows in regard to these three rules.

Let me start by considering Montola's "World Rule," which maintains that role-play is "an interactive process of defining and re-defining the state, properties, and contents of an imaginary game world."[6] The key part of this rule—at least, for the comparison at hand—is the reference to an "imaginary game world." For many wrockers, leaving behind the real world of "Muggles" for the imaginary world of "wizards" is part of the experience and thus of paramount importance. And it is generally the wrockers themselves who "define and redefine" this imaginary world, given that they are the ones performing in-character. Paul DeGeorge, for instance, told me that during concerts, "We're interested in … creating new environments when we perform. Within the confines of our show, we have the ability in that environment to manipulate it and give people different sensations and feelings. We really relish that role."[7]

This leads me to Montola's "Power Rule," which maintains that "the power to define the game world [in role-play] is allocated to participants of the game [who] recognize the existence of this power hierarchy."[8] Unlike many role-playing games such as *Dungeons & Dragons (D&D)*, wizard rock does not have one central authority whose job it is to decide what is allowed at any given moment. Instead, this power is decentralized, being distributed amongst the various players and performers. Of course, this is not to say that everyone has equal power to deem something "real," and during a wrock concert, the band who is performing more often than not "sets the stage," both figuratively and literally. This means that those individuals, be they wrockers or fans, who are successfully "playing along" will recognize the performing band's authority in this situation and respect their (albeit temporary) power to define the imaginary. Once that band walks off the stage and another one takes their place, the authority is transferred to that new group.[9]

Finally, let me consider Montola's "Character Rule," which states that "player-participants[10] define the game world through personified character constructs, conforming to the state, properties, and contents of the game world."[11] This is perhaps the most obvious connection between role-play proper and the behavior endemic among wrockers, as the members of the latter community often take on the role of distinct, fictional characters, whom they then perform as during bounded events (e.g., concerts). As mentioned above, wizard rock does not have a single, authoritative "dungeon master,"[12] meaning that these character constructs are almost always created and embellished by the individuals who make use of them.

While I do believe it is clear, given the above, that the behavior on display at wrock shows is a form of role-play, it must be noted that researchers like Montola, when they write about "role-play," are largely referring to role-playing *games* akin to *D&D*, *Call of Cthulhu*, *Warhammer*, or live-action role play (LARP)[13]—that is, "system[s] in which players engage in an artificial conflict, defined by rules, that [result] in a quantifiable outcome."[14] There are notable differences between these activities—which I refer to collectively as "traditional" forms of role-play—and wrock role-play. First, wrock role-play does not have any "end-goal"—that is, no one "wins" when they perform. And while certain events might host contests for the best "wrock band," by and large the bands and their fans are not competing to solve a puzzle or defeat an opposing team; they simply *are*. Second, traditional role-play is often defined by a certain make-it-up-as-you-go spontaneity. Wrock role-play, on the other hand, is often much more premeditated and rehearsed. Paul DeGeorge, for instance, told me, "We are often working from a script.... We try to pace our live shows in a very certain way."[15] Third—and perhaps most importantly—wrock role-play is often performed in a space that separates the performer from the audience (e.g., a concert venue),[16] whereas traditional role-play is usually carried out only amongst a closed group of players. In fact, many scholars assert that traditional role-play is something that people really can only *do*, rather than *watch*,[17] which stands in stark contrast to wrock role-play.

But regardless of these differences, the understanding of character inhabitation as role-play is popular within the community, as well as within many scholarly circles.[18] The wrocker Grace Dow, for instance, argued, "Some acts do emphasize role-play aspects [like] Draco and the Malfoys ... [or] Harry and the Potters.... I think there are definitely overlaps with role-play."[19] Lauren Fairweather concurred, telling me, "If [the bands] perform from the perspective of a character, then yes, it's role-play!"[20]

Interestingly, in an interview with Gilsdorf, Paul DeGeorge initially eschewed the "role-play" label, arguing that Harry and the Potters is simply "a band [that] performs."[21] He clarified by arguing, "What we do is a com–bination of acting and music. We do draw on Harry's personality [but] anything goes onstage. It's where we break furthest from Harry."[22] But then, after reading Gilsdorf's resultant book *Fantasy Freaks and Gaming Geeks* (2009), Paul began to see things differently. In a 2017 interview, he told me: "Following the experience of talking to Ethan [Gilsdorf] and reading his book and learning more about LARPing, [Joe and I] actually started to call ourselves 'LARRPers': 'live-action rock n' roll players.' So [now] I do think there is a truth in" connecting wizard rock with role-play.[23]

Wrock Role-Play and Its Relation to Cosplay

Given that most wrock bands supplement their role-play performances with costuming, I believe it is also necessary to consider this behavior in relation to another fannish phenomenon: cosplay, or, the act of dressing up as characters, generally from fictional media franchises. The connection between wrock role-play and cosplay is perhaps obvious to anyone who has

Wrockers (such as Joe DeGeorge of Harry & the Potters, left) can be compared to cosplayers (such as the author, right, who is cosplaying as Newt Scamander from Fantastic Beasts and Where to Find Them), as both often make use of costuming (courtesy Andrew Warren and Trina Thomas)

ever attended a wrock concert: at these shows, bands and fans alike often don Hogwarts robes, wave wands, and wear Harry Potter's trademark glasses. Even concert promoters will sometimes get involved, putting on the occasionally witch hat, or perching a stuffed owl on their shoulders. In other words, costumes are everywhere.

Where exactly does the tradition of cosplay come from? The answer is surprisingly complex and, as the fashion design theorist Theresa Winge argues, "blends.... Japanese and North American contributions."[24] Let me first begin by considering the North American side of things. While costuming in the West has a long tradition (e.g., Halloween, Carnival), the moment that is often cited as the beginning of "modern-day cosplay"—that is, dressing up as characters from pop culture—occurred at a masquerade ball in 1908 in Cincinnati, Ohio (of all places). At this event, a married couple named Mr. and Mrs. William Fell dressed up as the popular A.D. Condo cartoon characters "Mr.

Skygack from Mars" and "Diana Dillpickles," respectively. According to a short article later published in *The Spokane Press*, "Both the costumes [worn by the Fells] closely followed those of the comic characters."[25] Because everyone else was wearing mundane masks common at these sorts of events, the newspaper declared that the Fells were "the hit of the evening with the refreshing novelty of their disguise."[26]

Over the next few decades, as science fiction and fantasy increased in popularity and conventions were established to accommodate fans of these genres, more and more attendees began to follow the Fells' precedent by dressing up as their favorite characters. But while this behavior was gaining traction in the convention scene, it still did not have a universal, fandom-specific name (some called it "costuming," and still others considered it an offshoot of the aforementioned masquerade ball tradition).[27] This all changed in 1984, when Nobuyuki "Nov" Takahashi (a Japanese animation enthusiast and writer for *My Anime* magazine) travelled to the annual Los Angeles–based sci-fi convention WorldCon. At this event, hundreds of people were parading around dressed as fictional characters (many from the *Star Trek* universe).[28] Takahashi had never seen this sort of behavior before, and it struck him as fun and unique; in fact, so effected was Takahashi by his almost ethnographic encounter with costumed fans at WorldCon that he decided to write about it in a forthcoming issue of *My Anime*. Unfortunately, when Takahashi went to put pen to paper, he was stumped as to what he was going to call the behavior. After mulling over ideas, he eventually decided to combine the English words "costume" and "play," creating the Japanese portmanteau *kosupure* (which was eventually Anglicized into the now-familiar term "cosplay").[29]

Takahashi's *My Anime* article increased cosplay's exposure, causing its popularity to skyrocket. By the late 1980s the behaviour was spreading like wildfire across Japan, and by the early 1990s, it had become an integral part of fandom in the country. And as Japanese pop culture began to gain popularity in the U.S., the tenets of Japanese *kosupure* were eventually re-integrated into the pre-existing American costuming tradition, reinvigorating the practice and resulting in our modern understanding of "cosplay."[30] Today, this most unique behavior that is found at conventions the world over, and is often considered a fundamental aspect of fandom.

But *why* might fans engage in cosplay in the first place? To some, cosplay is just a quirk of fandom—an example of fans once again being too obsessed with some fictional character or universe. Others disagree, arguing that there is indeed some deeper meaning to the act that many miss. According to media theorist Paul Booth, cosplay is not merely the act of putting on a costume, but rather an elaborate performance in which the fan, via mental *and* physical mimesis, becomes a character. As one might imagine, the costuming is therefore an integral part of this performance, because it "emphasizes the fans' body as a site of transformative power."[31] In other words, the costumes used by cosplayers bring attention to the material aspect(s) of the fan, and in turn can be used as a tool to physically broadcast that some sort of mental identity transformation has simultaneously occurred. If this cosplay is successful, Booth quotes Scott Duchesne in saying, "Fan and [character] momentarily merge."[32]

Something of this nature can be observed at wrock concerts. During these shows, many bands don *Harry Potter*-esque clothing items. This gives the visual effect that fans and the bands alike have cast aside their "Muggle" identities, embraced new (mental) identities as "wizards," and are broadcasting this change through the use of (physical) techniques similar to those employed by cosplayers. This combination of mental and physical transformation allows the band members to be seen *as* those characters whom they are performing. To better understand this concept, consider Harry and the Potters' stage presence: when Paul and Joe DeGeoge put on their Gryffindor neckties and step out onto the stage, they are no longer the DeGeorge brothers, but rather two versions of Harry Potter himself. This role-playing is made manifest by their attire and is reinforced when the two each individually introduce themselves as the Boy Who Lived.

However, as with any comparison between two distinct types of behaviors, there are differences between wrock role-play and cosplay that need to be noted. For one thing, cosplayers often take part in competitions, in which they are judged against certain criteria such as quality of costume, energy of performance, etc. As we have previously noted, wrockers rarely compete to win prizes strictly for their role-playing. Additionally, cosplay is commonly a protracted and drawn out performance that often spans the entire duration of a convention, whereas wrock role-play mostly takes place only when a group is performing. But perhaps the most important divide between cosplay and wrock role-play is that the two groups ultimately consider different aspects to be of paramount importance: cosplayers emphasize the physical aspects of their performance, whereas wrock role-players focus more on mental inhabitation. This means that wrockers are not necessarily dependent on physical costuming and can still be said to role-play in situations where the emphasis is squarely on the auditory, rather than the physical (e.g., when a wrock band sings, records, or otherwise role-plays as a specific character without the use of costuming).

Identity Formation Through Performative Role-Play

In the eyes of some, wrock role-play is simply a way for people to briefly escape the burden of everyday "real" life: role-play, they argue, is thus a form of escape. When I asked my informants if they concurred with the last portion of that statement, most agreed that wrock role-play is at least partially a way for people to engage in escapist mental play, but they fervently rejected the idea that the behavior is only used to retreat from the problems present in the world. Perhaps Joe DeGeorge said it best when he described the *Harry Potter* series as:

> part of the bridge that brings that escapist world into a shared experience with which to reflect upon the prime world. When I'm [role-playing during] a concert, wizard rock brings the ideas and themes from these texts and amplifies them creating a visceral, physical and communal response.[33]

Other wrockers whom I interviewed—such as Ariel Factor Birdoff, Steph Anderson, and Christopher Bee—echoed the theme of Joe's statement, arguing that wrock role-play serves a dual purpose by both allowing people to escape into a fantastical world, while also allowing people to explore themes that relate to our world in unique and ultimately impactful ways.[34]

With statements like this, it is clear that wrockers and fans are pushing back against the problematic idea that escapist activities such as wrock role-play simply entail "checking out" of the difficult but ultimately real world and indolently drifting off into the soft world of the imagination. As Sarah Lynne Bowman argues, this sort of attitude about escapism is "not only condescending and derogatory, but also inaccurate"[35] because it fails to recognize the important psychological benefits of the activity—namely that wrock role-play can aid in identify formation.

According to Bowman, role-play in general "offer players the opportunity to self-express, co-create, and connect the magical worlds of their imaginations with facets of their own personalities.... Role-playing offers the opportunity, for short-or long-term periods of time, for individuals to explore aspects of themselves that normally remain dormant or under-expressed."[36] Taking Bowman's assertions and placing them in the narrower context of wizard rock, it seems reasonable to conclude that wrock role-play allows individuals to "put on" a specific character and through this process shape their own personal identity.

But how might something like role-play even bring about a major transformation in identity? The answer lies in wrock role-play's essentially performative nature. The term "performativity" was added to the social scientific lexicon in the 1950s by linguist J.L. Austin, who coined it to denote speech acts that actually *alter* the world in some real way (as opposed to just *describing* it).[37] The canonical example is the marriage proclamation, "I now pronounce you husband and wife."[38] This announcement does not just describe a wedding, but actually causes the marriage to come into being; after all, a ceremony that lacks this proclamation (or some variation of it) is not considered by most to be valid (think of the countless movies in which someone disrupts a wedding right before this proclamation). As one might imagine, Austin's argument—that language was not merely a tool of description but rather of active creation—was ground-breaking and drastically impacted the development of semiotics and linguistics in the mid–20th century.[39]

A few decades later, in her article "Performative Acts and Gender Constitution" (1988) and book *Bodies that Matter* (1993), the feminist philosopher Judith Butler borrowed and modified the term, using it as the cornerstone for her theory of gender identity. According to Butler, performativity refers to "the reiterative and citational practice by which discourse produces the effects that it names."[40] Butler then applied this understanding of performativity to gender, arguing that gender itself is created and maintained when people habitually—and often unconsciously—"cite" (that is, carry out) socially constructed gendered actions. The citation of these actions, in turn causes them to continue on as "the norm" for that gender. This means that gender performativity is not a one-off act that permanently fixes an individual's gender for the rest of their life, but rather a knotty and often circular enactment of gendered behavior that comes to construct an individual's gender identity throughout time via citational repetition.[41] In other words, gender is, as Nicolle Lamerichs puts it, "an expression of what one does, rather than what one is."[42] Consider, for example, the checking-off of one's gender on a form. According to Mal Ahern, writing for the Chicago School of Media Theory, such an act is performative, because we are citing some gendered norm to come to a conclusion about which gender to check, and by checking off that gender, we are actually *shaping* reality in that moment. Furthermore, by citing the norms associated with certain genders, we affirm their sociocultural impact, power, and authority, enabling them to persist into the future.[43]

While Butlerian performativity is frequently contrasted with performance, in that the former is often unconscious, ongoing, concealed, and pervasive, whereas the latter is self-aware, temporary, foregrounded, and bound,[44] it would be a mistake to say that a performance cannot also be performative. Indeed, there exist many examples of "performative performances" (to echo Derrida), such as weddings, trials, or baptisms, as these events, while bounded and often rehearsed, still manage to shape reality in some lasting way (e.g., a wedding literally *pronounces* two people as one, a trial *declares* someone innocent or guilty thereafter, a baptism *christens* someone with a new name). And an excellent example of a fannish behavior that can rightly be considered a "performative performance" is cosplay, because while it is indeed a bounded and rehearsed act in which a person temporarily but holistically inhabits the role of a separate character, it is also a complex, reiterative, and heavily citational activity that allows individuals to shape their own identity—identity which is eventually on display in the real world even when the person is not consciously performing.

This hypothesis was notably promoted by Lamerichs in her article "Stranger than Fiction," in which she wrote:

> Characters are used as signifiers of the fan's own identity. On the one hand, a costume shows off a player's attachment to a certain narrative or character [but] on the other hand, the associations connected with a character are transferred to the player. Expression through a costume of a fictional character is actually self-expression. Cosplayers decide what characters and values fit them.... What we see is that the identity of the fictional character rubs off on the identity of the player. The values or features of a character are projected onto the player by the spectators and player him- or herself.... Thus, when we speak of identity and identification in cosplay, we speak of two things. On the one hand, players actualize a narrative and its meaning; on the other hand, they actualize their own identities. To put it bluntly, by stating that a narrative or character is related to me—that I can identify with this particular story or person—I make a statement about myself.... It is through interaction with stories that we can imagine and perform ourselves.[45]

Booth argues something similar, writing, "These moments of costuming are not just in celebration of the [character] but are also a way for the fan to express self-affect, through fidelity (or not) to a character, and to discuss aspects of [the fan's] own identity."[46] He then quotes Cornel Sandvoss, who argued, "Being a [cosplayer] reflects and constructs the self."[47] In the eyes of scholars like Lamerichs, Booth, and Sandvoss, cosplayers refer to (or "cite") traits from fictional characters with which they either associate or wish to be associated. These traits are in turn transferred from the fictional character to the actual person, thereby establishing that fan's identity in the real world.

Given the relationship between cosplay and wrock role-play that was discussed in the preceding section, could Butlerian performativity also be applied to wrock role-play? Consider the case of Harry and the Potters. When they started their band, Paul and Joe DeGeorge purposely selected Harry Potter as the character whose role they would inhabit. And while they have largely remained true to the Harry of the books, by their own admission they have also emphasized and exaggerated certain aspects of the character, most notably his punk ethos.[48] Now, it is certainly true that the canonical Harry is defined by a certain DIY, anti-authoritarianism, but to many it might seem odd that the DeGeorges interpreted this to mean that Harry has the "soul" of a punk rocker[49]—that is, until one remembers that the DeGeorges consciously describe themselves as "com[ing] from punk rock."[50] It seems likely that when Paul and Joe DeGeorge first considered the character of Harry as a potential role-play candidate, they noticed this kernel of a character trait with which they themselves identified and wanted to further identify. They then amplified this trait and made it a central part of their role-play performance. Now, when they perform as Harry Potter, they are not only "actualize[ing] a narrative and its meaning" by bringing Harry Potter "into the real world," but they are also "actualize[ing] their own identities" by high-

Draco & the Malfoys, a band consisting of half-brothers Bradley Mehlenbacher (left) and Brian Ross, performing in 2008. On stage, the band memebers adopt the persona of the character Draco Malfoy (courtesy Jonathon Rosenthal).

lighting and citing that character trait with which they themselves want to be identified in the off-stage real world.[51]

But what about those bands who perform as otherwise despicable characters? Are the members of these bands performatively indexing their rather unsavory identities by choosing to role-play as particularly evil characters? Not so fast. Consider Brian Ross and Bradley Mehlenbacher of Draco and the Malfoys. The Draco that Mehlenbacher and Ross perform as is a caricature: an individual who is hyperbolically wicked and whose penchant for cruelty is rather overblown. For an example, consider the lyrics to their song "My Dad Is Rich, You Dad Is Dead":

> My dad's always there
> To open all my doors.
> You have to call a Patronus[52]
> Just to catch a glimpse of yours.
>
> My mom says she loves me,
> When she tucks me into bed,
> How's your mommy doing

> In the Mirror of Erised?[53]
> My dad is rich, and your dad is dead
> My dad is rich, and your dad is dead

Or what about the lyrics to "Dobby"?:

> Dobby
> Kicking you around was my favorite hobby
> But now you're not around, and I'm just a little bit sorry
> That kicking Dobby
> Is not my hobby
> Anymore

Given that in real life Mehlenbacher and Ross are nowhere near as diabolical as these lyrics suggest, the two are likely citing character traits with which they do *not* want to be associated and then inflating these traits to parodic proportions so as to explicitly mock them.[54] This creates a clear divide in the mind of the audience: on one hand, the evil in-universe band, and on the other, the good out-of-universe musicians. In this manner, Mehlenbacher and Ross's act is very much performative, but *via negativa*, as they are "actualize[ing] their own identities" by way of humorous irony.

But an important aspect of truly performative behavior is that it is often unconscious and concealed (even if at times made manifest by certain rehearsed enactments), as well as ongoing and pervasive. This means that if wrock role-play is to be considered a performative behavior, I need to demonstrate that it is still at work in subtle ways even after the explicit and bounded character inhabitation itself has come to an end; otherwise, such behavior would just be an elaborate but one-off performance with no lasting consequences.

In the proceeding paragraphs, I have established that by citing certain traits and acting in certain ways, wrockers are impressing into the minds of their audience specific qualities with which they wish to identify. But it is important to remember that when wrockers step off the stage, that connection between person and character does not instantly dissipate into the ether. In fact, it will continue for a time, *especially* if the role-play is habitually and citationally repeated in the future (i.e., if the band plays another show in-character). Once again, consider Harry and the Potters. As discussed earlier, the DeGeorge brothers perform as "punk rock Harry Potter" on stage and are seen in this light by their audiences. And because they have continuously and habitually performed as such for over fifteen years, they are now viewed by many as "punk rockers" when they are off stage, too.[55] Put another way, that trait that they have long been citing in their shows—that "punk rockerness"—has successfully come to define their identity in the real world. Consequently, because the effects of role-play continue to persist and play a major role in identify formation even when bands such as Harry and the Potters are not *explicitly* performing in a bounded environment, it is reasonable to conclude that such behavior is indeed an exercise in performativity.

A Different Kind of Transfiguration

Ultimately, wrock role-play is a rather unique form of fan behavior; on one hand, it mirrors the features of what one might call "traditional" role-play, whereas on the other, it breaks from traditional role-play by emphasizing a more open-ended style of performance that eschews competition and embraces spectators. Wrock role-play also borrows from and is informed by the phenomenon known as "cosplay," and this relationship is perhaps best demonstrated in wrockers' penchant for dressing up as character from within the *Harry Potter* universe. But perhaps the most important feature of wrock role-play is its performative nature, as the behavior is essentially an exercise in identity formation.

To consider a final example, turn once again to the vignette with which I opened this chapter. Even though our fellow wrockers returned to their "old selves" at the conclusion of the concert, their performances had nevertheless changed how Trina and I perceived them: We realized that Brian had humorously snarky side lurking beneath his composed exterior, we viewed Steph as a passionate and powerful proponent of justice, and we recognized that the Pisanis could be playfully provocative. In other words, by citing characteristics and traits from fictional characters with which they themselves want to be associated, these wrockers had effectively changed the way they were viewed by others, simply with a bounded and temporal performance. And perhaps most important was that this change in perception persisted, even when the performance itself had ended. Thus is the power of performative wrock role-play.

5

The Structure and Demographics of the Community

Ever since the wrock movement began, people have been interested in the community's structure and its internal makeup. Even today, forum posts and blog threads from yesteryear can be accessed online in which individuals advanced questions about wizard rock's make-up. But despite all this interest, the demography of wizard rock has never been studied in what one might call an extensive and scholarly manner. To rectify this issue, in the summer of 2017, I distributed a survey both online and in person to 150 random members of the wrock community,[1] asking specific questions about race, nationality, gender, sexual orientation, and representation. When the surveys were returned and their responses tallied, I then compared the results to the rhetoric of the community at large, looking in particular for instances where the beliefs espoused by the community failed to live up to the reality suggested by my survey, à la Kelli Rohlman (2010).

This chapter (which has been divided into sections about the structure of the community, as well as the nationality, race, gender, and sexual orientation of wrockers) considers the results of my demographic survey, concluding that while many within the wrock community affirm the importance of diversity and acceptance, as well as the dangers inherent in passively accepting hegemonic, repressive, or discriminatory social systems, the community is often subconsciously defined by those things against which it strives to fight. With that said, interviews with members of the community reveal that many are aware of issues that need to be rectified, and that measures are also being taken in the hopes of solving or at least ameliorating these problems.

Structure and Internal Division of the Community

Before exploring the scene's specific demographic data in greater detail, it would first be wise to consider how the wrock community is internally structured and divided. Beyond the obvious band/fan paradigm,[2] a number of wrock scholars, such as Kelli Rohlman and Aya Esther Hayashi,[3] have noted that in emic circles bands are divided into what are referred to as "tiers." A delineation of the tiers, synthesized from Rohlman and Hayashi's research, is as follows:

First (or "Top") tier: This tier comprises the most famous wrock bands, including many of the first groups, such as Harry and the Potters, as well as popular latecomers, such as Tonks and the Aurors. Most but not all of these musicians were seasoned "Muggle" performers before they discovered wizard rock. First-tier bands generally produce high-quality recordings, press up professional-looking CDs, have large social media presences, and are more likely to achieve financial success thanks to the size of their fanbases. First-tier bands also have the resources to make large-scale (and, in some cases, cross-continental) touring worthwhile.[4]

Second tier: Bands at this level, according to Rohlman, "do not enjoy the same level of commercial success as the Top Tier, but they have their own loyal, considerably smaller following[s]."[5] These groups are often musically competent, and release decently produced songs and albums. While second-tier bands are more likely to tour than third-tier bands, these tours are often smaller than those organized by first-tier bands.[6] Indexing their specific visibility and popularity within the scene, second-tier bands are often asked to open for first-tier bands at larger concerts. (In other words, these bands are big enough to play with more well-known groups but perhaps not famous enough to be the "main attraction.")

Third tier: Bands within the third-tier—often made up of wrock neophytes or green musicians—comprise most of the wrock community. These decidedly indie bands are typically very much underground, and they usually have limited, embryonic, or (more likely) nonexistent fan followings. These bands generally write only a handful of songs (which, if they are recorded, are usually defined by a certain lo-fi quality). They also rarely put out full-length records and are unlikely to perform live (let alone tour).[7]

As one can probably surmise, the division between each tier is fairly subjective, and, with a few exceptions (e.g., Harry and the Potters), wrock fans are not in unanimous agreement as to which bands belong in what tier.

"Upward mobility" is certainly possible: indeed, many contemporary first-tier bands began as third- or second-tier groups that worked their way to the top. For those bands who do reach the first tier, it is unlikely for them to "fall" from this apex, unless something causes the group to quickly and substantially lose favor in the community. An example of this most rare occurrence is the veritable *damnatio memoriae* imposed upon The Remus Lupins and Ministry of Magic. Both of these groups were at one point among the most popular (some might argue, *the* most popular) bands in the scene, but today are mostly disregarded by the community after it was revealed that certain members of these groups were sexually or emotionally abusive.

The tier system was initially a scandalous subject, as some within the community believed it threatened the idea that wizard rock was egalitarian—an idea that at the time was central to many people's understanding of the movement. This anxiety was on display in the comment section of the online wrock music critic Wrock Snob's article "Extended Thoughts: Women in Wrock, Part 1—In Defense of Men," published in 2010, when Kristina Horner of The Parselmouths wrote: "Can we not use tiers to describe wizard rock bands? I don't think that is a productive or even accurate way to 'rank' anyone."[8] A few comments later, Matt Maggiacomo wrote: "Who gives a fuck about tiers? Seriously. This topic really has been beaten to death over the past few years."[9] Both musicians are reiterating the same basic idea: fixating on the tiers requires focusing on a problematic hierarchy.

It seems likely that Maggiacomo and Horner's statements were made in good faith, but their assertions are nevertheless misguided. For one thing, abandoning the tier system does not make the problematic hierarchy go away—it just obscures it from view. Furthermore, both Horner and Maggiacomo are by most fans' reckoning a part of the first tier, meaning they necessarily have a privilege that those in lesser tiers do not. By denying the existence of tiers (or by proposing that they be disregarded), these musicians were thus inadvertently denying a system by which the community's hierarchy—and their position in it—could be constructively examined and productively critiqued. This is not to say that Horner and Maggiacomo are members of some sort of elite "wrock bourgeoisie," desperate to preserve their supremacy and fandom capital by consciously rebuffing their power. In fact, it is quite the opposite: their assertions are ultimately optimistic, based on the belief that wizard rock is something pure and special. Unfortunately, the reality is that wizard rock is a human institution, and thus it is not free from hierarchies, systems of oppression, processes of erasure, or other ills that befall all such institutions.

Nationality

As mentioned in this book's introduction, geographical constraints have not stopped the spread of wizard rock, and today, from Scandinavia to Oceania, there are wrock bands and fans to be found the world over. Nevertheless, the movement is more popular in certain parts of the world. Consider my survey results:

Table 1: Nationality of the Wrock Fandom (2017)[10]

	U.S.	U.K.	Australia	Canada	Sweden	Other
Number of Bands/Fans	119	8	3	3	8	9
Percent of Total Bands/Fans	79.3	5.3	2	2	5.3	6
n=150						

These numbers, in terms of percentages, are roughly similar to a breakdown of the bands listed on the Wizrocklopedia in 2012 by nation of origin[11]:

Nationality of Wrock Bands According to the Wizrocklopedia (2012)[12]

	U.S.	UK	Australia	Canada	Sweden	Other[13]
Number of Bands	551	55	24	22	18	31
Percent of Total Bands	78.6	7.8	3.4	3.1	2.6	4.4
n=701						

Despite considering different parts of the community (my survey was looking at both wrock *bands* and *fans*, whereas the data from the Wizrocklopedia relate only to *bands*), both of these charts show roughly the same patterns: The United States leads the pack, followed by the United Kingdom, and then Australia, Canada, and Sweden. The rest of the world accounts for only around 5 percent of the total community.

These results suggest that wizard rock is almost exclusively confined to the "Anglosphere."[14] Why is this the case? Many of my informants suggested that this is due to an English language barrier. They argued that the *Harry Potter* books—which were first published in the English language in an English-speaking country by an English-speaking author—were simply more likely to be popular in English-speaking nations due to their essentially English *nature*. And since these books did end up being more popular in these nations, and because reading the books is almost always a prerequisite for starting a wrock band, it stands to reason that these nations would simply have a greater number of wrock bands. While this is a common-sense argument, it still presents a problem: if English were the main factor as to where wrock bands form, why is the United States so over-represented? Should not the United Kingdom, being the birthplace of English (not to mention *Harry Potter*), be the epicenter of wizard rock? At the very least, should not the population of the United Kingdom be proportionately represented in the community?[15]

To account for wizard rock's disproportionate popularity in the United States, many point out that the first major wrock band, Harry and the Potters, was composed of two Americans, who, in their early years, almost exclusively performed shows in the United States to mostly American audience members. And because most of the ensuing wrock bands (e.g., The Parselmouths, Draco and the Malfoys, The Whomping Willows, The Moaning Myrtles) formed only after seeing Harry and the Potters perform live,[16] it follows that almost all these wrock bands would have been composed of Americans. In other words, wizard rock is so popular in the U.S. simply because it happened to start in the U.S. However, this presents yet another question: *why* did wizard rock start in the United States of all places? To find a suitable answer, then, it is necessary to reflect on a different topic: America's long-documented Anglophilic fascination with the British.

"Anglophilia" is defined as a love for anything British, and in the U.S. many people are proper Anglophiles, judging by the enormous popularity of British media in the country, as well as the fascination that many Americans have with the British royal family.[17] This Anglophilia is often indexed by a belief that anything British—be it history, culture, or a regional English dialect—is "sophisticated" or "classy." While this belief might come across as simply a harmless longing for a "posher" culture, the reality is that this sort of obsessiveness for anything British often belies a fixation with, as Elisa Tamarkin puts it, "the 'aura' of the British Empire."[18] These Americans often look toward the United Kingdom through a lens of "colonial ... fantasy," seeing the country and its peoples as superior, both in terms of perceived imperial might as well as culture.[19] Where does this sort of Anglophilia come from?

Anglophilia is most often found, not in the United Kingdom proper,[20] but rather in former British colonies. This is because it was in these places that the British spread their language, culture, and beliefs via systematic imperialism (factors generally considered essential to create the nostalgic longing that often defines Anglophilia).[21] But why, of all the British Empire's former colonies, is Anglophilia so strong in the United States? After all, the United States was the first major colony to actively—and successfully—reject British authority through a bloody revolution. Should not the United States loathe everything British? This seemingly bizarre contradiction has its roots in the period after the American Revolution, when white, upper-class, Protestant Americans began to develop a canonical "origin story" that cast the British Empire as both the tyrant to be fought against, as well as the progenitor of the American people. These shifts in perception caused many Americans to view the United Kingdom as the country that "started it all." This eventually created a sort of longing in the hearts of some Americans, who yearned to know more about and share in the perceived "blood ties" that supposedly existed between the U.S. and the United Kingdom.[22]

Unfortunately, because the United States was no longer under the rule of the Crown, British life and culture was somewhat inaccessible to the average American. The United Kingdom itself thus became a sort of exotic and almost magical place, and what was known about British life and culture—"the" accent, the literature, the monarchy, etc.—was fetishized into a concept that could then be idealized and fawned over.[23] This meant that anything British became a sort of celebrated novelty: for instance, individuals with British accents were assumed to be more intelligent or refined than "normal" Americans, and British popular culture was seen as more enjoyable. It is this sort of misguided and "culturally vicarious"[24] obsession with the United Kingdom that I mean when I use the term Anglophilia.

When *Harry Potter* was released, the books fit nicely into the American Anglophile's fetish, as they are undeniably British, and nostalgic to boot. As Genevieve Abravanel notes, "Although the Potter books reflect a wide range of reference, the magical world of *Harry Potter* would not be possible without the nostalgic visions of Englishness that have flourished in literature and public discourse over the past century."[25] The "nostalgic visions of Englishness" to which Abravanel refers is perhaps best illustrated in the books' main setting—Hogwarts—since the academy is clearly modelled on those boarding schools that the thrived during the peak of the British Empire. It was with these schools that the British used to instill a sense of identity and culture into their youth; this was especially the case during colonial times, when British aristocrats in far-off places wanted their children to have a "proper" British education.[26] This suggests that when American Anglophiles express their deep desire to attend Hogwarts, they are partially fixated with, to again quote Tamarkin, "the 'aura' of the British Empire"—albeit filtered through a lens of magic and fantasy. *Harry Potter*'s success in America was thus the result of a perfect storm of social and cultural conditions: the books were an Anglophile's dream, and Americans—with their documented history of strong, passionate Anglophilia—were the perfect audience.

But while this might explain why people ravenously scooped up the newest *Harry Potter* book when it was released in America, how exactly does it explain wizard rock's lopsided popularity in the U.S.? Quite simply, Americans, given their Anglophilic tendencies, are arguably more *likely* than individuals from many other places (including other Anglosphere nations)[27] to enjoy a decidedly British book series like *Harry Potter*. And a country whose citizens are more likely to enjoy *Harry Potter* is arguably more *likely* to host bands dedicated to *Harry Potter*. This ultimately results in a disproportionate number of wrock bands actually *being* from that country. In an interview, Paul DeGeorge told me that while he had never heard this argument before, it did possess explanatory power, saying, "It is possible that…. Anglophilia is part of what made *Harry Potter* so popular [in the U.S.], and so by extension it helped wizard rock along."[28]

Of course, it would be erroneous to assume that wizard rock is confined *only* to ex-British colonies or Anglophone nations. In fact, bands are to be found in countries as disparate as Denmark (e.g., Neville's Greenhouse), the Netherlands (e.g., Sigilum Serpentis), Russia (e.g., Hogwarts), Germany (e.g., Ethyln Gubrath), France (e.g., The Basilisk in Your Pasta), and Brazil (e.g., Potterock). With that said, these countries are nowhere near as represented as the aforementioned Anglophone countries.

The exception to this otherwise consistent rule is Sweden. In my 2017 survey, 5.3 percent of respondents identified as Swedish, and in 2012, 2.7 percent of the bands listed on Wizrocklopedia hailed from Sweden. While both of these percentages might seem small, they are disproportionally large when compared to the population of the country.[29] So popular is wizard rock in Sweden (a country that the music critic Wrock Snob has called the "underground hotbed of wizard rock")[30] that Harry and the Potters have toured in the country not once—a feat in and of itself for such a small, independent band—but rather three separate times.

For many this raises the question: why is the wrock scene so vibrant in Sweden? The answer is not quite clear, although it may have to do with a close network of active and devoted *Harry Potter* fans coming together following a painful blow to their community. According to Anna Fahlén of the Swedish band The Swedish Shortsnouts:

> Back in the early [2000s] there was a site called Hogwarts.nu, and until it closed in 2006 it was basically the *Harry Potter* forum in Sweden…. Literally everyone I'm friends with today was a member on that site…. The site basically closed down while activity on it was at its peak, the reason being technical site issues and bad economy I think…. For the users on the site, many in their teens (I was 14) this was devastating and there was really a sense of urgency to keep the community together and actually make things we wanted to happen really happen. We'd been following the international *Harry Potter* fandom as well, we listened to podcasts and wizard rock and knew about some of the cons in the US. And after our platform for fandom closed and the seventh and final book came out there was really a sense that if we don't try to do this now, we're never going to have any fandom events in Sweden and the com-

munity will disappear. This was at least 90% of the reason why [my brother, Erik, and I] started [The Swedish] Shortsnouts.³¹

According to the social scientists Brock Bastian, Jolanda Jetten, and Laura Ferris, "painful experiences" shared by a group often function as "social glue," which promote "bonding, solidarity ... cooperation" and—most importantly for the topic at hand—"group formation."³² Perhaps the closure of Hogwarts.nu was a painful enough event in the minds of its users that it united the Swedish wrock scene, motivating its members to build up a robust fandom in their country.

Race

In Oliver Boyd and the Remembralls' 2007 song, "Last Call," the band's lead singer Christian Caldeira passionately contends that wizard rock is "blind to," among other things, race. The sentiment is warm and well-meaning, and is often re-iterated by other wrockers, who hope to promote the idea that the wrock community is a safe and welcoming space for everyone. But while this optimistic belief pervades the scene, many of my informants confided in me their belief that the community is disproportionally white. Indexing their anxiety about holding such a belief, many of my informants qualified their statements, arguing that they were based on their own, personal observations, and that they did not have the demographic information to back up their assertions.

Does my survey confirm or refute these speculations? The results are as follows:

Race in the Wrock Community (2017)

	White		Asian	Indigenous North American	Black	Multi-Racial	No Response
	Non-Latinx	Latinx					
Number	124	10	4	2	1	5	4
Percentage	82.7	6.7	2.7	1.3	0.7	3.3	2.7
	89.3						
n=150							

The above data suggests that my informants' assertions were largely accurate and that the wrock community is, in fact, predominantly white.

Part of this racial disparity is likely due to systemic erasure of fans of color exacerbated by popular depictions of what it means to engage in fannish behavior. According to Mel Stanfill, fans are "culturally understood to be white" by the public at large.[33] This is mainly the result of pervasive media representation from the last thirty or so years, which has consistently depicted fans as such. While this may seem like an innocuous or even insignificant choice, it has had "major consequences for what fans are understood to be, both by nonfans and by fans themselves."[34] Most notably, it has resulted in many fans of color being alienated or relegated to the sidelines because they do not "fit the part."

In regard to wizard rock, this cultural understanding of what a fan "looks like" means that white wrockers are more likely to be elevated and celebrated because they are seen as representing the "reality" of the fandom, whereas wrockers of color are more likely to be overlooked because they do not conform to this "reality." This results in a highly problematic and often unconscious feedback loop: As wrockers of color are marginalized, the scene (and the representation thereof in people's minds) becomes increasingly white. This begins to alienate and drive away people of color, which results in less wrock bands of color forming. This in turn compounds the issue, causing the scene at large to be perceived as even *more* white. And thus the cycle continues *ad nauseum*.

The racial disparity found in wizard rock is also worsened by the fact that most of the main characters in the *Harry Potter* novels around which a wrock band might form are either commonly thought of as white or are depicted as white in the film adaptations.[35] Grace Dow notes:

> When I look around at the crowd at shows I've attended, the majority of the audience does seem to be white.... I can't help but notice the similarities with the source material. You have [a few characters of color, like] Dean Thomas, the Patil twins, Cho Chang, Kingsley Shacklebolt, and even, quite wonderfully, the new interpretation of Hermione as black.[36] But even so, the majority of the characters are depicted as white.[37]

Given that many studies suggest that people overwhelmingly relate and grow attached to characters that are like them, the overwhelming whiteness of the characters in *Harry Potter* means that people of color are less likely to relate and therefore less likely to grow attached to these characters. This is important to note, because, as Lauren Amanda Smith writes, "it is the ability to relate to and identify with the world of *Harry Potter* and its characters that produces the ability and desire" to create a wrock band.[38] With less people of color invested in characters, a disproportionately large number of wrock bands end up being composed of white individuals.

5. The Structure and Demographics   121

While the parent text marginalizes characters of color, wizard rock—being a medium through which fans themselves can create their own paratextual reinterpretations of the source material—has the potential to undo this marginalization. According to Smith, this "anti-erasure" potential can be seen in how many wrock songs are often written about minor characters who otherwise do not receive much attention in the books. Smith writes that those wrockers who write songs about these otherwise neglected characters are "'the new writers of *Harry Potter*' [who] correct marginalizations present in the canon texts."[39] This means that wizard rock's ability to "focus the spotlight" on lesser characters could also be used to bring to the forefront characters of color who are otherwise overlooked in the original text. Unfortunately, Smith notes:

> Those characters most often chosen to be brought from the margins to the center in wizard rock are [still usually] white. The songs dedicated to the Patil sisters, Lee Jordan or Cho Chang are rare (or more usually, nonexistent). Thus, while there is great subversive potential in the productive consumption of this community, it sometimes also subtly (and not so subtly) reifies hegemonic codes.[40]

In contemplating the racial disparity seen in the wrock scene, the relationship between race and access must also not be forgotten. In the United States, it is a reality that certain racial groups are systemically discriminated against, and this discrimination often hinders or blocks access to opportunities, resources, and materials that privileged groups take for granted. And for some people of color, this lack of access can extend to the *Harry Potter* books; Steph Anderson pointed this out in an interview when she told me, "[Consuming] *Harry Potter* during the time period where books were still coming out was a privileged action. To be able to gain access to hardcover books when they are released is a privilege that not everyone possesses."[41] Even today, there are communities of color that lack access to bookstores or libraries, where they might secure affordable or free copies of the series. Perhaps it goes without saying, but a person who is unable to access and therefore read *Harry Potter* is substantially less likely to create a wrock band.

Further exacerbating the situation is that people of color are less likely to have access to the Internet; Dana Floberg of the *Free Press* notes that "people of color comprise 32 million of the 69 million people in the United States who lack any form of home-internet access."[42] Floberg also notes that while 81 percent of white households are connected to the internet, this is the case for 70 percent of Latinx households and only 68 percent of black households.[43] What these statistics ultimately mean for the topic at hand is that not only are people of color less likely to have access to the online world in which the wrock community flourishes, they are also less likely to have the means of uploading wrock songs of their own creation.

Finally, wizard rock requires that a musician invest time and often money into the writing and recording of songs. This can disproportionately affect people of color, because these individuals—due to the unfortunate ways that long-term, systemic discrimination impacts people of color's social class, income levels, and employment opportunities—often find themselves impoverished or unemployed at a rate much higher than people who otherwise belong to a systemically privileged and hegemonic group.[44] There is a chance that members of groups with high poverty rates and low rates of employment might be less willing to spend time and valuable resources on what is for many people a fun but non-essential hobby.

However, it would be inaccurate to argue that wrockers are *only* white, as there are several wrock bands that include people of color. One such individual is Trina, who is of Filipina heritage. While discussing the intersection of race and wizard rock, she told me:

> I have never felt judged within the community because of my race. I've never felt judged because of my ethnicity or my cultural heritage. I love [wrock shows] because, while they by no means permanently fix racial issues, [they] create a ... safe place where everyone likes *Harry Potter*.... I know that this is a generality, but for me, I feel that everyone is welcome.[45]

At the same time, she tells me:

> It would be great to see more representation. As it stands, the community is very white. When we [i.e., The 8th Horcrux] started, I didn't see many [wrockers] who were like me at our shows [and now] I get really excited when we play if I see a young [wrock fan] who matches my racial identity! Now imagine if you're a kid and you see an adult who looks like you, singing about something you also love—that's cool! I hope that I can be that source of representation for someone else. [Also, more representation] would allow for a wider audience. Everyone—people from all racial or ethnic backgrounds—could benefit from ... listening to songs about *Harry Potter*![46]

While Trina is by no means representative of all wrockers of color, her comments are nonetheless telling. They suggest that while the community might welcome wrockers of color, there still is much work that needs to be done in regard to overcoming the racial disparity in wizard rock.

Gender and Sexism

Much like with race, the wrock community often conceives of itself as wholly egalitarian in regard to gender, dedicated equally to promoting both male- and female-fronted bands as well as stamping out any potential sexism. Take, for example, the words of Matt Maggiacomo, who in a 2009 discussion about the presence of sexism in the wrock community said:

I believe that there is no sexism inherent in the structure of the wizard rock community. If sexism exists, it's perpetrated by specific individuals who do not represent the values of the larger community.... I believe that sexism was never woven into the fabric of the community, deliberately or otherwise.... Wizard rock is a community in which any artist can thrive, regardless of gender.[47]

Such a declaration is undeniably idealistic, but how accurate is it? Is wizard rock the stronghold of gender equity that it conceives itself to be? The answer—as with almost all the issues covered in this chapter—is complicated.

First, consider the results of my survey:

Gender in the Wrock Community (2017)

	Cisfemale	Cismale	Non-Binary
Number	113	26	11
Percentage	75.3	17.3	7.3
n=150			

These data suggest that most wrock fans and band members are cisgendered women.[48] This higher percentage of women in the wrock scene is likely due to the similarity between wrock and other subjective and creative fandom outlets, like writing fan fiction—outlets in which fandom academics have long argued that women are more likely to take part. Henry Jenkins, for instance, writes, "Media fan [fiction] writing is almost always a feminine response to mass media."[49] Jenkins contends that this is due to how males and females are conditioned to analyze or "read" media: men read by focusing on "narrative organization and authorial intent," whereas women read by "reconstructing the textual world and understanding the characters."[50] This in turn leads to the two genders favoring different forms of participatory culture (to state in the most simplistic of terms: men are more likely to debate canon, whereas women are more likely to write their own stories).[51] Now, it should be acknowledged that Jenkins's consideration of gendered reading styles was in regard to fan fiction (and *Star Trek* fan fiction, in particular). However, it does not seem inappropriate to apply his ideas to wizard rock, given the movement's close relation to fan fiction.

Given the above, it may seem rather paradoxical to learn that most of the succcessful bands are composed entirely of or fronted exclusively by cisgendered men.[52] What is more, this imbalance is not a new phenomenon, but rather has existed since the genesis of the community. Of the first five major wrock bands (viz. Harry and the Potters, The Parselmouths, Draco and the Malfoys, The Whomping Willows, and the Remus Lupins), only one group was fronted by or even included women. While this looks damning, several individuals, including Rohlman and Wrock Snob, have pointed out that a majority of the first big wrock bands emerged from a small, but ultimately all-male coterie of relatives and friends. This means that the lopsided gender makeup of the early wrock bands was arguably due almost entirely to chance, and was not an intentionally sexist or exclusionary move.[53]

But regardless of whether this turn of events was deliberate or not, it is undeniable that a sort of male hegemony eventually developed in the world of wizard rock. This, in turn, resulted in female-fronted groups—who, it must be stressed, outnumbered their counterparts in large numbers—becoming less visible. For instance, Lauren Fairweather of The Moaning Myrtles said:

> Despite the fact that a very large majority of wizard rock bands are female-fronted, it seems like most of the bands who are booked to play at larger shows, especially in the earlier years, are [male-fronted]. In many cases back then, I was the only woman on the lineup, which [could] be a little bit discouraging.[54]

Female-fronted groups often learned of this inequity the hard way; for instance, some found that they had to approach potential venues to see if they could perform—while the very same venues were actively seeking out male-fronted groups.[55]

Thus, wizard rock ironically came to reflect the sort of androcentricism against which it claimed to fight. To further frustrate matters, a few of the biggest male-fronted[56] groups (who, it must remembered, held most of the power in the wrock community due to their status) contended that those pointing out and criticizing any sort of imbalance were not "real" fans because they were choosing to "see" rather than "look past" gender (this rhetoric was similar to that which sought to deny the existence of tiers in the fandom). According to Suzanne Scott, this self-identification of wizard rock as "sexism-free" often back-fired, blocking important conversations that might have improved the gendered make-up of the scene.[57]

But to exclusively blame male-fronted groups for this issue would be wholly unfair. For one thing, as Tammy Oler of *Bitch* magazine notes, "Many men who are involved in wizard rock actively support their female peers."[58] In fact, people like Matt Maggiacomo and Paul DeGeorge are among the most vocal opponents of sexism in the world of wizard rock. For another thing, this sort of top-down understanding of how the male hegemony formed fails to tell the whole story. Suzanne Scott, for instance, argues that "the complicity of female wrock fans ([herself] included) must [also] be acknowledged in perpetuating this imbalance."[59] Because female fans make up a larger majority of the wrock scene, they do have a certain power to influence which bands go on to be successful. What this means is that the consumptive choices of these female fans are indeed partially responsible for why male-fronted groups became popular.[60] But this cri-

5. The Structure and Demographics 125

tique can also be weaponized in the name of sexism, leading to the view that "wizard rock fangirls are simultaneously ... *the most* 'empowered' members of the community, and [consequently] *the source* of female wrockers comparative disempowerment" [emphasis added].[61] This is highly problematic because, while some female wrock fans may indeed be complicit, they are far from the only source of wizard rock's gender imbalance.

The good news is that in the last few years, the male hegemony in wizard rock has started to falter, and the scene has become more and more dominated by female musicians and female-fronted bands, such as Tonks and the Aurors, Tianna and the Cliffhangers, Losing Lara, Kirstyn Hippe, and The Lovegoods. And while many of the "biggest" bands (e.g., Harry and the Potters, Draco and the Malfoys) are still arguably the male-fronted groups, Fairweather notes that "right now ... nearly all the bands that are performing live (and touring) regularly are female-fronted, so that's changed quite a bit since I first started."[62] Part of the reason that female-fronted bands have gained greater visibility is because many of the "top tier" male-fronted acts have disbanded or stopped touring, such as Ministry of Magic or The Remus Lupins. However, to assume that this is the *only* reason would be to overemphasize the agency of men, relegating women to a mere passive role. Such a supposition would be erroneous, as the increased visibility of female-fronted bands is also—and perhaps mostly—the result of increased female activism.

Scott argues that "in recent years, female wrockers have made more of an organized effort to promote female-fronted wrock bands and cultivate a 'community of women supporting other women in their creative endeavors through wizard rock.'"[63] Scott writes that the first major example of this sort of activism was the establishment of the "Witch Rock" concert series by Tina Olson and Stacy Pisani (the former known in the wrock scene as "DJ Luna Lovegood," and the latter a member of the wrock band Swish and Flick) in 2009.[64] According to Maggie Hanna of the Wizrocklopedia:

> Why [organize a concert for] female wrock bands? Stacy informed me that her intention is not necessarily to simply promote female wizard rock bands, but to form a community of women supporting other women in their creative endeavors through wizard rock, as well as helping them grow musically. A "sisterhood" of wrockers, if you will. Since most of the wizard rock bands that come through New York City tend to be males, she saw this as an opportunity to help female bands in the wrock community showcase their talents on a somewhat larger platform.[65]

As the years wore on, gender-minded activism continued to increase, eventually leading to what Grace Kendall has dubbed "the feminist revolution of wizard rock."[66] Indeed, the impact of this revolution has been noticeable, and is clearly illustrated in the popularity and success of projects like Steph Anderson's "Yes All Witches!" organization, or the "Witch Rock" Twitter account[67] (an account that focuses exclusively on and retweets music by female wrockers).

It is important to remember that not everyone in the wrock community is cisgendered, and of the 150 people that I surveyed for this chapter, 11 individuals either did not adhere to the strict male-female gender dichotomy or did not self-describe as cisgendered. Unfortunately, these individuals have long been ignored, erased, or excluded from the larger wrock conversation despite their making up a small but significant percentage of the community. Luckily, the aforementioned injection of feminism into the scene has also led many to direct the spotlight on content creators who identify as transgender or non-binary, encouraging these individuals to put forth music that explicitly discusses their unique experiences as wrockers.

The 2017 release of Totally Knuts's album *Fresh, Spooky, and Queer* embodies this shift in many ways. TK Lawrence, the individual behind the band, wrote on Bandcamp, "As a non-binary queer person, I wanted to give the wrock world more representation for the LGBT community [with this album]."[68] The record contains the track "Trans Wizard," which makes these sentiments clear to all:

> I'm a non-binary wizard
> I'm a genderfluid witch
> I don't know what to call myself
> Except for maybe "wix"
> It seems as if we're harder to see
> Than a polar bear in a blizzard
> We need representation 'cuz
> My best friend's a trans wizard

In regard to non-binary representation in the wrock scene, Lawrence told me, "I think we're moving in the right direction, even if there might not be a ton of [songs discussing the topic] right now, I think in the (near?) future there will be more."[69]

Sexual Orientation

According to the feminist writer and critic Rebecca Traister, the wrock community has a "broad view of human ... sexuality."[70] Those within the community by and large concur with this assessment, and many of my informants were open about their acceptance of members regardless of sexuality, with TK Lawrence perhaps best epitomizing the comments that I received: "In my experience, the wrock community is absolutely accepting of the LGBT community.... Every wrocker I've talked to is super supportive and helpful."[71]

Lawrence's assertion is backed up by the fact that some wrock songs either take to openly discussing non-heteronormative relationships and pairings or are infused with LGBTQ+ themes; in fact, some of these songs are among the most well-regarded within the community. Kelli Rohlman argues that the quintessential example is "Dumbledore Is Gay (And That's OK!)" by Justin Finch-Fletchley and the Sugar Quills, which as the title suggests, discusses Dumbledore's outing and assures the listener that this revelation is progressive. The verse first goes as follows:

> Dumbledore's gay, and that's OK!
> I don't look at him any different than I did yesterday
> Dumbledore's gay, and that's OK!
> He's still the greatest freakin' wizard of his day!

According to the band's website, the song is beloved within the wrock community and "has become an anthem for wizard rock fans in promoting diversity, acceptance, and love for all kind, regardless of who or what you or they may be."[72] Rohlman reasons that the song's popularity is also due to the simple, and straightforward nature of the song's title and lyrics, which frankly reinforce the idea that queer sexual orientations such as Dumbledore's should not be stigmatized.[73]

The community has attempted to normalize queer sexual orientations through visual representation too. For instance, the cover to *Wizards and Muggles Rock for Social Justice, Vol. II* compilation album features cartoon versions of Dumbledore and Gandalf the Grey (the latter from J.R.R. Tolkien's *Lord of the Rings* series) holding hands. Surrounding them are a number of small hearts, garland that you might see at a wedding, and a number of cheering wrock band caricatures. At the bottom of the cover, the text reads: "A benefit for the Harry Potter Alliance and Marriage Equality Rhode Island." The implications of this cover are fairly clear: Dumbledore and Gandalf are getting married, and this is a *good* thing.

But as this chapter has shown several times before, simply because the community claims itself to be open and diverse does not actually make it so. Therefore, the question becomes: is wizard rock equally representative when it comes to non-normative sexual orientations? To answer this question, let me turn once again to my survey results, which are as follows:

Sexual Orientation in the Wrock Community (2017)

	Heterosexual	Homosexual	Bisexual	Asexual	Other	No Response
Number	77	4	38	16	12	3
Percentage	51.3	2.7	25.3	10.7	8	2
n=150						

Now contrast these results with that of two 2015 YouGov surveys that looked at sexual orientation in both the United States and the United Kingdom:

Sexual Orientation by Percentage in the United States and United Kingdom (2015)[74]

	Heterosexual	Homosexual	Bisexual	Other	No Response
United States	89	4	4	1	2
n=1000					
United Kingdom	88.6	5.7	2	0.7	3
n=1632					

These numbers are striking for a number of reasons. First, they show that while those who identify as heterosexual make up the majority of the wrock community, that majority as a percentage is substantially smaller than what is usually found in a normal[75] population. Second, the results indicate that those who identify as bisexual, asexual, or as some other, less-common orientation are, as a percentage, much more represented in the wrock community than they are in a normal population. Finally, the results show that the percentage of gay respondents was roughly half that in a normal population.

This last fact is particularly unexpected, given that most of the songs discussing non-normative sexuality in the community focus on the acceptance of homosexuality, specifically homosexual males. Rohlman hypothesizes that this particular emphasis is due to the influence of the *Harry Potter* books themselves, as the only canonical queer relationship that Rowling has confirmed was a one-sided infatuation that Albus Dumbledore harbored for Gellert Grindelwald when they were both in their youth.[76] But this assertion is problematized by the fact that most of the songs discussing/celebrating homosexual relationships are centered not on Dumbledore and Grindelwald, but rather Harry Potter and his school rival Draco Malfoy (a ship popular known as "Drarry").[77] In fact, according to Rohlman, "In Which Draco and Harry Secretly Want to Make Out" by The Whomping Willows (which was discussed in Chapter 2) was the first example of a "slash[78] wizard rock" song. Why exactly is Draco/Harry such a popular ship for wrockers? The answer is unclear (after all, canonically speaking, the two characters hold antithetical moral viewpoints and are openly antagonistic to one another).[79] Many of my informants speculated that this ship's popularity is due to the influence of fan fiction upon the wrock community, given that Draco and Harry slash fiction is particularly widespread on sites like FanFiction.com (although this still does not explain where exactly the ship came from and why it is so popular). Others speculated that wrockers are drawn to it because it affirms the "opposites attract" trope.[80]

Regardless, in the end it seems that Rohlman is correct when she writes, "The wizard rock community's attitudes toward sexuality are much more consistent than their attitudes about gender."[81] Not only is the community vocal in its support for queer sexualities, but wrockers and fans who identify as queer actually make up a sizeable portion of the scene. Of course, this is not to say that wizard rock is a medium that perfectly reflects the complexity and diversity of human sexual orientation (after all, while the community itself is diverse, most wrock songs that explicitly discuss relationships are still highly heteronormative). But these results do suggest that sexual identity is one topic wherein the rhetoric of the community and the reality of the community's make-up match up with one another, relatively speaking.

"The [Demographics] of [Wizard Rock] Don't Make Sense!"

While nationality, race, gender, and sexual orientation are all abtruse sociocultural topics that defy simple and tidy summations, the results of my demographic study heavily suggest the following: First, wizard rock is overwhelmingly centered in the United States, which I contend is at least partially a result of widespread and strong American Anglophilia. Second, most of those who participate in the community are white, which I argue is caused by popular depictions of fans as being entirely white, a relative lack of characters of colors in the *Harry Potter* books to which people of color might be able to better relate, and the fact that people of color often lack access to the books and the Internet at a greater percentage than white people. Third, in terms of gender make-up, there seems to be a veritable male hegemony at the heart of the movement, although in the recent years this has begun to falter in light of increased female activism. Fourth and finally, there is a fairly diverse and progressive representation of sexualities in the scene.

Ultimately, these results back up what Kelli Rohlman (2010) argued: while the community espouses a number of progressive principles in regard to many topics, it often falls short of these ideals. This is proof that the wrock community is susceptible to those same foibles which befall other human institutions. With that said, I believe it is important to remember the words of Kelli Rohlman, who concluded, "It does not ... appear as though the inconsistency between the rhetoric and the community behavior is intentional."[82] In fact, when presented with the reality that the community is not as egalitarian as it might otherwise conceive itself to be, many of my informants expressed a genuine and urgent desire to right these wrongs. This suggests that while the community may have its sometimes unacknowledged or unnoticed issues, it is more willing than others to engage in social activism when necessary. In the next chapter, I consider this sort of activism as well as how wrockers have managed to impact the world.

6

Wizard Rock and the "Muggle World"

On February 3, 2017, Bandcamp—the online music marketplace used by thousands of independent bands to distribute their music—announced that it would be donating 100 percent of the money that it earned that day to the American Civil Liberties Union (ACLU) Foundation of Southern California. This move—which was very much a political one, protesting the isolationist and xenophobic rhetoric of Donald Trump's presidential administration—resonated with hundreds of artists using the site, many of whom stood with Bandcamp and promised that they too would donate their earnings to the ACLU.

Among these bands was Harry and the Potters; on the same day that Bandcamp announced its intention to donate its earnings of the day, the group took to Facebook and broadcast to their fans that they too would follow suit so as to "support independent music and stand up for American values."[1] To entice their followers into making a wrock purchase, the DeGeorge brothers also uploaded a few rarities, like the "wiz-hop" EP *Lemon Drop.... The Beat* that they had recorded under the moniker Dumbledore in 2007, as well as a cassette tape that contained live tracks from their 2011 tour of Sweden. They also made their entire discography available for only $40.

Harry and the Potters' post was liked by over a hundred wrock fans and shared dozens of times. Soon, other bands began to follow suit, and within no time, the hashtag "#Wrock4ACLU" was on Twitter and trending. To keep the momentum of this ad hoc wrock charity drive up, popular wrock-centric Twitter accounts like Witch Rock and websites like the Wizrocklopedia began enthusiastically posting updates, alerting their followers as to which bands were donating their proceeds. Soon, wrock fans were taking to their various social media accounts and discussing the situation at hand, with many broadcasting to their friends and family just how much wizard rock they had actually purchased.

The morning of February 3 is still fresh in my mind: I was just about to clock in at work when I decided to quickly check my social media accounts. As soon as I opened my phone, I was astounded to see the sheer number of Bandcamp posts and ACLU hashtags zipping through cyberspace. At that moment, I realized that The 8th Horcrux had the potential to join in and help to affect change. I closed my browser and went to text Trina, but she must have had the same idea, for as soon as I began to compose a text, I saw a message from her reading: "Check out Bandcamp post. Profits go to ACLU." I quickly shot back: "Do you want us to do that?" Trina responded almost instantaneously, with only a single word: "YES."

I subsequently crafted both a Facebook post and a Tweet, letting our followers know what we were doing. By that evening we had raised around $20—by no means a massive amount of money, but a donateable sum nonetheless. After the funds finished processing in our PayPal account, Trina and I hit the "submit" button and sent the earnings straight to the ACLU Foundation of Southern California.

It was not until a few days later that we learned the full extent of the fundraiser: from Bandcamp's donations alone, the ACLU had earned almost $100,000, and this was not even counting the money privately donated by bands like us. And while, as I mentioned in the previous paragraph, the sum of money that Trina and I were able to donate was not much, it still felt good to be part of something larger—like a pile of disparate puzzle pieces coming together to make a beautiful portrait, or numerous strands of thread being woven into a lovely tapestry.

But in many ways, for the wrock community this fundraiser was par for the course; wrockers, after all, do have a long, documented history of charity work, political activism, and fundraising.

* * *

According to *Wired* magazine, "The portion of [the] *Harry Potter* fandom affectionately referred to as [wizard rock] is known for two things. The first is a joyous and unabashed celebration of the Potter mythos through music. The second is an equally fervent dedication to combating the social ills of the day."[2] For many outside of the wrock scene, the sheer intensity of the community's commitment to making their world a better place through social and political activism can be a bit of a surprise. After all, is not the wrock community just irreverent and wacky—made up mostly of nerds, geeky adults, and awkward (pre-)teens eager to discuss a series of books that they love? The answer is quite simply, no. In fact, a surprising number of wrock bands are not content with merely playing goofy songs and have instead used their status and power within the movement to impact the real world.

6. Wizard Rock and the "Muggle World"

A major reason wrockers are often so socially and politically active is simply because the *Harry Potter* novels are, in many ways, stories about activism and doing "what is right" when it really matters. Throughout the books, characters actively oppose unjust authority figures, castigate politicians who are failing to provide for the common good, admonish the abuse of politically sanctioned power, and demand democratization. Others fight for the rights of the enslaved, champion education reform, or deride the evils of racism. And because, to quote wrocker Ariel Factor Birdoff, "the [wrock community] is based on a series of books that in itself is about activism, it is only natural that fan produced content would champion the same causes that Harry, Ron, and Hermione also champion."[3] Furthermore, the socio-political themes of the *Harry Potter* books—works that, despite being fantastical, often parallel or resemble our own reality—can fairly easily be transplanted into our own world. Paul DeGeorge notes:

> Having a really solid text to work from, with both social and political themes *that are very rich and feel translatable to our own moment* is really advantageous. [When the wrock community is together] everybody is kind of on the same page. And that gives you an opportunity to make changes[4] [emphasis added].

This chapter looks at how bands that sing about *Harry Potter* have used their imaginative "wizardly" movement to affect change in the real world of "Muggles."[5] I begin by considering the penchant many wrockers have for social and political activism, namely their pro-literacy, pro-feminist, and anti-authoritarian beliefs. I then explore how wrockers have managed to translate their ideology into action through both the establishment of the Harry Potter Alliance and the distribution of charity compilations. The chapter concludes on a more somber note by looking at how some of those who had attained positions of influence within the wrock community have used their power to sexually assault members of the community, and how the community has reacted to these abuses and rallied around survivors.

"Fight Evil, Read Books": Pro-Literacy Efforts

While pro-literacy leanings have always been somewhat innate to the movement (given that wizard rock ultimately stems from a literary source), it was perhaps Alex Carpenter of The Remus Lupins who first made these sentiments most perspicuous when he claimed his band advocated for "the most awesome thing this side of invisibility cloaks: reading."[6] Eventually Carpenter boiled down this philosophy into an oft-quoted catchphrase: "Fight evil. Read books." And while Carpenter (whom many would argue should have perhaps listened to the first part of his own motto) has been all but shunned by the community due to abuse allegations, the sentiment he arguably formulized and popularized has remained strong with wrockers.

A number of wrock bands—including, among many others, Harry and the Potters, The Moaning Myrtles, Draco and the Malfoys, The Whomping Willows, and Tonks and the Aurors—have explicitly stated that, in addition to entertaining people with songs about a beloved book series, their goal is to promote literacy through music. This too is the goal of my band, The 8th Horcrux, and we have even released two openly and unequivocally pro-literacy parodies: "Reading" (a spoof of Sixpence None the Richer's '90s hit "Kiss Me") and "Bookworm" (a parody of Fifth Harmony's "Work from Home"), both of which extol the virtues of libraries and literature. We often perform these songs during the dénouement of our live shows, in the hopes that audience members will leave with a desire to go read a new book.

But wizard rock's pro-literacy activities have not been confined merely to encouraging listeners to sign up for a new library card (although, I must say, this *is* a noble goal). Rather, a number of concerts and record releases have been organized, whose proceeds have been donated to pro-literacy charities, such as: the Hallows and Horcruxes Ball (whose earnings went to the Geary County chapter of First Book, a nonprofit that gives books to impoverished children), the *Jingle Spells* compilation albums (the proceeds of which went to Get a Clue, a charity that raises funds for books and libraries in impoverished countries), and the Wizard Rock EP of the Month Club (which raised almost $15,000 for the aforementioned charity First Book). All-in-all, hundreds of thousands of dollars have been raised for pro-literacy charities over the course of wizard rock's mere fifteen-year existence.

Why has this pro-literacy campaign been so successful for wizard rock and the charities that they support? According to Kelli Rohlman, it is because the effort, while affecting real, positive change in the world, still manages to be "broad" and "neutral"; almost anyone can get behind "respect[ing] … the printed word," regardless of differences in political, religious, or social opinion.[7] However, in an age where some people zealously write-off any media—including books—with which they disagree as "fake news," perhaps this answer is a bit too idealistic. Approaching the question from a slightly different angle, the researchers Catherine Belcher and Becky Stephenson argue that wizard rock's pro-literacy activism has been so fruitful because it eschews "a class-based, exposure to 'classics' argument" by instead emphasizing "the social and fun aspects of being a part of a literary community."[8] This, Belcher and Stephenson claim, makes wrockers and their fans a unique and appealing "breed of literacy advocates."[9]

"Yes All Witches!": Feminism and the Fight for Gender Equality

At the onset of her book chapter "Embracing the Magic: Muggle Quidditch and the Transformation of Gender Equality from Fantasy to Reality" (2015), the theatrical scholar Jennifer Popple argues:

> In the *Harry Potter* universe, equal access for men and women appears to be a reality. With doors open to then, in education, employment, and social and political processes, women and girls in J.K. Rowling's series technically enjoy the "society between equals" that the liberal feminist John Stuart Mill called for in 1870. Two out of the four Houses at Hogwarts, Ravenclaw and Hufflepuff, are named after their female founders, and several women have served as Hogwarts headmistresses. Moreover, women occupy positions as respected teachers (such as Professors McGonagall and Sprout), highly trained Aurors in the Department of Magical Law Enforcement (Nymphadora Tonks), and even as powerful sorcerers among Voldemort's core group of Death Eaters (the most notable being Bellatrix Lestrange).[10]

As Popple's examples illustrate, the *Harry Potter* books portray a world where gender equality has been realized. Such an optimistic world has left an impression in the minds of untold readers, and many—including a large number of

Steph Anderson (foreground) and Andrew Boylan perform in front of a "Yes All Witches" banner at the 2017 LeakyCon. Yes All Witches was founded by Anderson, and is a grassroots fandom movement that embraces classic feminist idead to empower female members within the scene (courtesy Steph Anderson).

wrockers—have embraced ideals that stress the equality of all genders and that attempt to dismantle stereotypes about what women can or cannot do. And these ideals, combined with the fact that almost three-fourths of the scene identifies as female, have led to the wrock community becoming a bastion for feminist philosophical discourse and activism.

Sometimes, this feminist activism is subtle: Rohlman, for instance, identified several lines in the song "Transparent" by The Moaning Myrtles that can be construed as feminist (despite this not being the band's intention when writing the song).[11] Other times, this sort of activism can be quite obvious: for example, Tianna Mignogna released a single in 2012 entitled "Lily Evans, Feminist," whose title makes its subject matter patently clear. Similarly, in 2016, the Harry Potter Alliance put out the *Hex the Patriarchy* charity album that features a number of wrock bands singing songs about fictional female characters; the record was promoted with the tagline, "This is what a heroine sounds like." But regardless of whether the feminism is concealed or overt, it is undeniable that the philosophy has had a major impact on the wrock community at large.

Perhaps the best example of feminist activism in the wrock community is the Yes All Witches organization, established in 2014 by Steph Anderson of the band Tonks and the Aurors. Yes All Witches (which is a grassroots fandom movement that embraces feminist philosophy and activism to promote equality and empower female, PoC, and non-binary wrockers) can trace its origins back to a talk that Anderson gave in 2014 at the first Granger Leadership Academy. During her presentation (during which she actually introduced the phrase "Yes All Witches!"),[12] she discussed her experience as a female wrocker as well as how individual identity plays a part in the wrock experience. After the session, Anderson realized that the community needed to move from merely discussing equality to actually creating equality through action; in an interview, she explained: "There's been conversations about demographics of wizard rock in the past, but not much around actual feminism and active work towards diversity (beyond just getting more female representation) into wizard rock."[13]

Soon thereafter, Anderson founded Yes All Witches and within a relatively short span of time, it had evolved from an idealistic concept to a full-blown organization. Today, in cooperation with Feminist Apparel, Yes All Witches runs a micro-grant program, which bestows small but impactful allowances of $100 to underrepresented wrockers. As the Yes All Witches website puts it: "The goal is to continue to promote intersectional feminist ideals and also encourage our community to grow and evolve. Each grant [can be] put towards creating new, diverse wizard rock and releasing it into this world."[14] Potential recipients must submit an application that answers the questions: "How would receiving a Yes All Witches grant impact you and your art? What does your voice and your story bring to the fandom?"[15] Other than that, individuals are encouraged to be as creative with their application materials as they want. The first recipient of one of these micro-grants was TK Lawrence of the band Totally Knuts, who invested the money into the production of his 2017 album *Fresh, Spooky, and Queer.*

Yes All Witches has been positively received by the community (for instance, the musicologist Sarah Frances Holder, in her M.A. thesis "'Get Your Geek On,'" praised it as an "explicit enactment of a feminist inclusionary safe space"),[16] as have albums like *Fresh, Spooky, and Queer.*[17] Given this sort of reaction, it seems likely that the feminist spirit that has been guiding wizard rock for the last few years will continue to hold influence.

"Voldemort Can't Stop the Rock!": Resisting Authoritarianism

Considering that a major theme in the *Harry Potter* books is the repudiation of tyranny, many wrock bands have taken to writing political songs that criticize authoritarianism and what they perceive as despotic tendencies concealed within the hearts of some governmental figures.

Harry and the Potters are perhaps the premiere example of this.[18] While their first album was mostly apolitical, their sophomore effort, *Voldemort Can't Stop the Rock!* (released in 2004 and based on the fifth *Harry Potter* novel, *The Order of Phoenix*), contained a number of charged songs that disparage dictatorial sentiments. Chief among these tunes was the humorously titled "Cornelius Fudge is an Ass," in which Paul DeGeorge sings over twinkling keyboards and jangly guitars:

> You can pretend that the Ministry
> Knows what's going on
> You can convince yourself
> That the *Daily Prophet* has a clue
> But I think that the Quibbler
> Has a better grip on the truth

In a run-down of activist wrock songs, Kelly Ward of the Wizrocklopedia referred to this ditty as "the mother of all subversive" tracks due to its overtly political nature.[19]

While the song's title clearly indicates that the lyrics are directed at the titular Minister for Magic, the brothers have acknowledged that "Cornelius Fudge is an Ass" is also a direct critique of George W. Bush's 2001–09 presidency. In an interview, Paul DeGeorge told me:

> I was seeing these parallels with what was going on with the Bush administration. And I was thinking, like, "Oh! It's right here in the books let's make sure people recognize

that!" ... [We were also] wanting to connect young folks to politics [and help to engender] a political consciousness that hadn't quite developed yet. It's hard to make sense of global political movements and things like that—I'm almost forty years old and I have trouble making sense of it! What the hell is it like for a fifteen year old?[20]

According to Claudia Morales's excellent MTV article "Wizard Rock in the Age of Trump," when the band performed the song during the Bush years, they often reinforced the uncomfortable similarities between the *Order of Phoenix* and the real world by changing the last line of the above quoted verse to "You can convince yourself that *The Daily Prophet* has a clue/But I think they're a whole lot closer to Fox News"—directly referencing a real-life news network that is often accused of biased reporting that skews heavily to rightwing politics.[21]

But in 2008, Barack Obama became the Democratic candidate for president—an event that drastically altered the way the DeGeorges viewed the future of American politics. Around this time, Paul told the Wizrocklopedia, "[While] it's really easy for people to feel down on America, [Obama] represents hope and optimism and I think he truly recognizes the potential greatness about our country."[22] As Morales notes, this sense of newfound enthusiasm reached a fever pitch in the wrock community when Obama was

Harry & the Potters (Paul, left, and Joe DeGeorge) performing at an Occupy Boston protest (2011). Since their inception—and especially since the release of their sophomore album Voldemort Can't Stop the Rock (2005)—the band has been politically active (courtesy Chase Elliott Clark).

elected president in November of that year, and soon thereafter, the anti-authoritarianism of wizard rock was dialed down a bit. In fact, Harry and the Potters were so hopeful for the future that they dropped "Cornelius Fudge is an Ass" from their setlist, and for the majority of Obama's 8 years in office, the song remained untouched.[23]

The song would have likely remained in the band's vault had it not been for the 2016 political ascension of Donald Trump. Given this event, as well as the populist sentiment that was sweeping much of the world, Harry and the Potters decided to ratchet up their anti-authoritarian rhetoric by bringing "Cornelius Fudge Is an Ass" back into the fold when they performed that August at LeakyCon. And once again, the group changed the song's lyrics to convey their message, this time swapping out "Fox News" for "Breitbart," the far-right news outlet and mouthpiece for the former Trump advisor Steve Bannon. Morales's article paints a colorful picture of this performance, describing how at the song's conclusion, Paul DeGeorge grabbed the microphone, raised a fist in the air, and shouted: "Fuck Donald Trump!" to a cheering crowd.[24]

It is undeniable that this performance and the audience's reaction were indicative of a desire in the wrock community at large to oppose the rise of an authoritarian politician. Needless to say, the results of the 2016 U.S. presidential election—an election in which Donald Trump secured the presidency—had a major impact on the world of wizard rock, igniting within the hearts and minds of many an intense period of soul-searching. Paul DeGeorge, for one, began contemplating the significance of his songs that express anti-authoritarian sentiments, mentally recontextualizing and resituating them in a time that he and many would describe as politically dispiriting. He eventually came to the conclusion that the songs that repudiate authoritarianism and related evils have the most potential to comfort those who are otherwise living in fear, telling Morales: "I've seen a lot of people finding comfort in some of our music, and I'm thinking about the songs, in particular, that they're being comforted by—songs that speak to that fight against authority, that resistance to evil."[25] After more than a year of discussing these ideas, Paul and Joe began working on their long-awaited fourth studio album, which revolves around the plot of *The Deathly Hallows*. This album, among other things, stresses the necessity of resisting authoritarianism and its related evils. As of writing, this album has not been released, but a live performance of it at a house show on March 30, 2018, energized the crowd with its politically relevant message.

The actions of the DeGeorge brothers suggest that wrockers can use their own musical acts to actively push back against politicians that they oppose or laws that are oppressive. But wizard rock can also be used as an exercise in political empathy. In an interview, Myles Kane, who performs wizard rap in-character as the house elf Kreacher, expressed these ideas when he said:

> I think embodying a character like Kreacher ... certainly is an exercise in trying to shift perspectives and understand where certain extreme mindsets come from.... It was an opportunity to empathize with Kreacher and understand his actions in a way the [*Harry Potter* series] doesn't have time to explore. He's angry, he "hates" mudbloods[26]—anything "other." He's living in a frozen time, in a museum of the past, and has idealized his memories of "better days." There is a real parallel between his mentality and this "Make America Great Again" misguided nostalgia [that] Trump base supporters [feel] ... and the false strength that comes from drawing a line in the sand and saying "we're this" and "you're that." The Trump age has unfortunately seemed to only strengthen the divide.... What's great about Kreacher's story line is that he's forced into living with these people he despises and in the end, they find common ground and end up on the same side.[27]

By role-playing as Kreacher and trying to think as that character, Kane is thus able to better understand the 2016–18 political climate, the rise of Trump, and the nature of the president's supporters. And that sort of understanding is just as important as a stunning protest song in convincing people to join the resistance against authoritarianism.

With all this said, there are those bands that strive for political neutrality with their music. Generally, these groups eschew "taking a stand" because they view themselves as entertainers to all; they thus do not want to take sides and risk alienating their audience—an audience that may just want to hear silly song about *Harry Potter*. But Paul DeGeorge repudiates this view, arguing that, in reality, no one is neutral. In an interview, he expounded on this point by quoting the punk musician Victoria Ruiz (lead singer of the band Downtown Boys), saying, "All music is political. And if it is not making a statement, that's political too."[28] In other words, you can either take a stand with your music, supporting what you believe in and castigating that which you do not, or you can remain silent and implicitly convey your approval of the status quo. It is this mentality that has spurred Paul and Joe DeGeorge to infuse their quirky brand of tunes about a boy wizard with increasingly political statements; they want all to know that they are explicitly fighting against a world that they believe needs to change.

Changing the World

Unlike some other subcultures or genres whose members easily number in the hundreds of thousands, wizard rock is a rather diminutive community. So how, a skeptic might ask, can a community as small as wizard rock possibly hope to enact the change that it seeks to bring about in the world? After all, the sort of paradigm shifts on the scale of those that wrockers advocate almost

6. Wizard Rock and the "Muggle World" 141

always require huge swaths of time, legions of passionate individuals, and—perhaps most importantly—large sums of money to come about. Luckily for the musicians that I have discussed in this chapter, the wrock scene has found a number of ways to focus their efforts, and then magnify those efforts through the power of community and collaboration.

When discussing wizard rock's ability to enact change, it is perhaps best to start with a consideration of The Harry Potter Alliance (often abbreviated as "The HPA"), a charity that was co-founded by Paul DeGeroge of Harry and the Potters and activist/comedian Andrew Slack in 2005. While The HPA is not affiliated exclusively with the wrock community, it at least partially emerged from the scene and has worked intimately with a number of the biggest wrock bands many times. Thus, it would be wholly inappropriate for this book to overlook the organization.

The HPA has its origins in a bizarre encounter that DeGeorge had with Slack in 2005. In a YouTube video detailing the charity's history, DeGeorge humorously recounts:

> Sometimes people ask me about the early days of the Harry Potter Alliance, because [I was] there at the start, about five-and-a-half years ago. [It was] summer 2005. We had a Harry and the Potters show at an elementary school in Cambridge, Massachusetts. And this crazy looking guy came in, all sweaty, weird, and sticky. And he started talking real fast, and he said, "I have an idea! ... I want to start a real-world Dumbledore's Army,[29] and I want you to help me." And I said, "Hmmm crazy guy, this sounds like a good idea!" That guy was Andrew Slack.[30]

Slack was inspired to approach DeGeorge both due to his love of the *Harry Potter* series, as well as his desire to positively impact the world; in a video about The HPA's origins, Slack states, "I wanted to start something new while I was doing this comedy stuff and I [said to myself], 'You know what's finally going to be the thing? *Harry Potter* fans doing social justice!'"[31]

DeGeorge thought Slack's idea was a good one, and he quickly organized a charity show for Amnesty International, which managed to raise $300. While this sum was not huge, DeGeorge and Slack were pleasantly surprised, with the former explaining, "We all felt more gratified by the idea that we were building something a lot bigger."[32] Soon after, DeGeorge and Slack continued to develop their fledgling organization. During these first few months, things were a bit bumpy, as the charity was extremely small and operating with a shoestring budget, but because DeGeorge and Slack continued to pour resources into their pet project, the charity eventually stabilized. To get their message to even more people, Slack created a MySpace page and posted a bulletin informing the community of The HPA's goals; *Harry Potter* and wrock fans quickly discovered the message, and within just one day, Slack was receiving "hundreds if not thousands" of friend requests.[33] In time, the HPA's MySpace page had well over over 100,000 online "friends."[34]

Possibly taking a cue from the wrock community, The HPA began to work "within the structure of fandom."[35] They did this by expressing their goals via direct allusions to the characters and events from the *Harry Potter* novels: Those who were trying to do good were following in the footsteps of Harry, Dumbledore's Army, and the Order of the Phoenix. Real-world evil was personified as Voldemort, and specific ills were labelled his Horcruxes (e.g., the poverty Horcrux, the bullying Horcrux, the homophobia Horcrux).[36] And perhaps most notably, Slack dubbed the complacent and widespread mental state of those who are satisfied with the status quo the "Muggle Mindset," writing, "The 'Muggle Mindset' … is a system based on fear that sets normalcy as one's aspiration."[37] This "*Harry Potter*–izing" did two things. First, it allowed the HPA to gain (notably, younger) members by appealing to a popular fantasy series that millions were reading.[38] Second, by both fictionalizing reality and realizing fiction, The HPA helped to break down the barrier separating the "real world" and the world of "make-believe," thereby tapping into people's love for *Harry Potter* and channeling that love into projects that can make the world a better place. Henry Jenkins argued that this method allowed participants "to reconcile their activist identities with the pleasurable fantasies that brought the fan community together in the first place," leading to the creation of "a new form of civic engagement."[39]

In 2006, the HPA teamed up with Walmart Watch and began its first major campaign, entitled "Harry Potter and the Dark Lord Waldemart." The project sought to warn consumers about the predatory practices of the Wal-Mart Corporation by releasing three parody videos, each of which depicted Harry's struggle against the titular "Lord Waldemart": an evil wizard whose face is covered by Wal-Mart's signature smiley face logo.[40] The next year, The HPA, in tandem with The Leaky Cauldron fansite, organized concerts to call attention to the highly destructive War in Darfur (2003–present) and its associated genocide. Then, in 2009, The HPA began their now-annual "Accio Books!" charity drive, which to date has collected over a quarter-million books for the poor and disadvantaged.[41] Following the calamitous earthquake that laid waste to the Caribbean nation of Haiti in 2010, the HPA co-organized the "Helping Haiti Heal" campaign, which raised $123,754 for Partners in Health and enabled 50 tons of medical supplies to be quickly delivered to the reeling nation.[42] And in an attempt to resist authoritarianism and preserve American democracy, the HPA has also teamed up with a number of wrock bands (such as Harry and the Potters, Draco and the Malfoys, The Whomping Willows, The Moaning Myrtles, The Parselmouths, and Gred and Forge, among many others) to coordinate the "Wizard Rock the Vote" campaign during election season in the United States. This on-going project seeks both to register new voters at wrock concerts and also educate citizens about the major political issues of the day.[43]

Other major HPA campaigns have included increasing transgender awareness, supporting net neutrality, fighting against income disparity, and petitioning for marriage equality.[44] But perhaps The HPA's most famous campaign was its "Not in Harry's Name" movement, which started in 2011 and called for Warner Brothers to immediately cease using non-fair trade cacao (that was likely harvested by child slaves) in their chocolate frog candies[45]; HPA members cleverly argued that this business practice was equivalent to the wizarding world's (ab)use of house elves, and thus needed to end.[46] The HPA relentlessly waged this battle for several years before Warner Brothers finally acquiesced to the pressure in early 2015. This decision was big enough that the *Washington Post* ran an article entitled "How *Harry Potter* Fans Won a Four-Year Fight Against Child Slavery," in which the author, Alyssa Rosenberg, contended that the victory was "a fascinating symbol of what activism might look like when it's animated by fiction rather than political parties and when fans form coalitions with devoted advocates."[47]

Notably, the Harry Potter Alliance has even earned praise from J.K. Rowling herself; in a 2007 write-up about the author, *Time* magazine reporter Nancy Gibbs noted:

> When asked about [The HPA], Rowling practically levitates off the couch, spilling her coffee along the way. "It's incredible, it's humbling, and it's uplifting to see people going out there and doing that in the name of your character," she says. She's especially pleased by the group's choice of mission, and the old Amnesty International worker in her surfaces. "What did my books preach against throughout? Bigotry, violence, struggles for power, no matter what. All of these things are happening in Darfur. So they really couldn't have chosen a better cause."[48]

In fact, so touched was Rowling by the HPA's early efforts that on December 21, 2007, she bestowed the organization with an official "J.K. Rowling Fan Site Award," recognizing the HPA for "exemplify[ing] the values for which Dumbledore's Army fought in the books."[49]

Today, The Harry Potter Alliance is a sophisticated charity, staffed by six people and governed by a board of seven directors (including Melissa Anelli, the founder and headmistress of The Leaky Cauldron fansite, and Matt Maggiacomo of The Whomping Willows). With dozens of chapters and over 100,000 members worldwide,[50] it can thus call upon a great reserve of activism energy to continue the work that first made Rowling proud almost a decade ago.

For those wrock bands that do not have the resources of the vast Harry Potter Alliance (which is to say, almost all of them), a perhaps less grandiose but nevertheless effective method for increasing awareness or raising money is the compilation album. While charity records have long been a staple of the music industry, their application in the wrock community began when, according to Matt Maggiacomo, "Harry and the Potters created a sense in the first couple waves of wizard rock bands that [bands] needed to integrate some sort of charity or advocacy component into the community."[51]

While one could perhaps consider the first large-scale "charity compilation" to be the entirety of the 2007 Wizard Rock EP of the Month Club, the first bona fide wrock charity album was the inaugural volume of the *Wizards and Muggles Rock for Social Justice* compilation, released on July 1, 2007. Produced by Maggiacomo, this record brought together some of the biggest bands in wizard rock, making the record a veritable time capsule that accurately portrays the stylistic make-up of the scene at the time. Upon its release, the album was a smash success and his since managed to raise over $4,000 for the Harry Potter Alliance.[52] This achievement inspired Maggiacomo to release three subsequent volumes (in 2008, 2013, and 2017, respectively), and a best-of compilation (in 2013).

A few months after the release of *Wizards and Muggles Rock for Social Justice*, the Leaky Cauldron, a popular *Harry Potter* fansite operated by Melissa Anelli, released the next major charity album entitled *Jingle Spells*. The compilation has its origin in the Leaky Cauldron's annual "Get a Clue" literacy drive, in which money was raised to purchase books and construct libraries for needy people in impoverished countries. While this drive had previously taken on the form of a traditional fundraiser (i.e., fans donated what they could, often getting nothing in return), Anelli decided that the 2007 drive should be different, and in mid–October 2007, she made the following announcement:

> The holiday season is nearly upon us, so we asked 14 of the biggest and best wizard rock bands around to donate a Christmas or Holiday themed song for a very special compilation album [entitled *Jingle Spells*]. They all did so with enthusiasm, and what we now have to offer you for our fundraiser is one of the best holiday albums any of us has heard. Even if you don't like wizard rock, we're sure you're going to love this. We've had it on repeat for a few weeks now. It is all-new music, from 14 different bands, and buying the album is the *only* way you can hear the music on it. It's a perfect gift for yourself or anyone else you know who loves *Harry Potter*. It's for a good cause. It's a holiday gift and a holiday good deed, all rolled into one.[53]

The release was carefully curated, and the fourteen bands featured on the album—which included Harry and the Potters, Draco and the Malfoys, The Parselmouths, The Whomping Willows, and The Moaning Myrtles—were all handpicked by Anelli and her staff.[54]

Anelli ordered 3000 copies of the album and began advertising it on the Leaky Cauldron in late October 2007. Although a single copy cost 15 dollars, the album was quickly snatched up by fans and was out of print by the end of the year. When all was said and done, the compilation managed to raise over $30,000 for Book Aid International. This sum is particularly impressive when one realizes that it matched the earnings of the Leaky Cauldron's five previous "Get a Clue" drives *combined*.[55] The success of *Jingle Spells* ultimately led to the Leaky Cauldron releasing four more volumes in 2008, 2009, 2010, and 2011.

The bands that were featured on the first three *Jingle Spells* compilations were personally solicited by Leaky Cauldron staffers. However, when it came time to put together *Jingle Spells 4* (2010), Anelli decided to be less elitist, and so she set up a contest that allowed smaller bands to submit tracks for consideration. If these tracks were deemed worthy, they were included on the album next to songs by the bands who had previously been included on an "invite-only" basis, such as Harry and the Potters. And a year later, when *Jingle Spells 5* (2011) was being compiled, Anelli went a step further and opened up the entire album to submissions; those tracks which were selected were included on a physical release of the album, and those which just missed the cut were released as a free "supplementary" download.[56] Unfortunately, the 2011 volume of *Jingle Spells* would be the last. By 2012, interest in wizard rock had started to wane, and it seems that Anelli realized there might not be enough interest to justify the time, energy, and capital needed to produce a *Jingle Spells 6*.

Thanks to the resounding success of the *Wizards and Muggles Rock for Social Justice* and the *Jingle Spells* series, dozens of other wrock bands have been inspired to curate and release their own charity records, including but not limited to: *Rocking Out Against Voldemedia* (compiled in 2007 by the Harry Potter Alliance to sound alarms about media consolidation and extreme press bias), *Letters from Hogwarts* (compiled in 2008 by Steph Anderson of Tonks and the Aurors to benefit To Write Love on Her Arms), *Witches Wrock* (compiled in 2008 by the Leaky Cauldron to raise money for breast cancer research), *Siriusly Smiling: A Wizard Rock Charity Compilation* (compiled in 2008 by Jarrod Perkins of Gred and Forge to benefit the National Foundation for Facial Reconstruction/myFace), *Hogwarts Halloween* (compiled in 2010 by Brett Holden of Slytherin Soundtrack to benefit the Harry Potter Alliance), and *Wrock Hard Ditties* (compiled in 2011 by Anvil and the Hints to benefit the Pink Ribbon Day campaign).[57]

As this litany of charity records perhaps suggests, wrockers are ready and willing to donate their own music to compilations. Arguably, this is because there exists a deep desire in the hearts of many wrockers to "give back," or to contribute to causes about which they feel strongly. But in addition to altruistic reasons, it should be noted that many bands sign onto charity compilations because these records also serve as an excellent way to gain new audiences. Consider a hypothetical charity album featuring ten songs from ten different artists. Chances are that each band is going to promote the record to their fans—fans who might have never heard of the other groups on the record. This means that, in this hypothetical, a band would have the potential to magnify their audience by a factor ten. So in the end, charity albums help everyone involved: the causes that these records support get much-needed funding, and the bands that contribute get the opportunity to widen their fanbase.

The Dark Side of Wizard Rock

So far in this chapter, I have discussed how wrockers have used their imaginative movement to positively impact the "Muggle" world through political engagement, social activism, and humanitarian fundraising. But despite often viewing itself as being a pure force for good, the wrock community is not free from those who also attempt to abuse their popularity and act in decidedly wicked ways. In 2014, the community sadly learned this the hard way.[58]

In March of that year, Rosianna Halse Rojas, (an online vlogger and the personal assistant of the author and internet celebrity John Green) took to social media and bravely revealed that when she was 16, she had been in a toxic and abusive relationship with Alex Carpenter of The Remus Lupins, who at the time was well into his mid–20s.[59] Roja's story was a bomb shell, and it resulted in a number of other fandom members speaking out and revealing that they too had been mistreated by Carpenter. Horrifically, it turned out that many in the wrock community knew of Carpenter's (often-abusive) relationships, but that these same people had never once questioned his despicable behavior for whatever reason.[60] Following the subsequent Internet storm, Carpenter disbanded The Remus Lupins and retreated from the view of social media; soon thereafter, he was dropped from his label, DFTBA Records, by the label's co-owner Hank Green (the brother of John Green).[61]

The situation grew even darker when a few days later, Kristina Horner of The Parselmouths came forward and revealed that she had been in an emotionally and sexually abusive relationship with Ministry of Magic member Luke Conard for a number of years.[62] These allegations were later echoed by YouTuber Whitney Milam, who admitted that Conard had emotionally and sexually abused her, too.[63] Conard took to his Tumblr in an attempt to smooth things over, but his attempt at an apology was met with mostly negative reactions from online users, many of whom rightfully derided him for trying to excuse his repellent behavior by dabbling in victim-blaming.[64] The resulting outcry became so great that Conard's bandmate and friend Jason Munday renounced wizard rock as "one of the worst things [he had] ever encountered," effectively ending Ministry of Magic.[65]

6. Wizard Rock and the "Muggle World"

When news of these scandals broke, it raced like wildfire across the Internet and did two things. First, it shattered the illusion that many fans had had (even if they may have known in the back of their minds that it was unrealistic) about wizard rock being an egalitarian community, fueled by love and free from the evils that befall other sorts of movements. These once-optimistic fans quickly realized that wizard rock, despite its noble intentions, was a human institution and as with all human institutions, people can assume positions of power and then use those positions of power to take advantage of others.

But the news also had a second, more positive effect: hundreds of wrock content creators and fans alike refused to be bystanders and instead spoke out. Many of the *de facto* leaders in the community led this charge, arguing that fans and content creators—especially those who consider the wrock community as their home—have a moral duty to listen to and be compassionate toward survivors of abuse. The scene's leaders also encouraged those who wanted to see wizard rock be a safe place to reclaim their community. Matt Maggiacomo, for instance, wrote on his blog:

> I have always been willing to share my opinions on serious matters that have had the potential to negatively impact the wizard rock community and the greater HP fandom. This situation with all the allegations of abuse, coercion, and emotional manipulation against YouTube content creators is no different, and I have spent the last 36 hours trying to bring all my thoughts together to form something coherent. [I] think it's important that we remain focused on the most important thing, which is supporting those survivors of abuse who are brave enough to come forward with their stories.... To those who feel that wizard rock was the last refuge from the bullshit and is no longer a safe space, I say let's take time to heal and then let's take it back.... To my fellow male wrockers and fandom celebrities—if you're like me (i.e., introspective to a fault), you've probably spent the last 36 hours taking a long look at your past actions and engaging in some serious self-examination. I have gone through this process and emerged feeling pretty lousy. Nobody is perfect; everyone makes mistakes and I've certainly made my share. We can all strive to be better.
>
> So let's do that. Let's strive to be better, stronger, kinder, more generous and open and honest people. Let's view others as our equals and stop taking their support for granted. I have heard so many content creators speak of their fans and viewers as if they are nothing more than a paycheck, and this type of attitude is the first step toward dehumanizing people and feeling entitled to take whatever you want from them. Wizard rock has always tried to bridge the gap between band and fan in ways that are healthy and positive. We're supposed to be role models. Let's get back to owning that role.[66]

The Harry Potter Alliance likewise wrote:

> Sexual assault, sexual opportunism, and emotional manipulation are all unacceptable behaviors that should have no place in the *Harry Potter* fandom or anywhere else. The challenges we face on this front are systemic. They stem from deep-seated societal issues that are not unique to our community; they are a part of our culture. But

we have the opportunity to reject these aspects of culture. We can work to create solutions to these problems. Culture will evolve only when we play an active role in shaping it.

The Harry Potter Alliance is deeply committed to fostering a safe and healthy fan community. We are currently working with a Nerdfighter task force and LeakyCon to help make our fandom better, and seeking the advice and partnership of several professional organizations with experience handling these matters to make sure we do it right.

Being part of a fandom is a shared responsibility. If fandom is a place that you love and call home—if fandom is your Hogwarts—now is not the time to abandon it. Now is the time to stay and defend it.[67]

And perhaps most poignantly, Lauren Fairweather wrote:

This community is worth fixing. It's worth standing up for. And I'm not willing to walk away when it needs me most. I'm in this for the long haul. I'm not done fighting. But I can't do this alone.[68]

These individuals—and many more—recognized that what had happened was horrendous and that it could not be undone. At the same time, they realized that they could support those who had been hurt and also work to prevent things like this from happening again.

So how did it come to pass that a community which expressly prided itself on inclusion and egalitarianism produced this sort of abuse? The musicologist Aya Esther Hayashi pondered this exact question in her 2018 dissertation, "Musicking, Discourse, and Identity in Participatory Media Fandom." She argues that much of the literature surrounding fan spaces—including wizard rock—portrays these communities uncritically as "utopic" and "free of the conflicts that have been studied in other fan communities."[69] This understanding of fan spaces as utopic also extends to the fans who are a part of these spaces. Unfortunately, Hayashi notes that this is problematic: "When we idealize something too much, it can ultimately foster unsafe spaces [because we fail to] recognize that fan musical spaces are, in fact, also prone to creating hierarchies and inequalities."[70] It seems that this is exactly what happened with wizard rock. When abusers began preying on fellow members of the wrock community, many did not want to believe that this sort of behavior was happening in a community that they had (over-)idealized. This problem was compounded by some victims keeping quiet about the abuse that they had suffered for fear that others would criticize them for lying, seeking attention, or attempting to besmirch the name of wizard rock. But perhaps most damaging is that those who knew about the abuse often turned a blind eye to it, hoping not to rock the boat and destroy the community's reputation. This resulted in the perfect storm: for a time, abusers had the ability to target victims, relatively free from consequences.

The good news is that since 2014, many within the wrock community have been openly vocal in their support for abuse victims, as well in their condemnation of the abusers (almost all of whom have been driven from wizard rock by the consensus of the community). The scene has also become more vigilant and is thankfully less willing to excuse activities that might have previously gone uncommented upon. And while it would be completely foolish to say that wizard rock has reached a state of perfection or that the increased awareness somehow makes up for the horrendous transgressions of the past, it does not seem unreasonable to argue that the scene is now a better, safer, and more enjoyable place for wrockers and fans alike. Ultimately, the fact that the scene was able to re-evaluate itself and make itself safer for all members is, to quote Paul DeGeorge, "a testament to the strength and power of the overall community."[71]

"The Weapon We Have Is Love"

In the almost decade that I have spent as a wrocker, I have come across a handful of people who like to belittle or malign the movement. Often, in a tone dripping with condescension, they will ask me a variation of the following question: "Isn't it childish to sing songs about a kid's book? I mean, what do you hope to accomplish?" Whenever I get this question—which I am fully aware is meant to be deprecatingly rhetorical—I calmly inform them about organizations like the Harry Potter Alliance, or the *Jingle Spells* charity album series. I explain that while wizard rock may seem like a silly and foolish pastime, the members of the community have done much to make the world a better place. This answer does not always satisfy my detractors, but I am happy to say that it has numerous times managed to combat the smug attitude of critics.

I relay this story, not because I have an axe to grind, but rather because I believe it emphasizes the very point of this chapter: despite wizard rock's seemingly silly exterior, philanthropy and activism is at the heart of the movement, with many bands espousing the morals, ethics, and values that are to be gleaned from the *Harry Potter* novels. What is more, this reality is not only indexed by the sentiments that wrockers and wrock fans openly express, but also by what they literally do to bring about the change of which they speak. And even when some wrock band members abuse their positions of power, countless others within the community have shown the quality of their character by both repudiating behaviors that they believe are evil as well as by supporting victims of abuse.

7

The Wider World of Wizard Rock

In the fall of 2011, Trina and I enrolled as freshman at the University of Kansas, and after several months of growing pains, we finally became accustomed to university life. But while we spent most of our time prepping for exams or researching for papers, we never forgot about wizard rock, and we continued to dream up new parody ideas.

When classes concluded in December of that year, we retreated back to my house and began recording some of these tunes. By the spring of 2012, we had a third album completed, which we titled *Ridiculously Wicked*. After the rather laborious process of mixing our tracks and designing our album art, we slated the record for a summer release.

Our previous three albums had seen a somewhat limited circulation, given that we had really only sold them from our lockers at school and to people who we ran into at the local library. With *Ridiculously Wicked*, however, we were determined to make a splash; we wanted to get the wrock community's attention this time.

But how exact did we plan to do that? Our experience in the world of wizard rock had taught us that the scene is only partially about the musicians: in fact, there are many non-musically inclined wrock fans who lurk somewhat "behind the scenes," but who are nonetheless integral to the community's continuation—e.g., bloggers, critics, radio DJs, wrock encyclopedia editors. It was this portion of the wrock world that we turned to in our quest to maximize our album's impact.

We began our plan of attack in the winter of 2012 by first attempting to get our music played on the radio. To do this, we sent our parodies to the Whitman College radio station, 90.5 KWCW, based out of Walla Walla, Washington. Why of all available stations did we send our music there? Quite simply, because the station hosted a one-of-a-kind program known as The Witching Hour that played nothing but wizard rock; in fact, the DJs of the

7. The Wider World of Wizard Rock

program had previously reached out to us and let us know that they had played some of our spoofs on the air. The thought of making a few promo CD singles—an increasingly archaic practice in this day and age of digital media, and a practice practically unheard of amongst amateur wrock bands—was too enticing to pass up, and so we hand-crafted two singles for our songs "Crabbe and Goyle" and "If You Wanna Rock at Quidditch," respectively (each complete with unique covers, liner notes, and a few "rare" b-sides). We then dutiful shipped them to the station, and much to our excitement, both songs made their college radio debut in late January 2012.

Our second concern was contacting the various wrock encyclopedias and blogs that zealously catalogue every release in the community. The first site that we reached out to was the principal hub of wrock-related news, the Wizrocklopedia. In an impassioned and detailed email, we let the editors of the site know that The 8th Horcrux would soon be releasing a new album in the near future, and that we—in our own humble and highly unbiased opinions—thought this was our best record yet (alas, little did we realize that the site was on the brink of digital collapse). We also contacted sites like the French wrock zine *Poudlard Mag* and the Tumblr-based "news network" DFTBA News, scheduling interviews and holding promotional contests that we hoped would build up hype and entice readers to check out our new parodies.

Finally, we also took to Twitter and Facebook, not only to advertise our new music to our friends and fans, but to also reach out to those within the community who might have been able to influence others. We focused much of our effort on contacting Wrock Snob, the enigmatic reviewer of wizard rock. While the eminent wrock critic never did a full or official review of our album, they did post several positive tweets about our music, which at the time was good enough for us.

By the time our album came out on July 1, 2012, it felt as if we had journeyed to every corner of the greater wrock community, leaving no stone unturned in our (rather shameless, if I do admit) mission of self-promotion. And once we took the time to look back, we were quite astounded at how much ground we had covered. Who knew how substantial the non-musician side of wizard rock—the "wider world of wizard rock," as I have now come to call it—actually was?

* * *

Most treatments of wizard rock in popular media focus almost entirely on two things: the wrock bands, and the songs that they write. This is perhaps to be expected, as wizard rock *is* a type of music first and foremost. But by concentrating on only the most obvious aspects of the scene, these considerations often fail to shine a light on whole swaths of the wrock community.

This is problematic, because when one begins to explore the makeup of the community in a detailed manner, it becomes immediately apparent that it is not composed merely of bands, but also individuals who embrace various modes of fandom participation, and whose interests range from blogging all the way to documentary filmmaking. These individuals play a major part in the wrock community, but given that they are somewhat "behind the scenes," they are unfortunately often overshadowed by the bands whose existence they enable.

In an attempt to ameliorate this issue, the present chapter focuses minimally on major bands and musicians, instead devoting attention to what I like to call "the wider world of wizard rock" and those who make up this part of the community. The first portion considers "wrock radio" programs, such as *WZRD*, *The Witching Hour*, and wrockBOX. I then explore the importance of online wrock resources, like the Wizrocklopedia and *Your Wizard Rock Resource*, before discussing the creation and reception of wrock-centered documentary projects. The final portion of this chapter looks at music criticism within the wrock community, and award shows that have been established to celebrate musicians in the scene. With this chapter, it is my ultimate goal to show how wrock fans who might otherwise prefer disparate modes of fandom engagement still manage to come together and form a single community.

Radio

When you turn on the radio, what types of music do you normally hear? Rap? Rock? Generic pop? Image if you were to switch the dial and out from your speaker emanated not the latest top 40 hit, but rather a wrock song. Wizard rock is such an underground phenomenon that the previous sentence might seem like just a ridiculous thought experiment. However, a bona fide tradition that can only be described as "wrock radio" has indeed emerged over the last decade or so, and people all over the world have been tuning in.

Most people consider the origins of this "wrock radio" to be rooted not in a radio program at all, but rather a podcast by the name of *WZRD: The Wizard Rock Station*, which was created and hosted by Amy Snow and Jamie Walker from 2006–10. Prior to the founding of *WZRD*, Snow, a musician from Ireland, was pursuing a joint undergraduate degree in music and drama/theatre studies; in her spare time, she also played in her own wrock band, Romilda Vane and the Chocolate Cauldrons. Walker, on the other hand, lived in Illinois and was a student of digital media communications. Despite hailing from different continents separated by a vast stretch of ocean, the two came to know one another through an online *Harry Potter*-centered

7. The Wider World of Wizard Rock 153

LiveJournal community, and thanks in large part to their shared interest, they became fast friends.[1]

Snow had long been a fan of *Pottercast*, the official podcast of the Leaky Cauldron fansite, and in 2005 she began developing ideas for her own that would center on wizard rock. After sharing her idea with Walker, the two agreed to collaborate on the program, and following a few months of brainstorming and planning, *WZRD: The Wizard Rock Station* officially launched in March 2006.[2]

Each episode ran for roughly thirty-five minutes, and usually featured select tracks and wrock-related news, all of which was interspersed with Snow and Walker's commentary and general banter. Later episodes also featured "wrock celebrity" guest hosts, such as Lizz Clements (founder and webmaster of Wizrocklopedia), Grace Kendall (of the band Snidget), Doug "Jace" McDonald (frontman of Catchlove), and Mallory and Megan Schuyler (co-directors of *The Wizard Rockumentary*), among many others. And while *WZRD* was online-only (sans one show that was held live at the Terminus fan convention in Chicago), Snow and Walker strove to make it feel as much like a genuine radio station as possible. This included the soliciting of "bumpers" from famous bands (like The Moaning Myrtles, Snidget, and Peeved), which were then interspersed between songs.[3]

Producing *WZRD* was a somewhat laborious and time-consuming process, due to both technological as well as logistical issues, as Snow notes:

> It used to take hours to edit the sound files together, especially when there were multiple voices and microphones of varying qualities.... We had the best of intentions to release episodes on a regular basis, but with half the team in Europe and half in the States, it was impossible! People used to email us and ask when the next episode would be coming, and Jamie and I would guiltily MSN each other trying to get another one going.[4]

Snow and Walker worked on the project for about three and a half years. However, by the end of the podcast's run, Snow—who was increasingly busy setting up and running her own business teaching music—was finding less and less free time to dedicate to the production of *WZRD*; she eventually left the program a few months before Walker officially ended it in late 2009. In total, around 50 *WZRD* episodes were recorded and aired.[5]

Unfortunately, due to the transient nature of the Internet, much of *WZRD* has been washed away: online records of the station are incomplete, and the blip.tv site that once hosted the podcast's episodes has since expunged the files from its servers. Nevertheless, memories of *WZRD* are still cherished by many, including Snow:

> I loved [*WZRD* and] having the opportunity to connect with musicians.... It amazes me to this day when I get tweets or messages saying people remember WZRD.... The

most rewarding feedback for me is that people loved the parts when Jamie and I were just chatting about things.... We loved the bands, the material they were producing, the idea that everyone was coming together because of *Harry Potter* to do good things.[6]

Understandably, many bemoaned the passing of *WZRD* into Internet history. But fortunately for fans of wrock, the year after Snow and Walker's podcast went off the air, two students at Whitman College in Walla Walla, Washington, were dreaming up something even more extravagant.

The students in question were Mehera Nori and Sara Rasmussen, who met in 2008 during their first year at Whitman. Nori and Rasmussen—both of whom were *Harry Potter* fans—had fortuitously been placed in the same section of a class, and after Rasmussen noticed that Nori was wearing a Harry and the Potters shirt, the two struck up a conversation. Due to their mutual interests, they quickly became friends.[7]

A few years later, Rasmussen noticed an announcement from Whitman College's radio station 90.5 KWCW that actively encouraged students to participate in the running of the station; this included proposing ideas for and hosting unique programming. After pondering the announcement for a bit, Rasmussen approached Nori—who at the time was hosting her own show on KWCW—and asked if she had any interest co-hosting a program about *Harry*

Mehera Nori (left), Sarah Rasmussen (center), and Clair Riordan (right), broadcast an episode of The Witching Hour from Whitman College's KWCW radio station in 2011 (courtesy Ben Hovland).

Potter. Nori was amenable to the idea, and the two got to planning.[8] Initially, Nori and Rasmussen intended for their program to mostly focus on discussing the books, with the occasional Harry and the Potters' song thrown in for good measure, but according to Rasmussen: "Then we started really researching, and discovered so many more [wrock] bands. And it really grew from there. It began as a show about *Harry Potter* [but became] more about *Harry Potter* fan culture."[9]

They soon dubbed their project *The Witching Hour*, after a program of the same name that in the book series aired on the "Wizarding Wireless Network." The show launched in January 2010 and aired Monday nights. At first, *The Witching Hour* ran, as its name suggests, for an hour each week, but once the station recognized the sheer amount of material that Nori and Rasmussen had to work with, KWCW extended the program to two hours. During their time on the air, the show's hosts would spin a number of wrock tracks that they had handpicked the week prior. Most shows had some sort of overriding theme (e.g., "Gryffindor," "potions," "parody songs") around which all the songs selections would be based. During each episode, Nori and Rasmussen would play a string of songs before interjecting with their own insightful commentary. In particular, the two often discussed how the themes of the *Harry Potter* books could be applied to everyday life, and how many of the books' topics "intersect with political and social issues in the real world."[10] In regard to the latter point, Nori noted:

> It's great having … politics majors run the show, because there are just so many topics in the books that are so relevant. We've talked about racism, we've talked about sexism, we've talked about homophobia. My academic experience at Whitman meshes surprisingly well with the show and what we talk about on the air.[11]

The hosts also invited guest onto the program to discuss a wide range of subjects, including the *Harry Potter* series, its fandom, and the wrock community. Sometimes these guests were from Whitman, and sometimes they were not; one memorable instance of the latter occurred when Paul and Joe DeGeorge "took over" the show for a special midnight episode immediately preceding the release of *Harry Potter and the Deathly Hallows, Pt. I* (2010)—an episode which, according to Nori, "featured a lot of [the punk band] Fugazi."[12]

While much of the program's content was based around the output of the more popular wrock bands, like Harry and the Potters, Draco and the Malfoys, or The Remus Lupins, *The Witching Hour* was also willing to play tracks from lesser-known artists. This made it in many ways like a wrock version of Los Angeles's famous radio station KROQ in that *The Witching Hour* helped to expose smaller bands to a larger audience the world over.

To promote their show, Nori and Rasmussen employed fun, idiosyncratic, and creative methods, one of which included the hanging up of flyers that resembled Dolores Umbridge's "educational decrees" from the *Order of the Phoenix* film.[13] The decree, "No. 2011" (reflecting the year it was "issued"), demanded that "all students ... listen every week to *The Witching Hour*."

When they first started broadcasting, Nori claims that she and Rasmussen got either "one of two reactions: excitement and enthusiasm, or really judgy looks."[14] But while some people simply did not understand the point of a wrock radio program, many others—including, importantly, the management of KWCW—did. And after a few transmissions, wrock fans from outside the greater Walla Walla area began tuning in to the show. This increase in audience size might have been affected by the co-hosts' decision to post each show on iTunes as downloadable podcasts. Whatever the cause, *The Witching Hour*'s listeners quickly began to balloon, and by 2012, the program was being heard by a monthly audience of around 900 people—of which a surprising portion lived outside of the United States.[15] The program was even broadcast to the nearby Washington State Penitentiary, and much to the surprise of the program's co-hosts, a number of inmates became avid listeners and even sent in thoughtful fan mail.[16] The run-away success of the program combined with the breadth of its audience caught its hosts off guard; in a 2012, interview with Whitman, Nori exclaimed, "We were so surprised when we started hearing from people outside of Whitman. I'm still surprised to hear from people at Whitman!"[17]

Although *The Witching Hour* truly was Rasmussen and Nori's personal pet project—after all, they had almost single-handedly created, organized, and co-hosted the program for nearly two and a half years—the program luckily did not perish when they graduated in 2012. Instead, the torch was passed to Claire Riordan and Anu Lingappa, the former of whom had become a co-host in 2011, and the latter of whom had signed on in 2013.[18] In an interview, Rasmussen emphasized to me that both Riordan and Lingappa were instrumental in ensuring the continued success of *The Witching Hour*'s success, and that each managed to put their own unique spin on the show (for instance, Lingappa, who was a science student, hosted episodes on the "science of wizardry" and "magical maladies").[19]

Lingappa found the experience particularly therapeutic, telling me in an interview:

> *The Witching Hour* was special for me because of how genuinely happy I felt when I was there in the studio. Our Monday night time slot was directly after I got out of a three-hour organic chemistry lab. Every week I would show up frazzled, stressed out, and basically on the verge of tears (O Chem did not come naturally to me). However, having an outlet to revel in how much we all love *Harry Potter* without any judgment was probably the best form of self-care possible. The studio was a magical place in and of itself, where just entering would make me feel so light and unburdened. The things that made me sad and stressed out all belonged outside the studio.[20]

7. The Wider World of Wizard Rock 157

When it inevitably came time for Riordan and Lingappa to graduate, they too passed *The Witching Hour* onto their protégée, Erin Walters. (According to Lingappa, "I [met Erin] at a meeting of the campus feminist group, which seemed quite appropriate since I was first formally introduced to Mehera at one of those meetings. Erin made a very obscure and witty *Harry Potter* reference and I loved it. I knew she would be perfect for the show."[21]) This trend of "passing the torch" to a new cohort of radio hosts has continued to the present day, and as of April 2018, the program is in the hands of Megan Gleason and Jane Kern, who have devoted much of their energy into ensuring that Rasmussen and Nori's "noble and most ancient legacy"—to quote Walters—gets passed down "through generations of Whitman students [and] lives on."[22]

As one might imagine, projects like *WZRD* and *The Witching Hour* have done much to sate the desires of wrock fans who are eager to hear wrock in a traditional, radio(-esque) setting. But these programs unfortunately air only occasionally—sometimes once a week, sometimes once a month. What many wrock fans have yearned for is a 24-hour radio station that plays nothing but wizard rock. But while a desire like this might be viewed as an unrealistic pipe dream, the truth is that such a platform did at one point exist. It was known as wrockBOX, and during its brief existence in the early 2010s, it delighted wrock bands and fans alike.

wrockBOX was the brainchild of Keith Cardin,[23] the Executive Director of Wizarding Life Networks. He, along with Wizarding Life contributor "Apple-Tonks," worked tirelessly to create the website and compile its musical selection.[24] To acquire playlists, the two took to contacting wrockers and asking them if they would be willing to have their music streamed through the site. If the bands were amenable to this request, they were sent a Dropbox link, into which they could deposit their tracks.[25] These songs were then uploaded to the wrockBOX server, and fans who were listening to the stream could then use a feature called "Accio" to request songs that they wanted to hear.

wrockBOX advertised itself as an "Internet radio station," but it was more innovative than such a simple descriptor suggests. For one thing, Cardin structured the station so songs that were playing would link to their artists' existing social media accounts, resulting in a truly interconnected wrock experience. According to its website in early 2011:

> wrockBOX serves not only as an online radio station, but also a platform for both existing and emerging wizard rock bands to gather a new audience. Bands also have the ability to sync their songs with their iTunes singles, albums and even link to your social media sites like MySpace, Facebook and Twitter. Every time your song plays, the listener can see 'who,' 'from what album,' 'where can I buy it' and 'how can I find you?'[26]

The station also featured a simplistic but user-friendly chat room (which some called the "crackBOX" because it was "so addictive")[27] that enabled communication between listeners. Through this channel, listeners could talk with one another, discuss the station's playlist, and compliment the artists whose songs were being played. Some wrock bands even took to directly communicating with their fans through this feature.

The station had a soft opening on January 26, 2011, before "officially" launching on February 1. Within its first official week of operation, 88 wrock bands had uploaded their music to the station,[28] and roughly 2,000 wrock fans tuned in to give it a listen.[29] wrockBOX very quickly went from being an underground achievement to a smash success. And because it provided fans with a means to hear new songs, as well as fledgling artists with a way to broadcast their music to a wider audience, the station nestled itself snuggly into many a wrocker's heart. Grace Kendall, for instance, nostalgically recalls:

> [wrockBOX] was such a gift to the universe. We would turn on the station and try and guess which bands we were listening to. Sometimes it got stuck on having the same few bands play … but in general it got a good mix of lesser-known wizard rockers. [It was] such a great service for the community when it was live.[30]

And so beneficial was the program that a number of wrock bands have directly credited wrockBOX with increasing both the number of their fans as well as their record sales.

Unfortunately, only a few months after its debut, wrockBOX's server began struggling to keep up with the demand of its myriad listeners, and this technological strain resulted in the station going on- and off-line multiple times. To make matters worse, a number of these reboots resulted in the station's music server being wiped, meaning that bands had to re-upload their tracks if they wanted their music to be streamed. The deathblow, however, came in the summer of 2011, when wrockBOX suffered a technical difficulty that effectively derailed the station for a year. For reasons unknown, attempts to resuscitate wrockBOX were put on hold.[31]

But then, in July 2012, wrockBOX was re-launched as part of myHogwarts.co.uk, which had been created in the hopes of being an MMORPG fansite, complete with online wizarding classes.[32] From its new home, the radio continued to stream wizard rock 24/7, but this incarnation was more stripped down and streamlined. At the same time, the station also began to stream increasingly creative content, such as gag commercials for in-universe products, and "shoutouts from wizard rockers, talk shows, podcasts, real Quidditch matches, and DJ-hosted programming."[33] Unfortunately, during its myHogwarts.co.uk years, wrockBOX's playlist became extremely limited, largely due to the number of times its server had to be rebooted.[34]

wrockBOX and its newfound parent website lasted until the close of 2012; by the end of the year, lawyers from Warner Brothers, uncomfortable with myHogwarts.co.uk's online classes and fearing that they bordered on copyright infringement, asked that the site be taken offline. Not wanting to cause a scene, those who were running myHogwarts.co.uk obliged. Sadly, when myHogwarts.co.uk went down, so too did wrockBOX.[35]

Although wrockBOX was once again briefly resurrected in 2014 as a stand-alone website,[36] its return proved to be only temporary. Today the only thing that really remains of the radio station are archived webpages and scattered references to it on long-abandoned social media pages.

Online Encyclopedias

In a video discussing the loss of digital information and what one might call "digital decay," the author and vlogger John Green said, "I feel like we citizens of the Internet are in general better at creating stuff than we are at preserving, curating, and archiving it."[37] This quote is particularly important to consider in a book about the wrock community, because while a plethora of creative content was being unleashed upon the world during wizard rock's apex, many at the time did not recognize the need to archive or document that which was happening in the scene. Unfortunately, this oversight resulted in an untold amount of information being lost: key MySpace posts vanished, wrock blogs were deleted, and websites fell into disuse and eventually went offline. And while tools like the Internet Archive have certainly enabled wrock historians to recover some of this digital material, searching online for "lost" information can feel a bit like dredging the ocean: provided enough time and effort, bits of information will almost certainly be retrieved, but much of it has already been lost in a vast and impermeable void. Consequently, the importance of wrock encyclopedias—websites that have attempted to preserve the history of wizard rock for posterity—cannot be understated.

Perhaps the most important wrock encyclopedia is the appropriately named Wizrocklopedia (often affectionately referred to by fans as "The 'Pedia"), which was founded in September 2006 by Lizz Clements. According to its own website, the Wizrocklopedia exists for "the sole purpose of celebrating, promoting, and exploring wizard rock in all its aspects."[38]

The site has its origins in wizard rock's "golden age" (ca. 2005–06): a period in which dozens of bands were forming and recording songs. During this time, Clements—a writer by trade who was a wrock fan on the side—realized the very same problem that was touched upon at the start of this section: while a plethora of wrock content was being created, little if any of it was being documented by one central source. She thus took it upon herself to create the ultimate wrock resource, which could be used to both broadcast wizard rock-related news, as well as detail the burgeoning scene for those who wanted to know more about it.[39] In 2007, the site made its mission statement clear:

> While the *Harry Potter* fandom is well represented as a whole, we felt as if the current information being provided on wizard rock, the music, and the bands, was insufficient. We aim to record the past, present, and future of all things related to wizard rock and hope to shed more light on the movement itself. There has yet to be one place for those to discover the ins and outs of wizard rock. We intend to provide all the possible information a newcomer or seasoned veteran could wish to find.[40]

Clements took to discussing live shows, reviewing new albums, and posting links to fledgling bands' MySpace pages. Her audience at first was limited, but as word of wizard rock made its way throughout the *Harry Potter* fandom, Clements saw her readership grow dramatically, hitting a peak sometime in 2008.[41]

Within a year of its founding, the Wizrocklopedia was one of the most important wrock-related sites on the web (perhaps rivalled only by MySpace), for it was on this site that fans could read up on the history of the movement, learn about any bands in their area, or simply discuss wizard rock with other fans and musicians. And because the Wizrocklopedia became the go-to destination for wrock news—a veritable Wizard Rock MTV, if you will—bands who were hoping to make it big in the community often desperately sought to have their band name featured in any article that the site's writers might pen. Groups that were lucky enough to be mentioned or posted about often saw their popularity balloon overnight. Steph Anderson, for instance, told me, "In 2007, once Lizz first posted about Tonks and the Aurors, it made us. I saw the direct cause [and] effect with a huge surge of MySpace followers."[42] She further explained that being featured on the site "was the first indicator that you were officially in the scene."[43]

Initially, Clements ran the Wizrocklopedia by herself, but soon the world of wizard rock began to grow beyond what was reasonable for one person to cover. To ameliorate this issue, Clements sought outside help, and by 2007, the site had around 5–10 staff members posting news, penning reviews, and writing about newly formed bands.[44]

For almost half a decade, the Wizrocklopedia was the hub for all things wizard rock, but by 2010, it began to face increasingly challenging issues. For one thing, the cost of hosting the site grew and grew until it was more than the staff writers and editors could alone afford. On top of this, the site began to experience glitches and technical issues that its admins found themselves unable to easily resolve.[45] Eventually, the difficulties that the Wizrocklopedia faced grew so insurmountable that after July 13, 2010, the site stopped updating, and began to collect digital dust.[46] For many, this seemed like the end of the beloved site.

7. The Wider World of Wizard Rock   161

But the site was not dead just yet, and on April 18, 2013, it quietly returned. Senior editor Freya Fridy made the inaugural post on the rebooted site and revealed that Russ Benoit of the band Creevey Crisis had worked tirelessly to bring the Wizrocklopedia back. Fridy also took this opportunity to reveal that Benoit had been appointed the new editor-in-chief of the website.[47] From April 2013 until December 2014, the site posted updates, articles, and links, much as it had in the past. But while the site was back, it cannot be denied that it was a shade of its former self. Sadly, sometime after December 2014, this second version of the site went offline too, and within no time, the Wizrocklopedia domain[48] was also snatched up by a non–wizard rock–related blogger. For many, the Wizrocklopedia was finally a thing of the past.

But like Fawkes the phoenix[49] rising from (digital) ashes, the site simply refused to stay dead. In mid-2016, a new domain[50] was registered, and the information from the older site was transferred over to this new URL. Upon the site's third return in September 2016, staff writer Laura Dianiska posted a much-read update, which expressed the sense of optimism and reinvigoration that was sweeping the entire wrock community; she wrote:

> I can't speak for the entire team, but I know I'm super pumped to have the site back. I've been yearning for some fandom involvement since this summer, when I attended the Leviosa con in Las Vegas. I hadn't been to a con since Leaky 2012 and I was beyond overdue. I forgot how magical our little fandom was and still is. I forgot what it was like to sit in panels with like-minded folks and discuss our little book series through a critical lens. I forgot how it felt to sing along to Draco and the Malfoys with a room full of people doing the same thing.... All of this is to say, we're back wizards. We want to bring you some magical music news and reviews. We want to bring you new music you haven't heard yet. We want to throw it back and celebrate old-school wizard rock at its finest.[51]

In an update posted several months later, Dianiska admitted that her initial optimism had given away to a more pragmatic understanding of the technical and financial difficulties in running the site. Nevertheless, she affirmed the continuation of the site's wrock archive, and assured readers that the writers would try to publish more content in the future.[52] Soon thereafter, a GoFundMe fundraising page was set up, and ardent supports of the Wizrocklopedia managed to pledge $205 in just a few days—almost twice the amount needed not only to port the entire site over to a new server, but also to host it for an additional three years.[53] Given the role that the site had played in the development of wizard rock, it seems that long-time readers would simply not allow it to disappear into oblivion. And the site editors even openly poked fun at the number of times the site has almost gone under, writing, "We'll be here ... as long as someone is writing, recording, performing, posting videos of, or just plain discussing Wizard Rock. You can't really get rid of us, we've still got some more horcruxes left."[54]

As of writing, the Wizrocklopedia is still active. Unfortunately, its years-long vacillation between being on- and offline seems to have caused most of its former users—who were unsure as to the site's future—to permanently scatter and migrate to other corners of the Internet. This has led to a real need for a new encyclopedic site to emerge from the void and re-anchor the community in the digital sphere. On August 14, 2014, a site was founded that, today, looks like a possible contender: *Your Wizard Rock Resource*.[55]

The site was the creation of an Australian wrock fan named Susannah,[56] who by her own admission has "never attended a wrock concert in person" but who all the same is fascinated with collecting wrock song lyrics and album information.[57] Prior to her interest in wizard rock, Susannah had honed her transcription skills by listening to her favorite songs and then transliterating their lyrics; to ensure the quality of her transcriptions, she would then compare her results with official lyrics that she found online. Susannah continued this practice when she started listening to wizard rock, but quickly grew frustrated when she was unable to find an active, comprehensive, and accurate wrock lyrics site. To rectify this issue, she decided to create one herself.[58]

However, Susannah quickly learned why a site did not yet exist: much of the information that she was seeking was buried in the digital rubble of dead sites or tucked away in online recesses that were otherwise hard to access. And in the case of some bands, it was if they had completely disappeared. Susannah explained, "Sometimes I [would] Google a band name and all I [would] get are a few links, which lead to [only] passing mentions by the Wrock Snob. In those instances, it's more fruitful to ask people directly if they know anything about that band."[59] She surmises that this lack of information was likely caused by the sudden death of MySpace; after all, during wizard rock's heyday, many musicians used it as their *only* site. This means that these bands had taken to exclusively posting lyrics, news, and songs on their accounts. When MySpace purged their servers in 2013, much of this information was irretrievably lost, and for bands who had only used MySpace, it soon came to feel was if they had never existed in the first place.[60]

Regardless of these hurdles, Susannah has persisted in her quest to create the ultimate wrock lyrics site, and today *Your Wizard Rock Resource* contains listings for dozens upon dozens of bands. What is more, the site also includes links to bands' website or social media accounts, a constantly updated page that attempts to document every live wrock show, and a directory of ways through which one might be able to purchase songs and albums from their favorite bands. Susannah hopes to keep expanding in the future so that "the site [can be] as complete as possible."[61] To make her job a bit easier, she has considered opening up the website to other contributors, but as of 2017, she has not yet decided to go that route.[62]

Given the site's name and purpose, it seems undeniable that *Your Wizard Rock Resource* was heavily inspired by the Wizrocklopedia. At the same time, Susannah has attempted to differentiate her site from the latter and make it unique amongst wrock webpages. She explained:

> The 'pedia is a wonderful site, and I like it a lot, but because of its age, it tends to be big, overwhelming and tricky to browse unless you know what you're looking for. I try to make my site like, "You've heard of a wrock band and want to find all of its music? Here you go!" So, it's more a resource than a history. Simply put, I want to make it as easy as possible to find and learn about wrock.[63]

It should be noted that the Wizrocklopedia and *Your Wizard Rock Resource* are not the only wrock encyclopedia sources out there; indeed, in the almost two decades that wizard rock has been around, a sizable number of sites dedicated to documenting and preserving wizard rock sprung up, such as WizardRock.org and the Wizard Rock Wiki. With that said, most of these projects have collapsed over the years, either due to loss in interest, or lack of user participation. Given that wizard rock is experiencing something of a revival, it is possible that these currently defunct sites will be resurrected, but as of April 2018, this has not come to pass.

Documentaries

Encyclopedias were not the only way that wizard rock was being preserved for posterity. In 2007–08, two documentaries—*We Are Wizards* and *The Wizard Rockumentary*—were also filmed. Shot during wizard rock's golden age, these two films are unique and both function as visual and auditory time capsules that enable viewers to, in many ways, travel back to when wizard rock was arguably at its most popular.

The first of these projects, *We Are Wizards*, was the work of Brooklyn director Josh Koury, who was at the time best known as one of the co-founders of the Brooklyn Underground Film Festival. The origins of the film can be traced back to an idea Koury had initially developed with the film's eventual producer, Gerald Lewis, about making a documentary chronicling the *Harry Potter* fandom. The two liked the idea and felt that such a documentary would be fascinating, but they worried that they would be unable to holistically cover such a large and diverse subculture in a pithy hour-and-a-half film. After much deliberation, they decided to work on a film that would detail only some of the *Harry Potter* fandom's more quirky members, rather than the fandom at large. Eventually, they settled on wizard rock as one of their topics of interest.[64]

Despite their idiosyncratic subject matter, both Koury and Lewis were adamant from the onset that their film would not purposely depict *Harry Potter* fans as social degenerates or weirdos; in an interview with the

Independent Film Channel (IFC), Koury explained, "We didn't want to make a *Trekkies*-style documentary where you make fun of the nerdy kids. We wanted to focus our efforts and energy on finding people that we felt had something great to offer."[65]

Because Koury was largely a novice when it came to the *Harry Potter* fandom, he took to the Internet to find the right subjects for the film, eventually contacting a number of wrockers; many of these individuals agreed to appear in the documentary.[66] And while *We Are Wizards* does not focus only on wizard rock (the documentary also heavily focuses on Brad Neely, creator of the popular alternative soundtrack to *Harry Potter and the Sorcerer's Stone* entitled *Wizard People, Dear Reader*, as well as Caryl Matrisciana, an evangelical scholar who strongly opposes the *Harry Potter* series for religious and philosophical reasons), a vast majority of the film follows the antics of bands like Harry and the Potters and The Hungarian Horntails, by documenting a number of their live shows and interviewing their members.[67]

Of note, Koury et al. were not a part of the wrock community when they worked on *We Are Wizards*. And while this does mean that the film lacks a certain emic understanding of the wrock community, it also results in a slightly less biased representation of the scene: with his film, Koury was not trying to make wrockers look bad, but neither was he trying to make them look good. Kelli Rohlman argues that it is this feature that makes *We Are Wizards* truly unique, as other works that attempt to document wizard rock (e.g., the soon-to-be-discussed *Wizard Rockumentary*, or Melissa Anelli's 2008 book *Harry, a History*) often portray the community in an excessively upotic and—unfortunately—somewhat uncritical way.[68]

We Are Wizards was first screened in March 2008 at Austin, Texas's annual South by Southwest film and music festival. While those in the wrock community enjoyed the final cut for the most part, *We Are Wizards* polarized critics, a number of whom felt that it was too narrowly focused and would only appeal to, as Gabe Leibowitz of *Film and Felt* put it, "the most drooling of fanboys."[69] Others criticized the film for neglecting to explore why exactly wrockers do what they do. Conversely, several critics appreciated Koury's focus on those activities that occur on the peripheries of the *Harry Potter* fandom, with Lance Goldenberg of the *Village Voice* writing, "There's considerable pleasure to be had in spending time with these bizarre enthusiasts and watching the creative ways they find to express their obsessions."[70] And a vast majority of critics—even those who otherwise disliked the film—applauded the way Koury avoided mocking his subjects, by instead approaching them with kind-heartedness and genuine interest.[71]

In April 2008, only about a month after the release of *We Are Wizards*, another wrock documentary was released entitled *The Wizard Rockumentary:*

A Movie About Rocking and Rowling. This project was the brainchild of Mallory and Megan Schuyler, twin sisters from Spokane, Washington, who had been interested in wizard rock since around 2004. By 2006, the two had begun to seriously consider filming a documentary about the scene, both to record the antics of a quirky subculture with which they were fascinated, as well as to "expose the [wider *Harry Potter* fan] community to the joy that is wizard rock."[72]

The Schuyler sisters began their project in earnest in July 2006, spending five months documenting bands like Harry and the Potters, Draco and the Malfoys, The Switchblade Kittens, and The Whomping Willows. Along the way, Megan and Mallory also interviewed librarians, authors, Internet users, and "good ol' [wizard rock] fans from across the country and around the world."[73] Topics touched upon include "body image, musical aesthetic priorities, and the community's 'do-it-yourself' mentality."[74] Ultimately, it was the Schuylers intention for the film to be positive and encouraging towards the artists, and in an interview with author George Beahm, they expressed this sentiment as such: "If nothing else, we hope that this documentary will inspire people to follow their dreams and do what they love. You can start a band. You can write a book. You can make a movie."[75]

By early 2007, principle photography had wrapped, and the sisters focused their efforts on arranging and editing what they had captured; in an interview with Fantasy is Love, the sisters estimated that they had shot almost 40 hours of footage, which they were forced to cut down to an hour-and-a-half.[76]

The Wizard Rockumentary was first screened on April 11, 2008, at Spokane's Garland Theater to 125 enthusiastic wrock fans. At the premiere, the Schuylers also sold exclusive *Wizard Rockumentary* buttons, of which some of the proceeds were donated to Page Ahead (a charity, much like Book Aid International, that promotes children's literacy).[77] Unlike Koury's film, the release of *The Wizard Rockumentary* was decidedly more limited, resulting in significantly less attention from the general press. With that said, fans and critics who did see the documentary were mostly in agreeance that it was entertaining, enlightening, and made with what can only be described as a fans' love for the source material.[78]

And at a *New York Times* TimesTalk event on August 19, 2008, *Harry Potter* star Daniel Radcliffe himself was even given a copy of the DVD by a fan. His response? He laughed and told the bequeathing fan, "That's awesome! Thank you very much."[79]

Music Criticism

The wrock community is a fairly welcoming place, which means that even the most inexperienced of musicians are received with kind words and generous praise. After all, most people in the community want to make new initiates feel welcome and safe, and so they believe (with good reason) that making negative comments in regard to new music—even if one believes that such comments are well-deserved—can drive away younger musicians. While this attitude has successfully helped to stem (or at least limit) bullying and otherwise intimidating behavior, it has had the unfortunate side-effect of also limiting *constructive* criticism.

But there is one individual out there who habitually bucks the unspoken rule against criticism: Wrock Snob. As mysterious as they are outspoken, Wrock Snob is the pseudonym[80] for a wrock music critic—the equivalent of the scene's very own *Pitchfork*-personified.

Wrock Snob first laid out their mission statement in the inaugural post of their Wordpress page in May 2010, writing:

> It is very difficult to find negative opinions of any sort of wizard rock coming from wizard rock fans, and this is a lack that I believe is hurting the genre as a whole. I'm not a troll, and this site isn't purely to make fun of wizard rock, but I believe a hard examination of the music is something that is missing, because we're all one happy lovey-dovey Hufflepuffy community and we don't want to hurt anyone's feelings.... But if wrock is to grow as a genre ... there need to be more people taking a critical eye to it. I'm not saying I'm the only person for the job, but I'm the only one so far to volunteer.[81]

By taking on the title of wrock critic, Wrock Snob saw it as their job to applaud or to criticize all bands, albums, and songs that could otherwise be categorized as wizard rock.

Prior to their 2010 blog post, the Wrock Snob had merely been a mild-mannered wrock fan. In an interview, they explained

> In 2006, my church youth group went down to Alabama to help the Mennonite Disaster Service in their rebuilding efforts for a week. While down there, we listened to [the 1971 song "American Pie" by Don McLean] a whole bunch because, well, the song mentions levees and we had never heard of levees until the New Orleans levees became a national talking point. When I got home, one of the first things I did was jump on Wikipedia and look up the song to find out what any of it meant. At the bottom of the article was a list of significant parodies of the song. One of them was "Half-Blood Pie," a parody posted on Mugglenet. I listened to that song over and over and over. It was music—about *Harry Potter*! My jam! After a solid week of nothing but that song, I started tentatively googling to see if anyone else had made *Harry Potter* music, and I found Harry and the Potters. I downloaded a bootleg of one of their live shows and wore out my iPod shuffle listening to it. When I found the Wizrocklopedia, my fate was sealed.[82]

The Wrock Snob began to ravenously consume wrock song after wrock song. In time, they had developed strong opinions about the community, and so they created a Wordpress site onto which they could post these beliefs. Their first review was a caustic track-by-track takedown of the synth-pop wrock band Ministry of Magic's 2009 album *Onwards and Upwards* (an album that they thought was phoned in and ultimately insipid). Within a day of posting, the withering appraisal had gone viral, with some wrock bands and fans praising the honesty of the review and others condemning its severity.[83] Why did the review gain such immediate traction? Musicologist Aya Esther Hayashi suggests that it was due to the nature of the review: "The negative critique of one of the scene's most popular bands was new and incendiary."[84] It is also possible that the review was so popular because many people shared Wrock Snob's opinions but had been forced by community consensus to hold back their critiques for fear of injecting into the scene much-dreaded cynicism and negativity. Regardless, the cutting review cemented Wrock Snob's reputation as a no-holds-barred wrock critic. In no time, they were an important figure within the community.

A key element of Wrock Snob's style is their heavy use of comedic exaggeration and hyperbole, with praise often being excessively positive and criticism being scathingly brutal. The latter point is worth emphasizing, given that Wrock Snob, as mentioned above, gained a reputation in the world of wizard rock for being particularly critical. But these often fiery opinions do not come from a place of malice or hatred for the community—quite the opposite. On their website, they wrote, "I am a huge fan of wizard rock—so much of a fan, that I believe that it could be the best genre out there, and thus, [I] am very critical of it. It's tough love, basically."[85] It was this element of Wrock Snob that Paul DeGeorge of Harry and the Potters found so refreshing:

> Wrock Snob is great. I love Wrock Snob because nobody else actually looked at our scene through a critical lens. Like, he came from a place of real true love for wizard rock and he was not afraid to be critical. And as an artist creating, I'm often desperate for critical feedback—positive or negative. It's great that people like what we do, but sometimes you want to see it expressed in a way that's like, "I got all the jokes you made!" [Wrock Snob] would just do more detailed readings [of wizard rock] than I would usually get a chance to see.... To me, I felt really appreciated when I read what the Wrock Snob thought—even if it was negative.[86]

When asked, most in the wrock community have echoed the thoughts of Paul DeGeorge, arguing that Wrock Snob's analyses have made wizard rock much stronger in the long run.[87]

In September 2013, Wrock Snob announced "an extremely definite hiatus," saying, "I am currently at a point where I actually have the time, but I have neither the motivation nor the spirit to do Wrock Snob for a bit."[88] While they continued to blog thereafter, their output dwindled to around only one or two articles every few months—a substantially lower number than it had previously been. Today, the Wrock Snob is still active on sites like Twitter, where they post their thoughts not only about wizard rock, but also about politics and other facets of popular culture. Will today's second wave of wizard rock lead to a Wrock Snob renaissance? Only time will tell.

Award Shows

As was discussed in Chapter 1, by 2007, wizard rock was exploding in popularity. Realizing that there was not an effective way to reward the many bands who were releasing music, Lizz Clements of the Wizrocklopedia announced on January 18, 2007, the first annual "Wizard Rock People's Choice Awards" (often abbreviated simply as the WRPCAs).[89] This distinctive event allowed avid wrock listeners to vote for their favorite groups in 25 award categories, which ranged from "Best Male Vocals" all the way to "Best International Act" (and each year, two additional "special achievement" honors were also bestowed on deserving bands). Nominations for the first WRPCAs were held between January 22 and February 5, 2007. To ensure that the awards

Freya Fridy (left) and Dinah Weller honor Adam Dubberly of The Mudbloods with an award for the "Best EP" at the 2009 Wizard Rock People's Choice Awards. This award show was hosted by the Wizrocklopedia staff from 2007 until 2010 (courtesy Jonathon Rosenthal).

7. The Wider World of Wizard Rock 169

would be fair and that no one would try to rig the vote, the Wizrocklopedia instituted a "one person, one nomination" rule and monitored IP addresses to enforce this code of conduct.[90]

After the Wizrocklopedia staff members tallied the nominations and whittled them down to between five and seven contenders for each award, voting commenced on February 9 and lasted until the end of that month.[91] This was a period of much excitement, and nominated bands quickly took to their social media accounts, enthusiastically encouraging their followers to vote for them. Likewise, ardent fans bombarded anyone who would listen with petitions to cast a ballot for their group of choice. In the end, over 5,000 individuals took part in the voting process, the results of which were announced in March 2007 through the Wizrocklopedia. Bands who won in their respective categories were given "The Golden Broomstick": a digital banner that bands could showcase on their websites, letting potential listeners know of their success. (Wizrocklopedia staffers also gave out paper certificates of achievement to the winners.)[92]

The WRPCAs were held from 2007 until 2010.[93] At first, many in the wrock community found the event to be a wonderful way in which to recognize those contributing to the scene. However, as the years passed, dissatisfaction began slowly to grow. This rising discount became perhaps most vocal when in 2009 the synthpop band Ministry of Magic won nine out of the possible 36 categories; many voters felt as if the group and others like it—while undeniably popular—were preventing smaller bands from receiving warranted recognition. Other wrock fans were frustrated because the vast majority of the bands that were being honored at the WRPCAs were winning not because they were necessarily "better" or "more worthy" than their competitors, but simply because they had larger fanbases who could "stuff the ballot box" without violating any rules.[94] These sorts of complaints began to increase in number until organizing and hosting the awards became, to quote Steph Anderson, "a fairly thankless job."[95]

The year 2010 would be the final time that the WRPCAs would be hosted, as by July 2011, technical difficulties had derailed the Wizrocklopedia and eventually forced it offline.[96] To fill the void left by the implosion of the WRPCAs, Brett Holden of the band Slytherin Soundtrack organized "The Wizzies" in 2011. This award show was reminiscent of the defunct WRPCAs in many ways, although Holden implemented a number of reforms to differentiate his award show from that which had come before it. Perhaps most notably, Holden cut the number of award categories down to just nine (this was a substantial decrease from the 2010 WRPCAs' 29), and he required that award-winners actually take part in the ceremony; if they failed to do so, their award would be revoked and given to the runner-up. This stipulation ensured that bands wanting a Wizzie would actively take part in the event.[97]

When Holden first announced The Wizzies, the news was met with much excitement in the wrock community, as many had feared that an event like the WRPCAs would never again happen. Wrock Snob channeled these sentiments most clearly when they wrote on their website, "I'd given up all hope for the WRPCAs, and then, from the darkness sprang the Wizzies, like some wizard rock Batman.... Big 'events' like this [are] what [keep] the community running, and talking and discussing."[98]

Voting for The Wizzies officially commenced on June 17, 2011, and ended about a month later; over 300 individuals took part in the process.[99] When it came time to reveal the results, Holden and his assistants further differentiated their award show from the WRPCAs by actually organizing a "show" via Livestream (rather than merely unveiling the results via a blog post, as the organizers of the WRPCAs had done). Despite being a relatively small operation, the resulting stream was rather sophisticated, featuring staged video bits, and even pre-recorded performances from bands like Anvil and the Hints, Seen and Unforeseen, Slytherin Soundtrack, the Butterbeer Experience, Tianna Mignogna, and The Blibbering Humdingers.[100] Wrock Snob, in particular, applauded this unique format, writing before the show aired: "I really, really like how they're going to try and [make] a really, really low-budget Grammy's."[101]

The Wizzies award ceremony was streamed on July 31, 2011, and was hosted by Jesse Jorge.[102] Unfortunately, while the event was hyped by many in the wrock community, the show did not make much of a lasting impact. In the months after the award show, excitement about The Wizzies began to dry up, and on March 6, 2012, Holden took to Twitter to express his worries that there was not enough interest to justify a second show.[103] A little over a week later, the account went silent. Suffice it to say, no 2012 Wizzies were ever held. Today, most vestiges of this short-lived award show have been lost due to inevitable link rot: the award show's Blogspot domain no longer exists, the Livestream videos have been deleted, and even records of which groups won what awards are incomplete or nonexistent. All we really have left are the memories of those who organized the show, and those who watched the Livestream with bated breath, waiting to see if their band had won a Wizzie.

A Truly Magical Community

The world of wizard rock is often bigger than most people realize; interspersed between the solo acts streaming sets from their bedrooms and bands performing songs in libraries are a whole array of individuals—ranging from radio DJs to bloggers, encyclopedia writers to documentarians, critics to award show hosts—who have played an integral part in ensuring that the wrock world is alive. Unfortunately, given that wizard rock is conceived of by most as first and foremost a style of music, write-ups about the wrock movement and community have a tendency to accidentally overlook or unintentionally downplay the contributions of the aforementioned individuals.

With this chapter, I have attempted to do two things. First, I have attempted to rectify the aforementioned issue by bringing wider notice to individuals in the wrock community that I believe have been unfairly sidelined, ignored, or just plain overlooked. (After all, in a book dedicated to the wrock movement and its community, such a detailed and wide-ranging consideration of these peripheral aspects is of critical importance.) But second— and perhaps more importantly—I have attempted to show that wizard rock is not merely a group of like-minded *musicians*, but rather a diverse community that has idiosyncratically developed over the years to comprise a wide variety of people, all of whom focus their unique forms of fandom engagement on a single subject: music about the Boy Who Lived.

8

Why Do They Wrock So Hard?

So, far this book has covered much ground. I have surveyed the history of wizard rock, how wrockers act and operate, and the demographics of their unique society; I have explored wrock shows and the role-play that often takes place at these events; and I have taken a look at the peripheral but nonetheless important aspects of the community, like blogging, documentary film-making, and radio broadcasting. But one question has so far escaped direct and explicit consideration: *why* exactly do individuals flock to the wrock community? What is it about wizard rock that appeals to such a diverse range of people?

As discussed in this book's introduction, the question of "why" can often be the bane of a researcher. After all, explicating the reason a whole group of people do something is a daunting task—and a task that should not be taken lightly. But luckily, one of the strengths of social scientific and ethnographic research is that these sorts of "grand" conclusions need not be arrived at alone: indeed, the beliefs and opinions of the people being studied can and should be directly taken into account by the researcher. In this chapter, I consider some of the more commonly invoked reasons as to why people are drawn to the wrock community, interspersing each section with the testimony of wrockers and fans themselves.

While there are many elements that explain wizard rock's success, ultimately, it seems that most are drawn to the community due to its empowering nature, the fact that the scene often functions as a refuge from social alienation, and because wizard rock provides fans with an outlet through which they can express their "unlimited enthusiasm" for the *Harry Potter* series.

Promise of Financial Gain(?)

Before I expound the aforementioned reasons for why wizard rock has gained such a following, I think it best to briefly consider an explanation that I occasionally hear from proponents of rational-choice theory: wrockers are motivated only by the allure of money. *Harry Potter* is after all a multi-million-dollar franchise with an enormous fan-following. Perhaps it is common sense to view wrockers simply as shrewd businesspeople who have recognized that money can be earned by making music that caters to the vast sea of *Harry Potter* fans.

The idea that the community is predicated solely on profits is understandably anathema to many wrockers—myself included—but the assumption is not completely unfounded. Most forms of fan production circulate in what can be called the "gift economy"—a unique system of exchange in which products are given away by producer for free. The French sociologist Marcel Mauss was the first to formulate this idea in his work *Essay on the Gift* (1925), and while the concept was initially influential in the social sciences, it has since been considered in other disciplines, including fandom studies (notably by Karen Hellekson).[1] In this context, the aforementioned "products" take on the form of what the scholar Tisha Turk calls "creative labors" (e.g., fan fics, filk songs, fan art, user-created videos, Wikipedia articles), which are "given" freely to the fan community at large.[2] Wizard rock problematizes this understanding, since wrockers often seek some form of reimbursement for their creative labors (e.g., wrockers offer their music for purchase online, they sell merchandise at live shows, and they charge for tickets). By profiting off their creations, wrockers have thus reoriented the economy of their community by injecting into it a decidedly capitalist element.

But just because wrockers sell their products does not necessarily mean that they are *only* in it for the money, and such an assertion is ignorant for a number of reasons. For one thing, it makes the blanket assumption that *all* wrockers (or, at least, a vast number of them) are just opportunistic capitalists, motivated by nothing more than the exploitation of a market and the pursuit of wealth. While I do not doubt that there are some musicians out there for whom wizard rock is merely a means to a financial end, interpreting the movement *entirely* in the light of capitalism and rational self-interest fails to explicate the various and nuanced reasons that might inspire a person to write songs about *Harry Potter*. Might not, for instance, attachment to a beloved character or emotional resonance with a particular storyline motivate wrockers to pen songs just as much as—if not more so than—the allure of money?

For another thing, those who believe that wizard rock's popularity is due to entrepreneurs exploiting a possible market fail to understand the reality of financial success in the wrock community. While it is true that some bands (such as Harry and the Potters or Draco and the Malfoys) have shifted a substantial number of albums and sold thousands of tickets, the average wrock group is lucky to turn a small profit or break even, as recording and touring are often expensive endeavors. And this is not some closely guarded secret—on the contrary, most of the wrockers to whom I talked were quite open about the fact that they do not lavishly profit off their creations; many of my informants even told me that they were quite happy with this arrangement. The purpose of wizard rock, they argued, is not to make money, but rather to celebrate a book series that they and so many others love—If a band can make a living off their fannish tunes, then that is just an added bonus. While the assertion might sound like an overly utopic impulse on the part of my informants, I would argue that its veracity is bolstered by the fact that most wrockers are often more than content to release complimentary albums or play free shows. If wrockers were only shrewd capitalists, surely they would not let money slip from their hands so easily?

Given the above, it is perhaps best to view the capitalist element of wizard rock as simply a utilitarian necessity that enables the community to sustain itself. After all, if wrock bands did not charge for their creations, then these same bands would be less likely to invest in recording songs, pressing up albums for others, or touring extensively. This in turn would dramatically limit the scope and appeal of the wrock scene, ultimately causing it to dry up.

Potential for Empowerment

If economic incentives are unlikely to account for why people flock to the wrock community, perhaps more affective reasons should be considered. For instance, a number of my informants told me that wizard rock has made them feel confident and powerful, or that it has provided them with the self-assurance to do things that thought they might have never done before, such as performing music live in front of hundreds of people. Included in these numbers is Trina, who told me:

> Before wizard rock, I was quiet, shy, and vulnerable, and [prior to starting The 8th Horcrux] I was always worried about performing music in front of people.... I mean, aren't most of us worried that our creative endeavors won't be received well by others? ... And while at the time some of my high school peers thought [our music] was weird, I was introduced to other crowds who were more receptive.... Soon, I resolved to not be ashamed of [my band], but be confident in my own way.... I now feel like I can do anything![3]

This emphasis on empowerment is not confined to just the beliefs espoused by wrockers and fans in interviews; it can also be detected in the pervasive rhetoric of the community. Consider, for example, the words of Matt Maggiacomo that we discussed in chapter 2: "There are no bad wizard rock bands.... We should be encouraging [these bands] to have fun."[4] This assertion—which is oft-quoted and heavily cited by wrockers and fans online—emphasizes the do-it-yourself nature of the movement. Such a philosophy stresses the idea that anyone can make a band, anyone can write songs, and anyone can perform live in front of a group of people—no exceptions. Because the judgement that so many fear is effectively being stymied by these sort of sentiments, those in the community are made to feel equal with everyone else. This suspension of judgement in turn can empower members to branch out and try new things that they might have otherwise been scared to try for fear of mockery.

Wizard rock's empowering nature is also often referenced in the lyrics of songs. There are numerous examples of this—so many, in fact, that to actually list each instance would truly be a herculean task. Instead, I would like to consider perhaps the epitome of this phenomenon: "Transparent" by The Moaning Myrtles. While on the surface, the track uses terminology and phrases that the listener might quickly associate with the gloomy ghost Moaning Myrtle,

The song "Transparent" by The Moaning Myrtles (comprising Lauren Fairweather, left, and Nina Jankowicz) can be interpreted as a song extolling the empowering nature of the wrock community (courtesy Grace Kendall).

"Transparent" is actually a meta-wrock song, expressing how wizard rock has positively impacted the lives of band members Lauren Fairweather and Nina Jankowicz and given them a newfound sense of confidence. This sentiment is most notably on display in the song's chorus, which begins:

> Because of wizard rock, I wear contact lenses and Converse shoes
> Because of wizard rock, Harry asked me out and I refused

Kelli Rohlman reads the first line as indexing the band's belief that wizard rock has improved their self-esteem by encouraging them to wear clothing and other accessories that index what one might emically call "coolness." Now that they have found acceptance in a group, they have traded glasses—a stereotypical and often stigmatized symbol of the othered "nerd"—for contacts. Likewise, they have swapped out their older shoes for those which are fashionable.

The second line is doing two things at once: On the surface, it is referencing and inverting the canonical relationship between Moaning Myrtle and Harry Potter (in the books, it is the ghost who pines after Harry, not the other way around). On a deeper layer, however, the line is invoking the name "Harry" arguably as a metaphor for those things which Fairweather and Jankowicz may have been passive to in the past or may have previously not had the self-assurance to turn down; now, thanks to their experiences with wizard rock, the two have the courage and power to confidently stand up for themselves and, in effect, say "no."[5]

If the point of the song has so far been lost on the listener, the final two lines of the chorus make the message abundantly clear:

> Because of wizard rock, haunting bathrooms isn't such a bore
> Because of wizard rock, I don't feel transparent anymore

Once again, these two lines are doing double-duty, directly referencing the *Harry Potter* series while also poetically expressing a more personal meaning. The mention of "haunting bathrooms" purposely evokes the ghostly activity of Moaning Myrtle, but it also artfully describes what Fairweather and Jankowicz actually *do* as musicians—that is, sing songs from the perspective of a ghost who haunts bathrooms. And because the two wrockers are now part of a larger, welcoming group of like-minded enthusiasts, the activity is no longer lonely or isolating, but rather exciting. The overall message of the song is made manifest in the concluding line, which directly alludes to the literal transparency of Moaning Myrtle (who, as a ghost, is partially see-through), while also expressing Fairweather and Jankowicz's belief that the wrock community has transformed them from alienated wallflowers into empowered individuals.

Because "Transparent" details the unique, lived experiences of Fairweather and Jankowicz, its story is by no means representative of every single member of the wrock community, and should not be interpreted as such. Nevertheless, the song is an excellent case study, as it provides a clear example of how wizard rock has managed to successfully empower some of its members, and how that empowerment is in turn expressed to the scene at large.

Promise of Community and a Refuge from Social Alienation

In their book *Fangasm*,[6] the fan scholars Lynn Zubernis and Katherine Larsen write: "In fandom, we found … *others*—a group of people who, like us, had *always felt a bit different* [and who had] experienced [a] *sense of difference*" [emphasis added].[7]

I quote this passage here because the language that Zubernis and Larsen use—especially their reference to feeling "different"—is strikingly similar to that used by several of my wrock informants. Lauren Cook, for instance, told me, "When I had been younger, I was obsessed with *Harry Potter*, and *no one ever got it*. As an older teenager, I was really depressed, and *I felt so disconnected from, well, everything*" [emphasis added].[8] In the forward to her zine *Rocking the Room of Requirement* (in which she discusses the joy of becoming a member of the wizard rock community and "finding a home" at Brian Ross's wrock house shows), the wrock writer Claudia Morales expressed a similar feeling:

> Through middle school and high school [I] *long[ed] for just one night where I could sit on some couch or floor or kitchen counter and feel like I belonged in the crowd milling* about as I talked to friends or strangers and threw my head back and laughed and laughed.… [At that time in my life] I longed for a Hogwarts letter or at least a high school party. *I longed for friendship and belonging and a sense of home* beyond the star-cornered pages [of the *Harry Potter* books] I knew so well [emphasis added].[9]

Both Cook and Morales are describing in their own ways that feeling of separation from mainstream society—that "sense of difference"—and the sort of social alienation that this disconnect can create.

This feeling of disconnect is dangerous because it causes the fan—who feels as if no one around them shares their interests or desires—to fear that they are secretly a "freak" or somehow "weird [and] abnormal."[10] Such "othering" is psychologically damaging because, according to Zubernis and Larsen, it:

> … is closely connected to the experience of trauma—not just the stereotypical instances of natural disaster, car crash, sexual abuse, or physical injury, but trauma with a small "t"—those events that outpace our ability to [integrate] these events from the perspective of our dominant life narrative and thus make meaning of them, encompassing everything from a sprained ankle to a leaked email to divorce, addic-

tion, and poverty. We experience a sense of powerlessness, having been through an intrusive event we didn't anticipate and couldn't control. [As Judith Herman writes in *Trauma and Recovery*] healing depends on the opportunity to express emotions, engage in the grieving process that accompanies trauma, and reclaim a congruent sense of self and agency.... Unfortunately, that opportunity to feel the pain of loss and share it with another is complicated [by the fact that] the sense of otherness brings an internalized shame that encourages silence, which unfortunately intensifies the isolation and makes psychological difficulties more likely.[11]

It is thus a giant cycle: isolation engenders a feeling of being an "other," and that feeling of "otherness" engenders even more isolation. What then is a person to do?

To escape this mental spiral, many of my informants logged onto the Internet and reached out for a lifeline, grasping at anything that might alleviate their sense of loneliness and isolation. It was in this way that they discovered wizard rock. At first, this unique style of music was appealing simply because it provided them with songs about their favorite book series. But once these fans were able to interact with other, like-minded people through social media (and eventually at concerts), inter-personal networks began to form in no time. What this means is that while the content of wizard rock was appealing, it was really the *communal* aspect of wizard rock that made it function like a social medicine, allowing my informants—who had previously felt alienated or "othered"—to become a part of a group that finally understood them.

This acceptance has left an imprint in the minds of many wrockers, and even today its impact and importance is stressed within the scene, often via song. An often-discussed example is the track "It's Real for Us" by Lauren Fairweather.[12] The song was inspired by touching dialouge from the final *Harry Potter* book, *The Deathly Hallows* in which a young Severus Snape utters the titular phrase while revealing to his good friend Lily Potter that there is indeed a magical world into which they both fit. On a deeper level, however, the track can be interpreted as a celebration of the anti-alienating nature of the wrock community.[13] The end of the song goes as follows:

> I just can't wait to go and see
> So many people just like me
> 'Cuz all I've wanted for so long
> Is to find a place where I belong
> ...
>
> We can do magic, can do magic, can do magic
> If we stand together, stand together, stand together
>
> But it's real for us
> It's real for us
> Doesn't matter what the Muggles say
> 'Cuz it's real for us

It is important to note that "It's Real for Us" is an especially popular song, and when Fairweather plays it live, her concerts often turn into emotional sing-alongs. The classicist and wrock scholar Anne C. Smith argues that this is because the song enables wrockers and fans alike to "collectively [affirm] ... our own experience [by] choosing to emphasize not the feeling of alienation that we experience when 'Muggles' don't understand us, but instead the comfort of knowing that there is, in fact, a place for us, with people like us, the community of *Harry Potter* fans in general and of wizard rock fans in particular."[14] The popularity of "It's Real for Us" is thus a key piece of evidence that suggests wizard rock's appeal is at least partially due to its promise of community and its ability to function as refuge from a socially alienating world that does not understand an individual's unique, fannish interests.[15]

Now, it must be re-emphasized that the desire to escape this sort of social alienation and find a home in a like-minded group of people is not frivolous and unnecessary, but rather a very real, psychological, and deeply ingrained need that all humans have, given that we are social creatures. According to the Columbia University psychology professor Laurel Steinberg:

> Belonging to a fandom group helps ... define [a person's] identity and give a sense of purpose to what might be an otherwise routine lifestyle.... Connecting with people over shared passions and interests is good for mental and emotional health because it helps to create a fraternity-like or family-like sense of security.[16]

This means that it is not an exaggeration to say that the wrock community is central to the well-being—and possibly the survival—of many of its members.

Such an assertion is backed-up by the claims of my informants, many of whom directly credited wizard rock with helping them to cope with a diverse range of psychological, emotional, and mental ailments, such as crippling loneliness, social anxiety, and depression. For instance, one wrocker (who wished to remain anonymous) told me:

> I suffer from depression and social anxiety. When left to myself, my mental illnesses can get really bad—when I'm left alone with nothing to do, my brain starts to ruminate and I have bad thought spirals. I also get extremely lonely, and I feel lost. Luckily, being a part of the wizard rock community is a way to always be a part of something bigger than myself. As a wizard rocker, I feel like I'm less alone than I was before.... I don't feel so weird or different.... Being with other [wrock fans] makes me feel like I belong.[17]

Of course, I am not saying that wizard rock is some elixir for *all* the mental illnesses that plague humanity. Rather, I am suggesting that by providing a space where people can reach out and connect with one another, wizard rock has been reported to aid those who are suffering from these illnesses by helping them to not feel so different, othered, or otherwise hopelessly alone.

Outlet for "Unlimited Enthusiasm"

In May 2009, the noted author and vlogger John Green attended the inaugural LeakyCon (an annual *Harry Potter* fan convention, see Chapter 3), at which he watched a number of wrock bands play to enthusiastic crowds. After listening to original wrock compositions and meeting excited fans, Green was deeply struck by the earnestness of the wrock community. When the festivities were over, he posted a video on May 24 in which he exclaimed: "I was really inspired to spend a couple days with people who care about … making the world awesome … so completely without irony. Like, sometimes in our hyper-cynical world, we forget that it's okay to get enthusiastic about things."[18] After only two days in the middle of a sea of wrockers, Green had quickly recognized that the wrock movement was, in many ways, a stronghold of creative sincerity, providing individuals with a much-needed outlet for "unlimited enthusiasm."

The phrase "unlimited enthusiasm" has been around for quite a while,[19] but was first used in reference to wizard rock by Paul and Joe DeGeorge when they were organizing a large multi-band tour in 2008. In an interview, Paul explained:

> The Unlimited Enthusiasm Expo was a tour we did in 2008. We came up with the name because it felt like a good way to describe the common thread that connected all the bands … on the tour.… We really liked this branding and felt like it represented our outlook as creators and performers. I think it ties to wizard rock fairly simply because the foundation of fandom is enthusiasm. And when you are around like-minded fans, it often seems like that enthusiasm is unlimited.[20]

In this chapter, I have considered a number of hypotheses that seek to explain why the wrock movement has wedged itself snuggly into the hearts of so many, but I believe that the most satisfying answer is that wizard rock serves as an outlet through which fans can express this sort of "unlimited enthusiasm." After all, wizard rock at its core is a movement that encourages people to come together and unironically show love for the *Harry Potter* series by penning fun, fannish songs.

This very assertion is widely supported by the rhetoric of many wrockers and fans themselves. Consider, for instance, the opinion expressed by *BookRiot* writer and wrock fan Jesse Doogan in her article "Top 5 Wizard Rock Songs to Bring You Back to Hogwarts":

What I love most about wizard rock isn't necessarily the quality of the music, but their *unbridled enthusiasm for this imaginary world.…* I mean, really, *what's better than a group of people who are so excited about* Harry Potter *that they have to sing about it?* [emphasis added][21]

Such a sentiment strongly mirrors the feelings of numerous individuals whom I interviewed in the process of writing this book, such as Matt Maggiacomo (who revealed to me that it was, in particular, the crowd's "enthusiasm and supportive attitude" at the first Boston Yule Ball that convinced him to seriously commit to his band, The Whomping Willows),[22] or the wrock fan Spirit-Rose Waite, who told me:

> [Wizard rock] allowed me to forge links with others who cared about *Harry Potter* [on] *the level I did* … who also *enjoyed talking endlessly* about characters' morality and story arcs and fanfic etc. People who didn't try to shame me for *how important* Harry Potter *is to my life.* [emphasis added][23]

Even Trina has referenced these ideas before, saying in a 2015 interview that at its core, wizard rock is about "be[ing] enthusiastic about what you like" and knowing that "it's ok to like stuff."[24]

Perhaps unsurprisingly, wizard rock's full-on embrace of fanatical, fannish zeal has attracted many devotees of the *Harry Potter* series, who see the movement as a unique opportunity to unreservedly wax poetic about a book that they already held so dear. But what catches many people off guard is that a number of wrock musicians and fans were drawn to the community prior to their having read the *Harry Potter* books. While most of these individuals were aware of what *Harry Potter* was and how the basic story played out, they had never felt the need to read the books or dive head-first into aspects of the fandom—that is, until they witnessed the passion, earnestness, and the pure enthusiasm of the wrock community, in particular.

The wizard rapper Myles Kane performs at the inaugural LeakyCon (2009) under the stage name "MC Kreacher". Kane was inspired to write wizard rap after being struck by the sincerity and enthusiasm of the wrock community (courtesy Jonathon Rosenthal).

Myles Kane, who now performs "wizard rap" under the moniker MC Kreacher, was one of these individuals. In an interview with Kane, I learned that he had been introduced to wizard rock in 2008 while working on the documentary *We Are Wizards*. He explained:

> [Before] editing the film.... *I had never read the books....* The ... thing that really connected with me was the first live Harry and the Potters show we filmed at the NY public library. I went in thinking, "This is for kids; it's going to be nerdy and bad, obvious satire." But *I was blown away by their ability to be both comic and earnest in their performance.* And their effect on the crowd was magical. Yes, everyone in the theater was obsessed with *Harry Potter* and [they were] a very willing audience, but the band's music transcended that basic fandom, and was its own artful expression.... [*It was*] *sincere and also knowingly silly....* It was brilliant.... [It was] *obsession and fandom inspiring and feeding one's own creative spirit.*[25]

I feel that Kane's statement touches upon many of the same points that John Green made when he praised wizard rock in his May 2009 vlog. Wizard rock is a way for people to be "sincere and also knowingly silly." It is an opportunity for fans of *Harry Potter* to open their hearts and write songs about fictional characters and stories that mean so much to them. And it is a community that will not judge others for writing about otherwise "nerdy" topics. Ultimately, wizard rock is a place in which one can be unlimitedly enthusiastic.

Conclusion

In late September 2017, I was sitting on a couch with Trina in her apartment. Having taken a small break from the otherwise arduous task of planning the last few aspects of our wedding, we were scrolling absent-mindedly through old pictures that we had stumbled across on Facebook, reminiscing about when we were younger.

Somehow, we found ourselves browsing through an album that was dated fall of 2009. Within no time, the two of us had uncovered pictures we had taken while we were working on our first album: There was an embarrassing image of me—looking shaggy-haired and quite young—recording a vocal line. There was a shot of Trina intently laying down a guitar track on a bright pink Fender Squire. And there was a picture taken on the day we had received 100 professionally pressed up copies of our debut album *Potterwatch!* in the mail ...

While Trina and I were scanning these photos, it hit us: the two of us had been in a wizard rock band for almost a decade! *A decade.*

While I only started working on this book in earnest around the summer of 2016, it does not seem unreasonable to say that it has been in the works since 2009, for it was in this year that I became a full-fledged member of the wrock community. And in the years since, this most peculiar style of music has left a noticeable imprint on my life. I have made many good friends, written dozens of songs, and played numerous shows. Wizard rock even brought me and my wife together! As clichéd as it may sound, wizard rock is a part of me. And because it has played such a major role in my life, I have come to understand the wizard rock community on an arguably deeper level.

With this book, therefore, I have attempted to translate my insider knowledge so as to both provide a more thorough treatment of wizard rock as well as to combat some of the faulty conceptions that have been spread about it. I have striven to show that the movement is neither just a goofy hobby that keeps the more simple-minded entertained, nor an excuse for teenagers and grown adults alike to act like silly children, but rather a genuine community, replete with the complexities and struggles of supposedly "normal" modern life. Wizard rock is a bastion of creativity, encouraging people to engage with a book series that means so much to them and to create their own musical paratexts. It is a source of political consciousness, inspiring young individuals to become more civically and socially aware. Ultimately, it is an expression of human culture worthy of scholarly attention.

Chapter Notes

Preface

1. Carolyn Ellis, Tony E. Adams, and Arthur P. Bochner, "Autoethnography: An Overview."

Introduction

1. A "Muggle" is a person who has no magical abilities (*SS*, Chapter 1).
2. Harry and the Potters, *Mail Song #1*; Harry and the Potters, *Priori Incantatem*.
3. I do not discuss StarKid's 2009 *A Harry Potter Musical* in this book for two reasons. First, I believe it is more appropriate to consider this work in regard to YouTube culture and/or the musical tradition. Second, I believe that the musical functions first and foremost as a parody of the *Harry Potter* series and should be classified as such (cf. Valerie Estelle Frankel, "Parodying Potter," 59). This is not to say that fans of wizard rock do not listen to *A Harry Potter Musical*—quite the opposite!—or that *A Very Potter Musical* and wizard rock are completely incomparable; I simply believe it is beyond the scope of this work for me to discuss it. For a consideration of *A Harry Potter Musical* and other StarKid productions, see Aya Esther Hayashi, "Musicking, Discourse, and Identity," 118–22.
4. Rob Yoho, "Developing Community Through Wizard Rock," 221.
5. "Paving the Way for Wizard Rockers Everywhere."
6. Anne C. Smith, "It's Real for (All of) Us," 69; Do Rozario, "Wrocking," 269.
7. Anne C. Smith, "Playing [with] Multiple Roles."
8. Smith.
9. *My Immortal* is a piece of fan fiction that was originally published online in 2006. Riddled with grammatical and spelling errors, the work is borderline unreadable and is noted for its absurd plot points, its poorly written dialogue, and its blatant desecration of the *Harry Potter* canon. Many argue that the work is so terrible that it must have been the work of an Internet prankster.
10. In regard to Mignogna's work, Paul DeGeorge of Harry and the Potters told *Slug* magazine: "It was super interesting because [some of her songs] aren't [about] canon works.... I thought it was cool to see someone continue to innovate within the fan space in that way" (Ali Shimkus, "The Band that Live").
11. Of course, there *are* songs out there that reference, allude to, or focus entirely on *Star Wars* and *Lord of the Rings* (for instance, a number of heavy metal bands reference the works of Tolkien in their songs, and American parodist "Weird Al" Yankovic has written several tracks entirely about *Star Wars*). The point being made is that there are no widespread musical movements or genres dedicated *exclusively* to these works. One might counter that "Timelord rock" (trock)—a music genre based on the television series *Doctor Who*—exists, but this genre is nascent at best, and is arguably made up of only two notable band (i.e., Chameleon Circuit and Time Crash).
12. Melissa Anelli, "Rocking at Hogwarts," 111.
13. Henry Bial apud Nicolle Lamerichs,

"Stranger Than Fiction"; Mal Ahern, "Performance/Performativity."

14. E.g., the beginning of the song "Harry Potter" from the band's album *Live at the New York Public Library* (2011).

15. J.L. Austin, *How to Do Things with Words*, 6–7.

16. Judith Butler, *Bodies That Matter*.

17. Lamerichs, "Stranger Than Fiction."

18. Lamerichs.

19. Elizabeth D. Hutchison, *Dimensions of Human Behavior*, 446.

20. Hutchison. 446.

21. Jennifer Terrell, "Constructing Rooms of Requirement," 12.

22. It seems necessary to differentiate between author-created and non-author-created worlds, and so in this work, the physical and temporal world of human existence will often be referred to as the "real world." I will be the first to admit that such a term is often problematic—after all, it implies that the world of the mind, of imagination, and of group-play is fake or an illusion. While this very well might be a common-sense view of reality to hold, it is rather simplistic. It is undeniable that the imaginative world that wrockers temporarily inhabit during live shows or on their records is a fiction, but as anthropologist Clifford Geertz notes, a "fiction" can simply mean "'something made,' 'something fashioned.'" It does not have to mean that something is "false, unfactual, or merely [an] 'as if' thought" experiment" (Clifford Geertz, *The Interpretation of Cultures*, 16). After all, the fiction that wrockers embrace somehow manages to engender real beliefs, behaviors, and activities, which in turn manifest as action in the world of "truth" or "reality." To avoid the issue of denoting a "true" or a "false" reality, many in the wrock community have embraced (among other terms) the signifiers "wizards" and "Muggles" to differentiate between the created world that wrockers and their fans inhabit (the former), and the actual world in which all humans live (the latter). In sections of this book where emic terms are more desirable, these signifiers will be used in lieu of phrases like "the real world."

23. Terrell, "Constructing Rooms of Requirement," 12–13, 56–69.

24. Hutchison, *Dimensions of Human Behavior*, 446.

25. To succinctly quote Henry Jenkins on this matter, "Every [fan] knows that Hogwarts isn't real" (Henry Jenkins, "The Night of a Thousand Wizards," 120).

Chapter 1

1. Grace Kendall (musician, Snidget), interview by author, May 25, 2017.

2. There are exceptions to this tendency. Claudia Morales has written extensively about the relationship between wizard rock and punk, and Aya Esther Hayashi in her dissertation "Musicking, Discourse, and Identity in Participatory Media Fandom" makes a detailed and compelling argument that wizard rock is best understood within the context of a specific variant of punk rock: straight-edge (Hayashi, "Musicking, Discourse, and Identity," 64–66).

3. Ryan Cooper, "The History of Punk Rock Music"

4. Eric James Abbey, 67, 75; Stephen Duncombe and Maxwell Tremblay, *White Riot*, 88, 190, 203.

5. Cooper, "History of Punk"; Cf. Eric Jaffe, "The History of Punk Rock."

6. Cooper.

7. Fred R. Shapiro, ed., *The Yale Book of Quotations*, 492.

8. Cooper, "History of Punk"; Robert P. Marzec, ed., *The Mid-Atlantic Region*, 349; Stacy Thompson, *Punk Productions*, 16, 79; Ian Youngs, "A Brief History of Punk."

9. Cooper; Thompson, 19; Youngs.

10. Cooper; Jaffe, "The History of Punk Rock"; John Savage, "Punk"; Thompson, 10–32.

11. Cooper; Savage; Thompson, 42–80.

12. Matt Diehl, *My So-Called Punk*, 57; Thompson, 71–80.

13. Marzec, *The Mid-Atlantic Region*, 349.

14. Michael S. Foley, *Fresh Fruit for Rotting Vegetables*, 104.

15. Cf. Foley; Alessandro Moliterno, "What Riot?"

16. See comments on: Sarah Frances Holder, "I'm kind of mad..." Facebook, May 16, 2017, https://www.facebook.com/groups/1088071511244372/permalink/1586945428023642/.

17. Cf. Do Rozario, "Wrocking the Collaboration," 275; Russ Benoit, ed., "The History of Wizard Rock."

18. An "auror" is a "dark wizard catcher"; it is effectively the wizarding world's version of a CIA or MI5 agent (*GF*, Chapter 11). Nymphadora Tonks was a member of this elite brigade (*OP*, Chapter 3).
19. "Riot grrrl" is a feminist-infused offshoot of punk rock. Notable riot grrrl groups include Bikini Kill and Bratmobile (Thompson, *Punk Productions*, 58–70).
20. See comments on: Holder, "I'm kind of mad…"
21. The Shrieking Shack was a house built so that Remus Lupin could turn into a werewolf in peace. Due to Lupin's lycanthropic shrieks, it was widely believed to be haunted by violent spirits (*PA*, 14, 18).
22. Holly Casio (musician, The Shrieking Shack Disco Gang), interview by author, June 5, 2017.
23. "Quidditch" is a popular wizarding sport played on brooms (*SS*, Chapter 5).
24. Paul DeGeorge, "Bio."
25. "Harry Potter: What Is Wizard Rock?"
26. Marzec, *The Mid-Atlantic Region*, 349.
27. Henry Jenkins, "*Star Trek* Rerun, Reread, Rewritten," 39.
28. Jenkins, 37.
29. Jenkins, 39.
30. Sarah Elizabeth Rosenbaum, "Lit Punk."
31. Supposedly derived from a misspelling of "folk."
32. Henry Jenkins, *Textual Poachers*, 259.
33. Melissa Tatum, "Identity and Authenticity in the Filk Community."
34. Barry Childs-Helton and Sally Childs-Helton, "Filk Music."
35. Childs-Helton and Childs-Helton; Tatum, "Identity and Authenticity in the Filk Community."
36. Tatum.
37. Gary McGath apud Tatum.
38. For instance, Rebecca-Anne C. Do Rozario, "Wrocking the Collaboration," 265–76.
39. Cf. Catherine Hall, "Reading and [W]rocking," 194; Suzanne Scott, "From Filk to Wrock."
40. Hall, 194; Scott.
41. Scott Vaughan (musician, The Blibbering Humdingers), interview by author, January 30, 2018.
42. Tatum, "Identity and Authenticity."
43. Tatum.
44. Paul DeGeorge (musician, Harry and the Potters), interview by author, Lawrence, KS, May 25, 2017.
45. See comments on: Holder, "I'm kind of mad…"
46. Tatum.
47. Patrik Wikstrom and Christina Olin-Scheller, "To Be Continued…," 84.
48. Cf. Jenkins, "*Star Trek*," 42; See also: http://tvtropes.org/pmwiki/pmwiki.php/Main/FanFic?from=Main.FanFiction.
49. See: https://fanlore.org/wiki/Shipping.
50. Jenkins, "*Star Trek*," 55.
51. Jenkins.
52. Anelli, "Rocking at Hogwarts," 105–6.
53. Drama, "Switchblade Kittens and Harry Potter."
54. Drama.
55. Drama.
56. See comments on: Paul Thomas, "I'm in the final stages…" Facebook, September 8, 2017, https://www.facebook.com/groups/1088071511244372/permalink/1705355196182664/.
57. Drama, "Switchblade Kittens and Harry Potter."
58. Drama; See comments on: Thomas, "I'm in the final stages…"
59. Drama.
60. Drama.
61. Drama (musician, Switchblade Kittens), interview by author, February 26, 2018.
62. Elias Leight, "Hear Bruce Springsteen's Unreleased 'Harry Potter' Song."
63. Although "I'll Stand by You Always" makes no reference to the books' plots or characters, instead being based on the general *feeling* of the book (Leight).
64. After reading a draft of this chapter, Aya Esther Hayashi pointed out the "interesting paradox" of wrockers claiming Bruce Springsteen as part of wizard rock's history, while at the same time often opposing attempts by filkers to claim wizard rock (interview by author, February 15, 2018).
65. Anelli, "Rocking at Hogwarts," 106.
66. Anelli, 107, 111; Paul DeGeorge, "Other, Etc."; Paul DeGeorge (musician, Harry and the Potters), interview by author, June 12, 2018.
67. Joe DeGeorge and Andrew MacLeay, "About"; Joe DeGeorge and Andrew MacLeay, "Releases"; James Reed, "Singing of the Papal Smoke."

68. Anelli, "Rocking at Hogwarts," 112; Paul DeGeorge, interview, June 12, 2018
69. Anelli.
70. Anelli, 111–12.
71. Anelli; Joe DeGeorge (musician, Harry and the Potters), interview by author, June 29, 2017, May 25, 2017; Paul DeGeorge, interview, May 25, 2017.
72. Paul DeGeorge and Joe DeGeorge, "Old Interview I Found in Our Email."
73. Anelli, "Rocking at Hogwarts," 112.
74. Anelli, 112–13.
75. A "Time-Turner" is a small, hourglass-shaped time machine that creates boot-strap paradoxes (*PA*, Chapter 21).
76. Daytrotter, "Harry and the Potters—The Hogwarts Tonsil Hockey Team."
77. Anelli, "Rocking at Hogwarts," 112–13; Lev Grossman, "The Boy Who Rocked"; according to Paul DeGeorge, the band also performed an untitled song "about playing Quidditch in the snow," as well as "The Troll Song." These songs were never recorded, but the latter was often performed during the band's earliest shows (interview by author, June 14, 2018).
78. Anelli, 113–14; Paul DeGeorge (musician, Harry and the Potters), interview by author, January 9, 2018.
79. Anelli.
80. Paul DeGeorge, interview, January 9, 2018.
81. Anelli, "Rocking at Hogwarts," 115; DeGeorge, interview, May 25, 2017.
82. Anelli, 116.
83. Paul DeGeorge (musician, Harry and the Potters), interview by author, January 24, 2018.
84. DeGeorge.
85. Anelli, "Rocking at Hogwarts," 119.
86. Jessica Plummer, "Music Review: Harry and the Potters."
87. Paul DeGeorge, interview, January 9, 2018.
88. Anelli, "Rocking at Hogwarts," 120.
89. So popular was "The Human Hosepipe" that when it was later released on a free compilation, it was downloaded 200,000 times. See: Harry and the Potters, "@russtopherb haha! yeah, they're using the term 'sold' very loosely there. 'human hosepipe' was on a free comp and got DLed 200K times." Twitter, October 20, 2010, https://twitter.com/hollowgodric/status/967840675411779584.

90. Paul DeGeorge, interview, January 24, 2018.
91. Joe DeGeorge, interview June 29, 2017.
92. DeGeorge; Anelli, "Rocking at Hogwarts," 120–21; Emily Sweeney, "Sibling Musicians Bring out the 'Punk' in Harry Potter."
93. Paul DeGeorge, interview, January 9, 2018.
94. Anelli, "Rocking at Hogwarts," 120–21; Sweeney, "Sibling Musician."
95. Cf. Benoit, "The History of Wizard Rock."
96. Amy Phillips and Ryan Dombal, "Top Five Live Shows of 2005 (That Weren't Intonation)."
97. Anelli, "Rocking at Hogwarts," 121–23; Paul DeGeorge (musician, Harry and the Potters), interview by author, Lawrence, KS, June 12, 2018.
98. Née Brittany Vahlberg.
99. Anelli, "Rocking at Hogwarts," 121; Horner & Sonnett, "About"; Nicholas Jones, "The Best Bands of Wizard Rock."
100. Elisabeth Donnelly, "For Harry Potter Fans About to Rock, We Salute You."
101. Horner and Sonnet, "About."
102. Horner and Sonnet; Luke Winkie, "Never Forget Harry and the Potters and the Bizarre World of Wizard Rock"; for a critical look at Horner and Sonnett's self-conception of the limits to their authorial power, see Smith, "Playing [with] Multiple Roles."
103. "Wrock Spotlight: The Parselmouths."
104. Horner and Sonnet, "About."
105. Anelli, "Rocking at Hogwarts," 121.
106. Cf. http://tmbw.net/wiki/Dial-A-Song.
107. Anelli, "Rocking at Hogwarts," 121; Kristina Horner and Elle Viane Sonnet, "New Hotline," LiveJournal, August 4, 2004, https://theparselmouths.livejournal.com/3808.html; Elle Viane Sonnet, "Uhg!!," LiveJournal, July 29, 2004, https://theparselmouths.livejournal.com/1813.html.
108. Winkie, "Never Forget"; Paul DeGeorge (musician, Harry and the Potters), interview by author, June 21, 2018.
109. See: https://theparselmouthsband.wordpress.com/press/.
110. Anelli, "Rocking at Hogwarts," 123; Matt Maggiacomo, "Biography."
111. Bradley Mehlenbacher (musician, Draco and the Malfoys), interview by author, June 19, 2018

112. Mehlenbacher.
113. Mehlenbacher.
114. Anelli, "Rocking at Hogwarts," 123; "My Dad Is Rich" would eventually become Draco and the Malfoy's signature song.
115. The Whomping Willow is a violent, semi-sentient tree located at Hogwarts. The tree protects a secret passage that links the castle to the Shrieking Shack in the village of Hogsmeade (*CS*, Chapter 5; *PA*, Chapter 17); at his first "show," Maggiacomo referred to himself in the singular, before bowing to tradition within the budding community and amending his name with an "s" (Anelli, 128).
116. Maggiacomo, "Biography."
117. Maggiacomo.
118. Hayashi, "Musicking, Discourse, and Identity," 68; Mehlenbacher, interview, June 19, 2018.
119. Mehlenbacher, interview, June 20, 2018.
120. Anelli, "Rocking at Hogwarts," 124, 127–28.
121. Not to be confused with the wrock band "Remus and the Lupins," which is a side project of Draco and the Malfoys' Bradley Mehlenbacher. According to Mehlenbacher, "I did troll [Carpenter by forming] Remus and the Lupins … There was a message board thread where [Carpenter] said something like 'Enough of these "Something and the Somethings" bands!' … That's when I started my side project" (interview, June 20, 2018).
122. Anelli, "Rocking at Hogwarts," 128–29; Michelle Hunter, "Live from the Library."
123. Carpenter's openness with fans, however, later led to abuses. See chapter 4.
124. Aidan Bauernschmidt, "First-Year's Band 'Wrocks' as The Moaning Myrtles."
125. Anelli, "Rocking at Hogwarts," 129.
126. Anelli.
127. Bradley Mehlenbacher (musician, Draco and the Malfoys), interview by author, June 20, 2018.
128. Cf. Anelli, "In early 2005, Alex wasn't even a *Potter* fan … but that would change when … to impress a girl … he read the books. [Carpenter's] wasn't an all-consuming love…" ("Rocking at Hogwarts," 128).
129. Aya Esther Hayashi notes that the DeGeorges were uncomfortable with the way Carpenter attracted new fans by offering to "go on dates" with them via MySpace ("Musicking, Discourse, and Identity," 175).
130. Mehlenbacher, interview, June 20, 2018.
131. According to Hayashi, "Carpenter introduced [into wizard rock] an 'indie' commercialism" ("Musicking, Discourse, and Identity," 70).
132. Mehlenbacher, interview, June 20, 2018.
133. Anelli, "Rocking at Hogwarts," 129.
134. Anelli.
135. Anelli.
136. Anelli, 129–30.
137. Anelli, 130.
138. As mentioned earlier, Matt Maggiacomo changed his band's name to "The Whomping Willows," with an "s."
139. Mehlenbacher, interview, June 19, 2018.
140. Lizz Clements, ed., "Band Profiles."
141. E.A. Pyne, "Wizard Rock," 180–81; Hayashi, "Musicking, Discourse, and Identity," 93.
142. Jennifer Vineyard, "Harry Potter Fandom Reaches Magical New Level Thanks To Wizard-Rock Bands."
143. Lauren Fairweather (musician, The Moaning Myrtles), interview by author, June 7, 2018; Hayashi, "Musicking, Discourse, and Identity," 87.
144. Lauren Fairweather (musician, The Moaning Myrtles), interview by author, March 15, 2017.
145. Hayashi, "Musicking, Discourse, and Identity," 87.
146. Fairweather, interview, March 15, 2017; Hayashi.
147. Lauren Fairweather and Nina Jankowicz, "About."
148. E.g., Fairweather and Jankowicz.
149. Fairweather, interview, March 15, 2017.
150. Lauren Fairweather and Nina Jankowicz, "About."
151. Lauren Becker, "Interview: The Moaning Myrtles."
152. Paul DeGeorge, interview, January 9, 2018.
153. While each EP is assigned to a different month, EPs were actually shipped quarterly throughout the year.
154. Paul DeGeorge, interview, May 25, 2017.

155. DeGeroge; Paul DeGeorge, "Wizard Rock EP of the Month Club!"
156. Anelli, "Rocking at Hogwarts," 131.
157. Paul DeGeorge, interview, May 25, 2017.
158. Paul DeGeorge, "Albums."
159. DeGeorge.
160. Paul DeGeorge, "Holiday Sale!"
161. DeGeorge.
162. Joshua Zumbrun, and Sonya Geis, "Wizard Rock Has Fans in Hogwarts Heaven."
163. Matthew Cook, "Bang on the Drum All Day," 176; Joy Lambert and Annette Anderson-Ma, "Wizard Rocking the Library of Congress."
164. Arguably the most elaborate of these was Harry and the Potters' *Priori Incantatem*, a compilation that included rarities, b-sides, remixes, songs cut from previous albums, and a handful of new tracks. The physical release, which was limited to only 1000 copies, also included a second CD of demos. Complete with hand-typed liner notes and a beautifully matte-coated cover designed by Dan McCarthy, Georg Pedersen, and Meredith Moore, the record is a jewel and a must-have for any wrock collector.
165. "Wizard Rock."
166. Proma Khosla, "Wonderful, Weird."
167. Khosla; Note that two years later, a "Wrockstock Reunited" festival would be held.
168. Khosla.
169. Cf. Hayashi, "Musicking, Discourse, and Identity," 100, 101–102.
170. Hayashi, 101; Khosla, "Wonderful, Weird."
171. Hayashi, 102; Khosla; Grace Kendall (musician, Snidget), interview by author, May 26, 2017.
172. Khosla.
173. Mitchell Sunderland, "The Harry Potter Fans Still Making Music about Magic, Known as Wizard Rock."
174. Cf. Hayashi "Musicking, Discourse, and Identity," 102; Hayashi and I independently began to refer to this time period as wizard rock's "second wave."
175. This reveal occurred at Brian Ross's home during a wrock house party. According to those in attendance, the band performed around 12 new songs. Bradley Mehlenbacher—who along with Ross assisted the band in arranging parts of the album—later wrote on Facebook, "[Harry and the Potters] spent the last month [i.e., March] or so writing together, then [when] Paul was up [in New England] for the week, we spent [the 25–27th and the 29th of March] in Brian's basement putting it all together. We had everything down by Thursday, ran everything a few times, then it was showtime." See: Paul Thomas, "Yo, yo, yo!" Facebook, April 1, 2018, https://www.facebook.com/groups/1088071511244372/permalink/1913447442040104/.

Chapter 2

1. "Potterwatch" is a reference to the pirate radio station that offered support for Harry Potter and his allies during the Second Wizarding Wars (*DH*, passim). "Accio Awesome" is a reference to the *Accio* summon spell that enables the caster to retrieve a specified object (*GF*, Chapter 20).
2. A "Horcrux" is a receptacle into which a nefarious wizard can place a piece of their soul so as to attain functional immortality. To create such an object, a wizard must commit murder (*HBP*, Chapter 23).
3. Technically, the first Harry Potter parody song that I wrote was called "The Chosen One," a play on Green Day's "Know Your Enemy" (2009). I am not counting it here because I wrote the song before The 8th Horcrux formed.
4. Sam Ducharme (musician, Flitwick and the Charmers), interview by author, March 13, 2017.
5. Will Jackson (musician, DJ Gryf), interview by author, March 23, 2017.
6. Steph Anderson (musician, Tonks and the Aurors), interview by author, March 13, 2017.
7. Ducharme, interview, March 13, 2017.
8. Grace Kendall (musician, Snidget), interview by author, March 14, 2017.
9. Sarah Frances Holder argues this, too. See: "'Get Your Geek On,'" 64–65.
10. Smith, "It's Real," 71.
11. Cf. Rohlman, "Identity, Rhetoric, and Behavior," 38; Smith, "It's Real," 71.
12. Smith.
13. Smith.
14. This idea was discussed in personal interviews with both Aya Esther Hayashi and

Bradley Mehlenbacher, with the latter noting that "a demographics issue" is partially to blame. See: Paul Thomas, "Hey everyone!" Facebook, January 24, 2018, https://www.facebook.com/groups/1088071511244372/permalink/1840975385953977/.

15. Regarding the relationship between indie rock and whiteness, see: Sarah Sahim, "The Unbearable Whiteness of Indie"; regarding the relationship between punk rock and whiteness, see: Duncombe and Tremblay, *White Riot*.

16. See comments on: Paul Thomas, "Hey everyone!"

17. The latter being both a lyrical adaptation of Draco and the Malfoys' song "My Dad Is Rich, Your Dad Is Dead," as well as a parody of The Lonely Island's comedy single "I'm on a Boat."

18. According to the communications scholar Arthur Asa Berger, parody is "a form of … mimicry or imitation in which the style and mannerisms of some well-known [source] are ridiculed" (Arthur Asa Berger, *An Anatomy of Humor*, 44). In strictly legal terms, therefore, a musical parody must directly comment on or critique the original artist/song in some way. However, the colloquial use of the term "parody" usually refers to *contrafacta*, or songs that substitute "one text for another without substantial change to the music" (Robert Falck and Martin Picker, "Contrafactum"). Since the word "parody" is so widely used when referring to these types of spoofs, this book will use this term for simplicity.

19. Holder, "'Get Your Geek On,'" 65.
20. Mary Ann Rishel, *Writing Humor*, 201.
21. John Morreall, "Philosophy of Humor."
22. Lyndsey Havens, "The Magical Duo behind The 8th Horcrux."
23. Consider, for instance, what the music critic Wrock Snob wrote when reviewing a parody of Timbaland and One Republic's song "Apologize" by Ministry of Magic: "[The parody] makes a catchy but inane pop song tolerable by making it … all about *Harry Potter*!" (Wrock Snob, "My 25 Most Listened To Wizard Rock Songs").
24. Lauren Amanda Smith, "Wizard Rock."
25. Jenkins, *Textual Poachers*, 162–77.
26. Do Rozario, "Wrocking the Collaboration," 272–73; Smith, "Wizard Rock."
27. Smith.
28. Smith.
29. Jenkins, *Textual Poachers*, 165–68.
30. Jenkins, 167–68.
31. *We Are Wizards*.
32. Myles Kane (musician, MC Kreacher), interview by author, June 27, 2017.
33. Diagon Alley is a shopping district located in London. It can only be accessed by magical means (*SS*, Chapter 5)
34. Smith, "Wizard Rock."
35. Cf. Smith, "It's Real."
36. Joelle Paré, "Magical Musical Manifestations," 186.
37. Do Rozario, "Wrocking the Collaboration," 270.
38. Harry and the Potters, *Priori Incantatem*.
39. Holder, "'Get Your Geek On,'" 65.
40. The two are never explicitly identified as a couple in the books, although there are several references throughout the series that suggest this to be true, such as when the two go to the Yule Ball together (*GF*, Chapter 23), and when Draco is described as laying in Pansy's lap before the start of their sixth year (*HBP*, Chapter 7).
41. Smith uses very similar language, writing that with this lyrical sub-genre, wizard rock "step[s] in as a kind of productive consumption, *filling in the "gaps"* left by J.K. Rowling" ("Wizard Rock").
42. Jenkins, *Textual Poachers*, 162.
43. Jenkins, 163.
44. "Imperio," the first of the three "Unforgiveable Curses," puts the victim under the control of the caster (*GF*, Chapter 14).
45. The second of the three "Unforgiveable Curses," which causes the victim extreme pain (*GF*, Chapter 14).
46. A herbologist is a magical user who studies plants (*SS*, Chapter 8).
47. Ashley Barner, *The Case for Fanfiction*, 36; Jenkins, *Textual Poachers*, 171–73; see also: http://tvtropes.org/pmwiki/pmwiki.php/Main/MarySue.
48. Barner, 48–49; Jenkins, 173.
49. Kristina Horner and Elle Viane Sonnet, "About."
50. Jenkins, *Textual Poachers*, 175. It should be noted that the previously discussed "Brotherly Love" by Gred and Forge is a satire of this sort of fanon eroticization.
51. Cf. Jenkins, 162–77; Cf. "Fanfic."

52. Smith, "'Renting' a Room."
53. Jenkins, "*Star Trek*," 55.
54. See also: Do Rozario, "Wrocking the Collaboration," 271–72.
55. The headmistress of the Leaky Cauldron Harry Potter fandom website, and author of *Harry, A History* (2008).
56. Kristina Horner of The Parselmouths.
57. The frontman of The Whomping Willows.
58. Joe and Paul DeGeorge of Harry and the Potters.
59. Bradley Mehlenbacher and Brian Ross of Draco and the Malfoys.
60. Patrick Gill of The Hinky Punks.
61. Brandon Blair of Hollow Godric. On February 25, 2018, Blair himself noted that while this line was meant as a joke, it may nevertheless constitute the first recorded "wrock diss." See: Brandon Blair, "@whompingwillows it occurs [sic] to me that based on 'Wizard Rock Heart Throb'...," Twitter, February 25, 2018, https://twitter.com/hollowgodric/status/967840675411779584.
62. Smith, "'Renting' a Room."
63. "Nargles" are a (possibly fictitious) species, which Luna Lovegood and her father, Xenophilius, claim infest mistletoe and steal things (*OP*, Chapter 21).
64. Jackson, interview.
65. *The Wizard Rockumentary*.
66. "Wizard Rock » About."
67. "Wizard Rock » About."
68. Ducharme, interview, March 13, 2017.
69. Many in the community ascribe Ministry of Magic's professionalism to the fact that several of its members were formerly in major label bands.
70. Paul DeGeorge also told me in an interview that he and Joe were likely to record at least part of their fourth album in a professional studio (although parts of it were also recorded at the Lawrence, KS, Library) (interview by author, Lawrence, KS, April 6, 2018).
71. The former EP, reflecting the dark and foreboding tone of *The Half-Blood Prince*, operates on the premise that Harry Potter has started a hardcore punk band to convey his feelings about the murder of Albus Dumbledore at the hands of Severus Snape; the group thus infused the songs on the EP "with all the rage and dissonance [they] could muster" (Aleksandra Brzozowski, "Bowling with Bands: Harry and the Potters"; Harry and the Potters, *Priori Incantatem*). The latter EP features two songs by Harry and the Potters and two by The Zambonis, all of which revolve around Harry Potter and hockey, both literally (e.g., "Forbidden Forest Hockey League") and idiomatically ("Hogwarts Tonsil Hockey Team") (Harry and the Potters). In regards to the latter EP, Paul DeGeorge explained, "A few years into our band, I sent Dave—the guy behind the Zambonis—a message that said, 'Hey, check out our music. Love you guys!' And he invited us to play at a VFW hall in Connecticut, and then we started talking about doing something together. Then we recorded that EP. That's all there was to it."
72. Paul DeGeorge, interview, January 9, 2018.
73. Downloadable at: http://www.audacityteam.org/.
74. See comments on post: Paul Thomas, "Random question: were there any 'big' wrock albums that were recorded entirely in Audacity? What about Garageband?" Facebook, July 19, 2017, https://www.facebook.com/groups/1088071511244372/permalink/1655650894486428/.
75. See comments on post: Thomas.
76. While the group is not signed to the label, Harry and the Potters' merchandise and music is distributed though DFTBA Records (Paul DeGeorge, "We Are Excited to Announce That DFTBA Is Now...").
77. Many bands have created humorous vanity labels that give their bands the tongue-in-cheek veneer of professionalism. Examples include Indytronic Records (Ministry of Magic), Fueled by Pumpkin Juice Records (The 8th Horcrux, with its name being a parody of the alternative rock label Fueled by Ramen Records), Heat*Beat (Swish and Flick), WizNerd Records (KwikSpell), and AnEndOfSorts Music (Oliver Boyd and the Remembralls).
78. Eva Kurtz-Nelson, "'House of Awesome.'"
79. Dustin Walsh, "Under a Spell."
80. Walsh; Lizz Clements, ed., "More Wrock Bands Join Cheap Rent Family."
81. And some bands even have vinyl records pressed up (e.g., Harry and the Potters' 2011 release *Live at the New York Public Library*).
82. Fairweather, interview, March 15, 2017.

83. See: https://www.kickstarter.com/projects/1590372740/the-whomping-willows-1975-album-restoration.
84. See: https://www.kickstarter.com/projects/470278428/animals-that-have-left-me-10th-anniversary-vinyl.
85. Trina Thomas (musician, The 8th Horcrux), interview by author, Overland Park, KS, September 9, 2017.
86. Brenna Ehrlich, "How To: Get Your Music on iTunes."
87. Grace Kendall, "The 2016 Wizard Rock Sampler."
88. Ethan Gilsdorf, *Fantasy Freaks and Gaming Geeks*, 146.
89. Jackie Burrell, "Harry Potter Fans Tune in to Wizard Rock."
90. Virality is a popular folk view that media is transmitted like a virus. Memetics is a theory that was developed by evolutionary biologist Richard Dawkins in his book *The Selfish Gene* (1976), postulating that the "meme" (analogous to the gene in genetics) is the base unit of mental content; according to Dawkins, memes "live" or "die" per the principals of Darwinian evolution. Jenkins and many others criticize the concept of virality as well as the theory of memetics because they both either minimize or neglect altogether the important—and, arguably, central—role that human agents play in the creation and transmission of ideas. (Henry Jenkins, Sam Ford, and Joshua Green, *Spreadable Media*, 16–23).
91. Jenkins, Ford, and Green, *Spreadable Media*, 3.
92. Jenkins, Ford, and Green, 6.
93. Devon Glenn, "The History of Social Media from 1978–2012 [Infographic]."
94. Anelli, "Rocking at Hogwarts," 125.
95. Anelli.
96. Anelli, 128–29.
97. Anelli, 125–26.
98. Paul DeGeorge, interview, May 25, 2017.
99. Craig Smith, "MySpace Deletes Old User Content."
100. Russ Benoit, "Announcing the Wizrocklopedia Music Archive."
101. Cf. Hayashi, "Musicking, Discourse, and Identity," 107.
102. Terrell, "Constructing Rooms of Requirement," 27.
103. Although the live aspect of wizard rock is still very important.
104. Joe DeGeorge and Paul DeGeorge, "Golden Snitchwiches."
105. Zines (the name being short for "magazines" or "fanzines") are small, hand-made booklets. Usually self-published and released in limited numbers, zines are generally associated with underground or counter-culture subcultures like punk rock.
106. Suzanne Scott, "Revenge of the Fanboy," 235.

Chapter 3

1. The night of this concert—because I was so struck by the energy of the concert—I typed up a painstakingly detailed account of the show and posted it to Facebook as a note for my friends to read. I had no idea that eight years later, this ethnographic account—written when I did not even know what the word "ethnography" meant—would serve as the basis for this chapter's introduction.
2. Lauren Fairweather (musician, The Moaning Myrtles), interview by author, March 17, 2017.
3. Cf. Hayashi, "Musicking, Discourse, and Identity," 80, 108.
4. Jeffrey S. Debies-Carl, "Locating Punk Space," 175.
5. Debies-Carl, 127.
6. Debies-Carl, 126.
7. Sally Childs-Helton, "Folk Music in a Digital Age," 1.
8. DeGeorge, "Bio."
9. See comments on: Paul Thomas, "Wrockers: What Is...." Facebook, August 2, 2017, https://www.facebook.com/groups/1088071511244372/permalink/1670593169658867/.
10. Khosla, "Wonderful, Weird."
11. Amanda Finlaw (vlogger, Amanda Aesthetic), interview by author, May 28, 2017.
12. Sara Rasmussen (radio DJ, The Witching Hour), interview by author, May 29, 2017.
13. Anelli, "Rocking at Hogwarts," 126.
14. Anelli.
15. Edward Norbeck, "African Rituals of Conflict," 1254–55.
16. Max Gluckman, *Order and Rebellion in Tribal Africa*, 112.
17. Gluckman; Norbeck, "African Rituals of Conflict," 1254–55..
18. Halloween—a holiday in which children dress up in scary costumes, demand

candy, and threaten adults with pranks—might be as close as we get (Kottak, "Halloween"; Jennifer C. Mueller, Danielle Dirks, and Leslie Houts Picca, "Unmasking Racism," 315–35).

19. While the lyrics "Just ask Hermione Granger / What she would do when faced with a problem" might simply refer to the character's love of books, it must be remembered that Hermione was also the chief architect of the Society for the Promotion of Elfish Welfare (S.P.E.W.) (*GF*, Chapter 14). Perhaps, then, Steph Anderson is using Hermione's name as a metaphor for anyone working for the betterment of others.

20. For those interested, Morales's zine is perhaps the best emic account of wrock house shows.

21. Claudia Morales, *Rocking the Room of Requirement*, 5, 7.

22. Sam Ducharme (musician, Flitwick and the Charmers), interview by author, May 9, 2017.

23. Grace Kendall, interview, May 26, 2017.

24. Emily Cataneo, "Harry and the Potters Host Annual Yule Ball at Middle East Sunday."

25. Dan Shea, "5 Questions w/ Paul DeGeorge of Harry and the Potters."

26. Cataneo, "Annual Yule Ball."

27. Paul DeGeorge, "2008 Yule Ball CD/DVD Available Now!"

28. DeGeorge.

29. Paul DeGeorge, "We Are Excited to Announce the 2017 Yule Balls!"

30. Grace Kendall, "The Museum of Wizard Rock."

31. Abby Hupp (Wrockstock organizer), interview by author, August 7, 2017.

32. The name being a reference to the famous 1969 music festival, Woodstock.

33. Pyne, "Wizard Rock," 185.

34. Pyne, 185–86.

35. Kelli Rohlman, "Identity, Rhetoric, and Behavior," 29; *Wired*, "Our Weapon Is Love: Wrockstock 2008."

36. Gilsdorf, *Fantasy Freaks and Gaming Geeks*, 145; Abby Hupp (Wrockstock organizer), interview by author, September 30, 2017; Kelli Rohlman.

37. Abby Hupp (Wrockstock organizer), interview by author, August 8, 2017.

38. Pyne, "Wizard Rock," 185–86; Rohlman, "Identity, Rhetoric and Behavior," 16–17.

39. Rohlman, 16.

40. Wrockstock, "Wrockstock Reunited," Facebook, 2013, https://www.facebook.com/events/520551004647185/.

41. Logan Falletti, "Final 'Hallows and Horcruxes Ball' on Saturday."

42. ChALC. "The Hallows and Horcruxes Ball."

43. *The Collegian*, "Bands Entertain 'Harry Potter' Fans with Wizard Rock, Quirky Humor."

44. Falletti, "Final Hallows and Horcruxes; Jakki Forester, "Hallows and Horcruxes Ball Features Variety of Wizarding Activities for Avid 'Harry Potter' Fans."

45. Falletti.

46. Forester, "Hallows and Horcruxes."

47. Falletti, "Final Hallows and Horcruxes."

48. Falletti.

49. Forester, "Hallows and Horcruxes."

50. Scott, "Revenge of the Fanboy," 254; "Wrock Chicago."

51. Scott.

52. Pyne, "Wizard Rock," 186–89.

53. Pattie Beaven, "About."

54. Beaven; Pyne, "Wizard Rock," 186–88.

55. Melissa Anelli, "Presenting... LeakyCon 2009!"

56. Holder, "'Get Your Geek On,'" 3; Leaky-Con staff, "Top Young Adult Literature Authors to Meet Fans and Aspiring Writers at LeakyCon 2014"; Mischief Management staff, "LeakyCon Rebrands itself as 'GeekyCon' as Annual Fandom Convention Comes to A Close in Orlando Amid Sold-Out Crowd."

57. Hayashi, "Musicking, Discourse, and Identity," 51.

58. Grace Kendall (musician, Snidget), interview by author, February 1, 2018.

59. Paré, "Magical Musical Manifestations," 196.

60. Steph Anderson (musician, Tonks and the Aurors), interview by author, May 25, 2017.

61. Anelli, "Rocking at Hogwarts," 121–22.

62. Paul DeGeorge, interview, May 25, 2017.

63. Lauren Fairweather (musician, The Moaning Myrtles), interview by author, September 17, 2017.

64. See: https://www.kickstarter.com/projects/1590372740/riddikulus-2012-a-rolling-wizard-rock-festival.

65. See: https://www.kickstarter.com/projects/stephanderson/go-west-young-wizards-a-wizard-rock-summer-tour.
66. See: https://www.kickstarter.com/projects/stephanderson/yes-all-witches-route-66-edition.
67. *La conscience collective* in the original French. It is sometimes rendered as the "collective consciousness."
68. Kenneth Allan, *Explorations in Classical Sociological Theory*, 108; Émile Durkheim, *The Division of Labor in Society*, 63.
69. Ken Morrison, *Marx, Durkheim, Weber*, 169.
70. Durkheim, *Division of Labor*, 63.
71. Morrison, *Marx, Durkheim, Weber*, 169.
72. These two types are not mutually exclusive, and a society can be—and often is—some mix of both.
73. Durkheim uses the word "volume" to refer to the pervasiveness of the common consciousness.
74. Durkheim, *Division of Labor*, xxx; Morrison, *Marx, Durkheim, Weber*, 161–62, 151, 165.
75. Durkheim, xxx; Morrison, 166–68.
76. Trina Thomas (musician, The 8th Horcrux), interview by author, Overland Park, KS, June 13, 2017.
77. Anu Lingappa, "Violence in Harry Potter Community Calls for Barrier between Fans, Stars."
78. Fairweather, interview, March 17, 2017.
79. See comments on: Paul Thomas, "So, I'm meditating..." Facebook, August 18, 2017, https://www.facebook.com/groups/1088071511244372/permalink/1685964141455103/.
80. Émile Durkheim, *The Elementary Forms of Religious Life* (1915 [1912]), 214–15; Wendy Griswold, *Cultures and Societies in a Changing World*, 51–3; Morrison, *Marx, Durkheim, Weber*, 239–41.
81. Law, *Key Concepts in Classical Social Theory*, 166.
82. Morrison, *Marx, Durkheim, Weber*, 239–41.
83. Griswold, *Cultures and Societies*, 52–3.
84. Durkheim reference "collective sentiment" on a later page (Durkheim, *Elementary Forms* (1915 [1912]), 216); it has been moved here to make the point clear.
85. Durkheim, 215–18.
86. Émile Durkheim, *The Elementary Forms of Religious Life* (1995 [1912]), xli.
87. Griswold, *Cultures and Societies*, 53.
88. Cf. Yoho, "Developing Community," 223.
89. Arthur Buehler, "The Twenty-First-Century Study of Collective Effervescence," 70–97.
90. Tim Olaveson, "'Connectedness' and the Rave Experience."
91. Jeffrey May, "Pilgrims on Tour."
92. Jenkins, "The Night of a Thousand Wizards," 121; Sean McCloud, "Popular Culture Fandoms, the Boundaries of Religious Studies, and the Project of the Self," 187–206.
93. Durkheim, *Elementary Forms* (1915 [1912]), 382–83.
94. An anthropologist reading this section might wonder why I failed to mention Victor Turner's seminal idea of *communitas*. This is because I am of the same opinion as the Religious Studies researcher Tim Olaveson, who wrote that both Durkheim and Turner "were writing about the same phenomenon, although to differing degrees of depth and precision" (Tim Olaveson, "Collective Effervescence and Communitas," 106); For a brief consideration of *communitas* in the wrock community, see both Justin Clapp, "Collective Consumption," 53–60, and Yoho, "Developing Community," 222–23.
95. See: Thomas, "So, I'm meditating..."
96. See: Thomas.
97. See: Thomas.

Chapter 4

1. Astoria Greengrass grew up to marry Draco Malfoy (*CC*, Act One, Scene Four).
2. Gilsdorf, *Fantasy Freaks*, 148.
3. Yoho, "Developing Community," 224.
4. Markus Montola, "Social Reality in Roleplaying Games," 107.
5. Markus Montola, "The Invisible Rules of Role-Playing," 23–24.
6. Montola.
7. Paul DeGeorge, interview, May 25, 2017.
8. Montola, "The Invisible Rules," 23–24.
9. Authority can also be shared between two or more groups (e.g., if two wrock bands perform a song together, or engage in playful banter on stage while in character).

10. Montoloa notes that "participant roles include ... live musician[s]," among many other (Montola, "The Invisible Rules," 24).

11. Montola, 23–24.

12. A "dungeon master" (often abbreviated as the "DM") is the person who organizes a game of *Dungeons and Dragons*, controls the action, and makes most of the decisions (aside from those made by the other players).

13. "LARP" stands for "live-action role play." Unlike what one might call "traditional" role-play, in which much of the action unfolds in the shared imagination of the various participants, LARPing allows for participants to dress-up and act out the action in spatio-temporal "real life."

14. Katie Salen Tekinbaş and Eric Zimmerman, *Rules of Play*, 80.

15. Paul DeGeorge, interview, May 25, 2017.

16. Cf. Scott, "Revenge of the Fanboy," 249.

17. Sarah Lynne Bowman, "Discovering Your Inner Wizard," 95.

18. For an example of the latter, see: Rohlman, "Identity, Rhetoric and Behavior."

19. Grace Dow (fan), interview by author, June 1, 2017.

20. Fairweather, interview, April 17, 2017.

21. Gilsdorf, *Fantasy Freaks*, 146.

22. Gilsdorf.

23. Paul DeGeorge, interview, May 25, 2017.

24. Theresa Winge, "Costuming the Imagination," 66.

25. Luke Plunkett, "Cosplay Is Over 100 Years Old."

26. Plunkett.

27. Winge, "Costuming the Imagination," 66–67; Brian Ashcraft and Luke Plunkett, *Cosplay World*, 9.

28. Winge, 66; Chris Kincaid, "The History of Cosplay."

29. Winge, 66–67.

30. Winge, Ashcraft and Plunkett, *Cosplay World*, 6–8.

31. Paul Booth, *Playing Fans*, 151–52.

32. Scott Duchesne apud Booth, *Playing Fans*, 163.

33. Joe DeGeorge, interview.

34. Anderson, interview, May 25, 2017; Christopher Bee (fan), interview by author, May 26, 2017; Ariel Birdoff (musician, Madam Pince and the Librarians), interview by author, May 25, 2017.

35. Bowman, "Discovering Your Inner Wizard," 100.

36. Bowman, 87.

37. Igweonu and Okagbue, *Performative Inter-Actions*, 3.

38. John Warren, and Deanna Fassett, *Communication*, 94.

39. Austin, *How to Do Things*, 5–6.

40. Butler, *Bodies That Matter*, 2; Igweonu and Okagbue, *Performative Inter-Actions*, 4.

41. Butler; Lamerichs, "Stranger Than Fiction."

42. Lamerichs.

43. Ahern, "Performance/Performativity."

44. Igweonu and Okagbue, *Performative Inter-Actions*, 4.

45. Lamerichs, "Stranger Than Fiction."

46. Booth, *Playing Fans*, 163.

47. Cornel Sandvoss apud Booth.

48. Lacey Rose, "Wizard Rock."

49. Remember, Paul DeGeorge once claimed, "[Our band] kind of came out of the book. [...] I sort of saw a lot of [Harry's behavior] in my punk rock heroes" ("Harry Potter: What Is Wizard Rock?").

50. Gilsdorf, *Fantasy Freaks*, 144.

51. Cf. Lamerichs, "Stranger Than Fiction."

52. The "Patronus Charm" is a defensive spells used to protect the caster from a variety of nasty creatures (including Lethifolds and Dementors). The spell takes on the form of an animal with whom the caster holds a connection. Harry Potter's Patronus takes on the form of a stag, a creature into which his father was able to magically transform (*PA*, Chapter 12).

53. The Mirror of Erised is a mirror that shows the gazer their heart's true desire. In the case of Harry Potter, it shows him his deceased parents (*SS*, Chapter 12).

54. Rohlman, "Identity, Rhetoric and Behavior," 35.

55. One needs to only consider the countless newspaper and magazine articles about Harry and the Potters or the DeGeorge brothers in general that explicitly invoke the word "punk" in their title (e.g., Melody Joy Kramer, "Wizard Rock: Harry Potter Goes Punk".)

Chapter 5

1. This survey assumed a population size of 20,000 individuals. This was done because surveys considering populations equal to or

greater than this number all require roughly the same sample size to be statistically accurate, which makes 20,000 a "safe" estimation. Thus, with a sample size of 150 respondents, this survey's margin of error is ±6.7 percent (with a 90 percent confidence interval). Future surveys with larger sample sizes will be needed to more precisely document the demography of wizard rock.

2. Cf. Rohlman, "Identity, Rhetoric and Behavior," 23.

3. Rohlman; Hayashi, "Musicking, Discourse, and Identity," 91–101.

4. Rohlman; Hayashi, 91–92.

5. Rohlman, 25.

6. Rohlman; Hayashi, "Musicking, Discourse, and Identity," 92–94.

7. Rohlman; Hayashi.

8. Wrock Snob, "Extended Thoughts."

9. Wrock Snob.

10. These countries included: Argentina (1), Denmark (1), France (1), Germany (2), Ireland (1), Mexico (1), Norway (1), and Turkey (1).

11. The nationality of an additional 91 bands could not be determined, either because their websites did not list their nation of origin, or because their websites are no longer extant. However, because these groups represent only a fraction (11.5 percent) of the total bands, and because they were randomly scattered throughout the Wizrocklopedia's list, I would argue that their omission here is not statistically significant.

12. These numbers were shared with me by Russ Benoit of the Wizrocklopedia.

13. These countries included: Brazil (1), Denmark (2), Finland (2), France (2), Germany (8), Ireland (3), Italy (1), Japan (2), the Netherlands (2), Norway (1), Portugal (2), Russia (1), Slovenia (1), South Korea (1), and Spain (1).

14. That is, the portion of the world—generally said to include the United Kingdom, the United States, Canada, Australia, and New Zealand—where "the English language and cultural values predominate." See: *Merriam-Webster Online Dictionary*, s.v. "Anglosphere."

15. In 2012, the UK had a population of about 63.0 million and the United States a population of about 313.8 million, meaning that (in an evenly distributed world) bands in the U.S. should have outnumbered those in the UK by about 5 to 1. In actuality, the ratio was closer to 10 to 1. Likewise, in 2017, the UK had a population of about 65.6 million and the United States a population of about 326.6 million, meaning that the ratio of bands and fans in the U.S. to those in the UK should have again been 5 to 1. This year, the ratio was 15 to 1.

16. For instance, Lauren Fairweather told me, "I brought my best friend along with me to one of [Harry and the Potters'] shows and [afterwards] we decided to start The Moaning Myrtles together […] One of the most intriguing and inspiring things about wizard rock is getting to experience … concerts for the first time, and it's what drives a lot of new bands to start up in the first place" (Fairweather, interview, March 15, 17, 2017).

17. For American interest in the Royal Family, see: Rupert Cornwall, "The Regal Republic"; For American interest in British media vis-à-vis television, see: Virginia Harrison, "America's Love Affair with British TV" See also: Katharine W. Jones, *Accent on Privilege*, 77–80.

18. Elisa Tamarkin, *Anglophilia*, xxv.

19. Tamarkin.

20. Anglophilia never developed to such a degree in the United Kingdom itself because the aspects of every day British culture that Americans fawned over were seen by many Britons simply as banal.

21. Caroline Lee Schwenz, "Anglophilia."

22. Jones, *Accent on Privilege*, 77–80; Tamarkin, *Anglophilia*, xxiii–v.

23. Tamarkin, xxiv.

24. Compare this to the concept of "colonial vicariousness" in Tamarkin, xxv.

25. Genevieve Abravanel, *Americanizing Britain*, 162.

26. Scwhenz, "Anglophilia."

27. Many Anglosphere nations, such as Australia and Canada, have their own populations of Anglophiles. However, because these nations gained their independence much later than the United States, and because they are still tied to the United Kingdom in many ways (e.g., most have Queen Elizabeth as their head of state, most are members of the Commonwealth of Nations), their Anglophilia has not developed to the degree found in the United States.

28. Paul DeGeorge, interview, May 25, 2017.

29. In 2012, Sweden had a population of about 9.1 million and the United States a population of about 313.8 million, meaning that (in an evenly distributed world) bands in the U.S. should have outnumbered those in Sweden by about 34 to 1. In actuality, the ratio was closer to 31 to 1. Likewise, in 2017, Sweden had a population of about 10.0 million and the United States a population of about 326.6 million, meaning that the ratio of bands and fans in the U.S. to those in Sweden should have been 34 to 1. This year, the ratio was 14 to 1. These numbers suggest that, from 2012 to 2017, the wrock community in Sweden grew at a disproportionate rate.

30. See comments on: Sarah Frances Holder, "I mentioned before..." Facebook, April 22, 2017, https://www.facebook.com/groups/1088071511244372/permalink/1555907674460751/.

31. Anna Fahlén (musician, The Swedish Shortsnouts), interview by author, May 23, 2017.

32. Brock Bastian, Jolanda Jetten, and Laura J. Ferris, "Pain as Social Glue," 2084.

33. Mel Stanfill, "Doing Fandom (Mis) Doing Whiteness."

34. Stanfill.

35. In 1991 (when the first *Harry Potter* book is set), 93 percent of the United Kingdom identified as white. The largest minorities were people who identified as Asian (4 percent) and people who identified as black (3 percent) (ESRC Centre on Dynamics of Ethnicity, "How Has Ethnic Diversity Grown 1991–2001–2011?"). Per these demographics, and assuming that magical ability is found equally throughout all races and ethnicities, one could argue that Rowling is not replicating a racial bias in regards to the overrepresentation of white characters. However, the point being made here is that all the book's *main* characters (and the vast majority of secondary characters) are generally understood by readers to be white.

36. The decision to cast Noma Dumezweni—an English actress of color—as Hermione in the initial run of *The Cursed Child* led to a massive Internet debate. Some fans argued that the casting was an attempt to be "PC." However, many others logically countered that Hermione's race is not specified in the books, and thus the assumption that Hermione *has* to be white is either due to Emma Watson's popular portrayal of the character in the movies, or, more likely, blatant racial bias. Whatever the cause, this casting has led many fans to reinterpret the Hermione of the books as a black character. While it is too early to tell if this reinterpretation will encourage more people of color to form wrock bands, it is quite possible, given that it has reduced the excessive whiteness of the *main* characters.

37. Dow, interview.
38. Smith, "'Renting' a Room."
39. Smith.
40. Smith.
41. Anderson, interview, May 25, 2017.
42. Dana Floberg, "Digital Denied."
43. Floberg.
44. Bernadette D. Proctor, Jessica L. Semega, and Melissa A. Kollar, "Income and Poverty in the United States."
45. Thomas, interview, September 9, 2017.
46. Thomas.
47. Freya Fridy, "He Said/She Said."
48. In June of 2017, Joe DeGeorge shared with me his band's Facebook page statistics. Interestingly, the demographic spread of the band's fans roughly mirrors these results, with 73 percent of those who like the page identifying as women.
49. Jenkins, "*Star Trek*," 43.
50. Jenkins; Jenkins, *Textual Poachers*, 108–15.
51. Jenkins, *Textual Poachers*.
52. Holder, "'Get Your Geek On,'" 70.
53. Rohlman, "Identity, Rhetoric and Behavior," 72; Wrock Snob, "In Defense of Men."
54. Fairweather, interview, March 15, 2017.
55. Fairweather.
56. And some of the biggest female-fronted groups, too.
57. Scott, "Revenge of the Fanboy," 262; see also Hayashi (2017) and Rohlman (2010).
58. Tammy Oler, "Ladies Camp Rock," 67.
59. Scott, "Revenge of the Fanboy," 258.
60. Scott; this was also noted by Sarah Frances Holder in her M.A. thesis (Holder, "'Get Your Geek On,'" 70).
61. Scott, 261.
62. Fairweather, March 15, 2017.
63. Scott, Revenge of the Fanboy," 261.
64. Scott.
65. Maggie Hanna, "Wizrocklopedia Blog

Archive "A Sisterhood of Wrock"; Oddly, when discussing the concert, Pisani dismissed the idea that the event was combatting sexist or hegemonic structures within wizard rock itself, arguing that: "The only reason why the more popular wrock bands are male is because they are able to tour and promote. Female wizard rockers can tour and promote just as well as the males can, but we tend to have other commitments that keep us from doing so: school, family, work. It has little to do with gender—it just sort of ended up that way." As can be seen by this quote, there is still a desire in the wrock community to view the movement as wholly egalitarian. But attempting to reframe the gender issue so as to deny the existence of sexism only further reveals the problem. Why might women have more commitments than men? What allows men to get off the hook for things like "school, family, [and] work"? Scott argues that, were there not an underlying issue in the first place, the need for a female wrock showcase would be unnecessary ("Revenge of the Fanboy," 261).
66. Kendall, "The Museum of Wizard Rock."
67. See: https://twitter.com/witch_rock.
68. TK Lawrence, "Fresh, Spooky, and Queer, by Totally Knuts."
69. TK Lawrence (musician, Totally Knuts), interview by author, June 12, 2017.
70. Rebecca Traister, "Potterpalooza."
71. Lawrence, interview.
72. Justin Finch-Fletchley and the Sugar Quills, "Dumbledore Is Gay (and That's OK!)."
73. Rohlman, "Identity, Rhetoric, and Behavior," 76.
74. Derived from: YouGov, "Sexual Orientation" [UK]; YouGov, "Sexual Orientation" [U.S.].
75. "Normal" in the statistical sense.
76. Rohlman, "Identity, Rhetoric, and Behavior," 75.
77. Danika Ellis, "Queer and Feminist Wizard Rock"; It should be noted that there do exist other, less popular ships that have nevertheless gained a "loyal contingent" of fans (to borrow language from Rohlman, 77). These include Remus Lupin/Sirius Black and, more recently, Al Potter/Scorpius Malfoy.
78. Rohlman, 76; "Slash" is "a type of fan work in which two ... characters of the same sex or gender are placed in a sexual or roman-tic situation with each other" (https://fanlore.org/wiki/Slash). The name is derived from the unique usage of a slash mark to denote a ship. See: Rohlman, 76n59.
79. For a more in-depth consideration of this topic, see: Aaron Sohwabach, *Fan Fiction and Copyright*, 10–1, 69.
80. Do Rozario, "Wrocking," 269.
81. Rohlman, "Identity, Rhetoric and Behavior," 75.
82. Rohlman, 79.

Chapter 6

1. Joe DeGeorge and Paul DeGeorge, "Today we are excited…," Facebook, February 3, 2017, https://www.facebook.com/harryandthepotters/photos/a.407486277614.180035.13569222614/10154392562597615/?type=3.
2. *Wired*, "Our Weapon."
3. Birdoff, interview.
4. Paul DeGeorge, interview, May 25, 2017.
5. For another consideration of this point, see Hall, "Reading and [W]rocking," specifically 203–04.
6. Paré, "Magical Musical Manifestations," 196.
7. Rohlman, "Identity, Rhetoric and Behavior," 56.
8. Catherine Belcher and Becky Stephenson, *Teaching Harry Potter*, 153.
9. Belcher and Stephenson.
10. Jennifer Popple, "Embracing the Magic," 188.
11. Rohlman, "Identity, Rhetoric and Behavior," 73.
12. The phrase "Yes All Witches!" was based on the popular feminist hashtage #YesAllWomen, which gained prominence in May 2014 following the Isla Vista Killings and the rise of the hashtage #NotAllMen (Holder, "'Get Your Geek On,'" 71).
13. Anderson, interview, May 25, 2017.
14. Steph Anderson, "About."
15. Steph Anderson, "Apply for a YAW Grant."
16. Holder, "'Get Your Geek On,'" 69.
17. See for instance: http://www.wrocklopedia.com/2018/02/22/review-totally-knuts-fresh-spooky-queer/.
18. Cf. Rohlman, "Identity, Rhetoric, and Behavior," 61.
19. Kelly Ward, "Subversive Wrock."

20. Paul DeGeorge, interview, May 25, 2017.
21. Morales, "Wizard Rock"; Ward, "Subversive Wrock."
22. Chris Grosvenor, "Let's Get Political."
23. Morales, "Wizard Rock"
24. Morales; Ward, "Subversive Wrock."
25. Morales; Kelly Ward seemed to second DeGeorge's comments when she wrote on the Wizrocklopedia that politically conscious wrock songs—such as the aforementioned "Cornelius Fudge Is an Ass" or the other Harry and the Potters track "(Not Gonna Put on) The Monkey Suit" can "make [listeners] feel a little bit of hope even though these days are dark" ("Subversive Wrock").
26. "Mudblood" is a slur in the *Harry Potter* universe, referring to witches or wizards whose parents are Muggles.
27. Myles Kane (musician, MC Kreacher), interview by author, March 4, 2018.
28. Paul DeGeorge, interview, May 25, 2017.
29. "Dumbledore's Army" was an underground defense against the dark arts club that Harry Potter founded during his fifth year at Hogwarts to combat the draconian rule of Dolores Umbridge (*OP*, passim).
30. "The Harry Potter Alliance, A History."
31. "The Harry Potter Alliance."
32. "The Harry Potter Alliance."
33. "The Harry Potter Alliance."
34. Henry Jenkins, "How 'Dumbledore's Army' Is Transforming Our World."
35. Henry Jenkins, "'Cultural Acupuncture,'" 41.
36. Jenkins, 41, 43–44.
37. Jenkins, 43; Andrew Slack, "Harry Potter and the Muggle Activists."
38. Jenkins, 44–47.
39. Henry Jenkins, *Convergence Culture*, 207–8.
40. Jenkins; Stacy Takacs, *Interrogating Popular Culture*, 110; "The Harry Potter Alliance, A History."
41. "Success Stories."
42. Rohlman, "Identity, Rhetoric and Behavior," 60; "Success Stories."
43. "Wizard Rock the Vote 2016."
44. "Success Stories."
45. "Success Stories"; "The Harry Potter Alliance, A History"; "What We Do."
46. Henry Jenkins, "'Cultural Acupuncture,'" 46.
47. Alyssa Rosenberg, "How 'Harry Potter' Fans Won a Four-Year Fight against Child Slavery."
48. Nancy Gibbs, "Person of the Year 2007."
49. J.K. Rowling, "Section: Fan Sites: The HP Alliance."
50. Jenkins, "'Cultural Acupuncture,'" 39.
51. Matt Maggiacomo (musician, The Whomping Willows), interview by author, May 23, 2017.
52. Matt Maggiacomo, "Wizards and Muggles Rock for Social Justice."
53. Melissa Anelli, "Leaky's Sixth Get a Clue Fundraiser Now Open."
54. Anelli.
55. Melissa Anelli, "Jingle Spells Completely Sold Out."
56. Melissa Anelli, "The Great Jingle Spells Contest"; Melissa Anelli, "The Great(er) Jingle Spells Contest."
57. See the following for a fairly exhaustive list of released compilation albums: https://yourwizardrockresource.wordpress.com/compilations/.
58. For a thorough treatment of the 2014 sexual abuse scandal, its impact on the wrock community, and the reasons why it happened in the first place, see: Hayashi, "Musicking, Discourse, and Identity," 156–93.
59. Alanna Bennett, "Why The YouTube Community Is Standing Up Against Sexual and Emotional Abuse"; Hayashi, "Musicking, Discourse, and Identity," 156; Rosianna Rojas, "I am going to start with a redundant sentence..."; Aja Romano, Michelle Jaworksi, and Rae Votta, "A Guide to YouTube's 10 Biggest Sex Abuse Scandals."
60. Romano, Jaworksi, and Votta, "A Guide."
61. Hayashi, "Musicking, Discourse, and Identity," 157; Michelle Jaworski and Rae Votta, "The 9 Biggest YouTube Scandals of 2014"; Romano, Jaworksi, and Votta, "A Guide."
62. Bennett, "Why the YouTube Community Is Standing Up"; Hayashi, 156–57; Kristina Horner, "The Truth about ALL CAPS."
63. Hayashi, 157; Whitney Milam, "Awkward Boy Stories"; "Reference: List of Fandom Abuse Posts."
64. "Luke Conard Seemingly Both Apologies for and Denies Allegations, Internet Really Not Buying It"; "Reference: List of Fandom Abuse Posts."

65. Jason Munday, "My Experience with the Wizard Rock Community"; Jason Munday, "The wizard rock 'community' always was and somehow is still one of the worst things I've ever encountered. Glad it's dead," Facebook, March 31, 2014, https://www.facebook.com/jasonmundaymusic/posts/633263750061659.
66. Matt Maggiacomo, "Gah."
67. Andrew Slack, "Defense against the Dark Arts."
68. Lauren Fairweather, "Letters."
69. Hayashi, "Musicking, Discourse, and Identity."
70. Aya Esther Hayashi (musicologist), interview by author, August 29, 2017.
71. Paul DeGeorge, interview, May 25, 2017.

Chapter 7

1. Amy Snow (podcaster, *WZRD: Your Wizard Rock Station*), interview by author, June 26, 2017; Snow and Walker, "WZRD Info."
2. Snow.
3. Snow; Amy Snow and Jamie Walker, "Episodes."
4. Snow, interview.
5. Snow.
6. Snow.
7. Gillian Frew, "The Witching Hour"; Sara Rasmussen (radio DJ, The Witching Hour), interview by author, May 15, 2017.
8. Mehera Nori (radio DJ, The Witching Hour), interview by author, May 29, 2017; Rasmussen, interview, May 29, 2017.
9. Rasmussen, interview, May 15, 2017.
10. Frew, "The Witching Hour"; Nori, interview, May 29, 2017; Rasmussen, interview, May 29, 2017.
11. Frew.
12. Nori, interview, May 29, 2017.
13. The educational decrees were Ministry of Magic-approved "executive orders" that regulated Hogwarts. As Dolores Umbridge began to assume more power at the school, they became increasingly draconian (*OP*, passim).
14. Nori, interview.
15. Frew, "The Witching Hour."
16. Anu Lingappa (radio DJ, The Witching Hour), interview by author, October 10, 2017.
17. Frew, "The Witching Hour."
18. Frew.; Lingappa, interview.
19. Sara Rasmussen (radio DJ, The Witching Hour), interview by author, October 9, 2017.
20. Lingappa, interview.
21. Lingappa.
22. Erin Walters (radio DJ, The Witching Hour), interview by author, May 9, 2016; Varinia Balkins, "KWCW Spotlight."
23. He went by the pseudonym "Xavier Austrone" online.
24. "1st Week of WrockBOX Has Been Totally Awesome!!"
25. See comments on: Paul Thomas, "Does anyone remember WrockBox..." Facebook, May 8, 2017, https://www.facebook.com/groups/1088071511244372/permalink/1576126402438878/.
26. Keith Cardin, "WrockBOX | Wizard Rock Radio | 24/7 Internet Radio Station."
27. "1st Week of WrockBOX"
28. "1st Week of WrockBOX"
29. "Xavier's on YouTube?!"
30. See comments on: Thomas, "Does anyone remember WrockBox..."
31. See comments on: Thomas.
32. See comments on: Thomas; "About."
33. "About"; "Inside wrockBOX Wizarding Radio."
34. See comments on: Thomas, "Does anyone remember WrockBox..."
35. See comments on: Thomas.
36. wrockBOX, "It's official," Twitter, September 25, 2014, https://twitter.com/wrockbox/status/515393331845922816.
37. "What Should We Keep?"
38. Lizz Clements, ed., "Meet the Staff"; Lizz Clements, ed., "The Wizrocklopedia."
39. Clements; Clements.
40. Clements, "The Wizrocklopedia."
41. Based on Internet Archive snapshots.
42. See comments on: Paul Thomas, "Does anyone know..." Facebook, June 19, 2017, https://www.facebook.com/groups/1088071511244372/permalink/1620596091325242/.
43. See comments on: Thomas.
44. Clements, "Meet the Staff."
45. See here for a log of site issues: http://www.wrocklopedia.com/category/site-updates/.
46. This can be ascertained by noting gaps in the website's archives: http://www.wrocklopedia.com/archives/.

47. Freya Friday, "Creevey's Creevey Thursday."
48. Originally located at http://www.wizrocklopedia.com.
49. Fawkes was a Phoenix and Dumbledore's loyal familiar (*CS*, Chapter 12).
50. Now found at http://www.wrocklopedia.com.
51. Laura Dianiska, "'Pedia's Back! Send an Owl!"
52. Laura Dianiska, "State of the Pedia."
53. Laura Dianiska, "From the Editors: Thank You!"
54. Dianiska, "State of the Pedia."
55. Cf. Hayassi, "Musicking, Discourse, and Identity," 108.
56. Per her request, I have redacted her last name.
57. "FAQ."
58. Susannah (webmaster, *Your Wizard Rock Resource*), interview by author, May 27, 2016.
59. Susannah.
60. Susannah.
61. Susannah.
62. Susannah.
63. Susannah.
64. Nick Dawson, "Josh Koury, We Are Wizards."
65. Aaron Hills, "Interview: Josh Koury on 'We Are Wizards.'"
66. Hills.
67. Rohlman, "Identity, Rhetoric and Behavior," 6; *We Are Wizards*.
68. Rohlman, 4–6.
69. "We Are Wizards (2008)."
70. "We Are Wizards."
71. "We Are Wizards."
72. George Beahm, "The Wizard Rockumentary," 238.
73. Beahm, 237; Faith McKay, "An Interview with The Schuyler Sisters of The Wizard Rockumentary."
74. Rohlman, "Identity, Rhetoric and Behavior," 5.
75. Beahm, "The Wizard Rockumentary," 237.
76. McKay, "An Interview."
77. *Spokane 7*, "Documenting Harry's Spell"; Deborah Chan, "Wizard Rockumentary Review."
78. Chan.
79. Mallory Schuyler and Megan Schuyler, "In the News."
80. Per the request of Wrock Snob, I have redacted their name. I instead use their pseudonym where necessary.
81. Wrock Snob, "What Is This Shit?"
82. Wrock Snob (wrock music critic), interview by author, January 18, 2018
83. Wrock Snob; Hayashi, "Musicking, Discourse, and Identity," 99–100.
84. Hayashi, 99.
85. Wrock Snob, "What Is This Shit?"
86. Paul DeGeorge, interview, May 25, 2017.
87. I count myself among these community members. Early in my wrock career, I wrote a song called "Why'd You Do It, J.K.?" that tried to satirize the moral panic following J.K. Rowling's reveal that Albus Dumbledore was gay. When the song came to the attention of Wrock Snob, they called it "stupid" and negatively critiqued it for being problematic. While I was stung at the time—certain that Wrock Snob did not "understand" my art—I realize now that the criticism was completely valid, and that my attempt at "edgy satire" was dumb and offensive. Nowadays, I keep in mind Wrock Snob's critique, and I use it to write better, stronger songs.
88. Wrock Snob, "A Brief Respite."
89. Lizz Clements, ed., "The Wizard Rock People's Choice Awards."
90. Clements, "Wizard Rock People's Choice Awards"; Lizz Clements, ed., "The Wizard Rock Peoples Choice Awards: Fill Out the Nominations Form Now"; Lizz Clements, ed., "WR People's Choice Awards Nominations Open!"
91. Lizz Clements, ed., "WRPCA Voting Polls Open!!"
92. Clements, "Fill Out the Nominations Form"; Lizz Clements, ed., "Wizard Rock People's Choice Awards Results"; Lizz Clements, ed., "The Wizard Rock Peoples Choice Awards: Voting."
93. For a complete list of winners, see: "Susannah," *Your Wizard Rock Resource*, s.v. "Wizard Rock People's Choice Awards."
94. For a similar sentiment, see: Rohlman, "Identity, Rhetoric, and Behavior," 82.
95. See comments on: Paul Thomas, "I'm doing some research…" Facebook, April 13, 2017, https://www.facebook.com/groups/1088071511244372/permalink/1544778582240327/.

96. See comments on: Thomas, "I'm doing some research…"
97. Wrock Snob, "The Wizzies."
98. Wrock Snob.
99. Brett Holden, "We finally have the poll results! There were over 300 unique voters in final voting," Twitter, July 23, 2011, https://twitter.com/TheWizzies/status/94806199106682880.
100. "Wizzies Intro"; Wrock Snob, "The Wizzies."
101. Wrock Snob.
102. "Wizzies Intro."
103. Brett Holden, "It would appear that interest might not be at a high enough peak to justify putting together a show," Twitter, March 6, 2012, https://twitter.com/TheWizzies/status/177135770946113536.

Chapter 8

1. Jenkins, Ford, and Green, *Spreadable Media*, 65; Tisha Turk, "Fan Work."
2. Turk.
3. Trina Thomas (musician, The 8th Horcrux), interview with author, Overland Park, KS, October 23, 2017.
4. "Wizard Rock » About."
5. Rohlman "Identity, Rhetoric and Behavior," 57: Rohlman argues that the line may very well show traces of feminist philosophy, suggesting that the members of The Moaning Myrtles have realized that they do not need the approval or adoration of men to be successful or happy (57, 73).
6. While this book is focused mostly on the fandom surrounding the cult CW television series *Supernatural*, it is also interspersed with broader considerations of fans and fandom in general.
7. Lynn Zubernis and Katherine Larsen, *Fangasm*, 20.
8. See comments on: Thomas, "I'm in the final stages…"
9. Morales, *Rocking the Room of Requirement*, 4–8.
10. Larsen and Zubernis, *Fangasm*, 20.
11. Lynn Zubernis and Katherine Larsen, *Fandom at the Crossroads*, 105
12. For instance, the song is discussed in a similar way by both Smith (2017) and Hayashi (2018), who were writing separately from one another.
13. Hayashi, "Musicking, Discourse, and Identity," 87; Smith, "It's Real," 73.
14. Smith, 70.
15. Cf. Hayashi, "Musicking, Discourse, and Identity," 85–86.
16. Brianna Wiest, "Psychologists Say That Belonging To A Fandom Is Amazing For Your Mental Health."
17. Anonymous (musician), interview by author, September 20, 2017.
18. "WROCK!"
19. And is often attributed to Charles M. Schwab, an American steel magnate in the late 19th and early 20th centuries.
20. Paul DeGeorge (musician, Harry and the Potters), interview by author, October 17, 2017.
21. Jesse Doogan, "Top 5 Wizard Rock Songs to Bring You Back to Hogwarts."
22. Maggiacomo, interview.
23. See comments on: Thomas, "I'm in the final stages…"
24. Havens, "The Magical Duo."
25. Kane, interview.

Appendix A

1. "Susannah," *Your Wizard Rock Resource*, s.v. "Creevey Crisis."
2. According to Bradley Mehlenbacher: "[After] we played our first non-house party show in a theater in their home town of Norwood … a bunch of people came up to the merch table and were very sad that we didn't have CDs. … We knew [then] we needed to make an album. We put it together at Brian's house over the course of a month or two" (interview, June 19, 2018); "For the first record, and pretty much all of them, one of us would write a song, sometimes with a little input from the other (if we were stuck or unsure of a part or something). Then I would write the drum parts on a BOSS Dr. Rhythm drum machine, and then [we] record[ed] [the songs] at Brian's in GarageBand in his office. … Both of us would record guitars and vocals, depending on the song. For the most part we would sing lead on the songs we wrote. … I think we shared mixing duties" (interview, June 20, 2018).
3. According to Paul DeGeorge: "After spending months and months laboriously recording *Power of Love*, we wanted to get

back to basics and put something together in our parent's living room. 2007 was a busy year for us, so I think we just decided we'd spend a single weekend writing and recording this EP, which was for the Wizard Rock EP of the Month Club. We just wanted to do as many songs as possible, so we focused on writing really short songs. This was the first time we had Brad Mehlenbacher play drums for us on a recording. He'd been touring with us for most of the last year, so it was fun to finally get to record with him. We just set up the drums in the living room and recorded everything pretty quick and dirty. The first track is 'Harry Potter' and Joe starts it by saying, 'This song is called "Harry Potter," take one.' And that true. It was one and done, like most everything else on this EP. I think Brad had done his tracking [but] I still felt like we needed more songs, so I wrote 'Phoenix Tears' on acoustic guitar, recorded a demo, then took our sequencer up to my old bedroom and programmed the song while Joe was working on some other overdubs. Then I came downstairs and we cut the track" (interview, January 9, 2018).

4. According to Paul DeGeorge: "We decided to take things even more back-to-basics for this EP which we made for the 2008 Wizard Rock EP of the Month Club. Touring and recording is a lot of organization and scheduling and I think Joe and I were a bit sick of that by 2008, so we decided to just record this EP all by ourselves in our parent's basement. After coming off the publication of the final *Harry Potter* book, we felt there were still some unanswered questions. So most of the song content here is built around these kind of silly inconsistencies that we pulled out of the book. This is the kind of stuff that fans really obsess over and we just love that. So many unimportant unanswered questions. Let's get to the bottom of it! I don't remember why, but we wanted it to sound really raw. We recorded it live on cassette tape with a Tascam Portastudio 424. The only overdubs were a little drum part and maybe a guitar solo. I think we ran the vocals through a small guitar amp and put a mic on the amp to give it a bit more of that sharp edge. We wanted to push ourselves outside of our comfort zones a bit, so we switched up instruments where I played keyboard on a few and Joe played some guitar and we alternated on drums. He's a better drummer than I am, but we're both pretty terrible. I think the inconsistency of this recording actually makes it sound pretty fresh. The songs are sort of always on the verge of imploding. Most people probably find it terrible, but I love listening to these recordings. They feel really honest and true" (interview, January 9, 2018).

5. Justin Michaelman, "Justin Finch-Fletchley and the Sugar Quills."

6. Ethan Parker, "Kwikspell."

7. Birdoff, interview.

8. Kane, interview.

9. Adam Dubberly (musician, The Mudbloods) interview by author, February 7, 2018.

10. Kaitlin Mausser and Amanda Parrotte, "About."

11. Christian Calderira, "About."

12. In 2008, Sonnet, who was preparing for her wedding, reduced her commitments to the band. To make up for this, Eia Waltzer joined the group; the band's third album *Pretty in Pink (and Green)* featured all three on vocals. In 2009, Sonnet amicably left the band, and Alex Day helped The Parselmouths with their final album, *Spattergroit*.

13. The band later was expanded to include Toby Karlin, Tyler Nicholas, and Brandon Nicholas.

14. Casio, interview.

15. Kendall, interview, March 14, 2017.

16. Anna Fahlén (musician, The Swedish Shortsnouts), interview by author, July 8, 2017.

17. John and Stacy Pisani, "Swish and Flick," Facebook, accessed August 17, 2017, https://www.facebook.com/SwishAndFlick Wrock; John and Stacy Pisani, "Swish and Flick," Twitter, accessed August 17, 2017, https://twitter.com/swishandflick.

18. Anderson, interview, March 13, 2017.

19. Maggiacomo, interview.

20. Pyne, "Wizard Rock," 183.

Appendix A
List of Major Wrock Bands

Since 2002, over 1,000 wrock bands have formed, meaning that an exhaustive list is beyond the scope of this appendix. Instead, this section lists the larger wrock bands, chosen based on the number of albums they have released, the impact they have had on wizard rock, their activity within the community, and their relative popularity (ascertained from iTunes and Bandcamp rankings). Included with each band is also a short description of the group, the names of their members, and a list of their major releases.

Note: the symbol † denotes a Wizard Rock EP of the Month Club release. The symbol ✷ denotes a non-studio album release (excluding EPs, which are explicitly marked as such).

The Blibbering Humdingers

Hailing from Cary, North Carolina, The Blibbering Humdingers comprise husband and wife Scott and Kirsten Vaughan. The group was formed in 2007 after the Vaughns discovered wizard rock and were struck by the energy and passion of the groups they met. The Bibbering Humdingers' style is very eclectic, mixing elements of filk, new wave, rock, parody, doo-wop, folk, and swing.

Selected Discography

- *Nobody Expects the Blibbering Humdingers* (November 1, 2010)
- *Free Awkward Hugs* (March 26, 2012)
- *Just the Essentials* EP (July 9, 2014)
- *Raised by Nerds* (June 1, 2015)
- *Live at Dragon Con 2015* (December 16, 2015)✷
- *Fantastic Geeks and Where to Find Them* (January 1, 2018)

The Butterbeer Experience

Based in Pittsburgh, Pennsylvania, The Butterbeer Experience is the solo project of Lena Gabrielle. Gabrielle has a background in musical theatre, and many of her songs are at least partially situated in or inspired by this tradition. The band's name references the drink "butterbeer," a common beverage in the *Harry Potter* series.

Selected Discography

- *Non-Alcoholic* (December 26, 2007)
- *Accio Hot Guy* (August 6, 2008)
- *Songs from Beedle the Bard* EP (February 20, 2009)
- *Love Will Prevail: Songs from "The Final Battle"* (July 5, 2010)

Catchlove

Cathlove is a band that was formed in 2006 by Doug "Jace" McDonald, who hails from the Dallas–Fort Worth metro area in Texas. The band's name is a reference to the fictional character Greta Catchlove, who in the *Harry Potter* series wrote a book called *Charm Your Own Cheese*.

Selected Discography

- *OMG! It's Catchlove!* EP (June 8, 2007)
- *Where Do We Go from Here?* (July 17, 2007)
- *OMG! It's Christmas* EP (December 2007)
- *Wake Up Harry* EP (March 2008)†
- *It's Still Snowing* EP (December 2008)
- ♥ (July 15, 2009)

Creevey Crisis

Creevey Crisis is the solo project of Russ Benoit from Dartmouth, Massachusetts. The band is succinctly described on the Your Wizard Rock Resource blog as "often loud, occasionally acoustic, always original."[1] Of note, Benoit is also the current editor in chief of the Wizrocklopedia.

Selected Discography

- *Moving Photos and Memories* (October 2007)
- *Not Standing Silent* (June 2008)

- *Maybe in Four Years* EP (December 2008)
- *VII* (November 6, 2009)
- *Unfinished Spells* (February 28, 2010)
- *This Ship Has Sailed* EP (July 11, 2011)
- *Moving ... Again!* EP (July 11, 2013)
- *Throwing Eyes into Forests* EP (April 3, 2018)

Draco and the Malfoys

Among the first wrock groups to form, Draco and the Malfoys is made up of half-brothers Brian Ross and Bradley Mehlenbacher, who hail from Woonsocket, Rhode Island. As their name suggests, they play songs from Draco Malfoy's point of view. The band is known for their rock-influenced instrumentation and their ironic lyrics that extol Voldemort and the dark arts.

Selected Discography

- *Draco and the Malfoys* (June 1, 2006)[2]
- *Party Like You're Evil!* (July 1, 2007)
- *Family* EP (November 2007)†
- *An Anthology of Slytherin Folk Songs* (June 1, 2009)
- *It's a Slytherin World* (June 1, 2009)
- *Christmas Collection* (December 9, 2013)★
- *Cheat to Win* (July 29, 2014)
- *Best of Draco and the Malfoys* (June 30, 2016)★

The 8th Horcrux

The 8th Horcrux is a comedy wrock band from Kansas, comprising married duo Paul and Trina Thomas. Formed in 2009, the group bills itself as the "'Weird Al' Yankovic of wizard rock," as they specialize in writing *Harry Potter* parodies of Top 40 hits.

Selected Discography

- *Potterwatch!* (October 22, 2009)
- *Accio Awesome* (November 3, 2010)
- *Noize from the Cupboard* (July 1, 2011)
- *Pottermost!* EP (August 18, 2011)
- *The 8th Horcrux Live* (September 26, 2011)★

- *Ridiculously Wicked* (July 1, 2012)
- *Greatest Hits* (July 16, 2013)✶
- *Finite Incantatem!* EP (January 26, 2015)
- *Fantastic Beats and Where to Hear Them* (July 1, 2016)

Gred and Forge

Formed in 2007 by Jarrod Perkins, Gred and Forge is a wrock band from Asheville, North Carolina. The band's name is a spoonerism of "Fred and George," the names of the Weasley twins. Perhaps unsurprisingly, their music is sung from the perspective of the two characters.

Selected Discography

- *Half the Band I Used to Be* (September 1, 2007)
- *What Witches Want* EP (April 2008)†
- *We Had Class* EP (May 2008)
- *Pitches, Witches, Riches* (April 1, 2009)
- *Up to No Good* (August 1, 2011)

Harry and the Potters

Arguably the founders of wizard rock as it is known today, Harry and the Potters was formed in 2002 by brothers Paul and Joe DeGeorge of Norwood, Massachusetts. All their songs are sung from the perspective of Harry Potter. Musically, the band's songs are short, simple, and punk-infused, akin to the early music of They Might Be Giants.

Selected Discography

- *Harry and the Potters* (June 21, 2003)
- *Mail Songs #1* EP (October 2003)
- *Voldemort Can't Stop the Rock!* (July 1, 2004)
- *Harry and the Potters and the Power of Love* (July 4, 2006)
- *Scarred for Life* EP (July 4, 2006)
- Untitled split EP with The Zambonis (December 2006)
- *The Enchanted Ceiling* EP (July 2007)†[3]
- *In the Cupboard* EP (July 2008)†[4]
- *Priori Incantatem* (May 22, 2009)✶
- *Sonorus Cassette* series (August 31, 2009)✶

- *Harry and the Potters at the Yule Ball* EP/DVD (December 2009)†
- *Remixes* (November 18, 2010)*
- *Mail Songs #2* EP (April 22, 2011)
- *Live at the New York Public Library* (June 1, 2011)*
- *Live in Stockholm* (December 5, 2011)*
- *Hedwig Lives* EP (April 7, 2015)

The House of Black

The House of Black is an electro-rap group from Orlando, Florida, founded by Erin Pyne in 2007. Pyne is also notable in the wrock community for having authored the book *The Ultimate Guide to the Harry Potter Fandom* (2010). The band's name is a reference to the Black family, of which Sirius Black is a member.

Selected Discography

- *House of Black* (2009)
- *Beyond the Veil* (2012)

Justin Finch-Fletchley and the Sugar Quills

Justin Finch-Fletchley and the Sugar Quills is a band fronted by Justin Edward Michaelman, a musician from Providence, Rhode Island. Formed in 2006, the group's music is best described as acoustic rock, and according to their Bandcamp page, they "play songs about books, wizards, wizard books, pizza, parties, and pizza parties."[5] Michaelman has been very active within the wrock scene, and even helped package and mail the 2008 EP of the Month Club.

Selected Discography

- *Hufflepizza* EP (January 2008)†
- *Justin Finch-Fletchley and the Half-Blood Pizza* (May 27, 2009)
- *Pizzeria Hufflepoletana* EP (January 10, 2010)
- *Justin Finch-Fletchley and the HuffleWizard Christmas Songs* EP (December 25, 2011)

KwikSpell

KwikSpell is the solo project of Ethan Parker, who describes themself on their blog as being a "lone star wrockstar waiting on the first broom outta this town."⁶ KwikSpell was formed in 2008 in Austin, Texas, and dabbles mostly in acoustic guitar tracks.

Selected Discography

- *Magic 101* EP (May 20, 2008)
- *Good to See You Wallenby* (April 20, 2010)
- *Pretending for Real* EP (October 29, 2011)

The Lovegoods

The Lovegoods, hailing from Kitchener, Ontario, are part of wizard rock's "second wave." While they are one of the newest bands to form, The Lovegoods have made a splash in the wrock community for their musicianship and their performance skills. Most of their songs have a certain '90s alt-rock feel to them.

Selected Discography

- *The Lovegoods* EP (2017)

Madam Pince and the Librarians

Madam Pince and the Librarians is a New York–based band comprising Ariel Factor Birdoff and Kelly Foulds. According to Birdoff, the group formed after Wrockstock 2008: "I was playing Apples to Apples with other attendees, and I told them that if I ever had a wrock band it would be called 'Madam Pince and the Librarians.' They asked me why I hadn't done it yet, and I really had no answer. [Soon thereafter] the band was born."⁷

Selected Discography

- *Stacked!* (2010)

MC Kreacher

Although he has only issued one EP, MC Kreacher (aka Myles Kane of Brooklyn, New York) is one of the pioneers of "wizard rap." According to Kane, "My intro to *Harry Potter* was exclusively through wizard rock and the fan culture.... I told my film collaborators I was thinking about writing a wizard rap and who would be a good fit. They all suggested Kreacher, and then I [subsequently] ... wrote 'House Elf 4 Life,' which I figured would be a one off [but eventually] I wrote 5 more songs and tried to make one flow to the next as the portrait of Kreacher emerged."[8]

Selected Discography

- *Alone in the Dark* EP (May 2009)†

Ministry of Magic

Based in Ames, Iowa, Ministry of Magic was formed in 2007 by Luke Conard, Jeremy Jennings, Mark Jennings, Jason Munday, Aaron Nordyke, and Ryan Seiler. Musically, the band is situated in the synthpop genre. Around 2009, Ministry of Magic was arguably one of the most-popular wrock bands, but revelations in 2014 about abuse scandals caused them to fall from grace.

Selected Discography

- *The Tri-Wizard LP* (August 9, 2007)
- *Goodbye Privet Drive* (July 22, 2008)
- *Acoustiatus* (October 28, 2008)
- *Onward and Upward* (March 30, 2009)
- *Magic Is Might* (December 10, 2010)
- *Songs from Gringott's Vault* (December 13, 2011)★

The Moaning Myrtles

Founded in Hillsborough, New Jersey, by Lauren Fairweather and Nina Jankowicz in 2006, The Moaning Myrtles role-play as the unhappy ghost Moaning Myrtle. The group is notable for emphasizing the piano in most of their songs.

Selected Discography

- *Port-a-Potty* EP (May 2006)
- *Toilet Humor* (July 2007)
- *What About Myrtle?* (January 1, 2008)
- *Bathroom Acoustics* EP (August 2009)†

The Mudbloods

The Mudbloods are a band from Austin, Texas, made up of Adam Dubberly, David Matsler, and Brandon McCullough. Formed in 2005, the band originally wanted to take a "Weird Al approach" to songwriting by penning tunes in a variety of genres. However, they eventually settled on what Dubberly calls an "alt-country…. Tom Petty pop-rock sound with our Texas roots showing through."⁹ Of note, The Mudbloods were unaware of other wrock bands when they formed, and it was only after creating a MySpace page that they realized there was a larger wrock scene.

Selected Discography

- *Out of the Forbidden Forest* (2006)
- *The Animals That Have Left Me* EP (2007)
- *A War Amidst Pop Songs* EP (May 2008)†
- *Potosi* EP (October 2008)
- *The Complete Potion* (March 26, 2014)✶
- *The Time-Turner* EP (October 10, 2016)
- *The Animals That Have Left Me* vinyl re-release (2017)

Muggle Snuggle

Muggle Snuggle is a Pittsburgh, Pennsylvania, band that was formed in 2016 and comprises Amanda Parrotte and Kaitlin Mausser. The group—which is heavily inspired by folk and accordion music—humorously claims to "explain the wizard world through Muggle eyes."¹⁰

Selected Discography

- *Muggle Snuggle and the Philosopher's Songs* (2016)
- *Have a Very Harry Christmas* (2016)
- *Muggle Snuggle et les Chansons Secrètes* (2017)

The Nifflers

The Nifflers comprise Jake and Madison Kalbhenn, two siblings from Toronto, Canada; they play blues and acoustic rock. The band takes its name from the Niffler, a small mole-like creature in the *Harry Potter* universe with a duckbill that is attracted to shiny objects.

Selected Discography

- *Let's Make It Rock* EP (August 2008)†
- *Singing Songs and Clap-a-Longs* (December 31, 2008)

Oliver Boyd and the Remembralls

Oliver Boyd and the Remembralls were founded in Toronto, Canada, in 2006 by Christian Calderira. According to Caldeira, "I remember finding out about the whole wrock scene and thinking it was pretty funny. 'People are actually writing songs about *Harry Potter*?' I chuckled. Well, my face is surely red now."[11]

Selected Discography

- *Welcome to Wizard Rock* (November 21, 2006)
- *Back for the Fight* (July 10, 2007)
- *Open at the Close* EP (December 18, 2007)
- *The Slytherin* EP (June 28, 2008)
- *Bare Bones* EP (October 6, 2009)
- *Bare Bones, Vol. 2* EP (November 1, 2010)
- *End of an Era* EP (July 11, 2011)
- *The Bare Bones Collection* (November 1, 2014)*

The Parselmouths

The Parselmouths, founded in Renton, Washington, by Kristina Horner and Elle Viane Sonnet,[12] were the second wrock group to form, and the first to hail from the West Coast. Much of The Parselmouths' music emphasizes the acoustic guitar, although some of their songs contain elements of hard rock and indietronica.

Selected Discography

- *Sssss* (October 2006)
- *Broken Hearted Slytherins* (May 2007)
- *Illegal Love Potion* EP (June 2007)†
- *Pretty in Pink (and Green)* (July 7, 2008)
- *Spattergroit* (May 21, 2009)

The Puffskein Experience

The Puffskein Experience was formed by the Texan Miranda Caddell around 2013. The Puffskein Experience's music is mostly based around the ukulele. (Of note: Caddell now releases music under the moniker "Miranda Puffskein.")

Selected Discography

- *Live at Camp 9¾* EP (2013)
- *Just as Sane as I Am* EP (2014)
- *The Horcruxes* EP (2014)
- *The Fault* EP (2014)

The Remus Lupins

The Remus Lupins were formed in Beverly Hills, California, in 2005 by musician/actor-hopeful Alex Carpenter.[13] For many years, The Remus Lupins were one of the most-popular wrock groups, but revelations about sexual abuse scandals in 2014 caused Carpenter to disband the group.

Selected Discography

- *I'll Be at Hogwarts* EP (2005)
- *Spells from a Broken Wand* (2006)
- *I Was a Teenage Werewolf* (2007)
- *Horcruxes and Hand Me Downs* EP (March 2007)†
- *Nevermind the Furthermore* (2008)
- *The Rest Is Silence* (2009)

Roonil Wazlib

Roonil Wazlib is the project of Molly Newman, hailing from Sunnyvale, California. The band gets its name from a scene in *Harry Potter and the Half-Blood Prince* in which a malfunctioning Spell-Checking Quill accidentally misspells Ron Weasley's name on an essay.

Selected Discography

- *Muggle Knitting Patterns* (July 24, 2006)

- *Putting Fluffy to Sleep* EP (August 2007)†
- *Timeturner* (August 12, 2008)

Riddle™

Riddle™ is from Oxfordshire, England, and are perhaps the most well-known wrock band from the UK. Comprising sisters Georgia and Victoria Minnear, the band formed in 2007 and gained popularity after Lauren Fairweather of The Moaning Myrtles covered their song "Look at Me." The group's name is a play on and reversal of Voldemort's actual name, Tom Marvolo Riddle.

Selected Discography

- *More Magic* EP (2007)
- *Riddle Me This* (December 2008)
- *Secrets of the Darkest Art* (May 28, 2008)
- *Talons and Teacakes* EP (April 2009)†
- *This Time Around* (October 29, 2010)

Romilda Vane and the Chocolate Cauldrons

Romilda Vane and the Chocolate Cauldrons is the solo project of Amy Snow from Cork, Ireland. Snow is also known in the *Harry Potter* and wrock fandoms for hosting the WZRD podcast.

Selected Discography

- *Hogwarts, a Mystery* (2007)
- *Songs from Under the Stairs* EP (2010)

Seen and Unforeseen

Seen and Unforeseen is the solo project of Evie Džomba of Grand Rapids, Michigan. Formed in 2009, much of Seen and Unforeseen's music is acoustic guitar-based. (Of note: Džomba currently records solo work, including wizard rock, under her own name.)

Selected Discography

- *My Parents Are Muggles* EP (July 2011)
- *Worth Fighting For* (July 2012)

Shrieking Shack Disco Gang

Shrieking Shack Disco Gang is the "wizard" version of the "Muggle" band Cooties Attack!, made up of "Holly Horcrux" (i.e., Holly Casio) and "Hufflepuff Huw" (i.e., Huw Spink). The group formed ca. 2007 and was inspired by "DIY Casio pop punk type songs." The band took their name from one of the first songs they ever wrote, a tune about "having a party and coming together as the world is about to end."[14]

Selected Discography

- *Accio Pop!* (January 6, 2007)
- *Kabloomers! Destruction!* EP (January 2009)†

Slytherin Soundtrack

Slytherin Soundtrack is the solo project of Brett Holden from Springfield, Missouri. Holden is a prolific musician, and his albums are composed mostly of eclectic, guitar-based folk tracks.

Selected Discography

- *New Wizards* (December 2010)
- *A Pint of Magic* (March 2012)
- *Magical Beasts and Nice Giants* (April 2013)
- *Unplottable* (July 2013)
- *Unspeakables: Unreleased and B-Sides* (March 2014)✶
- *One More Butterbeer* (April 2014)
- *Scar* (November 2014)
- *The Golden Snitch, Vol. I* (March 2015)
- *The Golden Snitch, Vol. II* (March 2015)
- *Owls and Newts* (July 2015)
- *And the Missing Potion Ingredients* (April 2017)

Snidget

Snidget, a unique dulcimer-based band, is the solo project of Grace Kendall of Virginia that formed in 2005. According to Kendall, "I started performing under the name Snidget, named for the bird that predated the golden snitch [in Quidditch]. I loved that J.K. Rowling had built this backstory for this little bird.... I chose it because I was in my animal rights activist phase, and because it was so obscure."[15]

Selected Discography

- *To Dwell on Dreams* EP (June 10, 2007)
- *Live at Wrockstock* (March 26, 2014)*

The Swedish Shortsnouts

The Swedish Shortsnouts are a band made up of siblings Anna and Erik Fahlén, hailing from Borlänge, Sweden. The band was founded in 2007 after Anna and Erik realized that they could help keep the *Harry Potter* fan community afloat in Sweden by playing wizard rock. The band "sings catchy pop-rock songs about scandalously sidelined dragons and other magical things."[16]

Selected Discography

- *Magic Stuff* (June 20, 2016)

Swish and Flick

Swish and Flick is a New York "wizard rap" group made up of Stacy "DJ Swish" and John "Flick" Pisani. The band—which takes its inspiration from dance music, "old-school hip-hop," '80s synth-pop, and electronica—describes their music as "M-rated *Harry Potter* fan fiction that you can dance to."[17]

Selected Discography

- *In the House of Slytherin* (June 24, 2009)
- *With Love and Poison* EP (October 2009)†

Tianna and the Cliffhangers

Tianna and the Cliffhangers is the solo project of Tianna Mignogna from Pittsburgh, Pennsylvania. Formed in 2009, many of Tianna and the Cliffhangers' songs center around and celebrate queer and LGBTQ+ themes. (Of note: albums and EPs released prior to *Out of Character* were issued under the name "I Speak Tree.")

Selected Discography

- *Got Bark?* (September 3, 2010)
- *Trees Are Taller Than Me* (September 17, 2011)
- *Fangz 2 Raven* EP (January 15, 2012)
- *Out of Character* (September 9, 2013)
- *Picking Up Where You Left Off* (June 6, 2015)

Tonks and the Aurors

Often called the "Bruce Springsteen of wizard rock," Tonks and the Aurors is the project of Steph Anderson. Based in Cincinnati, Ohio, Tonks and the Aurors' songs are sung from the perspective of Nymphadora Tonks; Anderson explained, "Tonks and Remus [Lupin] are two of my favorite characters. There wasn't a popular Tonks band yet, so I decided to go that way and figured I could write from her perspective easily, being a young woman."[18] As of 2018, the band is one of the most popular in the wrock community.

Selected Discography

- *The Pink Album* (November 1, 2007)
- *The Hogsmeade Diaries* (August 6, 2008)
- *Tonks for the Memories* EP (March 2009)†
- *We Are Magic* (November 5, 2009)
- *A Familiar Beat* (June 10, 2012)
- *Huffleriot* (June 29, 2018)

The Whomping Willows

The Whomping Willows is the solo project of the Woonsocket, Rhode Island, musician Matt Maggiacomo. As the name suggests, most of The Whomping Willows' songs are sung from the point of view of the eponymous tree. According to Maggiacomo, "I first conceived the band around February 2005, but I didn't start writing music until October of that year. It wasn't until [the Boston Yule Ball] that I felt truly committed to the concept.... The crowd's enthusiasm and supportive attitude is what convinced me to commit to the band."[19] The band went on indefinite hiatus at the end of 2018.

Selected Discography

- *The Whomping Willows* (2006)

- *Welcome to the House of Awesome* (May 1, 2007)
- *III* (March 1, 2008)
- *Rock 'n' Roll Redux* EP (April 19, 2008)
- *Demons at the Helm* (2009)
- *Songs for Professors* EP (November 2009)†
- *Wizard Party Forever* (May 20, 2010)
- *1975* (July 29, 2014)

Witherwings

Witherwings was formed by the Washington, D.C.–based musician Mandala. In an interview with author Erin Pyne, Mandala explained that with her band, it was her intent to "write songs that make people feel the [emotion] I do after reading any of the [*Harry Potter*] books: pure happiness."[20]

Selected Discography

- *Stay Away* EP (2008)
- *Malfoy and Other Musical Creations* EP (2009)
- *On Lighter and Darker Matters* (2010)

Appendix B
Wizard Rock EP of the Month Club Releases

The Wizard Rock EP of the Month Club was founded by Paul and Joe DeGeorge of Harry and the Potters as a way to both raise money for charity as well as promote up-and-coming wrock bands to a wider audience. The club ran for three years and distributed 37 CDs and 1 DVD.

The 2007 Club

- Hungarian Horntails—*The First Task* (January 2007)
- Voldemort—*Evil Is Sexy* (February 2007)
- The Remus Lupins—*Horcruxes and Hand Me Downs* (March 2007)
- Remus and the Lupins—*Born to Howl* (April 2007)
- Ginny and the Heartbreakers—*Love Storm* (May 2007)
- The Parselmouths—*Illegal Love Potion* (June 2007)
- Harry and the Potters—*The Enchanted Ceiling* (July 2007)
- Roonil Wazlib—*Putting Fluffy to Sleep* (August 2007)
- The Fleur Delacours—*I Now Pronounce You Mrs. Bill Weasley* (September 2007)
- The Marauders—*Hogwarts 1975* (October 2007)
- Draco and the Malfoys—*Family* (November 2007)
- Dumbledore—*Lemon Drop.... The Beat* (December 2007)

One thousand copies were made of each EP: 800 were sent out to EP of the Month Club subscribers, whereas the other 200 were given to the participating bands free of charge. Frankie Franco III and Michael Golembewski served as the art directors.

The 2008 Club

- Justin Finch-Fletchley and the Sugar Quills—*Hufflepizza* (January 2008)
- Gryffindor Common Room Rejects—*Still Recruiting* (February 2008)
- Catchlove—*Wake Up Harry* (March 2008)
- Gred and Forge—*What Witches Want* (April 2008)
- The Mudbloods—*A War Amidst Pop Songs* (May 2008)
- The Hermione-Crookshanks Experience—*Penelope* (June 2008)
- Harry and the Potters—*In the Cupboard* (July 2008)
- The Nifflers—*Let's Make It Rock* (August 2008)
- Big Whompy—*Treestylin'* (September 2008)
- Tom Riddle and Friends—*Bob Hope Is a Vampire* (October 2008)
- The Basilisk in Your Pasta—*I Ate My Frog (Again)* (November 2008)
- The Giant Squidstravaganza—*Death to Humans* [double EP] (December 2008)

One thousand two hundred fifty copies were made of each EP. One thousand were sent out to EP of the Month Club subscribers, whereas the other 250 were given to the participating bands free of charge. Marty Allen, Joe DeGeorge and Frankie Franco III served as the art directors.

The 2009 Club

- Shrieking Shack Disco Gang—*Kabloomers! Destruction!* (January 2009)
- Mary and the GrandPrés—*Hymns of Truth and Light* (February 2009)
- Tonks and the Aurors—*Tonks for the Memories* (March 2009)
- Riddle™—*Teacakes* (April 2009)
- MC Kreacher—*Alone in the Dark* (May 2009)
- Peeved—*Nitwit! Blubber! Oddment! Tweak!* (June 2009)
- "Bob Dylan"—*"Bob Dylan" Sings the Songs of Harry and the Potters* (July 2009)
- The Moaning Myrtles—*Bathroom Acoustics* (August 2009)
- Danny Dementor—*Be a Wizard* (September 2009)
- Swish and Flick—*With Love and Poison* (October 2009)
- The Whomping Willows—*Songs for Professors* (November 2009)
- Harry and the Potters—*At the Yule Ball 2008* [CD/DVD set] (December 2009)

One thousand copies were made of each EP: 800 were sent out to EP of the Month Club subscribers, whereas the other 200 were given to the participating bands free of charge. Meredith Moore served as the art director.

Bibliography

Books, Journals and Scholarly Sources

Abbey, James Eric. *Garage Rock and Its Roots: Musical Rebels and the Drive for Individuality.* Jefferson, NC: McFarland, 2006.

Abravanel, Genevieve. *Americanizing Britain: The Rise of Modernism in the Age of the Entertainment Empire.* Oxford: Oxford University Press, 2012.

Ahern, Mal. "Performance/Performativity." In *The Chicago School of Media Theory Keywords,* edited by W.J.T. Mitchell. The Chicago School of Media Theory, 2003. https://lucian.uchicago.edu/blogs/mediatheory/keywords/performanceperformativity/.

Allan, Kenneth. *Explorations in Classical Sociological Theory: Seeing the Social World.* Thousand Oaks, CA: Pine Forge Press, 2005.

Anelli, Melissa. "Rocking at Hogwarts." In *Harry, a History,* 101–36. New York: Simon & Schuster, 2008.

Arthur, Kasandra. "'You, the Reader': Interpretative Authority, Rowling, and Her Fans." In *Harry Potter, Still Recruiting: An Inner Look at Harry Potter Fandom,* edited by Valerie Estelle Frankel, 94–103. Allentown, PA: Zossima Press, 2012.

Ashcraft, Brian, and Luke Plunkett. *Cosplay World.* Munich, Germany: Prestel Publishing, 2004.

Austin, J.L. *How to Do Things with Words.* Oxford, UK: Clarendon Press, 1962.

Barner, Ashley. *The Case for Fanfiction: Exploring the Pleasures and Practices of a Maligned Craft.* Jefferson, NC: McFarland, 2017.

Bastian, Brock, Jolanda Jetten, and Laura J. Ferris. "Pain as Social Glue: Shared Pain Increases Cooperation." *Psychological Science* 25, no. 11 (September 5, 2014): 2079–85. https://doi.org/10.1177/0956797614545886.

Bateman, Chris. *Beyond Game Design: Nine Steps Toward Creating Better Videogames.* Boston: Cengage Learning, 2009.

Beahm, George. "The Wizard Rockumentary: A Movie About Rocking and Rowling." In *Muggles and Magic: An Unofficial Guide to J.K. Rowling and the Harry Potter Phenomenon,* 3rd ed., 237–38. Charlottesville, VA: Hampton Roads, 2007.

Belcher, Catherine, and Becky Stephenson. *Teaching Harry Potter: The Power of Imagination in Multicultural Classrooms.* New York: Springer, 2011.

Berger, Arthur Asa. *An Anatomy of Humor.* Piscataway, NJ: Transaction Publishers, 1999.

Bial, Henry, ed. *The Performance Studies Reader.* Abingdon-on-Thames, UK: Routledge, 2004.

Boellstorff, Tom. *Coming of Age in Second Life: An Anthropologist Explores the Virtually Human*. Princeton, NJ: Princeton University Press, 2008.

Booth, Paul. *Playing Fans: Negotiating Fandom and Media in the Digital Age*. Iowa City: University of Iowa Press, 2015.

Bowman, Sarah Lynne. "Connecting Stage Acting, Role-Playing, and Improvisation." In *Analog Game Studies*, edited by Aaron Trammell, Evan Torner, and Emma Leigh Waldron. Pittsburgh, PA: ETC Press, 2017.

_____. "Discovering Your Inner Wizard: The Wide World of Harry Potter Role-Playing Games." In *Playing Harry Potter: Essays and Interviews on Fandom and Performance*, edited by Lisa S. Brenner, 86–107. Jefferson, NC: McFarland, 2015.

_____. *The Functions of Role-Playing Games: How Participants Create Community, Solve Problems and Explore Identity*. Jefferson, NC: McFarland, 2010.

Buehler, Arthur. "The Twenty-First-Century Study of Collective Effervescence: Expanding the Context of Fieldwork." *Fieldwork in Religion* 7, no. 1 (2012): 70–97. doi: 10.1558/fiel.v7i1.70.

Butler, Judith. *Bodies That Matter: On the Discursive Limits of "Sex."* Abingdon-on-Thames, UK: Routledge, 2014.

Camacci, Lauren. "The Prisoner of Gender: Masculinity in the *Potter* Books." In *Wizards Vs. Muggles: Essays on Identity and the Harry Potter Universe*, edited by Christopher E. Bell, 133–48. Jefferson, NC: McFarland, 2016.

Campbell, Patrick. *The Body in Performance*. Abingdon-on-Thames, UK: Routledge, 2014.

Childs-Helton, Barry, and Sally C. Childs-Helton. "Filk Music." In *American Folklore: An Encyclopedia*, edited by Jan Harold Brunvand, 548–9, Abingdon-on-Thames, UK: Routledge, 2006.

Childs-Helton, Sally. "Folk Music in a Digital Age: The Importance of Face-To-Face Community Values in Filk Music." *Scholarship and Professional Work* 60 (2016): 1. Accessed January 11, 2018. http://digitalcommons.butler.edu/librarian_papers/60.

Clapp, Justin. "Collective Consumption: An Ethnographic Examination of Consumption-Focused Social Relations." Ph.D. dissertation, University of Pennsylvania, 2012. http://repository.upenn.edu/dissertations/AAI3542792.

Cook, Matthew. "Bang on the Drum All Day: How Personal Interests Can Positively Impact Professional Development." In *Continuing Education for Librarians: Essays on Career Improvement Through Classes, Workshops, Conferences and More*, edited by Carol Smallwood, Kerol Harrod, and Vera Gubnitskaia, 172–79. Jefferson, NC: McFarland, 2013.

Debies-Carl, Jeffrey S. "Locating Punk Space: From Bars and Clubs to Cellars and Squats." In *Punk Rock and the Politics of Place: Building a Better Tomorrow*, 122–78. Abingdon-on-Thames, UK: Routledge, 2014.

Diehl, Matt. *My So-Called Punk: Green Day, Fall Out Boy, the Distillers, Bad Religion— How Neo-Punk Stage-Dived into the Mainstream*. New York: St. Martin's Press, 2013.

Do Rozario, Rebecca-Anne C. "Wrocking the Collaboration: Wizard Rock and the Work of J.K. Rowling." *Musicology Australia* 33, no. 2 (2011): 265–76.

Duncombe, Stephen, and Maxwell Tremblay, eds. *White Riot: Punk Rock and the Politics of Race*. New York: Verso Books, 2011.

Durkheim, Émile. *The Division of Labor in Society*. Edited by Steven Lukes. Translated by W.D. Halls. New York: Simon & Schuster, 2014 [1893].

_____. *The Elementary Forms of Religious Life*. Translated by Joseph Ward Swain. London: Allen and Unwin, Ltd., 1915 [1912].

_____. *The Elementary Forms of Religious Life*. Translated with introduction by Karen Field. New York: Free Press, 1995 [1912].

Ellis, Carolyn, Tony E. Adams, and Arthur P. Bochner. "Autoethnography: An Overview." *Forum Qualitative Sozialforschung* 12, no. 1 (November 24, 2010).

ESRC Centre on Dynamics of Ethnicity. "How Has Ethnic Diversity Grown 1991–2001–2011?" Manchester, UK: University of Manchester, December 2012. http://www.ethnicity.ac.uk/medialibrary/briefings/dynamicsofdiversity/how-has-ethnic-diversity-grown-1991-2001-2011.pdf.
Falck, Robert, and Martin Picker. "Contrafactum." *Grove Music Online*, October 20, 2006.
Farnel, Megan. "Magical Econ 101: Wealth, Labor and Inequality in *Harry Potter* and Its Fandom." In *From Here to Hogwarts: Essays on Harry Potter Fandom and Fiction*, edited by Christopher E. Bell, 28–53. Jefferson, NC: McFarland, 2016.
Foley, Michael S. *Fresh Fruit for Rotting Vegetables*. 33 1/3 105. New York: Bloomsbury Academic, 2015.
Frankel, Valerie Estelle. "Parodying Potter." In *Harry Potter, Still Recruiting: An Inner Look at Harry Potter Fandom*, edited by Valerie Estelle Frankel, 48–60. Allentown, PA: Zossima Press, 2012.
Geczy, Adam. "The Psychology of Cosplay." *Journal of Asia-Pacific Pop Culture* 1, no. 1 (2016): 18–36. doi:10.5325/jasiapacipopcult.1.1.0018.
Geertz, Clifford. *The Interpretation of Cultures*. New York: Basic Books, 1973.
Gilsdorf, Ethan. *Fantasy Freaks and Gaming Geeks*. Lanham, MD: Rowman and Littlefield, 2010.
Gluckman, Max. *Order and Rebellion in Tribal Africa*. Routledge Library Editions. Abingdon-on-Thames, UK: Routledge, 1963.
Griswold, Wendy. *Cultures and Societies in a Changing World*. Thousand Oaks, CA: Sage, 2012.
Hall, Catherine. "Reading and [W]Rocking: Morality and Musical Creativity in the Harry Potter Fandom." *Journal of Fandom Studies* 4, no. 2 (June 2016): 193–208.
Hayashi, Aya Esther. "Musicking, Discourse, and Identity in Participatory Media Fandom." Ph.D. dissertation, City University of New York (CUNY), The Graduate Center, 2018.
Hellekson, Karen, and Kristina Busse, eds. *Fan Fiction and Fan Communities in the Age of the Internet: New Essays*. Jefferson, NC: McFarland, 2006.
Henricks, Thomas. "Play." In *The Concise Encyclopedia of Sociology*, edited by George Ritzer and J. Michael Ryan, 444. Hoboken, NJ: John Wiley and Sons, 2010.
Hills, Matthew. *Fan Cultures*. Abingdon-on-Thames, UK: Routledge, 2003.
Holder, Sarah Frances. "'Get Your Geek On': Online and Offline Representations of Audiotopia Within the Geekycon Community." M.A. thesis, University of Tennessee, Knoxville, 2017. http://trace.tennessee.edu/cgi/viewcontent.cgi?article=5815&context=utk_gradthes.
Hutchison, Elizabeth D. *Dimensions of Human Behavior: Person and Environment*. Thousand Oaks, CA: Sage, 2008.
Igweonu, Kene, and Osita Okagbue. *Performative Inter-Actions in African Theatre 3: Making Space, Rethinking Drama and Theatre in Africa*. Cambridge: Cambridge Scholars Publishing, 2014.
Jenkins, Henry. *Convergence Culture: Where Old and New Media Collide*. 1992. Reprint, New York: New York University Press, 2008.
———. "'Cultural Acupuncture': Fan Activism and the Harry Potter Alliance." In *Harry Potter, Still Recruiting: An Inner Look at Harry Potter Fandom*, edited by Valerie Estelle Frankel, 48–60. Allentown, PA: Zossima Press, 2012.
———. "The Night of a Thousand Wizards." In *Harry Potter, Still Recruiting: An Inner Look at Harry Potter Fandom*, edited by Valerie Estelle Frankel, 115–23. Allentown, PA: Zossima Press, 2012.
———. "*Star Trek* Rerun, Reread, Rewritten: Fan Writing as Textual Poaching." In *Fans, Bloggers, and Gamers: Exploring Participatory Culture*, 37–60. New York: New York University Press, 2006.

_____. *Textual Poachers: Television Fans and Participatory Culture*. 2nd ed. New York: Routledge, 2013.
Jenkins, Henry, Sam Ford, and Joshua Green. *Spreadable Media*. New York: New York University Press, 2013.
Jones, Katharine W. *Accent on Privilege: English Identities and Anglophilia in the U.S.* Philadelphia: Temple University Press, 2001.
Kendall, Grace. "The Museum of Wizard Rock." Presented at MISTI-Con, Laconia, New Hampshire, 2017.
Kottak, Conrad Philip. "Halloween: An American Ritual of Rebellion." In *Anthropology: The Exploration of Human Diversity*. 6th ed. New York: McGraw-Hill Higher Education, 2012, 393.
Lambert, Joy, and Annette Anderson-Ma. "Wizard Rocking the Library of Congress." Presented at the California State University Fullerton (CSUF) Library, Fullerton, California, 2008.
Lamerichs, Nicolle. "Stranger than Fiction: Fan Identity in Cosplay." *Transformative Works and Cultures* 7 (September 20, 2010). http://journal.transformativeworks.org/index.php/twc/article/view/246.
Law, Alex. *Key Concepts in Classical Social Theory*. Thousand Oaks, CA: Sage, 2011.
Lee, Chin-Ting. "Keeping the Magic Alive: The Fandom and 'Harry Potter Experience' After the Franchise." In *From Here to Hogwarts: Essays on Harry Potter Fandom and Fiction*, edited by Christopher E. Bell, 54–77. Jefferson, NC: McFarland, 2016.
Marzec, Robert P., ed. *The Mid-Atlantic Region*. Westport, CT: Greenwood, 2004.
May, Jeffrey. "Pilgrims on Tour: Collective Effervescence in Concerts." B.A. honors thesis, University of Michigan, 2010. https://deepblue.lib.umich.edu/bitstream/handle/2027.42/77632/jefrober.pdf?sequence=1.
McCloud, Sean. "Popular Culture Fandoms, the Boundaries of Religious Studies, and the Project of the Self." *Culture and Religion* 4, no. 2 (2003): 187–206.
Mills, Albert, Gabrielle Durepos, Elden Wiebe, and Maréchal Garance, eds. "Autoethnography." *Encyclopedia of Case Study Research*. Thousand Oaks, CA: Sage, 2010. doi:10.4135/9781412957397.n19.
Moliterno, Alessandro G. "What Riot? Punk Rock Politics, Fascism, and Rock Against Racism." *Inquiries Journal* 4, no. 1 (2012). http://www.inquiriesjournal.com/a?id=612.
Montola, Markus. "The Invisible Rules of Role-Playing: The Social Framework of Role-Playing Process." *International Journal of Role-Playing* 1, no. 1 (2009): 22–36.
_____. "Social Reality in Roleplaying Games." In *The Foundation Stone of Nordic Larp*, edited by Eleanor Saitta, Marie Holm-Andersen, and Jon Back, 103–12. Halland, Sweden: Knutpunkt, 2014.
Moore, Chris. "Autoethnography of Objects." Cryptocommonicon. February 5, 2017. https://chrismoore.blog/2017/02/05/autoethnography-of-objects/.
Morales, Claudia. *Rocking the Room of Requirement, or Our House (In the Middle of Our Scene)*. Providence, RI: WizardPunkPress, 2017.
Morreall, John. "Philosophy of Humor." Edited by Edward N. Zalta. *The Stanford Encyclopedia of Philosophy*. Stanford, CA: Metaphysics Research Lab, Stanford University, 2016. https://plato.stanford.edu/archives/win2016/entries/humor/.
Morrison, Ken. *Marx, Durkheim, Weber: Formations of Modern Social Thought*. 2nd ed. Thousand Oaks, CA: Sage, 2006.
Mueller, Jennifer C., Danielle Dirks, Leslie Houts Picca, "Unmasking Racism: Halloween Costuming and Engagement of the Racial Other," *Qualitative Sociology* 30, no. 3 (2007): 315–35.
Norbeck, Edward. "African Rituals of Conflict." *American Anthropologist* 65, no. 6 (1963): 1254–79.

Olaveson, Tim. "Collective Effervescence and Communitas: Processual Models of Ritual and Society in Emile Durkheim and Victor Turner." *Dialectical Anthropology* 26, no. 2 (2001): 89–124.

_____. "'Connectedness' and the Rave Experience." In *Rave Culture and Religion*, edited by Graham St John. Abingdon-on-Thames, UK: Routledge, 2004.

Paré, Joelle. "Magical Musical Manifestations: A Literary Look at Wizard Rock." In *Harry Potter's World Wide Influence*, edited by Diana Patterson, 181–200. Cambridge: Cambridge Scholars Publishing, 2009.

Popple, Jennifer. "Embracing the Magic: Muggle Quidditch and the Transformation of Gender Equality from Fantasy to Reality." In *Playing Harry Potter: Essays and Interviews on Fandom and Performance*, edited by Lisa S. Brenner, 188–221. Jefferson, NC: McFarland, 2015.

Proctor, Bernadette D., Jessica L. Semega, and Melissa A. Kollar. "Income and Poverty in the United States: 2015." Washington, D.C.: United States Census Bureau, 2016. https://www.census.gov/content/dam/Census/library/publications/2016/demo/p60-256.pdf.

Pyne, E.A. "Wizard Rock." In *The Ultimate Guide to the Harry Potter Fandom*, 173–90. Winter Park, FL: What the Flux Publishing, 2010.

Rahman, Osmud, Liu Wing-sun, and Brittany Hei-man Cheung. "'Cosplay': Imaginative Self and Performing Identity." *Fashion Theory: The Journal of Dress, Body and Culture* 16, no. 3 (September 2012): 317–41. doi:10.2752/175174112X13340749707204.

Rishel, Mary Ann. *Writing Humor*. Detroit: Wayne State University Press, 2002.

Rohlman, Kelli. "Identity, Rhetoric and Behavior: The Contradictory Communities of Wizard Rock." M.A. thesis, Texas Tech University, 2010. https://ttu-ir.tdl.org/ttu-ir/bitstream/handle/2346/ETD-TTU-2010-12-1213/Rohlman_Kelli_Thesis.pdf?sequence=2.

Rowling, J.K. *Fantastic Beasts and Where to Find Them*. London: Bloomsbury Publishing, 2001.

_____. *Harry Potter and the Chamber of Secrets*. London: Bloomsbury Publishing, 1998.

_____. *Harry Potter and the Cursed Child—Parts 1 and 2, Special Rehearsal Edition Script*. New York: Little, Brown and Company, 2016.

_____. *Harry Potter and the Deathly Hallows*. London: Bloomsbury Publishing, 2007.

_____. *Harry Potter and the Goblet of Fire*. London: Bloomsbury Publishing, 2000.

_____. *Harry Potter and the Half-Blood Prince*. London: Bloomsbury Publishing, 2005.

_____. *Harry Potter and the Order of the Phoenix*. London: Bloomsbury Publishing, 2003.

_____. *Harry Potter and the Prisoner of Azkaban*. London: Bloomsbury Publishing, 1999.

_____. *Harry Potter and the Sorcerer's Stone*. London: Bloomsbury Publishing, 1997.

Savage, John. "Punk," Edited by Dale Hoiberg. *Encyclopædia Britannica*. Chicago: Encyclopædia Britannica, Inc., 2016. https://www.britannica.com/art/punk.

Schwenz, Caroline Lee. "Anglophilia." *Postcolonial Studies @ Emory* (blog). Emory University. April 2012. https://scholarblogs.emory.edu/postcolonialstudies/2014/06/20/anglophilia/.

Scott, Suzanne. "From Filk to Wrock: Performance, Professionalism, and Power in Harry Potter Wizard Rock." Presentation at the Console-ing Passions International Conference, Santa Barbara, CA, April 24–26, 2008.

_____. "Revenge of the Fanboy: Convergence Culture and the Politics of Incorporation." Ph.D. dissertation, University of Southern California, 2011. http://digitallibrary.usc.edu/cdm/ref/collection/p15799coll127/id/439159.

Serazio, Michael. "The Elementary Forms of Sports Fandom: A Durkheimian Exploration of Team Myths, Kinship, and Totemic Rituals." *Communication and Sport* 1, no. 4 (December 1, 2013): 303–25. doi:10.1177/2167479512462017.

Shapiro, Fred R, ed. *Yale Book of Quotations*. New Haven: Yale University Press, 2006.
Shuck, Raymond. "'The Anti-Racist-White-Hero Premise': Whiteness and the *Harry Potter* Series." In *Wizards Vs. Muggles: Essays on Identity and the Harry Potter Universe*, edited by Christopher E. Bell, 9–26. Jefferson, NC: McFarland, 2016.
Smith, Anne Collins. "It's Real for (All Of) Us: Wizard Rock and the Audience as Co-Creator." In *Harry Potter and Convergence Culture: Essays on Fandom and the Expanding Potterverse*, edited by Amanda Firestone and Leisa A. Clark, 67–76. Jefferson, NC: McFarland, 2018.
_____. "Playing [With] Multiple Roles: Readers, Authors, and Characters in 'Who Is Blaise Zabini?'" *Transformative Works and Cultures* 3 (September 14, 2009). http://journal.transformativeworks.org/index.php/twc/article/view/186.
Sohwabach, Aaron. *Fan Fiction and Copyright: Outsider Works and Intellectual Property Protection*. Abingdon-on-Thames, UK: Routledge, 2016.
Stanfill, Mel. "Doing Fandom (Mis)Doing Whiteness: Heteronormativity, Racialization, and the Discursive Construction of Fandom." *Transformative Works and Cultures* 8 (October 1, 2010). http://journal.transformativeworks.org/index.php/twc/article/view/256.
Takacs, Stacy. *Interrogating Popular Culture: Key Questions*. Abingdon-on-Thames, UK: Routledge, 2014.
Tamarkin, Elisa. *Anglophilia: Deference, Devotion, and Antebellum America*. Chicago: University of Chicago Press, 2008.
Tatum, Melissa L. "Identity and Authenticity in the Filk Community." *Transformative Works and Cultures* 3 (June 9, 2009). http://journal.transformativeworks.org/index.php/twc/article/view/139.
Tauber, Robert T., and Cathy Sargent Mester. *Acting Lessons for Teachers: Using Performance Skills in the Classroom*. Westport, CT: Greenwood Publishing Group, 2007.
Tekinbaş, Katie Salen, and Eric Zimmerman. *Rules of Play: Game Design Fundamentals*. Cambridge, MA: MIT Press, 2003.
Terrell, Jennifer. "Constructing Rooms of Requirement: The Ethnographic Study of Digitally Transmediated Sociality." Ph.D. dissertation, Indiana University, 2015. http://gradworks.umi.com/37/16/3716456.html.
_____. "The Harry Potter Alliance: Sociotechnical Contexts of Digitally Mediated Activism." In *Cyberactivism on the Participatory Web*, edited by Martha McCaughey, 41–61. Abingdon-on-Thames, UK: Routledge, 2014.
Thomas, Paul. "Paul Thomas, the 8th Horcrux." In *Harry Potter, Still Recruiting: An Inner Look at Harry Potter Fandom*, edited by Valerie Estelle Frankel, 166–8. Allentown, PA: Zossima Press, 2012.
Turk, Tisha. "Fan Work: Labor, Worth, and Participation in Fandom's Gift Economy." *Transformative Works and Cultures* 15 (2014). http://dx.doi.org/10.3983/twc.2014.0518.
Warren, John, and Deanna Fassett. *Communication: A Critical/Cultural Introduction*. Thousand Oaks, CA: Sage, 2010
Wikstrom, Patrik, and Christina Olin-Scheller. "To Be Continued..." In *Youth Culture and Net Culture: Online Social Practices*, edited by Dunkels Elza, 83–97. Hershey, PA: IGI Global, 2010.
Winge, Theresa. "Costuming the Imagination: Origins of Anime and Manga Cosplay." *Mechademia* 1 (2006): 65–76.
Yoho, Rob. "Developing Community Through Wizard Rock: An Interview with Wizard Rocker Lena Gabrielle." In *Playing Harry Potter: Essays and Interviews on Fandom and Performance*, edited by Lisa S. Brenner, 220–32. Jefferson, NC: McFarland, 2015.

YouGov. "Sexual Orientation" [UK], August 12, 2015. https://d25d2506sfb94s.cloudfront.net/cumulus_uploads/document/7zv13z8mfn/YG-Archive-150813-%20Sexuality.pdf.
———. "Sexual Orientation" [US], August 12, 2015. https://d25d2506sfb94s.cloudfront.net/cumulus_uploads/document/isqcugzp6d/tabs_OPI_Kinsey_Scale_20150813.pdf.
Zubernis, Lynn, and Katherine Larsen. *Fandom at the Crossroads: Celebration, Shame, and Fan/Producer Relationships*. Cambridge: Cambridge Scholars Publishing, 2012.
———. *Fangasm: Supernatural Fangirls*. Iowa City: University of Iowa Press, 2013.

Newspapers and Magazine Articles

Anderson, Eric. "Long-Running KWCW Shows." *The Whitman Wire*. May 12, 2017. http://whitmanwire.com/magazine-2/2017/05/12/long-running-kwcw-shows/.
Balkins, Varinia. "KWCW Spotlight: The Witching Hour." *The Whitman Wire*. November 16. 2017, https://whitmanwire.com/arts/2017/11/16/kwcw-spotlight-the-witching-hour/.
Bauernschmidt, Aidan. "First-Year's Band 'Wrocks' as the Moaning Myrtles." *Etownian*. March 29, 2007.
Becker, Lauren. "Interview: The Moaning Myrtles." *Shooting Stars Magazine*. October 31, 2007. https://shootingstarsmag.net/interview-moaning-myrtles/.
Bennett, Alanna. "Why the Youtube Community Is Standing Up Against Sexual and Emotional Abuse." *Bustle*. March 20, 2014. https://www.bustle.com/articles/18565-why-the-youtube-community-is-standing-up-against-sexual-and-emotional-abuse.
Brennan, Collin. "A Brief History of Punk Rock and Presidential Politics." *Consequence of Sound*. July 13, 2016. https://consequenceofsound.net/2016/07/a-brief-history-of-punk-rock-and-presidential-politics/.
Brzozowski, Aleksandra. "Bowling with Bands: Harry and the Potters." *Street Hawk Magazine*. Archived October 4, 2011. https://web.archive.org/web/20070807163434/http://www.streethawkmagazine.com/wpf/?p=36.
Burrell, Jackie. "Harry Potter Fans Tune in to Wizard Rock." *Contra Costa Times*. July 14, 2009. http://search.ebscohost.com/login.aspx?direct=true&db=n5h&AN=2W63924805835&site=ehost-live.
Carroll, Larry. "Harry Ramone? Iggy Voldemort? Band Splices Punk with Potter." *MTV*. September 8, 2005. http://www.mtv.com/news/1509166/harry-ramone-iggy-voldemort-band-splices-punk-with-potter/.
Cataneo, Emily. "Harry and the Potters Host Annual Yule Ball at Middle East Sunday." *MetroWest Daily News*. December 14, 2012. http://www.metrowestdailynews.com/article/20121214/News/312149411.
Chief. "We Are Wizards." Archived October 2007. https://web.archive.org/web/20071229005220/http://chiefmag.com:80/issues/9/profiles/We-Are-Wizards/.
Clements, Lizz. "A Beginner's Guide to Wizard Rock." *Examiner*. Archived July 10, 2016. http://web.archive.org/web/20160710170938/http://www.examiner.com/article/a-beginner-s-guide-to-wizard-rock.
The Collegian. "Bands Entertain 'Harry Potter' Fans with Wizard Rock, Quirky Humor." March 10, 2008. https://www.kstatecollegian.com/2008/03/10/bands-entertain-harry-potter-fans-with-wizard-rock-quirky-humor/.
Cornwall, Rupert. "The Regal Republic: Why Are Americans Obsessed with the Royal Family?" *The Independent*. April 24, 2011. http://www.independent.co.uk/voices/commentators/rupert-cornwell/the-regal-republic-why-are-americans-obsessed-with-the-royal-family-2274357.html.
Dawson, Nick. "Josh Koury, We Are Wizards." *Filmmaker Magazine*. November 14, 2008. https://filmmakermagazine.com/1342-josh-koury-we-are-wizards/.

Bibliography

Daytrotter. "Harry and the Potters—The Hogwarts Tonsil Hockey Team." *Paste*. May 28, 2006. https://www.pastemagazine.com/articles/2006/05/harry-and-the-potters-the-hogwarts-tonsil-hockey-team.html

Delsener, Mary. "Cellars by Wandlight: Harry and the Potters in a Cave." *The Phoenix*. Archived July 20, 2009. https://web.archive.org/web/20090720095301/http://thephoenix.com:80/BLOGS/onthedownload/archive/2009/07/15/cellars-by-wandlight-harry-amp-the-potters-in-a-cave.aspx.

Donnelly, Elisabeth. "For Harry Potter Fans About to Rock, We Salute You." *Salon*. July 14, 2007. http://www.salon.com/2007/07/14/wizard_rock/.

Ehrlich, Brenna. "How To: Get Your Music on Itunes." *Mashable*. May 20, 2011. https://mashable.com/2011/05/20/getting-music-on-itunes/.

Falletti, Logan. "Final 'Hallows and Horcruxes Ball' on Saturday." *The Collegian*. March 7, 2014. http://www.kstatecollegian.com/2014/03/07/final-hallows-and-horcruxes-ball-on-saturday/.

Filmmaking Focus. "Megan and Mallory Schuyler: Documenting the Culture of Wizard Rock." Archived May 10, 2007. https://web.archive.org/web/20070510152221/http://filmmaking-focus.com/megan-and-mallory-schuyler-documenting-the-culture-of-wizard-rock/.

Floberg, Dana. "Digital Denied: Systemic Discrimination Keeps Communities Offline." *Free Press*. December 13, 2016. https://www.freepress.net/blog/2016/12/13/digital-denied-systemic-discrimination-keeps-communities-offline.

Forester, Jakki. "Hallows and Horcruxes Ball Features Variety of Wizarding Activities for Avid 'Harry Potter' Fans." *The Collegian*. March 12, 2012. http://www.kstatecollegian.com/2012/03/12/hallows-and-horcruxes-ball-features-variety-of-wizarding-activities-for-avid-harry-potter-fans/.

Frew, Gillian. "The Witching Hour." *Whitman Magazine*. July 2012. https://www.whitman.edu/newsroom/whitman-magazine/2012/july-2012/campus-news/the-witching-hour.

Gibbs, Nancy. "Person of the Year 2007." *Time*. December 19, 2007. http://content.time.com/time/specials/2007/personoftheyear/article/0,28804,1690753_1695388_1695436,00.html.

Grossman, Lev. "The Boy Who Rocked." *Time*. August 3, 2009.

Harrison, Virginia. "America's Love Affair with British TV." *CNN*. March 12, 2015. http://money.cnn.com/2015/03/12/media/british-television-america/index.html.

Havens, Lyndsey. "The Magical Duo Behind the 8th Horcrux." Day in the Life. *University Daily Kansas*. 2015. http://www.kudayinthelife.com/8th-horcrux/.

Hookey, Avery. "Potter-Inspired Trio of Bands Rock Like Wizards at Library." *Tow Topics*. August 15, 2007. http://www.towntopics.com/aug1507/other4.php.

Humphries, Rachel. "Harry Potter 'Wrockers' Conjure Musical Magic." *ABC News*. January 8, 2007. http://abcnews.go.com/Business/FunMoney/story?id=3371717andpage=1.

Hunter, Michelle. "Live from the Library: Wizard Rock." *The Times-Picayune*. August 16, 2007. http://blog.nola.com/times-picayune/2007/08/live_from_the_library_its_wiza.html.

Jablonski, Natalie. "Woonsocket's Draco and the Malfoys." *Rhode Island Public Radio*. 2013. http://ripr.org/post/woonsockets-draco-and-malfoys.

Jaworski, Michelle, and Rae Votta. "The 9 Biggest Youtube Scandals of 2014." *The Daily Dot*. December 23, 2014. https://www.dailydot.com/upstream/youtube-scandals-2014/.

Jones, Nicholas. "The Best Bands of Wizard Rock." Tone Deaf. 2011. http://tonedeaf.com.au/the-best-bands-of-wizard-rock/

Khosla, Proma. "The Wonderful, Weird World of Wizard Rock." *Mashable*. November 20, 2016. http://mashable.com/2016/11/20/wizard-rock-harry-potter/.

Kramer, Melody Joy. "Wizard Rock: Harry Potter Goes Punk." *NPR*. July 13, 2007. http://www.npr.org/templates/story/story.php?storyId=11162595.

LeakyCon staff. "Leakycon Rebrands Itself as 'Geekycon' as Annual Fandom Convention Comes to a Close in Orlando Amid Sold-Out Crowd." PR Newswire. Aug 04, 2014. https://search.proquest.com/docview/1550793116?accountid=14556.

Leight, Elias. "Hear Bruce Springsteen's Unreleased 'Harry Potter' Song." *Rolling Stone*. February 10, 2017. http://www.rollingstone.com/music/news/hear-bruce-springsteens-unreleased-harry-potter-song-w466297.

Lingappa, Anuradha. "Violence in Harry Potter Community Calls for Barrier Between Fans, Stars." *The Whitman Wire*. April 17, 2014. http://whitmanwire.com/opinion/2014/04/17/fan-community-rife-with-sexual-violence/.

Milam, Whitney. "Harry Potter Fan Brings 'Deathly Hallows' to Life with Music." *Hollywood News*. July 4, 2010. http://www.hollywoodnews.com/2010/07/04/harry-potter-fan-brings-deathly-hallows-to-life-with-music/.

Mischief Management staff. "Top Young Adult Literature Authors to Meet Fans and Aspiring Writers at Leakycon 2014." PR Newswire. June 23, 2014. https://search.proquest.com/docview/1539266284?accountid=14556.

Morales, Claudia. "Our House." *Medium*. May 27, 2017. https://medium.com/wizard-punk/our-house-79bd90233bc5.

———. "Wizard Rock in the Age of Trump." *MTV*. November 28, 2016. http://www.mtv.com/news/2957858/harry-potter-wizard-rock-trump-election/.

Neuman, Steven. "'Wizard Rock' Casts Spell on Filmmakers." *The Spokesman Review*. Archived November 20, 2008. https://web.archive.org/web/20081120172250/http://stevenneuman.com/2007/07/wizard-rock-casts-spell-on-filmmakers.html.

Oler, Tammy. "Ladies Camp Rock: Wrocking'n'rowling with Wizard- and Twilight-Themed Bands." *Bitch*. Fall 2009.

Phillips, Amy, and Ryan Dombal. "Top Five Live Shows of 2005 (That Weren't Intonation)." *Pitchfork*. December 11, 2005. http://pitchfork.com/features/lists-and-guides/6215-2005-comments-lists-top-live-shows-and-music-videos/.

Plummer, Jessica. "Music Review: Harry and the Potters." *Barnard Bulletin*. Archived May 10, 2007. https://web.archive.org/web/20070510062634/http://www.columbia.edu/cu/barnardbulletin/archive/spring04/4-21/4-21music/4-21music.html.

Reed, James. "Singing of the Papal Smoke." *The Boston Globe*. May 14, 2005.

Riesman, Abraham. "The Bizarre, Unsolved Mystery of 'My Immortal,' the World's Worst Fanfiction Story." *Vulture*. March 12, 2015. http://www.vulture.com/2015/03/bizarre-unsolved-mystery-of-my-immortal.html.

Romano, Aja, Michelle Jaworksi, and Rae Votta. "A Guide to Youtube's 10 Biggest Sex Abuse Scandals." *The Daily Dot*. October 3, 2014. https://www.dailydot.com/upstream/youtube-sex-abuse-scandals-guide/.

Rose, Lacey. "Wizard Rock." *Forbes*. July 13, 2005. https://www.forbes.com/2005/07/13/rowling-potter-band-cx_lr_0713harryband.html#5328be24d3ce.

Rosenbaum, Sarah Elizabeth. "Lit Punk: Wiz Kids—Harry and the Potters Play the Space." *New Haven Advocate*. Archived December 19, 2010. https://web.archive.org/web/20101219004354/www.newhavenadvocate.com/music-articles/lit-punk-wiz-kids-harry-and-the-potters-play-the-space.

Rosenberg, Alyssa. "How 'Harry Potter' Fans Won a Four-Year Fight Against Child Slavery." *The Washington Post*. January 13, 2015. https://www.washingtonpost.com/news/act-four/wp/2015/01/13/how-harry-potter-fans-won-a-four-year-fight-against-child-slavery/?utm_term=.d305853695b9.

Sahim, Sarah. "The Unbearable Whiteness of Indie." *Pitchfork*. March 25, 2015. https://pitchfork.com/thepitch/710-the-unbearable-whiteness-of-indie/.

Shea, Dan. "5 Questions W/ Paul Degeorge of Harry and the Potters." *Boston Hassle*.

December 15, 2017. https://bostonhassle.com/5-questions-w-paul-degeorge-of-harry-and-the-potters/.
Shimkus, Ali. "The Band That Live: Paul Degeorge of Harry and the Potters." *Slug*. May 26, 2016. https://www.slugmag.com/music-features/harry-potters/.
Slack, Andrew. "Harry Potter and the Muggle Activists." *In These Times*. October 26, 2007. http://inthesetimes.com/article/3365/harry_potter_and_the_muggle_activists.
Spokane 7. "Documenting Harry's Spell." Archived July 17, 2009. https://web.archive.org/web/20090717053035/http://spokane7.com:80/music/stories/?ID=8242.
Sunderland, Mitchell. "The Harry Potter Fans Still Making Music About Magic, Known as Wizard Rock." *Broadly*. November 19, 2016. https://broadly.vice.com/en_us/article/the-harry-potter-fans-still-making-music-about-magic-known-as-wizard-rock.
Sweeney, Emily. "Sibling Musicians Bring Out the 'Punk' in Harry Potter." *The Boston Globe*. September 16, 2004. http://archive.boston.com/news/local/articles/2004/09/16/sibling_musicians_bring_out_the_punk_in_harry_potter/.
Traister, Rebecca. "Potterpalooza." *Salon*. June 1, 2007. http://www.salon.com/2007/06/01/phoenix_rising/.
Vineyard, Jennifer. "Harry Potter Fandom Reaches Magical New Level Thanks to Wizard-Rock Bands." *MTV*. Archived June 9, 2007. https://web.archive.org/web/20070609154648/http://www.mtv.com/movies/news/articles/1561855/20070606/story.jhtml.
Walsh, Dustin. "Under a Spell." *Detroit Metro Times*. July 11, 2007. http://www.metrotimes.com/detroit/under-a-spell/Content?oid=2187905.
Wiest, Brianna. "Psychologists Say That Belonging to a Fandom Is Amazing for Your Mental Health." *Teen Vogue*, July 20, 2017. https://www.teenvogue.com/story/psychologists-say-fandoms-are-amazing-for-your-mental-health.
Winkie, Luke. "Never Forget Harry and the Potters and the Bizarre World of 'Wizard Rock.'" Noisey. August 5, 2015. https://noisey.vice.com/en_us/article/rpy3nz/harry-and-the-potters-wizard-rock.
Wired. "Our Weapon Is Love: Wrockstock 2008." May 20, 2008. https://www.wired.com/2008/05/our-weapon-is-l/.
Youngs, Ian. "A Brief History of Punk." *BBC News*. December 23, 2002. http://news.bbc.co.uk/1/hi/entertainment/2601493.stm.
Zagier, Alan Scher. "Harry Potter Devotees Put Wizard Tales to Music." *USA Today*. June 18, 2008. http://usatoday30.usatoday.com/life/music/2008-06-18-539408079_x.htm.
Zumbrun, Joshua, and Sonya Geis. "Wizard Rock Has Fans in Hogwarts Heaven." *The Washington Post*. July 8, 2007. http://www.washingtonpost.com/wp-dyn/content/article/2007/07/06/AR2007070600500.html.

Webpages and Blogs

"About." myHogwarts.co.uk. Archived November 3, 2011. https://web.archive.org/web/20111103194423/http://www.myhogwarts.co.uk:80/about.
Anderson, Steph. "About." Yes All Witches. Accessed April 4, 2018. http://www.yesallwitches.org/about.
———. "Apply for a YAW Grant. Yes All Witches. Accessed April 4, 2018. http://www.Yesallwitches.Org/Apply-For-A-Yaw-Grant/.
Anelli, Melissa. "The Great Jingle Spells Contest." The Leaky Cauldron. October 1, 2010. http://www.the-leaky-cauldron.org/2010/10/01/the-great-jingle-spells-contest/.
———. "The Great(Er) Jingle Spells Contest." The Leaky Cauldron. October 19, 2011. http://www.the-leaky-cauldron.org/2011/10/19/the-greater-jingle-spells-contest/.

———. "Jingle Spells Completely Sold Out." The Leaky Cauldron. December 1, 2007. http://www.the-leaky-cauldron.org/2007/12/01/jingle-spells-completely-sold-out/.

———. "Leaky's Sixth Get a Clue Fundraiser Now Open." The Leaky Cauldron. October 14, 2007. http://www.the-leaky-cauldron.org/2007/10/14/leaky-s-sixth-get-a-clue-fundraiser-now-open-all-new-holiday-album-available-for-pre-order/.

———. "Presenting... Leakycon 2009!" The Leaky Cauldron. February 12, 2008. http://www.the-leaky-cauldron.org/2008/2/12/presenting-leakycon-2009/.

Backe, Emma Louise. "Consumption, Performance and Identity in Cosplay." *The Geek Anthropologist.* June 16, 2016. https://thegeekanthropologist.com/2016/06/16/consumption-performance-and-identity-in-cosplay/.

Bandcamp. "#Nobannowall: Over 400 Labels and Artists Join Us in Donating Today's Profits to the ACLU." Accessed September 11, 2018. https://daily.bandcamp.com/2017/02/02/nobannowall-over-150-labels-artists-join-us-in-donating-fridays-profits-to-the-aclu/.

Beaven, Pattie. "About." Wrock the Boat. Archived January 24, 2008. https://web.archive.org/web/20080124041206/http://www.wrocktheboat.com:80/about.html.

Benoit, Russ. "Announcing the Wizrocklopedia Music Archive." Wizrocklopedia. December 15, 2016. http://www.wrocklopedia.com/2016/12/15/announcing-wizrocklopedia-music-archive/.

Benoit, Russ, ed. "The History of Wizard Rock." Wizrocklopedia. Accessed June 22, 2018. http://www.wrocklopedia.com/the-history-of-wizard-rock/.

Bird, Neil, and James Shepherd, eds. "Harry and the Potters." wizardRock.co.uk. Archived March 10, 2012. http://web.archive.org/web/20120310120621/http://www.wizardrock.co.uk/BandInterviews/interview_hatp.htm.

Cardin, Keith. "WrockBOX | Wizard Rock Radio | 24/7 Internet Radio Station." WrockBOX. Archived January 30, 2011. https://web.archive.org/web/20110130063311/http://wrockbox.com:80/.

ChALC. "The Hallows and Horcruxes Ball." *Official Webpage of Kansas State's Children's and Adolescent Literature Community.* 2008. https://www.k-state.edu/chalc/Activities_archive.dwt.

Chan, Deborah. "Wizard Rockumentary Review: Hogpro Reporter Arabella Figg at Spokane World Premiere." Hogwarts Professor. April 18, 2008. http://www.hogwartsprofessor.com/wizard-wrockumentary-review-hogpro-reporter-arabella-figg-at-spokane-world-premiere/.

Clements, Lizz, ed. "Band Profiles." Wizrocklopedia. Archived February 17, 2007. https://web.archive.org/web/20070217040556/http://wizrocklopedia.com:80/?page_id=450.

———. "The History of Wizard Rock." Wizrocklopedia. Wizrocklopedia. Archived May 3, 2009. http://web.archive.org/web/20090503191131/http://wizrocklopedia.com/the-history-of-wizard-rock/.

———. "Meet the Staff." Wizrocklopedia. Archived October 6, 2007. https://web.archive.org/web/20071006083840/http://wizrocklopedia.com/index.php/about/staff/.

———. "More Wrock Bands Join Cheap Rent Family." Wizrocklopedia. September 10, 2007. http://www.wrocklopedia.com/2007/09/10/more-wrock-bands-join-cheap-rent-family/.

———. "The Wizard Rock Peoples Choice Awards." Wizrocklopedia. January 18, 2007. http://www.wrocklopedia.com/2007/01/18/the-wizard-rock-peoples-choice-awards-2/.

———. "The Wizard Rock Peoples Choice Awards: Fill Out the Nominations Form Now." Wizrocklopedia. Archived March 7, 2007. https://web- https://web.archive.org/web/20070307131211/http://wizrocklopedia.com:80/the-wizard-rock-peoples-choice-awards/.

Bibliography

———. "Wizard Rock Peoples Choice Awards Results." Wizrocklopedia. Archived March 7, 2007. https://web.archive.org/web/20070307131529/http://wizrocklopedia.com:80/wrpcawinners/.

———. "The Wizard Rock Peoples Choice Awards: Voting." Wizrocklopedia. December 14, 2013. http://archive.is/CH0RM.

———. "The Wizrocklopedia: Encyclopedia of Wizard Rock » About the Wizrocklopedia." Wizrocklopedia. Archived October 7, 2007. https://web.archive.org/web/20071007120511/http://wizrocklopedia.com/index.php/about.

———. "WR People's Choice Awards Nominations Open!" Wizrocklopedia. January 22, 2007. http://www.wrocklopedia.com/2007/01/22/wr-peoples-choice-awards-nominations-open-2/.

———. "WRPCA Voting Polls Open!!" Wizrocklopedia. February 9, 2007. http://www.wrocklopedia.com/2007/02/09/wrpca-voting-polls-open/.

Cooper, Ryan. "The History of Punk Rock Music." ThoughtCo. June 30, 2017. https://www.thoughtco.com/history-of-punk-rock-2803345.

DeGeorge, Joe, and Andrew MacLeay. "About." Eskimo Labs. Accessed July 26, 2017. http://www.eskimolabs.com/artists/ed/about.htm.

———. "Releases." Eskimo Labs. Accessed July 26, 2017. http://www.eskimolabs.com/artists/ed/releases.htm.

DeGeorge, Paul. "About." Harry and the Potters. Archived November 1, 2010. https://web.archive.org/web/20101101234820/http://harryandthepotters.com/about/.

———. "Albums." Wizard Rock EP of the Month Club. Accessed July 26, 2017. http://www.wizardrockclub.com/albums.html.

———. "Bio." Harry and the Potters. Accessed March 23, 2017. http://harryandthepotters.com/bio.

———. "Holiday Sale!" Wizard Rock EP of the Month Club. Accessed March 10, 2010. http://wizardrockclub.com/node/78.html.

———. "Live at Purgatory Chasm Bootleg!" Harry and the Potters. Archived November 23, 2010. https://web-beta.archive.org/web/20101123163032/http://harryandthepotters.com/news/page/7/.

———. "Other, Etc." Eskimo Labs. Accessed March 9, 2017. http://www.eskimolabs.com/etcetera.html.

———. "2008 Yule Ball CD/DVD Available Now!" Harry and the Potters. Archived November 23, 2010. https://web.archive.org/web/20101123152756/http://harryandthepotters.com/news/page/4/.

———. "We Are Excited to Announce That DFTBA Is Now..." Harry and the Potters. 2016. http://harryandthepotters.com/post/123573542469/we-are-excited-to-announce-that-dftba-is-now.

———. "We Are Excited to Announce the 2017 Yule Balls!" Harry and the Potters. November 2017. http://harryandthepotters.com/post/166850223969/we-are-excited-to-announce-the-2017-yule-balls.

———. "Wizard Rock EP of the Month Club!" Wizard Rock EP of the Month Club. January 25, 2007. http://www.wizardrockclub.com/node/27.html.

DeGeorge, Paul and Joe DeGeorge. "Golden Snitchwiches: Catch It in Your Mouth!!!" Snitchwiches.com. Accessed February 1, 2018. http://http://snitchwiches.com/.

———. "Old Interview I Found in Our Email." Harry and the Potters. Accessed June 14, 2018. http://harryandthepotters.com/post/26870261859/old-interview-i-found-in-our-email.

Dianiska, Laura. "From the Editors: Thank You!" Wizrocklopedia. January 3, 2018. http://www.wrocklopedia.com/2018/01/03/from-the-editors-thank-you/.

———. "'Pedia's Back! Send an Owl!" Wizrocklopedia. September 16, 2016. http://www.wrocklopedia.com/2016/09/16/pedias-back-send-an-owl/.

_____. "State of the Pedia." Wizrocklopedia. July 8, 2017. http://www.wrocklopedia.com/2017/07/08/state-of-the-pedia/.
Doogan, Jesse. "Top 5 Wizard Rock Songs to Bring You Back to Hogwarts." BookRiot. December 2, 2014. https://bookriot.com/2014/12/02/top-5-wizard-rock-songs-bring-back-hogwarts/.
Drama. "Switchblade Kittens and Harry Potter." Switchblade Kittens. Accessed March 9, 2017. http://www.switchbladekittens.com/friends/harry-potter.html.
Ellis, Danika. "Queer and Feminist Wizard Rock." BookRiot. September 7, 2016. http://bookriot.com/2016/09/07/queer-feminist-wizard-rock/.
Fairweather, Lauren. "Letters." *Lauren Fairweather* (blog). Tumblr. 2014. http://laurenfairweather.tumblr.com/post/79829581330/letters.
Fairweather, Lauren, and Nina Jankowicz. "About." *The Moaning Myrtles* (blog). Wordpress. December 19, 2006. https://moaningmyrtles.wordpress.com/about/.
"FAQ." *Your Wizard Rock Resource* (blog). Wordpress. Accessed August 1, 2017. https://yourwizardrockresource.wordpress.com/faq/.
Fridy, Freya. "Creevey's Creevey Thursday." Wizrocklopedia. April 18, 2013. http://www.wrocklopedia.com/2013/04/18/creeveys-creevey-thursday/.
_____. "He Said/She Said: The (Non?)Existence of Sexism in Wizard Rock." Wizrocklopedia. September 2, 2009. http://www.wrocklopedia.com/2009/09/02/he-saidshe-said-the-nonexistence-of-sexism-in-wizard-rock/.
Glenn, Devon. "The History of Social Media from 1978–2012 [Infographic]." *Adweek*. February 16, 2012. http://www.adweek.com/digital/the-history-of-social-media-from-1978-2012-infographic/.
Hanna, Maggie. "Wizrocklopedia » Blog Archive » a Sisterhood of Wrock." Wizrocklopedia. Archived February 27, 2009. https://web- https://web.archive.org/web/20090227093620/http://wizrocklopedia.com/2009/02/20/a-sisterhood-of-wrock/.
Harry and the Potters. "Voldemort Can't Stop the Rock!" Bandcamp. Accessed January 6, 2018. https://harryandthepotters.bandcamp.com/album/voldemort-can-t-stop-the-rock.
Hills, Aaron. "Interview: Josh Koury on 'We Are Wizards'" *IFC*. November 20, 2008. http://www.ifc.com/2008/11/josh-koury-on-we-are-wizards.
Horner, Kristina. "The Truth About ALL CAPS." *Oh Hey* (blog). Tumblr. 2014. http://italktosnakes.tumblr.com/post/79898322770/the-truth-about-all-caps-yes-another-post-about.
Horner, Kristina, and Elle Viane Sonnet. "About." *The Parselmouths Band* (blog). Wordpress. Accessed March 10, 2017. https://theparselmouthsband.wordpress.com/about/.
"Inside WrockBOX Wizarding Radio." myHogwarts.co.uk. Archived October 5, 2012. https://web.archive.org/web/20121005140412/http://myhogwarts.co.uk/inside/wrockbox/.
Jaffe, Eric. "The History of Punk Rock." In Music We Trust. Accessed August 14, 2017. http://www.inmusicwetrust.com/articles/08f04.html.
Jenkins, Henry. "How 'Dumbledore's Army' Is Transforming Our World: An Interview with the HP Alliance's Andrew Slack (Part One)." *Henryjenkins.Org* (blog). July 23, 2009. https://henryjenkins.org/blog/2009/07/how_dumbledores_army_is_transf.html.
KellyW. "Subversive Wrock: Using the Power of a Story to Influence the World." Wizrocklopedia. December 6, 2016. http://www.wrocklopedia.com/2016/12/06/subversive-wrock-using-power-story-influence-world/.
Kendall, Grace. *Wizard Rock Sampler* (blog). Tumblr. 2016. http://wizardrocksampler.tumblr.com/.
Kincaid, Chris. "The History of Cosplay." Japan Powered. October 16, 2016. https://www.japanpowered.com/otaku-culture/the-history-of-cosplay.

Bibliography

Koury, Josh. "About." We Are Wizards. Archived February 2, 2008. https://web.archive.org/web/20080202003503/http://wearewizards-themovie.com:80/pages/about/index.php.

———. "Talking Movies." Interview by Tom Brook, October 8, 2007.

Kurtz-Nelson, Eva. "'House of Awesome': A Wrock Ethnography." *Eva's Ethnography Extravaganza* (blog). Blogspot. December 13, 2007. http://ethnographyextravaganza.blogspot.com/2007/12/house-of-awesome-wrock-ethnography.html.

Lawrence, TK. "Fresh, Spooky, and Queer, by Totally Knuts." Bandcamp. Accessed June 12, 2017. https://totallyknuts.bandcamp.com/album/fresh-spooky-queer.

"The List." Potterglot. Accessed July 28, 2017. https://www.potterglot.net/the-list/.

"Luke Conard Seemingly Both Apologies for and Denies Allegations, Internet Really Not Buying It." *The YouTube Gazette* (blog). Tumblr. March 20, 2014. http://youtubegazette.tumblr.com/post/80171208536/luke-conard-seemingly-both-apologises-for-and.

Maggiacomo, Matt. "Biography." thewhompingwillows.com. Archived November 4, 2012. https://web.archive.org/web/20121104235410/http://thewhompingwillows.com/biography/.

———. "Gah." *Matt Maggiacomo* (blog). Tumblr. 2014. http://mattmaggiacomo.tumblr.com/post/79764336545/gah.

———. "Wizards and Muggles Rock for Social Justice." Bandcamp. Accessed August 23, 2017. https://thewhompingwillows.bandcamp.com/album/wizards-and-muggles-rock-for-social-justice-vol-1.

McKay, Faith. "An Interview with the Schuyler Sisters of the Wizard Rockumentary." Fantasy Is Love. Archived December 21, 2007. https://web.archive.org/web/20071221101749/fantasyislove.com/articles/wizardrock.php.

Michaelman, Justin. "Justin Finch-Fletchley and the Sugar Quills." Bandcamp. Accessed May 18, 2017. http://jffismybff.com/.

Milam, Whitney. "Awkward Boy Stories." *Wmilam* (blog). Tumblr. Archived January 18, 2017. https://web.archive.org/web/20170118001209/http://wmilam.tumblr.com/post/79987966729/awkward-boy-stories.

Moore, Chris. "Autoethnography of Objects." Cryptocommonicon. February 5, 2017. https://chrismoore.blog/2017/02/05/autoethnography-of-objects/.

Morales, Claudia. "Wizard Punk." *Claudia, More or Less*. 2016. http://claudiamoreorless.com/wizard-punk/.

Munday, Jason. "My Experience with the Wizard Rock Community." *Jasonmunday* (blog). Tumblr. April 2, 2014. http://jasonmunday.tumblr.com/post/81542693956/my-experience-with-the-wizard-rock-community.

Parker, Ethan. "Kwikspell." Weebly. Pretending for Real. Archived July 1, 2013. https://web.archive.org/web/20130701000000*/http://pretendingforreal.weebly.com/.

"Paving the Way for Wizard Rockers Everywhere." *Teaparty Boston* (blog). Wordpress. January 29, 2010. The Second Husk. https://secondhusk.wordpress.com/2010/01/30/harry-the-potters-only-playing-aztec-pyramids-from-now-on/.

Plunkett, Luke. "Cosplay Is Over 100 Years Old." Kotaku. May 16, 2016. https://cosplay.kotaku.com/cosplay-is-over-100-years-old-1777013405.

"Reference: List of Fandom Abuse Posts." *Glasgirl* (blog). Tumblr. March 21, 2014. http://glasgirl.tumblr.com/post/79915267203/reference-list-of-fandom-abuse-posts.

Rojas, Rosianna. "I Am Going to Start with a Redundant Sentence." *Hermionejp* (blog). Tumblr. March 15, 2014. http://hermionejg.tumblr.com/post/79604244628/i-am-going-to-start-with-a-redundant-sentence.

Rowling, J.K. "Section: Fan Sites: The HP Alliance." *J.K. Rowling Official Site*. Archived September 17, 2008. https://web.archive.org/web/20080917034614/http://www.jkrowling.com:80/textonly/en/fansite_view.cfm?id=20.

Schuyler, Mallory, and Megan Schuyler. "In the News." The Wizard Rockumentary. August 20, 2008. http://www.wizardrockumentary.com/news.html.

Slack, Andrew. "Defense Against the Dark Arts." *The Harry Potter Alliance* (blog). Tumblr. 2014. http://thehpalliance.tumblr.com/post/79879263737/defense-against-the-dark-arts.

Smith, Craig. "Myspace Deletes Old User Content… and Some People Actually Care." DMR. December 6, 2013. https://expandedramblings.com/index.php/myspace-deletes-old-user-content-and-some-people-actually-care/.

Smith, Lauren Amanda. "Wizard Rock: 'Renting' a Room in J.K. Rowling's Hogwarts." *The Jaded Hippy* (blog). Blogspot. December 10, 2010. http://jadedhippy.blogspot.com/2010/12/wizard-rock-renting-room-in-j-k.html.

Snow, Amy, and Jamie Walker. "Episodes." WZRDrock. Archived January 13, 2008. https://web.archive.org/web/20080113110457/http://www.wzrdrock.com:80/episodes.html.

———. "WZRD Info." WZRDrock. Archived January 13, 2008. https://web.archive.org/web/20080113110508/http://www.wzrdrock.com:80/info.html.

"Success Stories." The Harry Potter Alliance. Retrieved June 21, 2018. https://www.thehpalliance.org/success_stories.

"Susannah." *Your Wizard Rock Resource* (blog). Wordpress. August 19, 2014. https://yourwizardrockresource.wordpress.com/.

Vaughan, Kirsten, and Scott Vaughan. "About Us." The Blibbering Humdingers. Accessed May 22, 2017. https://blibberinghumdingers.com/.

Ward, Kelly. "Subversive Wrock: Using the Power of a Story to Influence the World." Wizrocklopedia. December 6, 2016. http://www.wrocklopedia.com/2016/12/06/subversive-wrock-using-power-story-influence-world/.

"We Are Wizards (2008)." Rotten Tomatoes. 2008. https://www.rottentomatoes.com/m/we_are_wizards/.

"What We Do." The Harry Potter Alliance. Accessed August 23, 2017. http://www.thehpalliance.org/what_we_do.

"Wizard Rock." Wizard Rock. Accessed March 13, 2017. http://wizardrock.org/.

"Wizard Rock » About." Wizard Rock. Accessed March 13, 2017. http://wizardrock.org/?page_id=2.

"Wizard Rock the Vote 2016." The Harry Potter Alliance. Accessed September 27, 2017. http://www.thehpalliance.org/wrockthevote.

"Wrock Chicago." Terminus 2008. Archived January 12, 2008. https://web.archive.org/web/20080112175926/http://www.terminus2008.org:80/events/wrock.html.

Wrock Snob. "Bard Questions: Is Wizard Rock Still Sexist?" *The Wrock Snob* (blog). Wordpress. August 19, 2013. https://wrocksnob.wordpress.com/2013/08/19/bard-questions-is-wizard-rock-still-sexist/.

———. "A Brief Respite." *The Wrock Snob* (blog). Wordpress. September 18, 2013. https://wrocksnob.wordpress.com/2013/09/18/a-brief-respite/.

———. "Extended Thoughts: Women in Wrock, Part 1—In Defense of Men." *The Wrock Snob* (blog). Wordpress. May 19, 2010. https://wrocksnob.wordpress.com/2010/05/19/extended-thoughts-women-in-wrock-part-1-in-defense-of-men/.

———. "My 25 Most Listened to Wizard Rock Songs." *The Wrock Snob* (blog). Wordpress. June 5, 2010. https://wrocksnob.wordpress.com/2010/06/05/my-25-most-listened-to-wizard-rock-songs/.

———. "What Is This Shit?" *The Wrock Snob* (blog). Wordpress. 2010. https://wrocksnob.wordpress.com/about/.

———. "The Wizzies." *The Wrock Snob* (blog). Wordpress. June 14, 2011. https://wrocksnob.wordpress.com/2011/06/14/the-wizzies/.

"Wrock Spotlight: The Parselmouths." MuggleNet. November 25, 2016. http://www.mugglenet.com/2016/11/wrock-spotlight-parselmouths/.

Bibliography

Videos

"1st Week of WrockBOX Has Been Totally Awesome!!" YouTube video, 9:03. Posted by "Appletonks," February 2, 2011. https://www.youtube.com/watch?v=FiBKBFQEjpE.

"The Harry Potter Alliance, a History." YouTube video, 11:48. Posted by "Thehpalliance" [Paul DeGeorge and Andrew Slack], January 9, 2009. https://www.youtube.com/watch?v=CddHOmhFXxQ.

"Harry Potter: What Is Wizard Rock?" YouTube video, 3:13. Posted by "Fuse" [Fuse TV], December 15, 2008. https://www.youtube.com/watch?v=ygZhuopX8SA.

"Music and the Collective Effervescence." YouTube video, 8:08. Posted by "Iuhiuhiuhiuh" [Alex Beam-Ward], December 15, 2008. https://www.youtube.com/watch?v=SPEVzR-Bljk.

We Are Wizards. DVD. Directed by Josh Koury. Brooklyn, NY: Brooklyn Underground Films, 2007.

"What Should We Keep?" YouTube video, 3:39. Posted by "Vlogbrothers" [John Green], May 30, 2017. https://www.youtube.com/watch?v=C6v-uNFF7dw.

The Wizard Rockumentary. DVD. Directed by Mallory and Megan Schuyler. Spokane: GryffinClaw Productions, LLC, 2008.

"Wizzies Intro" YouTube video, 1:07. Posted by "Thewizziesawards" [Brett Holden], July 21, 2011. https://www.youtube.com/watch?v=s9xQui-a6lk.

"WROCK!" YouTube video, 3:33. Posted by "Vlogbrothers" [John Green], May 24, 2009. https://www.youtube.com/watch?v=Bt2u7EK8ivg.

"Xavier's on Youtube?!" YouTube video, 2:25. Posted by "Xavier Austrone" [Keith Cardin], February 4, 2011. https://www.youtube.com/watch?v=E_nVG_FXnmc.

Songs and Albums

Draco and the Malfoys. "Dobby." On *Best of Draco and the Malfoys*. Compact disc. Woonsocket, RI: Self-released, 2016.

_____. "My Dad Is Rich." On *Draco and the Malfoys*. Compact disc. Woonsocket, RI: Self-released, 2005.

The 8th Horcrux. "Ginny, Are You OK?" On *Potterwatch!* Compact disc. Ottawa, KS: Fueled by Pumpkin Juice Records, 2009.

_____. "Potions Wizard." On *Potterwatch!* Compact disc. Ottawa, KS: Fueled by Pumpkin Juice Records, 2009.

_____. "Witch." On *Potterwatch!* Compact disc. Ottawa, KS: Fueled by Pumpkin Juice Records, 2009.

Fairweather, Lauren. "It's Real for Us." On *The Prince's Tall*. Compact disc. Providence, RI: Self-released, 2011.

_____. "Post-Potter Depression." On *Devil's Snare*. Compact disc. Hillsborough, NJ: Self-released, 2005.

Gred and Forge. "Brotherly Love." On *Siriusly Smiling: A Wizard Rock Charity Compilation*. Mp3. Asheville, NC: Self-released, 2008.

Harry and the Potters. "Bacon." On *Priori Incantatem*. Compact disc. Norwood, MA: Charming Records/Eskimo Laboratories, 2009.

_____. "Cornelius Fudge Is an Ass." On *Voldemort Can't Stop the Rock!* Compact disc. Norwood, MA: Charming Records/Eskimo Laboratories, 2004.

_____. *Mail Songs #1*. Digital liner notes. Norwood, MA: Charming Records/Eskimo Laboratories, 2009.

_____. *Priori Incantatem*. Liner notes. Norwood, MA: Charming Records/Eskimo Laboratories, 2009.

_____. "Rocking at Hogwarts." On *The Enchanted Ceiling* EP. Compact disc. Norwood, MA: Wizard Rock EP of the Month Club, 2007.

_____. *Scarred for Life* EP. Liner notes. Norwood, MA: Charming Records/Eskimo Laboratories, 2006.
Justin Finch-Fletchley and the Sugar Quills. "Dumbledore Is Gay (And That's OK!)." Bandcamp. Accessed May 18, 2017. https://justinfinch-fletchley.bandcamp.com/track/dumbledore-is-gay-and-thats-ok.
Losing Lara. "*Cursed Child* Isn't Canon." Bandcamp. Accessed June 20, 2018. https://losinglara.bandcamp.com/track/cursed-child-isnt-canon-explicit.
The Moaning Myrtles. "Transparent." On *What About Myrtle?* Compact disc. Woonsocket, RI: Cheap Rent, 2008.
The Mudbloods. "Imperius Regrets." On *Out of the Forbidden Forest*. Compact disc. Austin: Self-released, 2006
Oliver Boyd and the Remembralls. "Last Call." On *Back for the Fight*. Mp3. Toronto: Self-released, 2007.
Riddle™. "For Jo." On *Secrets of the Darkest Art*. Mp3. Oxfordshire, UK: Self-released, 2008.
Springsteen, Bruce. "I'll Stand by You Always" [identified on compact disc as "Song for Harry Potter"]. On *Bonus Tracks*. Compact disc. New York: Columbia Records, 2001.
Switchblade Kittens. "Ode to Harry" [internet single]. Mp3. Ventura, CA: Self-released, 2000.
Tianna and the Cliffhangers. *Fangz 2 Raven: An EP About* My Immortal. Mp3. Pittsburgh, PA: Self-released, 2012.
Tonks and the Aurors. "The Library Song" [internet single]. Mp3. Lebanon, OH: No Surrender Records, 2016.
Totally Knuts. "Trans Wizard." On *Fresh, Spooky, and Queer*. Mp3. Antioch, CA: Self-released, 2017.
The Whomping Willows. "In Which Draco and Harry Secretly Want to Make Out." On *Welcome to the House of Awesome*. Compact disc. Woonsocket, RI: Cheap Rent, 2007.
_____. "Wizard Rock Heartthrob." On *Welcome to the House of Awesome*. Compact disc. Woonsocket, RI: Cheap Rent, 2007.

Index

Ableton Live *see* digital audio workstations
Abravanel, Genevieve 177
abuse scandals *see* sexual abuse scandals
access *see* race
Accio Books! 142
ACLU *see* American Civil Liberties Union
American Civil Liberties Union 131–32
Amnesty International 141, 143
Anderson, Steph 22, 26, 50, 79, 88, 96, 100, 106, 121, 125, 135, 136–37, 145, 160, 169, 194*n*19, 218
Anderson-Ma, Annette 44
Anelli, Melissa 5, 40, 44, 59, 67, 78, 143, 144–45, 164
Anglophilia 116–18, 197*n*20, 197*n*27
Anglosphere 115, 118, 197*n*14, 197*n*27
Anvil and the Hints 145, 170
Apple 65
asexuality 127–28
Audacity *see* digital audio workstations
Audition *see* digital audio workstations
Austin, J.L. 16, 106
Austin, TX 164, 210, 212
Australia 17, 92, 115, 162, 197*n*14, 197*n*27
Austrone, Xavier *see* Cardin, Keith
authoritarianism 137–40
autoethnography *see* ethnography

Bad Religion 21
band naming 49–51
Bandcamp 64, 65–66, 68, 69, 126, 131–32, 205, 209
Bantu peoples 78–79
Barnard College 33
The Basilisk in Your Pasta 118, 221
BBC 29, 88
BDSM 98
Beaven, Pattie 86–87
Bee, Christopher 106
Bellwether Manufacturing 32
Benatar, Pat 53

Benoit, Russ 161, 197*n*12, 206
Beverly Hills, CA 39, 214
Birdoff, Ariel Factor 76, 78, 106, 133, 210
Bitch 124
"Bitch" (song) *see* Brooks, Meredith
The Blibbering Humdingers 25, 26, 92, 94, 170, 205
blip.tv 153
blogging 152, 162–63, 172
Blogspot 170
Blood Brothers 42
BlöödHag 31
BookRiot 180–81
Booth, Paul 104–5, 108
Borders Bookstore 32, 33
Boston Public Library 33, 34
Bowman, Sarah Lynne 106
Boyd, Alex 26, 97
Brazil 118, 197*n*13
breast cancer 145
Breitbart 139
British Empire 116–17
Broadly 45
Broadway 87
BroadwayCon *see* LeakyCon
Brooklyn, NY 163, 210
Brooks, Meredith 53–54
Brown, Jerry 21
Bush, George W. 138
Butler, Judith 2, 16, 99, 107–8
The Butterbeer Experience 50, 63, 99, 170, 206

Caldeira, Christian 119, 213
California 21, 28, 39, 44, 131, 132, 214
California State University Fullerton 44
Call of Cthulhu 101
Cambridge, MA 42, 81, 141
Canada 34, 115, 197*n*14, 197*n*27, 210, 212–13
canon 13–14, 27–28, 35, 54–55, 56–59, 121, 123, 128, 176, 185*n*9, 185*n*10

241

Cardin, Keith 157
Carpenter, Alex 39–40, 59, 67, 133–34, 189n121, 189n128, 189n129, 214; abuse allegations against 146, 189n123, 189n129, 214
Casio, Holly 22, 216
Catchlove 87, 153, 221
CD Baby 65
Chang, Cho (character) 53, 98, 120, 121
charity albums *see* compilation albums
Cheap Rent 63
Childs-Helton, Sally 75
Church, Brian 42
Cicierega, Neil 43, 81–82
Claire, Cassie 33
Clare, Cassandra *see* Claire, Cassie
Clements, Lizz 153, 159–60, 168
Collective Effervescence 76, 92–94, 95
Columbia University 179
common consciousness 90–92, 195n67, 195n84
Commonwealth of Nations 197n27
community: definition 17; importance 16–18, 171, 177–180
compilation albums 127, 133, 134, 143–46, 188n89, 200n57
Conard, Luke 41, 146, 211
Condo, A.D. 103
cons *see* fan conventions
contrafactum 191n18
Cook, Lauren 94, 177
cosplay 2, 16, 99, 102–105, 107–8, 111
Creevey Crisis 161, 206

D&D *see* Dungeons and Dragons
The Daily Prophet 137–38
Danny Dementor 52, 221
Darfur 142, 143
DAW *see* see digital audio workstations
Dawkins, Richard 193n90
The Dead Kennedys 21
Debies-Carl, Jeffrey S. 75
The Decemberists 34–35
de Certeau, Michel 23
DeGeorge, Joe 9, 15–16, 22, 26, 30–43, 56, 59, 71, 72–74, 81, 102, 103, 105, 106, 108, 138–40, 155, 180, 192n70, 198n48, 204n3, 204n4, 208, 220, 221
DeGeorge, Paul 9, 13–14, 16, 22, 23, 26, 30–35, 37–40, 42, 43–44, 56, 59, 61, 68, 71, 72–74, 81–82, 101, 102, 105, 108–11, 118, 124, 133, 137–40, 141, 149, 155, 167, 180, 185n10, 188n77, 190n175, 192n58, 192n70, 192n71, 196n49, 204n3, 204n4, 208, 220
Demographics 114–130
Denmark 118
DFTBA News 151
DFTBA Records 146, 192n76
Diana Dillpickles 104
Dianiska, Laura 161
digital audio workstations 62–63
digital decay 159

DiscMakers 48, 63, 70
dissing 192n61
DistroKid 65
DIY *see* Do-it-yourself ethos
DJ Luna Lovegood *see* Olson, Tina
DM *see* dungeon master
Do-it-yourself ethos 20, 22, 47–71, 108, 216
Doctor Who 87, 185n11
documentaries 3, 4, 44, 55, 88, 152, 163–65, 170, 172, 182
Doogan, Jesse 180–81
Dow, Grace 102, 120
The Downtown Boys *see* Ruiz, Victoria
Doylsetown, PA 34
Draco and the Malfoys 1, 37–40, 43, 44, 45, 47, 50, 51, 52, 55, 56, 62, 66, 70, 76, 80, 83, 84, 86, 87, 88, 96–98, 102, 116, 123, 125, 134, 142, 144, 155, 161, 165, 174, 189n121, 191n17, 207, 220; formation 37–39; performativity 109–10
Drama 28–29
Dubberly, Adam 57, 168, 212
Ducharme, Sam 49–50, 61, 80
Duchesne, Scott 105
Dumbledore (band) 43, 52, 220
Dumezweni, Noma 198n36
dungeon master 101, 196n12
Dungeons and Dragons 101, 196n12
Durkheim, Émile 2, 75, 90–94, 195n73, 195n84, 195n94

Ebrahimi, Farhad 42
Ed in the Refridgerators 30
egalitarianism 114, 122, 124, 129, 147, 148, 198n65
The 8th Horcrux 3, 26, 46, 50, 53–54, 55–56, 62, 68, 77, 89, 91, 96–99, 122, 132, 134, 151, 174, 190n3, 192n77, 207–8; formation 7–8, 47–50
Eminem 52
empowerment 3, 125, 135–36, 172, 174–77
encyclopedias 3, 45, 150–51, 159–63, 170
erasure 114, 120–21
eroticization 57–58
ethnography 3–4, 172, 193n1
Ethyln Gubrath 118
expanding the series timeline 56

Facebook 69, 76, 84, 94, 131–32, 151, 157, 183, 190n175, 193n1, 198n48
Fahlén, Anna *see* The Swedish Shortsnouts
Fahlén, Erik *see* The Swedish Shortsnouts
Fairweather, Lauren 41–42, 59, 64, 74, 80, 85, 89–90, 92, 102, 124–25, 148, 175–77, 178–79, 197n16, 211, 215
fan conventions 24, 46, 81–90, 153, 180
fan fiction 1, 11, 13–14, 20, 27–28, 33, 58, 63, 123, 128–29, 181, 185n9, 199n78, 217
fan non-fiction *see* zines
fangirls 124–25
Fangz 2 Raven 14, 58, 218

Index

fannish cosmology 18
fanon 57, 191*n*50
Fantastic Beasts and Where to Find Them 46, 65, 69, 103
SS *Fantasy* 86-87
Fawkes the phoenix 161, 202*n*49
feminism 125-26, 135-37, 187*n*19, 199*n*12, 203*n*5
filk *see* filk music
filk music 1, 20, 23-27, 75, 91, 97, 173, 187*n*64, 205
Finlaw, Amanda 77-78
First Book 43, 84, 134
first tier *see* tier system
FL Studio *see* digital audio workstations
The Fleur Delacours 43, 220
Flitwick and the Charmers 46, 49, 51
Floberg, Dana 131
Foley, Michael Stewart 21
folk music 23, 91, 187*n*31
Ford, Sam 66
Fox News 138-39
France 118, 197*n*10, 197*n*13
Fresh Fruit for Rotting Vegetables 21
Fresh, Spooky, and Queer 126, 137
Fridy, Freya 161, 168
Fugazi 155
Fuse 22

Gabrielle, Lena 99, 206
Game of Thrones 87
GarageBand *see* digital audio workstations
GeekyCon *see* LeakyCon
Geertz, Clifford 186*n*22
gender 2, 16, 57, 107, 112, 122-26, 129, 135-37, 198*n*65
gender equality in *Harry Potter* 135
gender of wrockers 122-26
genre 16-17, 51-53
Germany 21, 118, 197*n*10, 197*n*13
Get a Clue 134, 144-45
The Giant Squidstravaganza 55, 221
Gibbs, Nancy 143
gift economy 173
Gilsdorf, Ethan 98, 102
Gleason, Megan 157
Gluckman, Max 78-79
God 13, 21
GoFundMe 161
golden age 40-46, 68, 159, 163
Goldstein, Tina (character) 46
Gonzalez, Yaritza 21-22
Granger, Hermione (character) 10, 11, 28, 54, 58, 79, 120, 133, 194, 221; ethnicity 198*n*36
Greater Boston area 32, 34
Gred and Forge 13, 40, 63, 84, 142, 145, 191*n*50, 208, 221
Green, Hank 146
Green, John 146, 159, 180, 182
Green, Joshua 66
Green Day 21, 54, 190*n*3

Grint, Rupert 11
Gryffindor 33, 36, 50, 55, 73, 105, 155, 221

Haiti 142
Halloween 87, 103, 145, 193*n*18
The Hallows and Horcruxes Ball 2, 36, 84-86, 134
hardcore punk 192*n*71
Harry, a History 5, 40, 44, 78, 164
Harry and the Potters 1, 7-8, 9, 12, 26, 29, 33-35, 37-43, 46, 47, 50-51, 55, 56, 61-62, 66, 67, 70-71, 72-74, 76, 81-82, 86, 88, 89, 98, 102, 105, 113, 116, 118, 123, 125, 131, 134, 154, 155, 164-167, 174, 182, 185*n*10, 190*n*164, 190*n*175, 192*n*58, 192*n*71, 192*n*76, 192*n*81, 197*n*16, 200*n*25, 208-9; formation 30-33; fourth studio album 46, 139, 190*n*175, 192*n*70; performativity 15-16, 108-9, 110-11, 220-21; punk influence 22, 51, 108-9, 196*n*55; socio-political activism 137-141, 142, 144-45
Harry and the Potters and the Power of Love 42-32, 74, 208
Harry and the Potters at the Yule Ball 2008 81, 209, 221
The Harry Potter Alliance 43, 82, 83, 127, 133, 136, 141-43, 144, 145, 147-48, 149
Harry Potter and the Cursed Child 46, 58-59, 198*n*36
A Harry Potter Musical 185*n*3
Harvard Square 42, 44
Harvard University 98
Hayahsi, Aya Esther 5, 45, 113, 148, 167, 186*n*2, 187*n*64, 189*n*129, 189*n*131, 190*n*174, 190*n*14, 203*n*12
heterosexuality *see* sexual orientation
Hillsborough, NJ 41, 211
Hinsey, James 94
Hippe, Kirstyn 90, 125
hockey 192*n*71
Hogwarts 5, 10, 12, 15, 31, 41, 47, 55, 62, 72, 97, 98, 100, 103, 117, 118, 119, 135, 145, 148, 177, 180, 186*n*25, 189*n*115, 192*n*71, 200*n*29, 201*n*13, 214, 215, 220
Hogwarts (band) 118
Hogwarts Halloween 145
Holden, Brett 145, 169-70, 216
Holder, Sarah Frances 5, 137, 198*n*60
Hollow Godric 59, 118, 192*n*61
homosexuality *see* sexual orientation
horcruxes 54, 56, 142, 161, 190*n*2
Horner, Kristina 35-37, 67, 114, 146, 188*n*102, 192*n*56, 213
house parties 37-39, 79-81, 190*n*173
The HPA *see* Harry Potter Alliance
Hufflepuff 100, 135, 166, 216
The Hungarian Horntails 43, 164, 220
Hupp, Abby 82-84
Hutchison, Elizabeth D. 17

identity 26; formation 105-111

244　Index

IFC *see* Independent Film Channel
Indiegogo 64, 89
Internet Archive 159, 201*n*41
Isla Vista Killings 199*n*12
iTunes 65, 156, 157, 205

Jackson, Will 50, 52, 60
Jankowicz, Nina 41–42, 175–77, 211
Japan 103–4, 118, 197*n*13
Jenkins, Henry 5, 23, 27–28, 54–58, 66, 94, 123, 142, 186*n*25
Jennings, Jeremy 41, 211
Jennings, Mark 41, 211
Jingle Spells 134, 144–45, 149
Jorge, Jesse 170
Justin Finch-Fletchley and the Sugar Quills 40–41, 70, 84, 87, 90, 125, 127, 209, 221

Kane, Myles 55, 139–40, 181–82, 210–11
Kansas City, MO 89, 96
Kansas State University 84–86
Kendall, Grace 19, 50–51, 66, 80, 87–88, 125, 153, 158, 216–17
Kern, Jane 157
Kickstarter 64, 89
Kierkegaard, Søren 53
Kim, Ernie 32, 42
Korg Digital 12 track 32, 33, 61
Koury, Josh 88, 163–64
Kunaki 63–64
KWCW *see* The Witching Hour
KwikSpell 51, 192*n*77, 209–210

labels *see* record labels
Lambert, Joy 44
Lamerichs, Nicolle 107–8
LARP *see* live-action role-play
Larsen, Katherine 177
Last.fm 64–65
Lawrence, KS 7, 72,
Lawrence, TK 126, 137
Lawrence Public Library 72–74
The Leaky Cauldron (fansite) 5, 87, 142, 143, 144–45, 153, 192*n*55
LeakyCon 2, 87–88, 139, 148, 180, 181, 194*n*56
Lepelstat, Amanda Leigh 22
Les Savy Fav 42
Let's Lumos! 50
Letters from Hogwarts 145
Levine, Jenn 19
Lewis, Gerald 163
LGBTQ community 126–29
libraries, importance of 76–79
Library of Congress 43
LiL iFFy 52
Li'l Wayne 60
Lingappa, Anu 91, 156–57
live-action role-play 101, 102, 196*n*13
Live at the Yule Ball 43, 72, 81, 209, 221
live concerts 72–95
LiveJournal 33, 36, 153

Logic *see* digital audio workstations
Lollapalooza 86
London, UK 46, 191*n*33,
The Lonely Island 191*n*17
Lord of the Rings 14, 127, 185*n*11
Los Angeles, CA 39, 104, 155
Losing Lara 58, 125
The Lovegoods 46, 125, 210
Ludo Bagman and the Trash 46
lyrical sub-genres 2, 54–60
lyrics *see* lyrical sub-genres

Madam Pince and the Librarians 62, 210
maggi, Maggie 125
Maggiacomo, Matt 37–39, 59, 61, 63, 85, 114, 122, 124, 143–44, 147, 175, 181, 189*n*115, 189*n*138, 218
"Make America Great Again" 140
Malfoy, Draco (character) 38, 56, 57–58, 97, 109–10, 128, 207
Malfoy Manor 80
The Man 21, 23, 78
Manhattan, KS 84–86
marginalization 55, 120–21
Marsh, Dave 20
Mary Sue characters 57
masquerade 103–4
Matrisciana, Caryl 164
Mauss, Marcel 173
MC Gryf 50, 52–53
MC Kreacher 52, 55, 181–82, 210–11, 221
McCloud, Sean 94
McDonald, Doug "Jace" 153, 206
McGath, Gary 24
McLean, Don 166
mechanical solidarity *see* solidarity
media consolidation 145
Mehlenbacher, Brad 37–39, 40, 43, 46, 55, 59, 76, 109–10, 189*n*121, 190*n*175, 190*n*14, 192*n*59, 203*n*2, 204*n*3, 207
memetics *see* Dawkins, Richard
merch *see* merchandise
merchandise 2, 19, 35, 40, 69–71, 86, 89, 173, 192*n*76
metawrock 59
Micka, Kevin 42
The Middle East Downstairs 81–82
Mignogna, Tianna 14, 58, 76, 136, 170, 185*n*10, 217–18
Milam, Whitney 146
Mill, John Stuart 135
mimesis 15, 99
Ministry of Magic (band) 45, 61, 83, 84, 114, 125, 146, 167, 169, 191*n*23, 192*n*69, 192*n*77, 211; formation 41
Mischief Management *see* LeakyCon
Mr. Skygack from Mars 103–4
MISTI-Con 19
Moaning Myrtle (character) 41–42, 175–76
The Moaning Myrtles 1, 35, 63, 64, 70, 83, 84, 116, 124, 134, 142, 144, 153, 203*n*5, 211, 215,

221; formation 41–42, 197n16; "Transparent" 136, 175–77
Montola, Markus 99–101, 196n10
moral economy 27
Morales, Claudia 80, 138–39, 177, 186n2, 194n19
The Mortal Instruments 33
motivation of wrockers 172–82
MTV 9, 41, 138, 160
The Mudbloods 41, 46, 57, 63, 64, 84, 168, 212, 221
"Muggle Mindset" 142
MuggleNet 34, 166
Munday, Jason 41, 146, 201n65
Museum of Wizard Rock 19
My Anime 104
My Immortal 14, 58, 185n9
myFace *see* National Foundation for Facial Reconstruction
myHogwarts.co.uk 158–59
MySpace 2, 17, 25, 39, 45, 48, 65, 66, 67–69, 80, 141, 157, 159, 160, 162, 189n129, 212

name *see* band naming
National Foundation for Facial Reconstruction 145
nationality of bands 2, 114–19, 197n11, 197n13, 197n15, 198n29
Nazi Germany *see* Germany
Neely, Brad 164
Nelly 52
The Netherlands 34, 118, 197n13
Neville's Greenhouse 118
New York (city) 125, 210
New York (state) 217
The New York Dolls 20
New York Public Library 186n14, 192n81, 209
New York Times 165
NOFX 21
Nordyke, Aaron 41, 211
Nori, Mehera 154–57
Norwood, MA 9, 30, 203n2, 208
Not in Harry's Name 143
#NotAllMen 199n12
NPR 9

Obama, Barack 138–39
OCs *see* original characters
The Offspring 21
Olaveson, Tim 195n94
Oler, Tammy 124
Olin-Scheller, Christina 27
Oliver Boyd and the Remembralls 119, 192n77, 213
Olson, Tina 125
One Republic 191n23
organic solidarity *see* solidarity
original characters 27, 57
othering 177–80

Paré, Joelle 56

Parkinson, Pansy 35, 36, 56, 191n40
parody songs 7, 24, 26, 47–48, 53–54, 91, 97, 134, 150–51, 155, 166, 185n11, 190n3, 191n17, 191n18, 191n23, 205, 207
The Parselmouths 1, 43, 51, 53, 57, 63, 67, 83, 84, 114, 116, 123, 142, 144, 146, 192n56, 204n12, 213, 220; formation 35–37
The 'Pedia *see* The Wizrocklopedia
Peeved 153, 221
performance, definition of 15–16
performativity 16, 99, 106–8; of Draco and the Malfoys 109–10; of Harry and the Potters 108–9, 110–11
Perkins, Jarrod 145, 208
personalization 57
Phantom of the Opera 51
Phoenix Rising 82
Pink Ribbon Day 145
Pisani, John 96–98, 111, 217
Pisani, Stacy 45, 52–53, 96–98, 111, 125, 198n65, 217
Pitchfork 34, 166
Plummer, Jessica 33
podcasts 45, 118, 152–54, 156, 158, 215
political activism *see* activism
pop punk 12, 21, 28, 54, 216
Popple, Jennifer 135
Potosi, MO 83, 212
Potter, James 11
Potter, Lily 11, 136, 178
"Potter Mobile" 34
Potter Puppet Pals 43, 82
Pottercast 153
"Pottermania" 11, 14, 44, 87
Potterock 118
Poudlard Mag 151
Poughkeepsie, NY 34
PreSonus *see* digital audio workstations
privilege 3, 114, 121–22
pro-literacy 133–34
Pro Tools *see* digital audio workstations
Prophecy (symposium) 84
punk rock 1, 8, 20–23, 31, 32, 34, 51, 53, 75, 78, 108, 110, 140, 155, 186n2, 187n19, 191n15, 192n71, 193n105, 196n49, 196n54, 208, 216
Pyne, Erin Anne 83, 209, 219

Queen of England 21, 197n27
Quidditch 22, 70, 73, 135, 151, 158, 187n23, 188n77, 216

race 119–22
Radcliffe, Daniel 11, 165
radio 150–51, 152–59
The Ramones 21, 22
Rancid 21
Rasmussen, Sara 78, 154–57
rational choice theory 173–74
Ravenclaw 135
"real world" 2, 186n22
recontextualization 56

246 Index

record labels 28, 30, 40, 44, 63, 192n77
recording 14, 32, 42, 48, 60–63, 203n2, 204n3, 204n4
Red Bubble 70
refocalization 55
religion and fandom 94
The Remus Lupins 1, 43, 45, 50, 67, 83, 84, 86, 114, 123, 125, 133, 146, 155, 214, 220; formation 39–40
Renton, WA 35, 213
The Restricted Section 22
Riddle™ 59–60, 215, 221
Riddle, Tom *see* Voldemort
Riordan, Claire 154, 156–57
riot grrrl 22, 28, 43, 97, 187n19
Rishel, Mary Ann 53
rituals of rebellion 78–79
Rocking Out Against Voldemedia 145
Rohlman, Kelli 5, 113, 124, 127–29, 134, 136, 164, 199n77, 203n5
Rojas, Rosianna Halse 146
role of the Internet 14
role-play 2, 15–16, 31, 33, 36, 41, 51, 96–111 140, 172, 196n13, 211; definition 99–100; "Three Invisible Rules" 100–1
Romilda Vane and the Chocolate Cauldrons 62, 152, 215
Room of Wrockquirement 83
Rosenberg, Alyssa 143
Ross, Brian 37–39, 46, 52, 59, 76–77, 80, 87, 97, 109–10, 177, 190n175, 192n59, 203n2, 207
Rowling, J.K. 1, 9–11, 13–14, 22, 27, 45, 46, 56–60, 98, 128, 135, 143, 191n41, 198n35, 202n87, 216
Ruiz, Victoria 140
Russia 17, 118, 197n13

St. Louis, MO 84
Salon 35
Sandvoss, Cornel 108
Scamander, Newt 46, 103
Scandinavia 89, 114
Scarred for Life 61, 208, 192n71
Schopenhauer, Arthur 53
Schuyler, Mallory *see* the Schuyler sisters
Schuyler, Megan *see* the Schuyler sisters
the Schuyler sisters 44, 153, 165
Schwab, Charles M. 203n19
Scott, Suzanne 5, 25, 71, 86, 124–25, 198n65
Seattle, WA 31, 35, 37
second tier *see* tier system
second wave 45–46, 168, 190n174
The Secrets 30
Seen and Unforeseen 46, 170, 215
Seiler, Ryan 41, 211
The Sex Pistols 21
sexism 122–26, 155, 198n65
shipping 27, 128–29, 199n77, 199n78
The Shrieking Shack Disco Gang 22, 216, 221
Sigilum Serpentis 118

Siriusly Smiling: A Wizard Rock Charity Compilation 145
Sisley, Anne 85
Slack, Andrew 83, 141–42
"slash" fan fiction 128–29, 199n75
"slash" fiction 128–29, 199n78
Slytherin 36, 38, 50, 207, 213
Slytherin Soundtrack 145, 169, 170, 216
Smith, Anne C. 13, 51, 179
Smith, Lauren Amanda 54–60, 120–21, 191n41
Snidget 19, 50, 90, 153, 216–17
Snitchwiches 70
Snow, Amy 152–54, 215
social activism *see* activism
social justice themes in *Harry Potter* 132–33
social media 2, 12, 17, 40, 41, 49, 65, 66–69, 71, 75, 113, 131–32, 146, 157, 159, 162, 169, 178
solidarity 2 90–92, 119
Soltero 30, 37
Sommerville, Alisha 84
Sonnet, Elle Viane 35–37, 67, 188n102, 204n12, 213
Soundtrack Boston 61
South Africa 78
South by Southwest 164
spatio-temporal reality *see* real life
Spokane, WA 104, 165
spreadable media 5, 66–69
Springsteen, Bruce 29–30, 42, 97, 187n64, 218
Stanfill, Mel 120
Star Trek 23, 27–28, 104, 123
Star Wars 14, 185n11
Steinberg, Laurel 179
sticking it to the Man *see* the Man
The Stooges 20
Supernatural 203n6
Sweden 115, 118–19, 131, 198n29, 217
The Swedish Shortsnouts 118–19, 217
Swish and Flick 45, 50, 52, 53, 83, 96, 98, 125, 192n77, 217, 221
Switchblade Kittens 1, 28–29, 54, 86, 165

Takahashi, Nobuyuki 104
Tamarkin, Elisa 116
Tatum, Melissa 24–26
Terminus 86, 153
Terrell, Jennifer 5, 69
textual poaching 5, 23
They Might Be Giants 37, 208
third tier *see* tier system
Thomas, Trina 7–8, 47–49, 54, 64, 68, 72–74, 77, 85, 91, 96–98, 111, 122, 132, 150–51, 174, 181, 183–84, 207
Tianna and the Cliffhangers 217, 239
tier system 113–14
Timbaland 191n23
TIME 143
Timelord rock 185n11
To Write Love on Her Arms 145

Index

Tonks, Nymphadora 97, 100, 135, 187n18, 218
Tonks and the Aurors 22, 43, 46, 50, 62, 79, 83, 84, 86, 90, 96–98, 113, 125, 134, 136, 145, 160, 218, 221
Totally Knuts 126, 137
touring 34, 88–90
traditional role-play *see* role-play
Traister, Rebecca 126
transgender individuals 126
Trekkies 164
trock *see* Timelord rock
Trump, Donald 131, 138–40
Tumblr 48, 146, 151
TuneCore 65
Turk, Tisha 173
Turner, Victor 195n94
38th Parallel 41
Twitter 2, 17, 69, 125, 131, 151, 157, 167, 170
2016 presidential election 139

Umbridge, Dolores 156, 200n29, 201n13
Uncle Monsterface 61
"Undesirable No. 1" 52
United Kingdom 34, 89, 115–18, 197n20, 197n27, 198n35
United States 17, 34, 67, 88, 115–18, 121, 128, 129, 142, 156, 197n14, 197n15, 197n27, 198n29
University Daily Kansan 53
University of Chicago 8
University of Kansas 150
unlimited enthusiasm 3, 37, 172, 180–82
Unlimited Enthusiasm (expo) 180

Vahlberg, Brittany *see* Sonnet, Elle Viane
vanity labels 192n77
Vans Warped Tour 29, 86
Vassar College 34
Vaughan, Kirsten 25, 205
Vaughan, Scott 25, 92, 94, 205
The Velvet Underground 20
virality 66, 193n90
virtual geography 17
Voldemort (band) 51, 220
Voldemort (character) 10, 12, 18, 22, 33–34, 42, 47, 54, 73, 97, 135, 137, 142, 207, 208, 215
Voldemort Can't Stop the Rock 33–34, 42, 137–38, 208

Waite, Spirit-Rose 181
Walker, Jamie 152–54
Walla Walla, WA 150, 154, 156
Walmart Corporation 142
Walmart Watch 142
Walters, Erin 157
Wampum Willow 83–84
Ward, Kelly 137
Warner Brothers 22, 27, 35, 39, 40, 46, 71, 143, 159
Washington Post 44, 143

Washington State Penitentiary 156
Watson, Emma 11, 198n36
We Are Wizards 44, 55, 88, 163–64, 182
Weasley, Ginny (character) 28, 42, 54–55, 66, 71, 74
Weasley, Ron (character) 10, 11, 28, 54, 133
The Weird Sisters 29
Westman, Karin 84–85
whiteness of characters 120–21, 198n36
Whitman College 91, 150, 154–57
The Whomping Willows 1, 50, 57–58, 59, 61, 62, 63, 64, 70, 80, 83, 84, 86, 90, 116, 123, 128, 134, 142, 143, 144, 165, 181, 189n138, 192n57, 218–19, 221; formation 38–40
Wikipedia 166, 173
Wikstrom, Patrik 27
Williams, John 12
Wired 132
Witch Rock (concert series) 125, 198n65
Witch Rock (Twitter) 125, 131
Witches Wrock 145
The Witching Hour 91, 150–51, 152, 154–57
With Confidence 12
wiz-hop *see* wizard rap
Wizard People, Dear Reader 164
wizard rap 43, 50, 52–53, 55, 96, 139–140, 181–82, 210–11, 217
Wizard Rock EP of the Month Club 3, 43–44, 81, 134, 144, 204n3, 204n4, 205, 209, 220–21
The Wizard Rock People's Choice Awards 168–69, 170
Wizard Rock Revival (Facebook group) 21, 69
Wizard Rock Samplers 66
Wizard Rock the Vote 142
Wizard Rock Wiki 163
The Wizard Rockumentary 44, 61, 153, 163, 164–65
Wizarding World of Harry Potter 11
WizardRock.org 163
Wizards and Muggles Rock for Social Justice 127, 144, 145
The Wizrocklopedia 45, 66, 68–69, 80, 115, 118, 125, 131, 137, 138, 151, 152, 153, 159–62, 163, 166, 168–69
Wizrocklopedia Music Archive 68–69
The Wizzies 169–70
Woonsocket, RI 37, 80, 207, 218
Wordpress 166
WorldCon 104
wrap *see* wizard rap
Wrock Chicago 2, 86, 87
Wrock Hard Ditties 145
Wrock Snob 114, 118, 124, 151, 162, 166–68, 170, 191n23, 202n87
Wrock the Boat 2, 86–87
wrockBOX 152, 157–59
Wrocklopedia *see* The Wizrocklopedia
Wrockstock 2, 38, 45, 60, 82–84, 88, 190n167, 210, 217

Wrockstock Reunited *see* Wrockstock
Wrockstock Spooktacular *see* Wrockstock
The WRPCAs *see* The Wizard Rock People's Choice Awards
WZRD 152–53

Yankovic, "Weird Al" 7, 24, 47, 185n11, 207
Yes All Witches! 90, 97, 125, 135–37, 199n12
YMCA Trout Lodge 83

Yoho, Rob 13
Your Wizard Rock Resource 152, 162–63
YouTube 65, 78, 141, 146, 147, 185n3
The Yule Ball (concert) 2, 39, 43, 72, 81–82, 87, 181, 209, 218, 221

The Zambonis 31, 61, 192n71, 208
zines 71, 193n105
Zubernis, Lynn 177

www.ingramcontent.com/pod-product-compliance
Ingram Content Group UK Ltd.
Pitfield, Milton Keynes, MK11 3LW, UK
UKHW041936140426
5217IPUK00014B/506